Praise for *Union 1812*

"We are in Langguth's debt for this vivid retelling of the story of a war that still has everything to do with who we are and how we got this way. Langguth . . . paints human portraits with skill and grace. *Union 1812* is a Plutarchan undertaking, with the larger story of politics and war told through the lives of presidents Washington, Adams, Jefferson and Jackson, the Madisons, and lesser-known figures such as Zebulon Pike. The book has a lovely narrative pace. . . . Reading Langguth, one is reminded anew of how relevant and resonant the past can be."

—Jon Meacham, *Los Angeles Times Book Review*

"Popular history at its most accessible, full of colorful anecdotes and pithy quotes. . . . Langguth practically brings the War of 1812 to life again, a literary accomplishment that would have made the old Yale diplomatic historian Samuel Flagg Bemis proud. . . . Besides being a good read, *Union 1812* allows you to discover the second wave of our founders with a renewed sense of awe and surprise."

—Douglas Brinkley, *Washington Post Book World*

"*Union 1812* offers to give readers . . . all they want to know about America's second major war. . . . Langguth shows that victory in battle depended, time and again, on the personalities of the human leaders. . . . Langguth capably juggles multiple fronts, diplomatic maneuvers, social observations, and the eyewitness testimony, fragmentary but vivid, of lesser figures."

—Richard Brookhiser, *The New York Times Book Review*

"This is the fascinating saga of a war that tested the nation's ability to set aside political differences and survive its inevitable second confrontation with a better-prepared foe eager to avenge earlier defeat. Langguth provides rich historical detail and unforgettable insights into the event and those who assumed leadership during this pivotal period in American history."

—Larry Cox, *Tucson Citizen*

"In *Union 1812*, Langguth makes the case that 'Mr. Madison's War' was a second war of independence, one that rescued 18 states and forged them into a nation. He makes history come alive with his accounts of the people and events that made that happen."

—Pat McCoid, *The News Tribune* (Tacoma, Washington)

"A. J. Langguth has done a fine service . . . with *Union 1812*, a sweeping narrative history of key personalities and the events that led to the war. . . . An excellent work and a fascinating read."

—Kim Crawford, *The Flint Journal* (Michigan)

"Langguth superbly conveys the growing pains of the United States as it came of age. Characters from our grade-school history books come alive under his pen."

—Richard J. Ring, *The Providence Journal*

"This is a book that is not just for those who love history but for those who love a good story with great characters. . . . Each and every person that Langguth writes about is written as if he knows each of them personally, 'warts and all.' . . . Langguth, with the skill of a fiction writer, sets the scene."

—Connie Martinson, *Beverly Hills Courier*

"A fast-paced account of the War of 1812. . . . Langguth's prose is vivid, and he brings to life a panoply of personalities, from Dolley Madison to Tecumseh. . . . A panoramic view of a decisive event in American military and political history."

—*Publishers Weekly*

"Expertly guides readers through American history from the country's unsteady years as a sovereign nation to the culminating victories of the War of 1812. In vivid and richly detailed prose that can read like fiction but is based in well-researched fact, Langguth portrays a host of Federalist politicos and young America's many struggles. . . . As he did in *Patriots*, Langguth here relies heavily on letters, personal journal entries, speech transcripts, and other primary sources that are uniformly fascinating and enlightening. While in no way revisionist, this is well-done history and a worthy addition to any academic library's American history collection."

— Library Journal

"An engaging survey of interesting times. . . . Langguth does a nice job of introducing to modern readers characters who had influence in their time but are mostly forgotten today. . . . Nicely complicates our understanding of many iconic figures."

— Kirkus Reviews

"Never again after this masterly work will 1812 be a forgotten war. Langguth brilliantly restores the war to its rightful place in American history while at the same time giving us a rousing good story that holds our attention from beginning to end."

— Doris Kearns Goodwin, author of Team of Rivals

"A. J. Langguth is incapable of writing a dull sentence. Here he brings rousingly to life the perilous, fascinating years between America's first and second wars of independence. With an artist's flair, a scholar's rigor, and the narrative genius of a born storyteller, he gives us presidents and their wives, Redcoats and frontier Caesars, heroes and scalawags—an unforgettable portrait gallery of young America."

— Richard Norton Smith, author of Patriarch: George
Washington and the New American Nation

"A. J. Langguth's *Union 1812* is an excellent companion volume—and handy sequel—to his fine *Patriots*, which entertained and enlightened readers with its cast of characters from the Revolutionary War. Anyone now looking for an equally engaging and reliable guide to the principal figures and events surrounding the War of 1812 need look no further. This is it."

— Benson Bobrick, author of Angel in the Whirlwind:
The Triumph of the American Revolution

"*Union 1812* both fills a gaping hole in our early history and inventively and persuasively anchors the War of 1812 to the founding process, giving us portraits not only of players like Madison, Tecumseh, Jackson, and Harrison, but also of the revolutionary heroes Jefferson, Adams, and Washington, whose contributions take on new meaning in light of this 'second war of independence' and the true opening of the American West."

—William Hogeland, author of *The Whiskey Rebellion*

Also by A. J. Langguth

Our Vietnam: The War 1954–1975 (2000)

A Noise of War: Caesar, Pompey, Octavian and the Struggle for Rome (1994)

Patriots: The Men Who Started the American Revolution (1988)

Saki: A Life of Hector Hugh Munro (1981)

Hidden Terrors (1978)

Macumba: White and Black Magic in Brazil (1975)

Marksman (1974)

Wedlock (1972)

Jesus Christs (1968)

The Americans Who

Fought the Second

War of Independence

UNION
-1812-

A. J. Langguth

SIMON & SCHUSTER PAPERBACKS

New York London Toronto Sydney

For Alice E. Mayhew

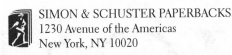
SIMON & SCHUSTER PAPERBACKS
1230 Avenue of the Americas
New York, NY 10020

First Simon & Schuster trade paperbacks edition November 2007

SIMON & SCHUSTER PAPERBACKS and colophon are registered trademarks
of Simon & Schuster, Inc.

For information about special discounts for bulk purchases,
please contact Simon & Schuster Special Sales at
1-800-456-6798 or business@simonandschuster.com.

Designed by Jaime Putorti

Manufactured in the United States of America

10 9 8 7 6 5 4 3 2 1

The Library of Congress has cataloged the hardcover edition as follows:

Langguth, A. J., 1933–
    Union 1812: the Americans who fought the Second War of Independence / A. J.
Langguth.
        p. cm.
    Includes bibliographical references and index.
    1. United States—History—War of 1812. 2. United States—History—War of
1812—Influence. I. Title.

E354.L34 2006
973.5'2—dc22   2006040340

ISBN-13: 978-0-7432-2618-9
ISBN-10:   0-7432-2618-6
ISBN-13: 978-1-4165-3278-1 (pbk)
ISBN-10:   1-4165-3278-1 (pbk)

Photo credits will be found on page 480

Contents

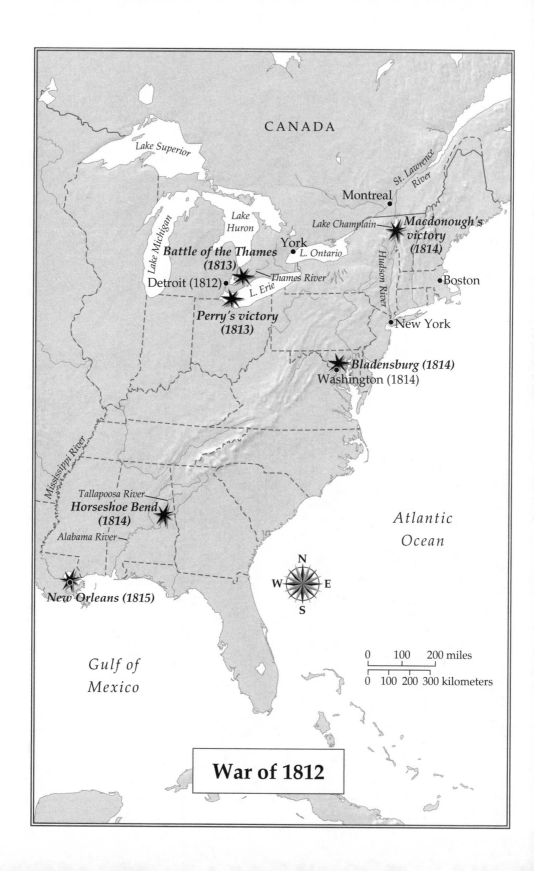

CANADA

Lake Superior

Montreal

St. Lawrence River

Lake Michigan

Lake Huron

Lake Champlain — ***Macdonough's victory (1814)***

York
• *L. Ontario*

Battle of the Thames (1813)

Detroit (1812) •

Thames River

L. Erie

Hudson River

• Boston

• New York

Perry's victory (1813)

Bladensburg (1814)
Washington (1814)

Mississippi River

Tallapoosa River

Horseshoe Bend (1814)

Alabama River

Atlantic Ocean

N
W • E
S

New Orleans (1815)

Gulf of Mexico

0	100	200 miles
0	100 200	300 kilometers

War of 1812

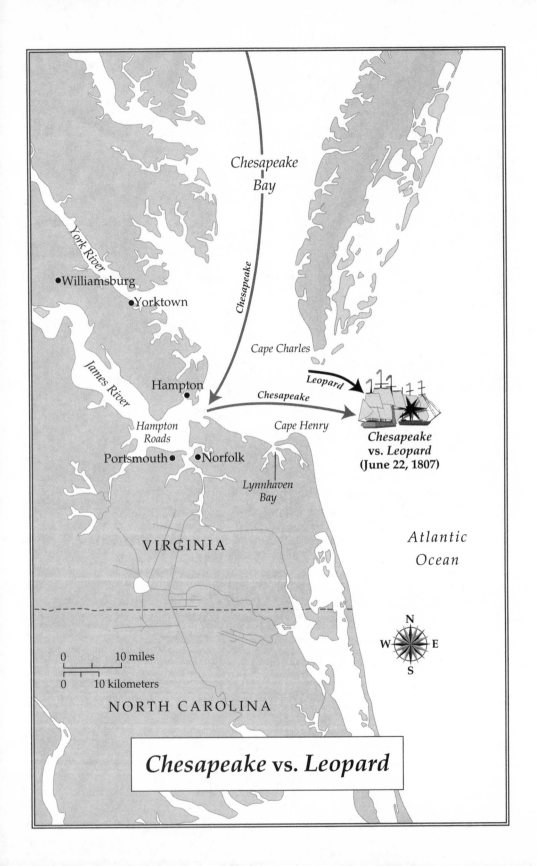

Chesapeake
Bay

York River

•Williamsburg

•Yorktown

James River

Hampton
•

Hampton
Roads

Cape Charles

Chesapeake

Leopard

Chesapeake

Cape Henry

Chesapeake
vs. Leopard
(June 22, 1807)

Portsmouth •   • Norfolk

Lynnhaven
Bay

VIRGINIA

Atlantic
Ocean

N
W   E
S

0   10 miles

0   10 kilometers

NORTH CAROLINA

Chesapeake vs. Leopard

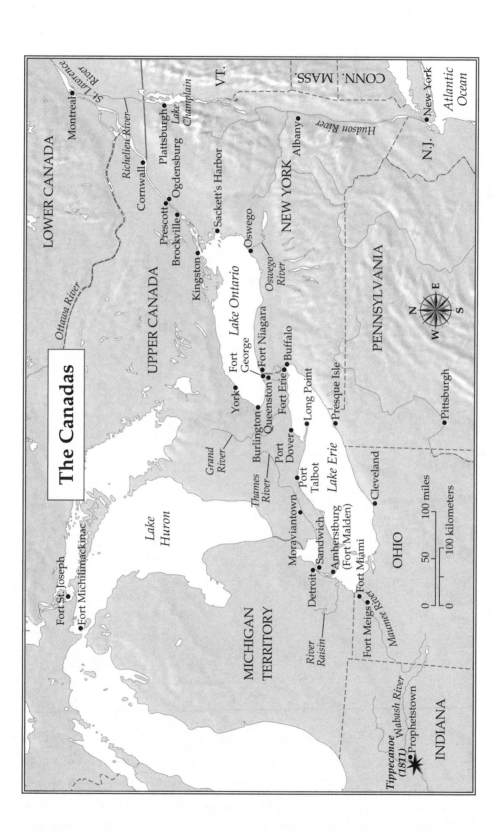

The Canadas

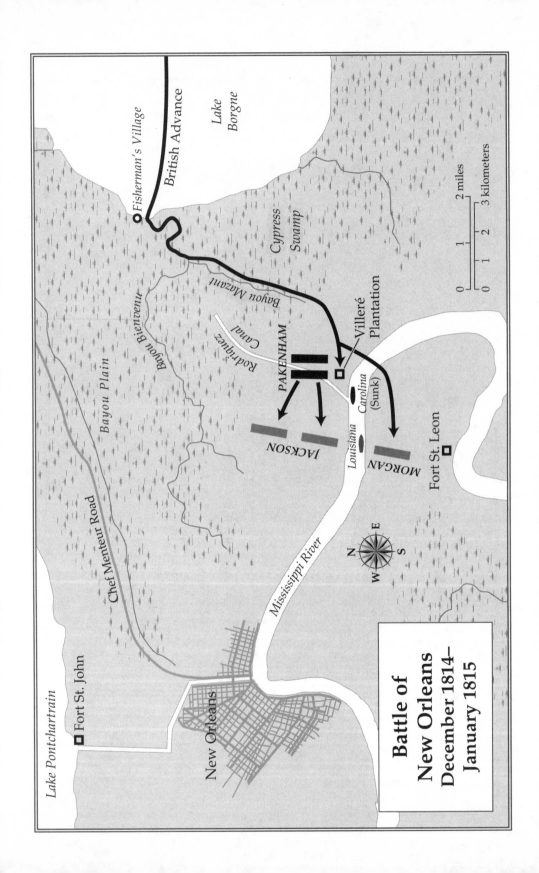

Lake Pontchartrain

Fort St. John

Chef Menteur Road

Bayou Plain

Bayou Bienvenu

Fisherman's Village

British Advance

Lake Borgne

Cypress Swamp

Bayou Mazant

Rodriguez Canal

PAKENHAM

Villeré Plantation

JACKSON

Louisiana

Carolina (Sunk)

MORGAN

Fort St. Leon

Mississippi River

New Orleans

N E S W

2 miles

3 kilometers

1

2

0

1

2

0

1

Battle of New Orleans December 1814– January 1815

UNION

When their rejoicing died away, the creators of the United States of America faced the hard fact that winning a war had been easier than governing their new country.

The crusade against Great Britain had united poor and rich, abolitionists and slave owners, clergy and godless. And yet the Articles of Confederation, their first experiment at unity, had barely seen them through to the peace treaty of 1783. With their common enemy gone, the states were proving to be fatally suspicious and envious of one another. But to take their place among the world's great powers, Americans needed to turn their infant republic into a mature nation.

Four presidents spent the next three decades pursuing the goal of an enduring union. Along with their ambitious vision and hard-fought compromises, success would mean uprooting the continent's native tribes and maintaining a willful blindness to slavery.

By 1812, America's leaders also came to believe that national honor required a second war with England.

The Washington family at Mount Vernon

Chapter One

HOMECOMING
(1783–1787)

For George Washington, America at peace was proving to be a disappointment. When he resigned his command of the Continental Army in December 1783, he expected to ride off to the perfect plantation life he had envisioned throughout the Revolutionary War. But after the challenges and glory of the past eight years, civilian routine could sometimes seem humdrum. And from Mount Vernon, Washington watched appalled and helpless as the nation he loved began to fall apart.

The reasons were hard for him to accept. As a Virginian, Washington had overcome his initial dislike of New Englanders in the early days of the war and led them in a united cause. He had believed that after enduring such a painful birth, the new nation would develop a unique American character, dedicated to independence and justice. And yet greed and regional hatreds were threatening to destroy his dream.

On his first night at home, Washington started up anxiously in bed before dawn. It took a moment or two for him to realize that "I was no longer a public man, or had anything to do with public transactions."

As a tranquil isolation settled over Mount Vernon, Washington had to admit that he missed the stir and bustle of the old days. To Thomas Jefferson, who was headed for Paris to represent the United States, Washington complained of his "torpid state" and solicited any political gossip: "If you have any news that you are likely to impart, it would be charity to communicate a little of it to a body."

Meantime, Washington was left with time to reflect on his inevitable death. He was fifty-two, with his great work finished, and men in his family did not survive into old age. Writing to Gilbert Lafayette in Paris, he confided to the twenty-six-year-old marquis, "I am not only retired from all public employment, but I'm retiring into myself." When Lafayette came to America the following year, Washington found his visit all too short and predicted that they might not meet again because he "might soon expect to be entombed in the dreary mansions of my fathers."

In retirement, Washington passed his days by restoring and expanding his estate, which had suffered from his long absence. He struck a bargain with his bibulous gardener that if the man would stay sober, Washington would allow him a dram of liquor in the morning and a drink of grog at night, along with four dollars at Christmas to let him get drunk for four days and nights.

Although Washington was a private citizen, admiring visitors constantly showed up at his door. He kept a hundred cows at Mount Vernon, but the crowds came in such numbers that he was forced to buy butter for their meals. With the stream of guests so unrelenting, a year and a half passed before the day that Washington could dine alone with his wife.

He would greet everyone courteously and offer refreshment to men and women who were often unfamiliar to him. With strangers, Washington would withdraw to his chambers soon after supper while his guests remained at the table. But when Washington felt entirely comfortable with the company, he might take enough champagne to lower his reserve and get him laughing.

To accommodate his new life as his country's most admired citizen, Washington added bedrooms in the attic of the main house and raised the roof for two new wings. In leisure moments, he unleashed French hounds, a gift from Lafayette, to chase the gray foxes Washington bred as quarry. A superb horseman, he was hunting three days a week until that palled and he passed his time instead by answering the rising volume of letters.

Washington also had to cope with the artists and sculptors who importuned him for a chance to capture his likeness. Protective of his role in history, Washington usually agreed to receive them and showed both respect and curiosity for men with a temperament so different from his own. One of them, Joseph Wright, made busts from face masks, and Washington stretched out reluctantly on a cot to let the artist oil his face and daub it with plaster. But when Martha Washington came into the room unexpectedly, her cry of alarm made Washington smile, which he said explained the slight twist to his mouth in Wright's finished statue. Another explanation might have been the false teeth he commissioned from a favorite craftsman named John Greenwood.

Obliging as Washington tried to be, he resisted when the eminent French sculptor Jean-Antoine Houdon wanted to depict him in Roman garb. Washington apologized to Jefferson, who had arranged the commission, that although he understood that togas were "the taste of connoisseurs," he preferred something more modern. Houdon compromised on a military cloak but insisted on another life mask. Even though his assistant later dropped the cast, Houdon's finished statue captured Washington's broad brow and firm chin, the straight line of his mouth, and his steady gaze. It also conveyed a trace of the shy diffidence that, despite his public austerity, had won Washington so many admirers.

For Martha Washington, two children in their household supplied a welcome diversion. After her twenty-seven-year-old son, Jacky Custis, died just before the American victory at Yorktown in 1781, the Washingtons agreed to raise his two younger children—five-year-old Nelly and her three-year-old brother, George Washington Custis, nicknamed "Wash" or "Tub." Although Washington enjoyed "the little folks," he balked at adding one other relative to the household.

His mother, Mary Washington, had complained for years about the way that her George had forsaken her and gone off to fight a war. All the same, Washington had been a dutiful son even when her demands exasperated him. Now, nearing eighty, she was threatening to vacate the house that Washington had bought for her in Fredericksburg and move in with him. For once, Washington found a value in the assault of visitors on Mount Vernon. He wrote urgently to assure her that the constant hubbub would interfere with the serenity that should be her first concern.

Mary Washington accepted that argument and stayed on in Fredericksburg until her death from breast cancer. Washington waived the hundreds of pounds in debts that her estate owed him, but a year passed before he sent for the few mementos she had bequeathed to him. Putting on a black armband of mourning, Washington expressed to his sister "a hope that she is translated to a happier place."

Since Washington had more property than ready cash, his finances were always precarious. Yet he rejected a plan by officials in Pennsylvania to petition the Continental Congress for money on his behalf. Nothing must tarnish his reputation as a patriot who had never exploited his service to the nation. Washington explained that his attitude toward such rewards "had been long and well known to the public." He then made an even greater sacrifice by turning down grants of land that the Congress was awarding other Revolutionary War veterans.

As Washington had learned, wilderness land was not always a lucrative investment. He had once bought thirty-two thousand uninhabited acres on the Ohio and Great Kanawha rivers, along with other tracts in the same territory where he had fought for Britain as a young

officer during the French and Indian Wars. When he rode out to inspect his holdings, however, Washington was confronted by squatters
who had been living on his property for the past ten years. They had
cleared the land and built sturdy log houses and refused to accept
Washington, hero or not, as their landlord.

He hired a lawyer and fumed for the next two years until he won
his case. But upon hearing that the squatters were "now in my power,"
Washington declined "to distress them further" and repeated his earlier
offer to rent them the land. The experience taught him how contentious the frontier had become, and he resolved to sell off his western investments. When no buyer was willing to pay thirty thousand
English guineas for his acreage, Washington was forced to hire an
overseer, and that man managed to turn a profit on the land. All the
same, Washington's debts forced him to dispose of his accumulated
stocks at one-twentieth of their face value.

In retirement, Washington had begun to keep a squire's diary, usually
limited to the day's weather and the condition of his crops. If he
recorded the names of his many guests—for example, on Friday, May
20, 1785, "A Mr. Noah Webster came here in the afternoon and stayed
the Night"—Washington seldom bothered with why they had called or
what they talked about. In Webster's case, the lexicographer had come
to present in person his plan for a new system of government.

When James Madison, a Virginia planter in his mid-thirties, rode
to Mount Vernon to spend a weekend, Washington recorded no more
than his arrival and the fact that he had left Monday morning after
breakfast. Madison was normally no more expansive than his host, but
he had observed Washington attentively during his visit and concluded
that the scope of his new projects—including a plan for Virginia and
Maryland to join in improving navigation on the Potomac—"shows
that a mind like his, capable of grand views, and which has long been
occupied with them, cannot bear a vacancy."

Madison also saw that a political crisis confronting the United
States could force Washington out of retirement and compel him to
address again the great issues of his time.

✻   ✻   ✻

That crisis had been building even before the war ended, but Washington's hopeful nature had persuaded him that the "unsettled and deranged" state of affairs under the Articles of Confederation would be resolved. In the meantime, he could only suggest electing representatives wisely and supporting their attempts to preserve a union welded among the fractious individual states.

But Washington's trip west had reminded him how little was binding one state to another. War had given them a common enemy, but now the country had to base its identity on more than opposition to British rule. Without a common purpose, western settlers, who were likely to be immigrants, might feel no bond with the original states. Washington saw such men standing on a pivot. "The touch of a feather would turn them any way." They might even join with the Spanish colonists further down the Mississippi, although at the moment the Spaniards seemed blind to their opportunity.

Washington longed for a nation united by high principle. To depend on mere commercial self-interest pointed up a central weakness of the Articles because one state's dissenting vote could kill any legislation. Not only was unanimous agreement required, but if a state's delegates did not show up for a debate, their absence was recorded as a negative vote.

That flaw was proving particularly damaging to tax policy. In 1781, the Continental Congress had tried to pay the interest on the federal debt by levying a 5 percent tax on all imports. Every state approved the legislation except Rhode Island. Two years later, congressional leaders tried again with a tax limited to twenty-five years. By then, the opposition had grown until New York, Maryland, and Georgia joined Rhode Island in rejecting the measure.

Washington had endorsed those attempts to raise revenue for his army and watched in the following years as deadlocks and inertia grew only worse. "The Confederation appears to me to be little more than a shadow without substance," Washington complained, dismissing the fears of southerners that they were being dominated by New England. "We are either a united people, or we are not," Washington wrote to Madison in 1785. "If we are not, let us no longer act a farce by pretending to be it." Perhaps his countrymen would have to admit that the

British had been right all along when they predicted that the American experiment could not last.

To Madison, a major shortcoming in the Articles had been setting up the Continental Congress with only one chamber and then expecting it to act as both legislative and executive branches of government. And he considered the way representation was apportioned to be blatantly unfair. His state of Virginia had sixteen times more residents than Delaware, yet their votes in the Continental Congress counted as the same. Even to amend the Articles required unanimous agreement by all thirteen states.

When an economic depression struck and no federal legislation controlled the nation's economy, states passed local laws aimed solely at protecting their own interests. Britain was violating terms of the peace treaty of 1783, but when Massachusetts tried to retaliate by imposing taxes against British shipping, Connecticut defeated that strategy by declaring that its ports would remain free. New Jersey undercut New York in the same way, as Delaware undercut Pennsylvania.

Washington was outraged by state legislators who were short-sighted as well as selfish. "My *opinion* is," he wrote in the spring of 1786, "that there is more wickedness than ignorance in the conduct of the states."

Even though sentiment was growing that the Articles had failed, challenging them might be denounced as an assault on the government itself, even as treason. A scant three years after John Jay signed the peace treaty with Britain, he was urging Washington to speak out for amending the Articles. Jay admitted, though, that he could not say whether "the people are yet ripe for such a measure."

Washington might be braced for a second revolution, but James Madison—short and unimposing, a victim of persistent fevers, stomach ailments, and occasional seizures—seemed an unlikely crusader to lead it. After graduating from the College of New Jersey at Princeton, Madison had been a state delegate in Virginia before winding up, at age twenty-nine, in the Continental Congress for the last three years of the war.

Apart from his height, calculated generously at five feet five, Madison had none of the public stature of the "Signers," those men whose names adorned the Declaration of Independence. He was almost twenty years younger than Washington and fifteen years younger than John Adams. Thomas Jefferson was only eight years older and had become a close friend, but Jefferson was already a towering figure from that legendary era.

And yet it was falling to Madison to argue that the jerry-built Articles could not be salvaged. They must be scrapped. America must start over again. His position was radical, but Madison had already shown an intellectual courage that could not be intimidated.

After leaving the Continental Congress, he had returned to Virginia to study law, hoping to earn his own living and stop depending on income from Montpelier, his family's estate. Madison soon found law practice narrow and unsatisfying and doubted that his thin voice and dry manner promised success. Like Washington, he turned to land speculation. His partner was the Revolutionary War hero "Light Horse Harry" Lee, but their venture proved ill-fated, and Madison escaped gratefully to a seat in the Virginia Assembly in Richmond.

Madison's first cautious step toward sweeping reform was to join his state's call for a convention in Annapolis, Maryland, to examine the nation's trade policies. Earlier, he had missed a session that Washington had convened at Mount Vernon to explore jurisdiction over the Potomac River because Governor Patrick Henry had neglected to inform the delegates in time.

That Mount Vernon conclave had failed, and the response in Annapolis was just as discouraging. Only nine of the other twelve states agreed to send delegates, and representatives from only five of those states made it to Annapolis.

But the men who did arrive shared Madison's longer-range objectives. They called on the Continental Congress to sponsor another convention in May 1787. Aware of the resistance if their true goal were known, they claimed that their gathering would limit itself "to the sole and express purpose of revising the Articles of Confederation."

Washington approved of any attempt to extend control by the Continental Congress over the nation's commerce. But he warned that change would come hard. "It is one of the evils of democratical government," he wrote, "that the people, not always seeing it & frequently misled, must often *feel* before they can act right." The slow progress toward a remedy was lamentable, Washington added, and yet forcing change before the people were ready could bring about political "convulsions" that would destroy liberty.

Then, before the delegates could gather in Philadelphia, an uprising in western Massachusetts made their convention more urgent than ever.

The Massachusetts legislature had been meeting its Revolutionary War debts by imposing steep taxes that could be paid only with hard money. Lenders were not required to accept the devalued Revolutionary dollars that had become a bitter joke. Such stringent measures left farmers facing foreclosure of their land, even jail. Petitioning for relief, they asked that paper money be honored and that repayment deadlines be eased. But the legislators cared chiefly about protecting the state's creditors and, for two years in a row, had rejected the farmers' appeals.

By 1786, the widespread discontent revived the same slogans that had aroused Massachusetts against the British only a decade earlier. Beginning with indignant town meetings, the protests grew until bands of armed men surrounded several country courthouses to stop the courts from collecting debts or carrying out foreclosures.

The state's governor, James Bowdoin, responded with force, just as Britain's provincial governors had done, and sent troops to open the courts. In late January 1787, a retired Revolutionary army captain from Springfield named Daniel Shays reacted by marching twelve hundred angry men to seize their town's federal arsenal.

The result was a reenactment of the Boston Massacre. State militiamen fired into the crowd, killing four protesters. After ten days of uproar, another Revolutionary War veteran, General Benjamin Lincoln, brought in enough troops to quell the brief rebellion. Lincoln's actions led to no casualties but a hundred men were taken prisoner. Another

790 rebels were allowed to clear themselves by swearing an oath of allegiance.

That option was not extended to Shays and his fellow ringleaders. They were convicted of high treason and sentenced to death. But the Massachusetts legislature at last voted relief for the state's debtors, and the men were pardoned.

As America's envoy in Paris, Thomas Jefferson was observing the far greater turbulence that was threatening King Louis XVI and his queen, Marie Antoinette. From the safe distance of the French capital, Jefferson could dismiss Shays's uprising with a romantic metaphor. "I like a little rebellion now and then," he wrote to Abigail Adams, although John Adams's downright wife was unlikely to agree. "It is like a storm in the atmosphere."

More than once, Jefferson had let his pleasure in a striking phrase overtake his more humane instincts. To the Adamses' son-in-law, he had written, "The tree of liberty must be watered from time to time with the blood of patriots and tyrants. It is its natural manure."

James Madison was not given to fanciful language, and more profound differences distinguished him from his good friend. Jefferson was tall and youthful, with reddish hair that never seemed combed. Though he was somewhat shy in company, Jefferson's unmistakable warmth with friends and his lively curiosity drew men and women to him.

Burdened with a pinched severity, Madison possessed unfailing good manners but little charm. He had been described, not unfairly, as "a schoolteacher dressed up for a funeral." One critic carried the image further: "a country schoolmaster in mourning for one of his pupils whom he had whipped to death."

Washington Irving, a young businessman with literary aspirations, would compare him one day to shriveled fruit—"a withered little Apple-John."

Both men enjoyed good wine, and they imported choice vintages from France. Jefferson spoke French well, but Madison was uncomfortable in the language because he had been taught by a Scottish teacher who left him speaking with a pronounced burr.

Jefferson's optimism and vivid imagination let him embrace many fresh enthusiasms. Madison's caution and reserve could make him seem the older of the two and kept him perpetually anchored in the practical world.

But the two men were also alike. Their health was a matter of life-long concern to both of them—Jefferson's blinding migraine headaches, Madison's painful intestinal disorders. And for Jefferson, good humor ranked as the highest virtue in a friend—even above integrity. Madison possessed a dry wit, and from his college years had retained a fondness for racy jokes. He told them, in male company, exceedingly well.

Politically, little separated the two. When Jefferson sailed to France to represent the United States, Madison had taken up in the Virginia Assembly the battle for religious liberty that Jefferson had once waged. Madison's opponent was Patrick Henry, the Revolution's foremost orator, who had introduced an assessment bill that would support Christian churches by letting Virginians assign a share of their taxes to their own congregations.

Madison saw the legislation as a way for clergymen to feed again on state revenues as they had done under the British. When the Anglican Church dominated Virginia before the Revolution, Presbyterians had fought any favoritism. Now they seemed to want their share.

At Madison's urging, the bill's final passage was delayed long enough for him to write a rebuttal that he titled "Memorial and Remonstrance Against Religious Assessments." Madison had heard reports that even churchgoing Christians were uneasy about Henry's bill, and he played on their distrust of government.

"Who does not see," Madison wrote, "that the same authority, which can establish Christianity, in exclusion of all other religions, may establish with the same ease any particular sect of Christians in exclusion of all other sects?"

Madison sent a copy of his argument to Mount Vernon. Because he did not know Washington's views, he pretended not to be its author. Washington said he believed that Henry's proposal was divisive, but in principle he saw no harm in Christians—or, for that matter, Jews and Mohammedans—receiving tax relief for supporting their religion.

Before the showdown, Patrick Henry had been elected governor, which prevented his hypnotic voice from being heard in the legislature. Madison won the vote with a public response so favorable that he introduced an even stronger guarantee of religious freedom, one that Jefferson had first drafted six years earlier. It, too, passed easily.

While Jefferson was in France, he and Madison had devised a private code for their letters. Using it, Madison described the way Patrick Henry was trying to thwart their vision for America. Jefferson had always considered Henry something of a charlatan, but he had never questioned his genius as an orator. His reply to Madison was characteristically extravagant:

"What we have to do I think is devoutly to pray for his death."

Shays's rebellion, together with a similar uprising in Rhode Island, had left Madison even more determined to reform the federal government. He worried, though, that some delegates might arrive in Philadelphia favoring a monarchy for the United States. Instead, Madison offered what he called a "lesser evil"—partitioning the federal government into three separate and powerful branches.

To bolster his arguments, he had been studying a range of political philosophies. Montesquieu made the case for small republics, but Madison preferred the Scottish philosopher David Hume's essay "On the Idea of a Perfect Commonwealth." Hume, who had died just as America was claiming its independence in 1776, derided Plato's *Republic* and Thomas More's *Utopia* because they were predicated on changes in human nature that Hume considered highly unlikely.

He argued instead that, while a man in his personal life might be virtuous, in politics he should be considered a knave who must be controlled by a constitution. But Hume could also envision a great-hearted leader who would suppress his personal ambition in order to establish a truly free state.

Madison was sure Washington was such a man.

Without Shays's rebellion, Washington might not have been inclined to risk his reputation by going to Philadelphia. But what he had heard about the unrest in Massachusetts alarmed him enough to bring on fever and pains for the first time since his return to Mount Vernon. "I am mortified beyond expression," Washington wrote, "when I view the clouds that have spread over the brightest morn that ever dawned upon any country."

Although the Massachusetts revolt had been put down, Washington was receiving reports of other movements that threatened to break up the states into two or even three distinct nations. After all, the separatists argued, the United States already comprised a territory larger than the combined size of Britain, Ireland, France, Spain, and Italy.

To prevent that sort of splintering, Washington agreed that a conference might be valuable. Nothing might come of it, but a thoughtful discussion could be influential later, when the people were more prepared to make drastic changes. His friends, however, urged Washington not to attend in person. They reminded him that he had pledged never again to accept a public position. To join Virginia's delegation in Philadelphia could be seen as breaking his word.

By now, Madison could read Washington adeptly and suspected that he would end up going to Philadelphia. Washington's view of his own importance was entirely realistic, but he had never wanted to be seen as grasping or ambitious. He must be persuaded and then allowed to give way with a becoming reluctance.

As Washington raised objections, one did weigh heavily on him: He had already told the Society of the Cincinnati, a new fraternal order, that he would not be going to Philadelphia for the society's convention. How could he now show up in the city and shun their meeting?

The issue was delicate because the membership included men who had served loyally under Washington during the Revolution, but he did not approve of the direction in which they were headed.

The society had been named by Washington's great friend Henry Knox for Lucius Quinctus Cincinnatus, the Roman general who defeated his country's enemies before returning to civilian life. America's Cincinnati intended to aid distressed veterans and maintain ties with military allies in France. Since cheery Henry Knox himself would pose no threat to the Republic, Washington at first had agreed to preside over the society, even though its membership was limited to former Revolutionary War officers.

That restriction provoked suspicion among civilian politicians, and in New York and Philadelphia they formed clubs called the Sons of Saint Tammany to offset the society's influence. And when the Cincinnati voted to deed their membership to their eldest sons, Washington realized why outsiders might regard it as intended to become a home-grown aristocracy. He announced his opposition to hereditary membership and called for an end to national Cincinnati conventions.

It was after the state chapters resisted his reforms that Washington made excuses for not attending their Philadelphia gathering. Now, if he went to the Constitutional Convention instead, he might offend a group of men for whom "I shall ever feel the highest gratitude & affection."

Martha Washington was leaving the decision to her husband, but she let him know that, with the war over, she had expected him to grow old at her side. She certainly would not be leaving her grandchildren to accompany him to Philadelphia. Even Madison, although he wanted him there badly, understood the stakes for Washington if the Philadelphia meeting were to fail as Annapolis had. He wrote that Washington should not "participate in any abortive undertaking."

But Madison could report that he had persuaded the suspicious members of the enfeebled Continental Congress to sanction the proposed convention. That concession at least would protect against any charge of illegitimacy. To ease Washington's fear that he would be embarrassed by a poor showing of delegates, Madison assured him that, at the very most, only three states would refuse to send representatives — Connecticut, Maryland, and Rhode Island.

And, finally, if Washington still declined to participate, a substitute chairman was available. Benjamin Franklin, the one American whose renown compared with Washington's, had returned from France. He had been deified there for his talents and adored in Parisian society for flirtations that turned, more often than he might have wished, into avuncular friendships.

The French reverence for Franklin was so great that Jefferson had won instant acclaim for his reply whenever Parisians asked whether he had come to replace Dr. Franklin. "No one can replace him, sir," Jefferson would say. "I am only his successor." But writing in code to Madison, Jefferson noted that John Adams had opened his eyes to Franklin's vanity and his other less admirable qualities.

For Madison and his colleagues, Franklin's announcement that he would attend the convention was heartening, although, at eighty-one, he was too frail to take an active role in the debate. But, as Franklin wrote to Jefferson, the convention must succeed or "it will show we have not the wisdom among us to govern ourselves."

At last, Washington notified his friend Edmund Randolph, who had agreed to join the Virginia delegation, that he, too, would be making the trip to Philadelphia—"contrary to my judgment."

With Washington committed, Madison spelled out to him in a private letter what the convention must accomplish. He acknowledged that several of his proposals were "radical," especially those that stripped away many state powers and transferred them to one strong federal executive. But if that were not done, Madison predicted that the states would "harass each other with rival and spiteful measures dictated by mistaken views of interest."

Madison wanted to extend federal supremacy to the courts as well and produce a government of well-organized and balanced powers. But he did not expect his eminently rational plan to convince the individual states, and he knew that a new federal government could not rely entirely on the power of persuasion. Madison stressed to Washington that whenever a state balked at a specific provision, the central government must be able to resort to force; the "right of coercion should be expressly declared."

Madison addressing the Virginia Convention

Chapter Two

PHILADELPHIA
(1787–1788)

Madison's bold plan was waiting for the delegates as they arrived in Philadelphia. Only Rhode Island had refused to send representatives; the leaders of that smallest state suspected that any change in the Articles would come at their expense. Patrick Henry had also stayed home, complaining that he smelled a rat.

John Hancock, now governor of Massachusetts, would not be making the trip, either, nor would Samuel Adams, another Revolutionary firebrand. Adams understood the inadequacy of the Articles and complained to his cousin John that Americans might be zealous for liberty but were unwilling to work or pay for it. But Sam Adams had always been suspicious of Washington's popularity as a general, and he feared that a tyrannical national government would replace the current amalgam of sovereign states.

Madison did not regret Henry's boycott or the absence of either Adams. John Adams, who had been representing the United States abroad since 1777, had sent home an ambitious analysis of various possible governments. Madison granted that Adams's prestige might make his tract influential, but he himself saw little to recommend it. "Men of learning find nothing new in it," Madison wrote caustically. "Men of taste, many things to criticize. And men without either, not a few things which they will not understand."

Most of the fifty-five delegates anticipated a pleasurable stay during the convention. Among the world's English-speaking cities, Philadelphia was second only to London in size and comforts. Madison also could expect most delegates to be well-informed since thirty-nine had served in the existing Congress. Well-to-do lawyers would predominate in Philadelphia, but unlike thirty-one of them, James Madison had never practiced law and would be one of the least prosperous men in the hall. At thirty-six, he was not the youngest of the leading figures, however; Alexander Hamilton from New York was thirty-two, and Charles Pinckney from South Carolina only thirty.

Convinced that Virginia must take the lead, Madison reached Philadelphia on May 2, the first delegate to arrive. Washington got to town on the thirteenth and made note of the church bells that were ringing to welcome him. He had intended to lodge in a boardinghouse until Robert Morris, said to be the richest man in the country, induced him to move into his brick mansion on High Street.

When the session opened on May 14, only delegates from Pennsylvania and Virginia were on hand to watch as local convicts from the Walnut Street jail carried Benjamin Franklin into the hall in a sedan chair. The lack of punctuality by the other members irked Washington, but Madison reminded him of the bad weather and muddy roads that he had encountered in getting there.

It took another eleven days for a quorum of delegates from seven states to arrive. Madison expected that their number would fluctuate

Alexander Hamilton

from day to day, but on May 25, 1787, twenty-nine men were present and the convention could begin its deliberations.

As Virginia was pressing for a Constitutional Convention, Alexander Hamilton had also been insistent in New York about repairing the federal government. Not much taller than Madison, Hamilton was a far showier presence, and his relations with Washington dated from the war years when he had served as the general's chief aide.

Hamilton's childhood on the Caribbean island of Nevis had been more exotic than those of the other delegates in Philadelphia. His mother, a local beauty named Rachel Faucette, had abandoned her older husband to take up with James Hamilton, the scapegrace fourth son of a Scottish laird. Drifting away from Nevis ten years later, Hamilton left behind two sons. The older boy was apprenticed to a carpenter. The younger, Alexander, had inherited his father's freckled complexion and a bulge to his forehead, a knobby chin, and close-set blue eyes that he thought kept him from being handsome.

Alexander's illegitimate birth had ignited in him a consuming desire to escape from the island, an ambition that led eventually to the assignment with Washington at Valley Forge. But the circumstances of his birth had also fostered a touchy pride that made him easily offended.

Even dealing with Washington had provoked Hamilton to flareups. After one petty misunderstanding, Hamilton's influential father-in-law had to pressure him to return to Washington's side. When he did, Hamilton remained churlish and insisted for a time on a distant formality.

Washington valued Hamilton's ability highly and forgave him unconditionally. He had refused Hamilton's requests for a military command only because he could not replace the young man's knowledge of French and his skill at ghost-writing graceful letters. As the war wound down, however, Washington relented and assigned Hamilton to a newly formed battalion under Lafayette at the battle of Yorktown. Despite his stature, Hamilton wore his uniform well, and he won over his men with his courage and high spirits.

In the West Indies, Hamilton had never developed an allegiance to any one state. He viewed America as a unified nation, and the men of his battalion had also shed much of their parochialism. When they drank, a favorite toast was "Cement to the Union!"

As early as 1780, Hamilton had been warning about defects he saw in the Articles of Confederation, and when peace came, the state of America's economy troubled him deeply. He argued that the new nation's debts could only be repaid by a concerted effort from all thirteen states. Since few of his fellow New Yorkers shared his enthusiasm for increasing the federal government's powers, Governor George Clinton would have preferred to keep Hamilton away from Philadelphia entirely. His reputation required naming him to the delegation, but the other New Yorkers were instructed to limit themselves "to the sole and express purpose of revising the Articles of Confederation." And since they were to be bound by a unit rule, the vote of an individual dissident like Hamilton would go unrecorded.

*   *   *

The federal convention was meeting in a historic chamber, the east room of Philadelphia's State House, where the Declaration of Independence had been signed. When delegates arrived at ten o'clock each morning, the square forty-foot chamber with its high plaster ceiling was still cool, and blinds were drawn on the two tall side windows against the sun. No matter how high the temperature rose, those windows would be kept shut to guard against eavesdroppers. Delegates were seated in groups of three and four at tables in front of the presiding member, whose chair was decorated with a sunburst painted on its tall back.

Delegates had adopted an oath of secrecy so strict that Madison felt he must apologize to Jefferson in Paris for not being able to inform him about the proceedings. Annoyed, Jefferson complained to John Adams that the restrictions were "abominable," but he expected that whatever came out of Philadelphia would be "good and wise."

When Virginians presented the Madison proposals, the first challenge came from New Jersey, determined to protect small states from being overwhelmed. The Virginia Plan would determine the number of representatives in the lower house by a state's population. Those men, in turn, would select the upper chambers.

For the time being, Hamilton remained silent. His agenda focused on a central government that could levy taxes for the entire union. In his view, local legislators were suited for only the most mundane chores—building roads, hiring policemen.

Convention delegates had chosen as their secretary William Jackson, one of Washington's former military aides, but when Jackson's recording of the debates proved slipshod and sparse, Madison took on the chore of keeping a fuller account for himself. Since he knew nothing of shorthand and since the delegates were seldom short-winded, Madison chose a seat directly in front of the presiding officer so that he could hear clearly every argument to both his left and right. He used abbreviations and strove to be legible. After each session adjourned, he hurried at once to his rooms to write out his notes more fully while the debates were fresh in his mind.

When Madison's account was published many years later, some

readers credited him with writing the entire Constitution. Madison protested, modestly but accurately, that the document should be regarded as "the work of many heads and many hands."

But his transcript revealed how quarrelsome those heads could be and how often those hands were raised in protest. Pinckney from South Carolina was equally conspicuous for his wealth and his vanity, and Madison disliked the way he seemed to lust after fame and popularity.

At the convention, however, Pinckney spoke impressively—as an American rather than as a southerner—and two dozen of his recommendations were incorporated into the Constitution's final draft. It was Pinckney who came up with names for the executive and legislative branches: President, House, Senate.

For Madison, tiring days filled with difficult compromise were followed by nights devoted to the transcribing. Although he was not given to exaggeration or self-praise, Madison said afterward that keeping the minutes had almost killed him. Only his belief in the uniqueness of the undertaking in Philadelphia sustained him. He was convinced that if a firsthand account of the nation's birth pangs could be preserved and if historians were capable of doing them justice, America's early history could offer more valuable lessons than the story of any other nation in any other age.

That sense of obligation made Madison especially attentive on Monday morning, June 18, 1787, when Hamilton rose to speak for the first time.

He began by explaining that his silence during the first three and a half weeks had been due to his respect for his elders and to the delicacy of disagreeing with his fellow delegates from New York. But now, Hamilton said, the crisis was too severe to indulge those scruples any longer.

As early as 1780, with the war still raging, Hamilton had called for a convention like this one, since the Declaration of Independence, undeniably stirring, was only an advertisement for the new nation, not its blueprint. Hamilton scoffed at amending the Articles or adopting the Virginia Plan. The result, he said, would be only "pork still, with a little change of sauce."

He then outlined his own plan: Two legislative bodies, with members in the lower assembly elected for three years. In the upper chamber, senators would be elected for life and unseated only for bad behavior. The elected chief executive also could be removed only for serious lapses of conduct.

Hamilton recommended that judges be able to nullify any state law that ran counter to his proposed constitution; they, too, would hold office for life unless they misbehaved.

In describing the immense powers of the executive, Hamilton made the tactical mistake of referring to that person as a "monarch," although an elected one. Recovering himself, he tried to make the position sound less threatening by calling the man simply "governor."

That governor, however, could veto any law. If the legislature approved, he could launch wars, sign treaties, and appoint outright the heads of the departments of Finance, War, and Foreign Affairs. Only lesser posts like ambassadorships would require Senate approval. And he could pardon men convicted of every offense except treason; for that offense, the Senate would have to agree.

Madison worried that Hamilton was trumpeting his ideas so indiscreetly that Madison's own proposals would be jeopardized by his bald honesty. Certainly the New Yorker was not tactful. "Take mankind in general," Hamilton said, describing the human clay available for shaping a government. "They are vicious—their passions may be operated upon." Driving home that point, Hamilton added, "Our great error is that we suppose mankind more honest than they are."

In a rash moment, he praised the British system as a desirable model because of its built-in balances. Since men were ruled by ambition and self-interest, government's role was to guarantee that those passions served the public good. When Madison summarized Hamilton's remarks, he retained their sense but toned down their harsher assessments of human nature.

Hamilton's ideas visibly appalled Elbridge Gerry of Massachusetts and George Mason of Virginia, men dedicated to protecting the rights of the states. For some other delegates, his six-hour speech—the longest oration anyone had made at the convention—established

Hamilton as an American Cicero. In any case, New York's unit rule left him powerless within his own delegation.

Before the month was out, Hamilton returned to his law practice in New York, leaving Madison behind to mollify the delegates who suspected that he shared Hamilton's scheme to weaken the states to the point of abolishing them. As discord threatened to destroy the convention, George Washington regretted having been lured to Philadelphia. He had long ago mended the rift with Hamilton and wrote to him candidly, "If to please the people, we offer what we ourselves disapprove, how can we afterwards defend our work?"

Washington concluded his letter, "I am sorry you went away. I wish you were back."

As the humid heat persisted, delegates spent most of their time wrangling over the potential danger in creating a strong chief executive. They finally decided to define the president's powers more sketchily than they had when they adopted Benjamin Franklin's crucial compromise in forming the legislature. Franklin had proposed equal representation for all states in the Senate, with the condition that bills involving money originate in the House, where membership would reflect each state's population.

Madison agreed to an Electoral College when it was put forward as a safe, indirect way to choose the new executive that protected his election from runaway democracy. Senators from each state would select a slate of disinterested citizens to vote for two men on a single ballot. The winner would become president, the runner-up vice president. Since the number of those electors would reflect their congressional representation, the smaller states could prevent the election of a demagogue. Madison hoped that the cumbersome system would also reduce the risk of legislators' becoming kingmakers who undermined the balance of powers.

By August, the convention could no longer avoid the issue of slavery. Madison had come to acknowledge that the greatest division at the convention "did not lie between the large and small states: it lay between the Northern & Southern."

The first shipload of twenty Negroes had arrived in Virginia in 1619, and forty years later, the status of blacks as slaves was established by law. In 1663, Maryland had ruled that their children, as well, were slaves for life.

Now, a Pennsylvania delegate objected to calculating congressional seats by the formula of the Articles of Confederation, which counted a slave as three-fifths of a white voter. Were the slaves citizens? If so, why were they not equally represented? If they were simply property, why were they represented at all?

Since slaves could not vote, apportioning congressional seats by the three-fifths clause gave slave owners about one-third more seats in the House than their numbers alone would justify. But Pinckney warned that South Carolina could never accept any plan that jeopardized the institution of slavery. Oliver Ellsworth of Connecticut suggested that since the Articles had not "meddled with this point," he saw no reason to do so now. "The morality or wisdom of slavery are considerations that belong to the states themselves."

Ellsworth's Connecticut colleague, Roger Sherman, agreed. He disapproved of slavery, Sherman said, but it was "expedient to have as few objections as possible to the proposed scheme of government." Sherman argued that it was "best to leave the matter as we find it."

The subject was too emotional simply to be tabled. Like Washington and Madison, George Mason came from the slave-holding state of Virginia. Yet he called slavery an "infernal traffic originated in the avarice of British merchants." Looking back to the Revolution, Mason noted that if the British had agitated more adroitly, America's slaves could have proven highly dangerous. When Mason cited slave revolts in ancient Greece and Sicily, Pinckney countered slyly that Mason's examples merely proved that "if slavery be wrong, it is justified by the example of all the world."

Mason had the final rebuttal: "Every master of slaves is born a petty tyrant."

Ellsworth of Connecticut raised the stakes. He himself had never owned a slave, he said, and could not judge the effects of slavery on a man's character. But if morality was the issue, perhaps the convention should go further and free all of the slaves. Instead of that drastic step, however, he favored relying on the passage of time. As the number of free workers increased in America, they would eventually replace slave labor.

By maintaining his usual silence, Washington avoided revealing his conflicted feelings. He had first excluded free black volunteers from the Revolutionary army until they came to his headquarters in Cambridge, Massachusetts, to protest. Washington reversed himself and explained to the Continental Congress that if he did not accept the men, the British would recruit them.

At the time that he was struggling against his own disdain, Washington invited to call on him at his Cambridge military headquarters a black poet named Phillis Wheatley, whose work was being hailed through the Northeast. She had written a tribute to Washington, which he said exhibited "a striking proof of your great poetical talents." His enthusiasm was not shared by most other southerners, including Jefferson, who found her poems "below the dignity of criticism."

Washington's closest black companion throughout the war had been his slave William Lee, who rode into battle at the general's side. In 1768, Washington had purchased Billy as a teenager for sixty-one pounds, fifteen shillings. He soon saw that his new acquisition, besides acting as his valet, could keep up with him on horseback.

When they returned from the war, Lee became a smiling fixture at the mansion, laying out Washington's clothes each morning and brushing his hair, pulling it back in a tight queue and tying it with a ribbon. But during their time in the North, Lee had lost his heart to Margaret Thomas, a free black cook from Philadelphia, and he prevailed on Washington to invite her to live at Mount Vernon. Although Washington agreed reluctantly, the letter sending for her reflected his distaste for the woman and his skepticism about their bond:

"The Mulatto fellow William, who has been with me all the war, is attached (married, he says) to one of his own colour. . . . They are both applying to me to get her here and tho' I never wished to see her more, yet I cannot refuse his request (if it can be complied with on reasonable terms) as he has lived with me so long and followed my fortunes through the War with fidelity."

Margaret Thomas may have had second thoughts about giving up freedom for the life of a slave's wife, since Washington's meticulous records made no further mention of her.

Only the previous spring, Billy Lee had fallen and broken his knee. Washington got him onto a sled, paid a surgeon to operate, and found a new role for him since he was too crippled for his usual chores.

Washington's concern for Lee would not have surprised at least one subsequent guest at Mount Vernon. A Polish nobleman came to visit much later with a letter of introduction from General Tadeusz Kościuszko, who had served with Washington in the war. During his ten days at Mount Vernon, the visitor toured Washington's slave quarters and observed the contrast between the gracious life at the manor house and the condition of the 120 slaves who made those comforts possible:

"We entered one of the huts of the Blacks," he wrote, "for one cannot call them by the name of houses. They are more miserable than the most miserable of the cottages of our peasants."

Even so, the visitor has seen enough other estates to know that "General Washington treats his slaves far more humanely than do his fellow citizens of Virginia. Most of those gentlemen give to their Blacks only bread, water and blows."

Washington may not have permitted his slaves to be whipped, but in his younger years he had sold them on the market. And after his victory at Yorktown, he made a point of recovering several of the seventeen slaves who had escaped from Mount Vernon during the war.

The Polish guest was also astounded by the high spirits of the slaves, who played vigorous games every Sunday after working all week in the fields. "Either from habit," he speculated, "or from natural humor disposed to gaiety, I have never seen the blacks sad."

Lafayette knew that slavery weighed on Washington's conscience and had written after the war to suggest that the two of them buy a small estate together and experiment with freeing its slaves and hiring them instead as tenant farmers. Washington had put him off.

Three years later, when Lafayette bought land in the South American colony of Cayenne to put his plan into action, Washington wrote to congratulate him on "a generous and noble proof of your humanity." He added that he wished Lafayette's spirit would spread throughout the United States. "But I despair of seeing it."

And yet, Washington concluded, "to set the slaves at float at once would, I really believe, be productive of much inconvenience and mischief." He had decided that slaves should be freed only by degrees and then only by the act of a state legislature.

As the debate over slavery persisted, Randolph of Virginia suggested appointing a committee to seek a compromise. Most delegates supported that maneuver, except for the determined abolitionists from New Hampshire, Pennsylvania, and Delaware. The Massachusetts delegation abstained.

Like Washington, Madison had been struggling with the immorality of slavery throughout his life. Three years earlier, his father had given him a tract of 560 acres, even though farming held no attraction for him. To a friend, Madison wrote that he wanted "to depend as little as possible on the labor of slaves," which was why he had turned to land speculation. But that alone could not support his life at Montpelier.

As a member of the committee to reach a compromise, Madison hoped to keep Georgia and South Carolina committed to the new Constitution by going along with a provision that would permit the importing of slaves for the next thirteen years — until the year 1800. But when the full convention took up the matter again, delegates voted to add another eight years and allow the slave trade to continue until 1808.

Madison foresaw "all the mischief" that the next twenty years was sure to bring. He claimed that a delay that long would dishonor America's character more than if the new Constitution did not mention slavery at all.

One final committee was formed to resolve every other nettlesome issue that had been postponed, and Madison was chosen to represent Virginia. His colleagues had watched throughout the summer as he worked tirelessly but unobtrusively to ease discord and search out points of agreement. When a vote went against him, Madison yielded with no show of temper.

His fellow Virginians did not share his equitable nature. Randolph said he doubted whether he could vote for the proposed Constitution since several of its provisions were "odious." George Mason said that he would sooner chop off his right hand than sign the document as it stood.

And yet, by calm persuasion among allies and opponents, Madison had achieved much of what he had come to Philadelphia to accomplish. What's more, the success had come in the record time of three months and twenty-three days—with Sundays observed as days of rest and a two-day hiatus to mark the Fourth of July. To write and modify the Articles of Confederation and then persuade the last state to ratify them had taken five years.

Madison remained troubled that the small states had been able to force an equal vote for themselves in the new Senate, and he regretted that Congress was not given the power to veto state laws. But he agreed when Benjamin Franklin said that prolonging this convention was unlikely to achieve a better result.

Even so, Madison's summation to Jefferson in September was less than jubilant. Yes, he wrote, the outline of America's new Constitution was attractive, but Madison was not betting on its success since state governments retained a great capacity to thwart it.

As the convention completed its work on Monday, September 17, 1787, Madison toted up the statistics that testified to his stamina. By adjournment day, some delegates had already left on family business, others to protest the proceedings. Of the original delegates, only thirty-eight had remained regularly in the hall. But as Madison put it, he had not been "absent a single day, nor more than a casual fraction of an hour in any day." During the convention's eighty-six days, he had risen to speak on seventy-one of them.

Hamilton had come back to Philadelphia to sign a four-page engrossed copy of the new Constitution, and Franklin was also on hand, aware of another fateful moment in his nation's history. Franklin could no longer muster the strength to take the floor, but he had written out remarks for James Wilson of Pennsylvania to read into record:

"I confess that there are several parts of this Constitution which I do not at present approve," Franklin's statement began, "but I am not sure I shall never approve them." He had lived long enough, he said, to have changed his opinion often on important subjects because of better information or further reflection. "It is therefore that the older I grow, the more apt I am to doubt my own judgment, and to pay more respect to the judgment of others."

Franklin touched lightly on religion. He had always held his personal beliefs close to the point of smothering them. Now he observed that most men think they know the truth, and he quoted a quip that the only difference between Catholics and Protestants was that the Church of Rome was infallible and the Church of England was never wrong. Franklin segued to the story about a French woman who ended a family quarrel by complaining, "I don't know how it happens, sister, but I meet with nobody but myself that's always in the right."

Franklin then offered a neat summation:

"Thus, I consent, Sir, to this Constitution because I expect no better and because I am not sure that it is not the best."

Some members complimented Doctor Franklin's remarks even as they refused to sign the document. Three of the holdouts—Gerry of Massachusetts and Madison's two fellow Virginians, Mason and Randolph— said they feared the powers being given to the new central government. Since Gerry took pride in having signed both the Declaration of Independence and the Articles of Confederation, he was distressed to be withholding his signature from the Constitution.

But his resistance to a standing army remained great. To him, America's militia provided defense enough, and yet this new document authorized Congress to raise money for a federal army. Looking west, Gerry saw territories arising that could dominate a national government. If the settlers acquired power, he warned, they would "like all men, abuse it. They will oppress commerce and drain our wealth into the western country."

Hamilton rebuked his opponents by pointing out that no one's ideas were further from the finished product than his own but that the choice was between "anarchy and convulsion on the one side, and the chance of good to be expected from the plan on the other."

Franklin had promised that his earlier criticism would stay within those walls and urged other delegates to return home and support the new Constitution wholeheartedly. His colleagues knew that, however sincere Franklin's vow, secrecy might be impossible for him. At suppers around town, he had often spoken so expansively about the day's deliberations that a delegate had to be assigned to ward off his indiscretions.

One evening, Franklin entertained a guest by displaying a snake with two heads that he kept preserved in a jar. Imagine the dilemma of that snake, Franklin said, chuckling, if one head chose to go to one side of a bush and the other was adamant about going to the other side. In fact, he said, the snake's quandary reminded him of something that had happened that very day at the convention. Before he could finish the story, his minder broke in to remind Franklin about his oath of silence.

For Washington, discretion was inbred and congenial. His diary entries had been limited to "Attended convention" or, for variety, "Attended the convention," "In convention," and, with the suggestion of a sigh, "In convention as usual."

But he had shown how seriously he took the need for secrecy when a delegate brought him a copy of the early Virginia Plan that had been dropped accidentally outside the chamber. At his iciest, Washington brandished it before the delegates.

"I know not whose paper it is," Washington said. "But here it is. Let him who owns it, take it."

With that, he threw down the document on a desk and strode from the hall. The owner did not come forward.

Washington's show of irritation was unusual. Presiding over the convention, he had considered his proper role to remain silent during the debates. But his face was no impenetrable mask. Men noted that when he was bored, Washington's eyes went blank, but if tempers rose, he looked anxious and solicitous. He relaxed again only after a compromise had been reached.

With the delegates about to return home, Washington asked what they wanted to do about the convention minutes; reports of acrimony might give ammunition to men who wanted to retain the Articles. One delegate recommended either burning the records or entrusting them to Washington for safekeeping. A majority of delegates speculated that the minutes might be needed one day to refute allegations about what had just transpired, and they voted to hand them over to Washington. The only exception was Maryland, whose delegates had been instructed to report publicly on the proceedings.

Delegates had stipulated that the new Constitution be ratified in each state at popularly elected conventions. When nine of the thirteen states approved it, the Constitution would immediately replace the Articles.

As members signed off on the document, Franklin pointed to the painting of the sun on the president's chair. Often during the course of the sessions, Franklin said, he had been uncertain about the direction in which the sun was moving. "But now, at length," Franklin concluded, "I have the happiness to know that it is a rising, and not a setting, sun."

The time had come for the delegates to sell their handiwork to the suspicious states. They could make the valid claim that most elements of their new Constitution had been recycled from earlier documents. They had drawn on the Articles themselves and on various state constitutions. They had also consulted the Northwest Ordinance that the Continental Congress had passed two months earlier. Vermont and Kentucky were already in line for statehood, and the ordinance set out procedures for eventually absorbing the territories north and west of the Ohio River. Even though the ordinance also prohibited slavery north of the Ohio, every southern congressman voted for it, suggesting that they knew and endorsed the compromise reached in Philadelphia.

And yet the power given by the Constitution to a strong executive and to the judicial branch meant that the document was no mere cobbling together of familiar ideas. Its novelty began with its first seven words drafted by Gouverneur Morris of Pennsylvania: "We the people of the United States." They served notice that these were principles, unlike the Articles, that transcended state boundaries. On behalf of the American people, Morris continued, the Constitution would "form a more perfect union, establish justice, insure domestic tranquility, provide for the common defence, promote the general welfare, and secure the Blessings of Liberty to ourselves and our posterity."

Signing the document, Hamilton shared Madison's doubts that it would be ratified. He expected men deeply in debt to resist a fiscally sound government since the reforms would stop them from cheating their creditors. Yet if the Constitution were defeated, Hamilton could imagine a British prince accepting an invitation to cross the Atlantic and rule over the United States. The best protection against that calamity lay in the fact that Washington would probably be the first president. With a touch of complacency, Hamilton predicted that "this will insure a wise choice of men to administer the government and a good administration."

With debate raging from state to state, attacks grew personal. In mid-October 1787, Hamilton appealed to Mount Vernon for help because Governor Clinton's supporters were claiming that he had first palmed himself off on Washington as an aide and then been dismissed from the general's official family. Resurrecting their six-year-old rift, a newspaper article described Hamilton—although not by name—as "a superficial, self-conceited coxcomb." Washington did not want to take sides between Hamilton and Clinton, but he issued a rebuttal of the specific charges and expressed again his highest regard for his former aide.

As the controversy continued in America, Lafayette in Paris described for Hamilton the growing tension between Great Britain and France. Lafayette recommended a friendly neutrality as America's best strategy. But if the new nation were forced into war, Lafayette hoped the hostilities lasted long enough for the United States to annex Canada and Newfoundland.

From what Jefferson was hearing in Paris, the new Constitution sounded verbose, even comical. He thought everything useful in it could have been added to the Articles as three or four new provisions. He wrote mockingly to John Adams in London that "their President seems like a bad edition of the Polish king." Jefferson was careful to be less dismissive to Madison, who sent a long letter in which at last he could lay out the reasoning behind the Constitution's inevitable compromises.

Jefferson was not persuaded. He faulted the Constitution for not showing proper respect for popular opinion but, inconsistently, he also objected because no limit had been established for the number of times this new president might seek reelection to a four-year term. Jefferson complained that letting voters retain the same man in office was an invitation to tyranny.

Most troubling of all was the absence of a specific list of rights that no administration could violate. Jefferson's concern was so great that he urged states not to ratify the Constitution until that unforgivable omission had been corrected.

Before the convention, Madison had been content to walk a step behind the author of the Declaration of Independence, and his correspondence remained modest and conciliatory. But Madison had spent four grueling months in Philadelphia while Jefferson was enjoying himself in Paris. Having thought longer and deeper about the issues, Madison lectured his friend on the role of government for a country that was already large and growing larger.

Madison favored a system neutral enough to prevent any single segment of society from denying the rights of any other. But he also wanted to ensure that the government was kept within its own limits.

In launching their ratification campaign, Madison, Hamilton, and John Jay took the name "Federalists" and prepared a series of articles to appear throughout the country. In New York journals, they published twenty-seven letters signed "Publius," in honor of Publius Valerius, who had founded a republican government in Rome after the fall of its last Tarquin king. Their recent immersion in the pertinent issues allowed Madison, Hamilton, and Jay to write quickly. Hamilton planned for their articles to appear four times a week, a tidal wave of propaganda that would sweep the Constitution to ratification. He expected the three men to meet regularly at his house at the corner of Wall Street and Broadway, but deadline pressure often required that an essay go directly to the printer without their consultation.

When Hamilton took a break to tend to his law practice, Madison stepped in and wrote numbers 37 to 58 by himself. Jay, who became ill, contributed only number 64 in a later series. Then, as Madison left New York in March 1788, Hamilton resumed the assignment, apologizing unnecessarily for any repetition or lapses in logic.

Hamilton had expected to print twenty to twenty-five essays in book form. As the number crept to eighty-five, printing costs increased to eight times the original estimate, but publication went forward. The volume was now called *The Federalist*.

With the essays generating momentum slowly, several state conventions had already approved the Constitution before the most controversial articles appeared. Washington admired their high intellectual tone, which was far removed from the inflammatory political tracts that were being passed around in cities and towns. He predicted that posterity would pay attention to the essays as long as men were concerned about the ingredients of a civil society.

In Massachusetts, both Samuel Adams and Governor John Hancock inspected the new Constitution warily. Its advocates also had to overcome Elbridge Gerry's argument that governing such a diverse collection of states would lead inevitably to an authoritarian regime. To offset Hancock's resistance, the Constitution's supporters played to his notorious vanity and suggested that, if it were approved, he might one day become president.

With Sam Adams, the key was his well-known sympathy for Boston's workers and tradesmen. Paul Revere remained famous for sounding the alarm against the Redcoats, and he called at Adams's house to report that a mass meeting at a popular tavern had backed the Constitution.

Adams asked how big the crowd had been.

"More, sir, than the *Green Dragon* could hold," Revere replied.

"And where were the rest, Mister Revere?"

"In the streets, sir."

That show of popular support persuaded Sam Adams to join Hancock at the ratification convention on January 31, 1788. The two men had been estranged, but each had recently lost a son, and grief had

helped to reconcile them. Hancock endorsed the Constitution but proposed nine amendments to limit the power of the new federal government; Adams applauded Hancock's position.

Even with the backing of Boston's Revolutionary lions, ratification
in Massachusetts passed by only nineteen votes, 187 to 168.

Despite their close friendship, Madison had not revealed to Jefferson
his role in writing *The Federalist*. That anonymity allowed him to challenge in print one of Jefferson's most cherished principles—that "the
people" should meet often to resolve any difficult issue. Madison was
wary of the same passions that Jefferson celebrated so cheerfully. His
own careful temperament persuaded Madison that it was the role of
leadership to channel the public's unruly emotions.

Washington's endorsement had been essential, but it did not prevent attacks on the Constitution from Patrick Henry or from George
Mason, a man both Jefferson and Madison respected for his devotion
to republican government.

Six states, led by Delaware, had already ratified the Constitution
before Virginia's delegates met in Richmond on June 2, 1788. Henry
would be pitted against Madison, whose thin voice barely carried to
the walls of the chamber. As Henry launched his attack, he was so mes-
merizing that the convention's stenographer became transfixed and
laid down his pen.

The new empire would suck the people's blood with taxes, Henry
cried, and crush them with its standing army. Turning to the subject of
slavery, Henry became carried away by his own forebodings and
shouted, "They'll free your niggers!" His audience only laughed at his
hysteria and shrugged off the threat.

Henry was on firmer ground in mocking the theoretical safeguards
written into the Constitution: "What can avail your specious, imagi-
nary balance, your rope-dancing, chain-rattling ridiculous ideal checks
and contrivances?"

Exhaustion and stress sent Madison to bed for a few days. When he
returned to the fray, his voice was barely a whisper. He had marshaled
his arguments with his customary precision, but the stenographer
recorded eight times that Madison spoke so softly that he could not be

heard. Madison himself worried that Henry's rebuttal—his dramatic pauses and disbelieving shakes of the head—would undo an hour of Madison's best efforts.

Yet Madison seemed to be carrying the convention. Whenever his voice dropped too low, delegates got up from their chairs and drew closer to hear him. When Henry objected that only three-fourths of the states were required to adopt the Constitution, Madison asked, "Is it not self-evident that a trifling minority ought not to bind a majority? Would the honorable gentlemen agree to continue the most radical defects in the old system because the petty state of Rhode Island would not agree to remove them?"

During the twenty-four days of debate, light moments were rare. But Madison appreciated a newspaper's caricature of one of his allies, George Nicholas, who was short, sharp-tongued, and shockingly fat. When Madison saw the cartoon of Nicholas as a plum pudding on legs, he laughed until tears came to his eyes.

A sticking point for Virginians became whether the new document should be accepted before or after it was amended. Despite Jefferson's pressing for a bill of rights, Madison had resisted, preferring to rely on the sweeping statement that every power not mentioned in the Constitution was reserved to the people.

From Paris, where agitation against the king was mounting, Jefferson wrote to George Washington that not itemizing a citizen's rights in the Constitution had been a fatal error. And gradually, Madison was coming to understand that to deflate the opposition required a plain statement of those rights. As a proud author of the Constitution as it stood, however, he could not truly believe that omitting a bill of rights had been a serious defect.

Finally, to defuse the issue, Madison and his allies agreed that at the next Congress they would present amendments to guarantee specific liberties. But Henry found their pledge easy to ridicule. "Do you enter into a compact first," he asked, with a sneer, "and afterwards settle the terms of the government?"

His answer came on June 25, when Virginia's convention voted 89 to 79 for the new Constitution. Delegates did not know that a favorable vote in New Hampshire had already guaranteed its adoption.

From Poughkeepsie in New York, Hamilton had been keeping a close check on the New Hampshire vote. Out of his own delegation of sixty-five members, he considered only nineteen reliably committed to the Constitution, despite his public predictions that if it was not ratified, the country would collapse in civil war. Hamilton had paid a rider on horseback to rush New Hampshire's result to Poughkeepsie, but even after that decisive vote, the deliberations in Virginia and New York remained crucial. A lasting union would require their wealth and prestige.

Burnt-out but determined, Madison set off for New York, hoping to sway its convention. Governor George Clinton was leading his state's opposition and trying to make ratification conditional on the proposed amendments. No, Madison protested, the Constitution required adoption "in toto and forever."

Hearing of the ratification by Virginia broke up Clinton's bloc, and the Constitution won in New York, 31 to 29. But delegates insisted that their votes were being given "in full confidence" that amendments would be added.

North Carolina and Rhode Island still held out, and opponents in other states were clinging to the idea of a second convention. Since Madison considered that a ploy to return power to the states, he and his Federalists countered with a decisive concession: The first session of the Congress convened under the new Constitution would, in effect, constitute a second convention because it would address any unfinished business left over from the first.

The people of New York celebrated the Constitution by paying lavish tribute to its local champion. Carpenters at the shipyard fashioned a miniature replica of a ship, twenty-seven feet long and exact in every detail, which they christened the *Alexander Hamilton* and paraded down Broadway with full sails and waves fashioned from canvas crashing against its hull.

The effect was marred by a mishap during the launch when an

arm of the statue representing Hamilton broke off—the arm holding the Constitution.

The reconstituted Congress was scheduled to meet in February or March of 1789. Beforehand, Madison rode again through the winter chill to consult with Washington at Mount Vernon. They spent a companionable few days, disturbed only by Madison's attack of hemorrhoids. Since it was inevitable that Washington would be elected president, Madison wrote a draft of an inaugural address for him to deliver at New York's city hall, which had been renamed Federal Hall.

The man receiving the second-largest number of electoral votes would win the vice presidency. John Adams seemed the probable choice for the post, and the results went as Madison expected: A unanimous 69 votes for Washington as president, 34 for Adams to serve with him.

The speech that Madison prepared resonated with the elevated language that came naturally to Jefferson but that Madison could achieve only because Washington would be delivering it. "The preservation of the sacred fire of liberty," Madison wrote, "and the destiny of the republican method of government, are justly considered as deeply, perhaps as finally, staked on the experiment entrusted to the hands of the American people."

Madison had hoped to take one of Virginia's seats in the House of Representatives without having to wage a campaign. Then he learned that Patrick Henry was backing another candidate, James Monroe, who had been one of Madison's friends and business partners.

A protégé of Jefferson, who had tutored him in law, Monroe was thirty years old, six feet tall, and a veteran of the Revolution. He had been badly wounded at Trenton, then survived the winter with Washington at Valley Forge. Until he married Elizabeth Kortright early in 1786 and immediately began a family, Monroe had enjoyed flirting with young women, but they often found him stuffy and plain-looking, although they admired the pronounced dimple in his chin.

When he and Madison served together in the Continental Congress, Monroe had written to complain privately to Jefferson that Madison regularly undercut him, and he had been disappointed not to be chosen as a delegate for the Constitutional Convention in Philadelphia. Recruited now to run for Congress, Monroe assured himself that he was opposing Madison only because of his own commitment to a citizen's bill of rights.

When Monroe's supporters began claiming that Madison actively opposed those amendments, Madison's friends prevailed on him to end his complacency and launch a gentlemanly campaign. He won easily and resumed cordial relations with Monroe. But as he took his seat in Congress, Madison was finally convinced of the need for a definitive bill of rights.

During the ratification process, Madison's reputation had swelled across the nation. Less than a year earlier, his four-page letter had sketched out for Washington a new form of government. Now he was being called upon to give it shape—creating executive departments, developing a system of taxation, establishing the role of federal judges.

John Adams had recently returned from London to join in the task. The vice president–elect had a well-known weakness for pomp, and he was being accompanied from Massachusetts by a gratifying cavalry escort as he headed for New York and America's rebirth.

Washington reviewing the Whiskey Rebellion army

Chapter Three

WASHINGTON
(1789–1797)

To serve as America's first president, Washington would be giving up the pleasures of country life for a rented house in New York. It was a sacrifice with one consolation: The costs of maintaining Mount Vernon were outrunning his current income. Washington intended to decline the presidential salary, as he had refused to accept pay for commanding the Continental Army. But his new expense account would underwrite his daily living and the entertaining that had become a burden.

As Washington prepared for his trip, he learned the extent of his financial straits. He was refused when he applied for a loan of a thousand pounds to pay off his local debts and had to appeal to an acquaintance for five hundred pounds. Then he had to ask for another hundred simply to get to New York.

During his ride north, Washington stopped in Philadelphia at the house of one financier who had never failed him. In 1781, Robert Morris had established the first U.S. bank, with a capital of four hundred thousand dollars, fifty thousand of it his own money. That transaction restored America's credit and allowed the war to continue.

But the United States now owed more than $1.6 million in back interest payments on European loans and almost $1.4 million in current payments on the principal. At home, the Continental Congress had run up a debt of $41 million, and the individual states had issued another $25 million in paper.

That was the country's bleak economic picture when Washington asked Morris to become his secretary of the treasury. Morris refused but assured Washington that he knew someone better—"a far cleverer fellow than I am"—Alexander Hamilton.

Washington was startled. "I always knew Colonel Hamilton to be a man of superior talents," he said, "but never supposed he had any knowledge of finance."

Happy to be off the hook, Morris grew expansive. "He knows everything, sir. To a mind like his, nothing comes amiss."

The new regulations stipulated that the electors' ballots must be counted in front of both the House and the Senate. Those bodies were coming together so slowly, however, that for more than a month America was left without a government. The delay troubled Washington, not least because the country was losing three hundred thousand pounds sterling in tax revenue.

By April 26, 1789, the inauguration could go forward. Jubilant crowds turned out along his route to cheer Washington as he made his way to New York. In Trenton, a row of girls, each dressed in white and carrying a basket of flowers, was joined by a row of young women in the same costume, while behind them stood a throng of married women. Their theme was spelled out in blossoms: "The Defender of the Mothers Will Be the Protector of the Daughters."

When Washington reached Federal Hall, the state's chancellor,

Robert Livingston, led him to a balcony where a crowd was waiting in the rain. Livingston administered the oath of office to the first president, and at its conclusion Washington said, "I solemnly swear." He repeated the oath himself and added, "So help me God." With that, Washington bent forward and kissed the Bible on which he had sworn.

"It is done!" Livingston shouted to the crowd. "Long live George Washington, President of the United States!"

Washington bowed and went inside to the Senate chambers, took the chair designated for him, and began a low-pitched and somewhat embarrassed reading of his twenty-minute speech.

In the audience was Fisher Ames, a thirty-year-old member of the new Congress from Dedham, Massachusetts. In recent days, Ames had been taking the measure of the men who would be serving with him. Not surprisingly, because Ames had been an ardent backer of the Constitution, Madison struck him as a man of sense and integrity. But he also found Madison physically "little and ordinary," and his politics seemed timid and shaped by a concern with retaining his popularity in Virginia.

At the sight of George Washington, however, Ames became again the wide-eyed schoolboy who had been admitted to Harvard College at the age of twelve. "Time has made havoc upon his face," Ames wrote to a friend. "His aspect grave, almost to sadness, his modesty, actually shaking; his voice deep, a little tremulous, and so low as to call for close attention." Ames said that he sat entranced. "It seemed to me an allegory, in which virtue was personified." He was sure that "no man *ever* had so fair a claim to veneration as he."

The veneration turned out to be not universal, and Washington found the next eight years as vexing and uncongenial as he had anticipated. From the time the Revolutionary War ended, Washington had hoped fervently that a spirit of unity would prevail over any political divisions. Whenever he saw a fissure opening, as had happened with the Cincinnati, Washington did his best to heal it. The society had survived but, with Washington distancing himself, never became the menace its critics had feared. As president, Washington intended to be equally alert to other schisms that might threaten the union.

                              *   *   *

During his years in France, Jefferson had found much to admire, not least Maria Cosway, the blond twenty-seven-year-old wife of an English artist. When Jefferson analyzed the nature of a Frenchman's passion—"only moments of ecstasy amidst days and months of restlessness and torment"—he might have been summing up his own blighted romance with Mrs. Cosway.

Although that affair drifted to an end, Paris continued to fascinate and charm Jefferson. "Here, it seems a man might pass a life without encountering a single rudeness," he wrote to a professor at William and Mary College. "In the pleasures of the table, they are far before us, because, with good taste they unite temperance. They do not terminate the most social meals by transforming themselves into brutes. I have never seen a man drunk in France, even among the lowest of the people. Were I to proceed to tell you how much I enjoy their architecture, sculpture, painting, music, I should want for words."

If anything, the rumblings of revolution only increased Jefferson's admiration for his hosts. At home, many of his countrymen shared his optimism about the protests against King Louis XVI and were inclined to welcome a French version of America's challenge to monarchy. Around the United States, supporters banded together in "Democratic Clubs" to praise France's Jacobin movement and urge that their government extend aid to the French rebels.

After the Bastille was stormed in 1789, Lafayette made a gift to Washington of a key to the prison. In those early days, Washington also was impressed by this popular uprising that promised the birth of another constitutional government. He called the development in France so wonderful that the mind could scarcely grasp it. And yet Washington had misgivings. This first paroxysm of liberty had been triumphant, but he worried that it would not be the last.

"The Revolution," Washington wrote, "is of too great a magnitude to be effected in so short a space and with the loss of so little blood." Very soon, he was also entertaining doubts about the influence on America of the new Democratic Clubs.

                              *   *   *

As the impassioned flights of Jefferson's pen indicated, the prospect of more blood running in Parisian gutters did not dismay him. He was willing to see "half the earth desolated," Jefferson once wrote, "were there but an Adam and Eve left in every country, and left free, it could be better than it is now."

In the early days of French unrest, Jefferson had blamed the king's problems on the tendency of his queen, Marie Antoinette, to involve herself in politics. "The tender breasts of women," he wrote to an American friend, "were not formed for political convulsions." To Madison, Jefferson offered a mixed judgment on Louis XVI. The king was irascible and rude, certainly, and religious to the point of bigotry. He loved his people but was governed too much by his wife, who was willful and dissipated.

While Jefferson deplored the meddling of women, John Adams had a different complaint about the unrest in France. He resented the unseemly ambition that the revolution was awakening in its men. Adams had labored his whole life to lift himself from being an obscure small-town lawyer to becoming an American statesman. Now he was ready to raise the drawbridge against other men's aspirations. "Every man should know his place," Adams wrote, "and be made to keep it."

People gossiped that Adams longed to marry his daughters to European aristocrats. Whether that was true or not, opponents jeered at his fixation on titles and gave him one based on his heft—"His Rotundity." Adams regretted that the stark designation of "president" had been chosen for his nation's leader. He was convinced that—whatever lofty-minded philosophers might think—if George Washington were introduced to the common people of foreign countries by so meager a title as president, "they will despise him to *all eternity*."

Contemptuous of Adams's enthusiasm for American titles, Jefferson remarked that he wished Adams had been in France lately to watch the nobility fleeing for their lives from Versailles. "If he could then have had one fibre of *aristocracy* left in his frame, he would have been a proper subject for *bedlam*."

As France's revolution progressed, Jefferson sent Madison day-by-day accounts of life in Paris. Their judicious tone did not mask his pleasure at being recognized as the godfather of French liberation. How different was Jefferson's reputation now from when he had been received in England. There, during an audience with King George, he had felt he was being snubbed as the author of the Declaration of Independence.

In private, Jefferson was advising Lafayette on his draft of a "Declaration of the Rights of Man." The composition owed much to the American declaration, but although Lafayette spoke English well, his French could not match Jefferson's felicity. "Nature has made man free and equal," Lafayette's first point began, but with an immediate qualification: "Any distinction necessary to the social order to be founded on its utility."

Freedom of speech and the press became man's right to "the communication of all his thoughts by all possible means." Happiness was considered a "quest" rather than a pursuit.

Jefferson boasted to Madison that the American Revolution was being viewed by French insurgents "as a model for them on every occasion." America's authority, he added, "has been treated like the Bible, open to explanation but not to question."

Jefferson had already requested permission from Congress to return to the United States, but after a mob cut off the heads of officials at the Bastille, he noted, "Indeed, the scene is too interesting to be left at present."

Excitement struck closer to home when the apartments in Jefferson's building were robbed at three different times. He ordered bars and alarm bells installed on his windows and joined with his neighbors in requesting a police guard.

Jefferson objected to a growing feeling among New Englanders that France was owed no special favors despite her decisive aid during the American Revolution. To say that gratitude should not affect national conduct was a principle from the dark ages, Jefferson argued. How could one honestly equate Britain—a country he had derided to Abigail Adams as "rich, proud, hectoring, swearing, squibbing, carnivorous"—with France, which, having spent "her blood and money to save us, has opened her bosom to us in peace."

By the time Congress granted Jefferson's earlier request to come home, he was sure that Louis XVI would accept a constitutional monarchy and was sorry he would miss the peaceful end to another triumph of the people.

As Jefferson prepared for the voyage, Madison sounded him out about accepting a position in Washington's administration. Jefferson declined with considerable force since he hoped to return to France the following spring.

His personal life, however, was presenting Jefferson with a more wrenching decision. Sally Hemings, his lovely and light-skinned slave, had come to Paris to look after his motherless daughters, then seventeen and eleven. Sally was half-sister to Jefferson's late wife, and now, nearing seventeen herself, she was pregnant with her first child. Much later, she told her family that she had refused to leave Paris until Jefferson promised to free her children when they turned twenty-one. For Jefferson, that turmoil, combined with the prospect of returning to Virginia, became so stressful that, with bags packed and ready to sail, he suffered his first migraine headache since he had left America.

Until Jefferson landed in Norfolk and picked up the newspapers, he did not know that Washington had gone ahead and nominated him to be secretary of state. Wending his way slowly to Monticello with his entourage, Jefferson wrote to Washington that he foresaw only criticism of his performance at the Department of State and would much prefer—unless the president insisted—to return to France.

As usual, Washington prevailed. But before Jefferson went to take up his duties at State, he developed another migraine that lasted six weeks. He arrived at last in the capital in March 1790, to find that the enthusiasm of Democratic Club members for France's revolution matched his own. But in Paris, he had kept current with American politics only by mail and had missed the emerging nuances of personality and self-interest within the new government.

When Jefferson went to call on the president one day, he encountered Alexander Hamilton on the street. Hamilton seemed in despair, and for an hour he harangued Jefferson as he paced back and forth in front of Washington's door. The problem was economic. Hamilton said that divisions in Congress about the nation's credit and about retiring the debt were so intense that he could imagine some representatives withdrawing from the session and even from the union. Jefferson heard out Hamilton sympathetically, not fully aware of a widening breach in their philosophies.

Hamilton's opponents were especially critical of his plan for the federal government to assume outstanding state debts going back to the days of the colonies and the Articles of Confederation. Hamilton had told congressmen and wealthy friends about his proposal, and some of them began to buy up the bonds of veterans and farmers who had assumed the paper would never be redeemed.

Madison was outraged by a cynical speculation that rewarded government insiders, but Hamilton argued that it was impractical to try to hunt down the original owners of the bonds, and he claimed that the future credit of the country depended on paying those who actually had the bonds in their possession. He went even further, suggesting that it was the speculators who had shown the stronger faith in America's future.

Jefferson volunteered to set up a meeting so that Hamilton and Madison, once firmly allied in their *Federalist* days, could resolve their differences. Over dinner, an unlikely compromise was struck. Madison and another holdout in the Congress agreed to drop their opposition to Hamilton's policy of debt assumption in return for Hamilton's support for moving the nation's capital to a tract of land along the Potomac River.

The Constitution had stipulated a federal district ten miles square but had not specified where it should be located. George Washington was known to favor strongly the building of that "Federal City" within an easy ride from Mount Vernon, but congressional wrangling had blocked a decision until, at dinner, Hamilton agreed to transfer the government to the Potomac by the year 1800. For the decade until then, its offices would move from New York to Philadelphia.

Despite the opposition in Congress, Hamilton's performance at the Treasury was justifying Morris's high praise. He planned a national Bank of the United States that would strengthen the central government by combining state and federal debts and paying them off with federal securities. Hamilton also recommended taxes on imports and distilled spirits, on the theory that they were more acceptable to farmers than a tax on land. To guard against Indian raids on the frontier, he urged that the government borrow enough money to underwrite an effective army.

Practical as Hamilton's financial theories appeared to be—and Washington had been won over by them—Jefferson was becoming convinced that they would move the United States toward the dubious British model. Worse still, Hamilton might be among those men who hoped one day to see America ruled by a king. Jefferson had never lost his belief that men who tilled the earth were "the chosen people of God" and that the most genuine virtue resided only in their breasts.

When Washington contracted pneumonia in May 1790 and appeared to be near death, discreet jockeying began among his possible replacements beneath their cries of alarm. As vice president, John Adams was the logical choice, although his wife dreaded the prospect. Abigail Adams confided to her sister that the government was not cemented strongly enough to last, and Washington's death would have "most disastrous consequences."

John Adams viewed Hamilton at the Treasury as a wildly ambitious and irresponsible intriguer. Hamilton, in turn, regarded Jefferson's disavowal of interest in the presidency as a sham and considered himself the more popular choice. And Jefferson had repeated to Madison Benjamin Franklin's evaluation of Adams: "Always an honest man, often a great one, but sometimes absolutely mad."

To everyone's professed delight, Washington made a full recovery. But he was debating whether to accept a second term. At sixty, Washington spoke of himself as already growing old and confessed to Jefferson that his physical health was declining. More alarming were new lapses in a memory that Washington had always considered faulty. He wondered whether other men were noticing a mental decline that was not yet clear to him. But Washington was realistic enough to forgo false modesty, and he knew that a struggle to replace him might tear the government apart.

From the start of the Revolution, Washington had feared and detested political factions. And yet Jefferson and Madison already seemed to be pulling away from staunch Federalists like Hamilton

and Adams and aligning themselves instead with the Democratic
Clubs that backed the French Revolution. Despite the clubs' name,
Jefferson and his allies—the majority of them southerners—were
being called Republicans. Only years later would their label change
to "Democrats."

Upheaval in France was sharpening those divisions within the
United States. And in the British Parliament, Edmund Burke described Lafayette's "Declaration of the Rights of Man" as an essay that
would "disgrace the imbecility of school boys." By that time, Jefferson
was too canny to acknowledge his role in framing the declaration, but
he quietly promoted newspaper articles praising France.

The partisan spirit engulfing politics had led to combative newspapers
sprouting up around the nation until printers were now turning out
hundreds of weeklies. As early as 1785, a thirty-six-year-old Bostonian
named John Fenno had moved to New York to launch the *Gazette of
the United States*. His paper ran no advertisements, unless one
counted Fenno's unstinting praise for Hamilton and Adams and the
way he treated any scrap of news about the president and Mrs. Washington as bulletins from a royal court. Readers could expect admiring
details about the president's Tuesday receptions, Martha Washington's
soirees on Friday evenings, and their regular outings to the theater,
where *School for Scandal* was a particular favorite.

To counter the influence of Fenno and other Federalist editors, Jefferson induced Philip Morin Freneau, a friend of Madison's from Princeton, to become a translator in the State Department. That job would
pay his keep while he launched a newspaper devoted to boosting Jefferson's Republican faction. Freneau, just turning forty, showed a
marked talent for vituperation. His *National Gazette* reveled in personal attacks on the Federalists—Alexander Hamilton for his long
nose, John Adams for his "breadth of belly."

Writing under several pseudonyms, Hamilton retaliated with attacks on Jefferson for underwriting Freneau with a government job
and for opposing the Constitution before it had been adopted. Madison and James Monroe were delegated to rebut the charges, but the

public rift was hastening the evolution of America's two-party system.

Jefferson sounded an injured note, claiming that, unlike Hamilton, who signed some essays "An American," he always put his name to anything he wrote. In fact, Jefferson had tried to keep his own contributions to the *Gazette* anonymous until a printer inadvertently revealed his connection. That exposure obliged Jefferson to apologize to Freneau's targets and led Washington to suggest to him that perhaps Freneau should not be holding a job in the same government he denounced so regularly.

Jefferson listened without committing himself, but he had resolved not to fire Freneau. "His paper has saved the Constitution which was galloping fast into monarchy," Jefferson wrote in his journal. "It is well and universally known that it has been that paper which has checked the career of the Monocrats."

Freneau's broadsides were reinforced by those from Benjamin Bache, Benjamin Franklin's grandson and a disappointed office seeker. Going after leading Federalists in his *General Advertiser* and later the *Aurora*, Bache was candid that his object was "to destroy undue impressions in favor of Mr. Washington." He attacked the president's love of praise, his ostentatious piety, his "farce of disinterestedness"— charges with a kernel of truth. But he added absurd denunciations of Washington for his "spurious fame" and his "insignificance."

Another editor, James Thomson Callender, took up the game with his claims that Washington had authorized "the robbery and ruin of the remnants of his own army." Worse yet, Washington had destroyed the Constitution; he was, in fact, a traitor to his country.

Even Thomas Paine joined the chorus, convinced that Washington had never adequately rewarded Paine's eloquence in the fight for American independence.

Mortified by the insults when he felt he deserved only praise, Washington denounced the articles as "infamous." And yet, he pressed Congress to enact postal laws that would increase "the transmission of newspapers to distant parts of the country." Hurtful attacks aside, the president said he continued to believe in "the infinite blessings resulting from a free press."

*   *   *

Washington was also being vexed regularly by the hostility of many tribes along the frontier. In October 1790, an army general who tried to terrorize Indians in Ohio had been badly defeated. A year later, General Winfield Scott led volunteers from Kentucky in raids along the Wabash, and General James Wilkinson staged other attacks.

By September 1791, subduing the tribes had fallen to General Arthur St. Clair, governor of the Northwestern Territory. He had gone off to lead two thousand men against Indians in the Ohio lands, and Washington was waiting impatiently for news of his campaign.

Late one afternoon in November, an officer rode up to the house that Washington now occupied in Philadelphia and told the servant that he must hand over a sheaf of papers to the president personally. The Washingtons were entertaining that evening, but Washington went to the door and returned with the dispatches. Glancing through them, he moved with the company from the dinner table to his wife's drawing room, where he made his customary point of speaking courteously with every female guest. Visitors knew that the Washingtons retired early, and they were gone by 10 p.m.

As the last carriage left, Washington steered his secretary, Tobias Lear, to his private parlor. A twenty-three-year-old Harvard graduate, Lear was the latest young aide to act as a surrogate son to the childless president. He watched as Washington paced the room, more agitated than Lear had ever seen him.

"It's all over," Washington blurted out. The dispatches told of a total rout of the American army. St. Clair had been surprised in his camp, his officers and men butchered. The general himself had apparently escaped.

"That brave army!" Washington was pounding his forehead with his fists. "That brave army cut to pieces! O God!"

The president's body was shaking. "It's too shocking to think of. And a surprise!" Thinking of St. Clair, he burst out, "O God! O God! He is worse than a murderer! How can he answer for it to his country? The blood of the stain is upon him! The curse of widows and orphans! The curse of Heaven!"

Washington seemed shocked by the depth of his own emotion. He sat on a sofa and gestured to Lear to sit. "It was here, sir, in this very room," Washington said, more calmly, "that I conversed with St. Clair on the very eve of his departure for the west.

"I remarked, 'I shall not interfere, General, with the orders of General Knox and the War Department. They are sufficiently comprehensive and judicious. But as an old soldier, as one whose early life was particularly engaged in Indian warfare, I feel myself competent to counsel:

" 'General St. Clair, in three words: Beware of surprise. Trust not the Indian. Leave not your arms for a moment. And when you halt for the night, be sure to fortify your camp. Again and again, General, beware of surprise.'

"And yet that brave army surprised and cut to pieces! O God!"

Washington knew many of St. Clair's officers and named them in a sorrowful litany: Butler, Ferguson, Kirkwood. "Such officers are not to be replaced in a day." He looked to Lear, embarrassed by his outburst. "This must not go beyond this room."

Washington's thoughts turned to his own days on the frontier during the French and Indian Wars, when a blunder had almost ended his fledgling military career. "General St. Clair shall have justice," he said quietly. "I looked hastily through the dispatches. I saw the whole disaster but not the particulars."

Half an hour had passed, and Lear thought Washington seemed entirely calm once again. "I will hear him without prejudice," the president promised. "He shall have full justice."

As more detailed accounts of the debacle reached the capital, Washington learned that St. Clair had flung himself into the midst of the heaviest fighting. Although he was not wounded, the battle left him so weak that men had to carry him from the field. By the time St. Clair came to Philadelphia to face his commander-in-chief, Washington held out his hand to him. St. Clair limped to his side and grasped the president's hand in both of his own. Washington had decided that St. Clair's valiant past service gave him a claim to the nation's allegiance. But justice required a trial by a government commission.

Bache's *General Advertiser* used the defeat to question America's right to invade Indian lands, especially with the expense so great in money and men. Although Bache did not ignite a political debate, the public mood seemed to favor more peaceful dealings with the tribes.

When a military panel examined St. Clair's behavior, its members exonerated him. They ruled that he had been merely unfortunate.

France's government now called itself the Directory, and its excesses were straining Jefferson's loyalty. Maximilien Robespierre, leader of the Jacobins, had demanded that Louis XVI and Marie Antoinette go to the guillotine on January 21, 1793, and a reign of terror had spread throughout France.

Caught in the middle, suspected for his moderation, Lafayette had fled France, intending to return to the United States. Instead, he was imprisoned in Austria as an enemy of Europe's monarchies.

Despite France's crucial aid to the colonies during America's Revolution, Washington was determined to stay uncommitted when France declared war on Great Britain. He found an excuse in a treaty the United States signed with France in 1778, which provided that America would support France only in her defensive wars.

On April 22, 1793, Washington issued a Proclamation of Neutrality, which gratified Hamilton but outraged those Americans pledged to the French. Writing in the press as "Helvidius," Madison argued that only Congress, not the president, had the authority to issue such a proclamation.

The debate soon became less abstract when the Directory sent its first envoy, Edmund Genêt, who arrived in Charleston, where the population included a large number of French refugees. Red-haired, blue-eyed, and broad-shouldered, Genêt had been sent in his early twenties as chargé d'affaires to the Russian court of Catherine the Great. At first, she had been charmed enough to present him with diamond knee buckles until his fervent antiroyalist politics got him sent home.

Now twenty-nine, Genêt was on his way to Philadelphia when he learned of Washington's proclamation, but his boisterous welcome from Democratic Clubs along his route misled him about the president's current popularity. Genêt began privately to dismiss Washington as *le vieillard*, the old man.

He expected support for his mission to come instead from Jefferson: Genêt had been ordered to collect America's $2.5-million debt to France but was authorized to accept that payment in the grain his country badly needed. The president, however, had instructed Jefferson to use every means to avoid embroiling America with either France or Britain, reminding him that the secretary of state was to "endeavor to maintain a strict neutrality."

Washington knew where Jefferson's sympathies lay and had once approached him about returning to France to represent America through this difficult time. Jefferson had declined. He could never again cross the Atlantic, he said, and since Genêt was coming to the United States, he would be more useful at home.

With Jefferson's bias in mind, Washington concluded his remarks about neutrality with unusual asperity: "I therefore require that you will give the subject mature consideration."

Washington demonstrated his own diplomatic touch when another prominent French revolutionary wrote that he was coming to the United States and requested a letter from the president that would introduce him to the American people. Washington obliged him:

"C. Volney needs no recommendation from
George Washington."

Citizen Genêt tried to further France's interests with indirect challenges to Washington's authority that would deflate the president's reputation. In South Carolina, he commissioned ships to sail against the British. He set up French consuls at American ports and authorized them to turn over any seized vessels to France, which meant that the Directory was now claiming to preside over American soil. Spurred on by local support, Genêt next set about recruiting volunteer troops to attack Spain's holdings in Louisiana and Florida.

Those provocations drove Washington to act. *Little Sarah*, a British privateer captured by the French, was discovered illegally loading cannon bound for France. For that violation of neutrality, American authorities ordered the ship not to leave its position on the Delaware River outside Philadelphia. Despite Genêt's assurance that the captain would not be departing, the ship suddenly sailed for home. Washington seemed to suspect, unfairly, that Jefferson had abetted its escape.

In the heated debate that followed, Hamilton argued for forty-five

minutes that the Directory should be instructed to recall Genêt at
once. Determined to avoid an open break with France, Jefferson
scoffed privately at Hamilton's oratory—"as inflammatory & declamatory as if he had been speaking to a jury."

But the next day, Washington was handed a satirical article from a
pro-French faction that predicted that he would meet the same fate as
Louis XVI. Jefferson was fascinated by the article's effect on the president. He was already convinced that constant adulation had left Washington unable to deal with being contradicted or even being offered
advice he had not asked for.

Now Jefferson watched as Washington "got himself into one of
those paroxysms when he cannot command himself." The president
complained that he was fed up with the personal abuse being heaped
upon him and swore that *"by god he had rather be in his grave than in
his present situation. He had rather be on his farm than to be made
emperor of the world!"*

Washington shut down the French admiralty courts, returned the
confiscated ships to their owners, and sent army troops to stop any in-
fringement of America's neutrality along its southwestern borders.

When Washington revoked the papers of the French consul in
Boston for flagrantly ignoring the neutrality act, Genêt threatened to
go over the president's head and take his case to what he believed was
the sovereign state of Massachusetts. Hamilton arranged the publication of that high-handed threat, and the country was outraged. Genêt
tried to recover the initiative by demanding that Washington deny the
threat had ever been made. In response, Washington simply turned
over their entire correspondence to the newspapers, and the Directory
recalled Genêt.

Rather than go home, where lately the Jacobin faction had denounced him as a criminal, Genêt became the first person to ask for
political asylum in the United States. After Washington granted his request, Genêt moved to New York, married one of Governor Clinton's
daughters, and spent the next four decades as a gentleman farmer.

At the height of the Genêt affair, Jefferson had informed Washington
that he intended to resign at the end of September. Now with the trou-

blesome matter resolved, he met with the president to confirm his decision. Long before the arguments over Genêt, Jefferson had been defeated regularly during cabinet meetings in the jousting over policy matters. Much as Washington tried to be diplomatic, he clearly leaned more to the thinking of Hamilton and the Federalists than to that of Jefferson and his Republicans.

Even the planning for the new Federal City on the Potomac had become a battlefield. Washington himself had picked the location and persuaded its owners to donate part of the land and sell the remainder at twenty-five dollars an acre. To design the city, Washington named a French engineer he had known when the man was a young volunteer in the Continental Army. Major Pierre Charles L'Enfant shared Washington's vision of the great capital that America deserved, and he envisioned a small center that could be expanded as the nation grew. Having been a surveyor in his youth, Washington understood the logic behind L'Enfant's concept, and Hamilton was endorsing it enthusiastically.

To Jefferson, however, the result would be only one more northern city, another New York or Philadelphia, without the leafy charm of Williamsburg. He may have expected his fellow Virginian to agree, but Washington had showed Jefferson's alternative sketch to L'Enfant without telling him who had proposed it. L'Enfant looked over Jefferson's design—a park at its center and streets radiating out in strict parallel lines—and was unimpressed. The regularity of the streets, when they were extended to accommodate a growing population, would "become at last tiresome and insipid," he said. The plan lacked "a sense of the really grand and truly beautiful."

Although Jefferson lost that round, L'Enfant soon proved impossible to work with. He alienated owners of the land he needed and rebuffed the president's attempts to smooth matters over. Urging Washington to take a firm stand with L'Enfant, Jefferson said, "He must be subdued." But Washington saw L'Enfant as an artist and remarked that "the feelings of such men are always alive." In the president's view, it was wise "to humor them or put on the appearance of doing it."

Pursuing that approach, Washington made even more concessions.

Finally, though, L'Enfant refused to compromise and shouted at Tobias Lear, who had come to plead with him on the president's behalf. As Genêt might have told him, insulting Washington was not a winning strategy. L'Enfant's appointment was terminated.

The unmistakable signs that Washington favored Hamilton over Jefferson hurt and offended the man who had enjoyed a worshipful standing among France's revolutionaries. Both Hamilton and Jefferson had lost their fathers at a young age, and Washington could provide an idealized replacement, as he had showed in forgiving the young Hamilton for his pettish rebellion. To Jefferson, Hamilton was not only younger by fourteen years, he was brash and untrustworthy. If Hamilton succeeded in delivering the country to northern speculators, wouldn't he expect to share in the tainted profits? Jefferson and his Republicans were convincing themselves that Hamilton must be corrupt.

There was another consideration that Jefferson would not confront directly. In Virginia and Massachusetts, where bloodlines conferred social rank, Hamilton's illegitimate birth was never entirely forgotten. John Adams had called him "the bastard brat of a Scotch peddler."

And yet Washington, evaluating both of his secretaries with a steady eye, seemed to find Hamilton the more impressive.

In announcing his departure, Jefferson at first simply pleaded an urgent need to look after business matters at home. It was an excuse any Virginia planter could understand, although Washington pointed out that he himself was being called upon to forsake Mount Vernon for another four years.

Because Washington hated to hear about strife in his official family, he had cut off Jefferson's earlier complaints about Hamilton. But since he was leaving, Jefferson took the opportunity to recite in detail the reasons for his distrust. Washington professed to be unaware that differences between the two men had passed from philosophical to personal. Then, assuring Jefferson that it was essential he stay in the cabinet as a check on the opposing faction, the president offered to try to resolve any ill feelings.

Jefferson said the breach was too serious for mediation because Hamilton and his Federalists wanted to establish a monarchy in America. Washington could not take that threat seriously. He was convinced, he said, there were not ten leaders in the entire country who entertained such thoughts.

No, Jefferson persisted, there were many more than the president imagined. He himself had heard Hamilton say that the Constitution was "a shilly-shally thing of milk and water, which could not last. It was only good as a step to something better." And now, Jefferson added, not only was Hamilton conspiring to let the executive branch swallow up the legislature, but those very lawmakers had become corrupt. He offered one remedy: Restructure the Congress to prevent men from voting on any bill that affected their own interests. Washington listened but was not encouraging. He said he doubted that such conflicts could ever be avoided.

Hamilton's victory in establishing the Bank of the United States still rankled with both Jefferson and Madison. In leading the opposition, Madison had challenged Hamilton's plan to organize the proposed bank with a combination of government money and private investment. Before he had been persuaded to drop his objections, Madison had called the result unconstitutional. And yet, only a few years earlier Madison had endorsed a doctrine of implied powers, an interpretation that would make the bank legal. Congress had agreed with his earlier argument and approved the bank by a margin of two to one.

When Jefferson raised the issue of the bank one last time, the president reminded him that he had entertained his own doubts. Washington had even asked Madison to draft a veto message and then had held off on authorizing the bank until the last possible day. But it was done. Now only experience would settle the question of how well the bank functioned.

They were being called to breakfast. Because Washington's reputation already soared above all others, he could forget the more human sentiments from his own youth—a need for praise, a craving for position, a desire for power. These days, Washington would not insult other men by suggesting that their motives might be less lofty than his own.

Before they parted, Washington asked Jefferson to remember that men could disagree and remain civil. "I will frankly and solemnly declare," the president assured him, "that I believe the views of both of you are pure and well meant."

As the country turned increasingly westward, tribal wars were not Washington's only concern on the frontier. His reputation as a modern Cincinnatus was tested again when residents of the Allegheny region of western Pennsylvania refused to pay the federal taxes on whiskey — which they produced and consumed in great quantities. The memory of British taxation was fresh in Washington's mind, and to a degree he could sympathize with them.

But as president he was responsible for keeping America solvent. To ease the crisis, Washington approved a slight lowering of the excise laws and issued a proclamation urging national unity. For a while, those overtures seemed to temper local hostility to the federal government.

But Hamilton informed him from the Treasury that the United States marshal in Pennsylvania had issued thirty-nine writs for failure to pay taxes. Each case had been settled quietly until a fortieth writ set off a violent protest that could not be ignored. Local officers killed the leader of the resistance, a retired army major, and warned the rioters that their Whiskey Rebellion amounted to treason.

Washington saw the challenge starkly: "If a minority, and a small one too, is to dictate to the majority, there is an end put, at one stroke, to republican government."

Pennsylvania's governor attempted to handle the crisis with the assistance of a thirty-three-year-old Swiss-born negotiator named Albert Gallatin. A graduate of the University of Geneva, Gallatin had come to America at nineteen to enlist in the Revolution. After the war, he worked as a French tutor at Harvard before settling in western Pennsylvania and rising in Republican politics.

Gallatin reached a tentative settlement, but his pact called for a full pardon for the rebels and forgiveness for all unpaid back taxes. That leniency was unacceptable to Hamilton, who held an appointment these days as secretary of war in addition to his post at the Treasury. He persuaded Washington to order up the militia, which brought the available troop strength to twelve thousand men.

In the Roman legend, Cincinnatus had also been called to arms a second time—to fight not against foreign enemies but against his own countrymen. Dismayed by that prospect, Washington hoped to put down the rebellion with as little bloodshed as possible. Stopping at an inn on his way to join the militia, the president raised a toast: "A happy issue to the business before us."

During his journey, Washington received welcome news from General Anthony Wayne, who had scored victories over the Indians of the Northwest Territory. The deaths of St. Clair's men had been avenged, and Wayne was hoping the new luster to his reputation would convince Congress to station a large and permanent army along the frontier. Wayne said that he favored making peace overtures to the tribes, but if they were rejected, the only answer was a standing army. Otherwise, "we have fought, bled and conquered in vain."

Washington intended to arrest the Pennsylvania rebels only after he had displayed his full strength and could round up the ringleaders in one sweep. The sight of that overwhelming federal force had the effect Washington counted on, and the spirit went out of the rebellion. By late October 1794, Washington was sure the uprising had been quelled. After being gone from the capital for three and a half weeks, the president rode home to resume civilian life.

Once Washington left, Hamilton seized whiskey stills and launched mass arrests. He began with the twenty most prominent leaders and continued until he had another 150 in custody. All were sent to Pittsburgh for civil trials.

With the crisis past, Hamilton recommended that Washington use the rebellion as an excuse to censure the antiadministration Democratic Clubs, but Madison argued successfully in the House that such an action would violate the Constitution. For Madison, power rested with the people to censure their government, not with the government to censure its people.

In his annual address to Congress in December, Washington devoted twenty minutes to the Whiskey Rebellion, reporting gratefully that "the misled have abandoned their errors and pay the respect to our Constitution and laws which is due from good citizens to the public authorities." They had been found guilty of treason, but Washington welcomed them back into the union by commuting their death sentences.

On Christmas Day, the last of the "Whiskey Boys" were marched through the streets of Philadelphia by the New Jersey Light Horse troop. One week later, Washington read a proclamation drafted for him by Hamilton that called for a day of public prayer to give thanks that the United States once again enjoyed domestic tranquillity.

As time for his reelection approached, Washington seemed resigned to accepting a second term if he could be sure he had national support and would not have to campaign for the office. He sent Tobias Lear to make inquiries in the northern states, and Lear returned to say that if anyone mentioned Washington's stepping down, it was only with apprehension. Washington had already sounded out Jefferson before he left the cabinet, and that foremost anti-Federalist assured him that any other candidate would be considered no more than a partisan political figure.

On February 13, 1793, the Electoral College again chose Washington unanimously. He acknowledged afterward that he would have been chagrined not to have received "a pretty respectable vote." John Adams won another term as vice president, despite the fact that Hamilton and his allies were tepid about Adams and backed him only because his opponent was New York's governor George Clinton. All the same, Adams won overwhelmingly, with seventy-seven electoral votes against a total of ten for his opponents.

Even though Washington felt that Jefferson and the Democratic Clubs were turning on him, he maintained his cordial feeling for Madison in the House of Representatives and was pleased when it appeared that Madison would soon be enjoying the domestic tranquillity that Washington had extolled during the day of public prayer.

By the age of forty-three, Madison had seemed destined to be a life-long bachelor, and local hostesses had given up trying to arrange a match for him. Almost a dozen years earlier, he had been engaged briefly to a New York congressman's teenage daughter, Catherine

Floyd. But while Madison was in Virginia preparing for the wedding, Kitty Floyd fell in love with a medical student closer to her own age and broke off the engagement.

Jefferson had tried to console Madison with an oblique reference to other fish in the sea. But, sorely disappointed, Madison never courted again until he set his sights on a buxom young widow named Dolley Payne Todd.

Dolley Payne had grown up in eastern Virginia, in a house sold to her struggling family at a cheap price by Patrick Henry, her mother's cousin. By the end of the Revolutionary War, Dolley was fifteen and slender, with dark hair, blue eyes, and remarkably fair skin. As a Quaker teenager, she was forbidden to wear jewelry, but her mother appreciated the allure of a pale cheek and always sent her outdoors in a hat and long white gloves. If the sun's glare was particularly strong, she tied a linen mask across Dolley's face.

Quaker austerity could not repress Dolley's love for amusement. Her indulgent grandmother had slipped bits of jewelry to her, which Dolley kept in a bag around her neck until the day that she lost it while playing in the woods. And although her parents had locked up the ballroom at the top of the house, Dolley learned to dance in secret and passed on the steps to other girls.

When Dolley's devout mother persuaded her husband to become a Quaker, John Payne took up the faith with a convert's zeal. Once the Revolution was won, he freed his few slaves and moved the family to Philadelphia. Despite its many attractions, Philadelphia's thirty-five thousand residents were crowded into seven thousand houses built within something less than one square mile, with open sewers that provided breeding grounds for typhoid and yellow fever. When Dolley's brother died abruptly, John Payne fell into a long depression. He ran up debts he couldn't repay, then took to his bed and never left the house.

But he encouraged a handsome Quaker lawyer named John Todd to court his daughter. Dolley was well aware that men stared after her in the street, and yet when Todd proposed, she put him off until her father called her to his bedside and pointed out that young Todd had shown him great kindness during his time of distress. At the age of twenty-one, Dolley obeyed her father and got married; a year later, her father died.

The heavy rains of spring 1793 had left behind pools of stagnant water, but residents did not connect the increase in mosquitoes to the yellow fever that raged throughout the city. People of means fled for the countryside, and seventeen thousand left in less than two weeks. President and Martha Washington retreated to Mount Vernon, and John Todd took Dolley, their year-old boy, and a second infant son by litter across the fourteen miles to a resort called Gray's Ferry. When Todd's parents, who remained behind, fell ill, he rushed back to be with them. Dolley wept and pleaded that he get out of the city at once, but Todd stayed on to close his law office and help other afflicted friends. He swore, though, that once he had done his duty, he would never leave her again.

Todd made it back to Gray's Ferry only long enough to feel unmistakable signs of the fever. To protect his family, he left again and died several days afterward. By the time the epidemic eased, Dolley had also lost her baby. She and her mother, two widows, returned to Philadelphia with Dolley's surviving son, Payne. Her mother ran a boardinghouse on North Third Street, taking in the legislators who came to Philadelphia as temporary bachelors.

Besides her striking looks, Dolley enjoyed a reputation as a diligent reader, and she spelled better than many of the men who sought her company. Moving into her mother's house, she came to know a former boarder, Aaron Burr, who had left his family behind in New York to serve as his state's senator.

Courtly and charming, Burr himself was not blind to Dolley Todd's appeal, but he was married to a woman who fascinated him far more. Entering Dolley's life as her friend and adviser, Burr soon found her an eligible suitor.

Madison had spotted Dolley while she was out for a stroll and prevailed on Burr to arrange an introduction. Burr agreed sardonically and Dolley reflected his tone in the note she sent to recruit a chaperone:

"Dear friend," Dolley wrote to another young Quaker woman. "Thou must come to me. Aaron Burr says that the great little Madison has asked to be brought to see me this evening."

After supper, Dolley dressed carefully in a gown of mulberry satin, with a silk kerchief around her neck for propriety and a cap that allowed an errant curl to escape. Dolley was now twenty-six, and possibly—given a habitual imprecision about her age—Madison thought she was even younger. In any case, he kept calling on her until Philadelphia's matrons heard rumors of their unlikely romance.

Two years earlier, one of Dolley's sisters, fifteen-year-old Lucy, had married George Steptoe Washington, the president's nephew. Family members believed it was that connection that gave Martha Washington license to quiz Dolley about Madison's courtship. Martha had become a formidable social arbiter in Philadelphia and took the responsibility seriously. Whenever Washington entered a room, his wife invariably rose and announced, "The president."

According to family legend, Martha Washington had summoned Dolley to her side and asked whether she and Madison were engaged.

The pointed question rattled Dolley. "No," she said, "I think not."

"If it is so," Mrs. Washington said, "do not be ashamed to confess it. Rather, be proud." She predicted that Madison would make her a good husband, all the better for being so much older. "We both approve of it," she added. "The esteem and friendship existing between Mr. Madison and my husband is very great."

Washington was more circumspect than his wife in offering matrimonial advice. He had decided that a woman only asked for an outsider's opinion when she had already made up her mind and expected approval for her decision. Hearing anything else, Washington concluded, she would go ahead and marry anyway.

On September 15, 1794, Dolley married Madison, aware that she would be disowned by the Quakers for marrying outside her faith.

One last crisis faced Washington in his second term before he could escape from the presidency. Britain and France were now openly at war, and America's neutrality was proving hard to maintain. In London, William Pitt the Younger announced an Order in Council, a decree that authorized the seizure of any neutral ships doing business with the French West Indies. In a matter of months, the British took some 250 American ships.

With resentment running high, Congress debated reprisals, but Washington and his cabinet wanted to avoid waging another war against Britain only a decade after the Revolution. In the spring of 1794, Washington sent John Jay to London as envoy extraordinary. In forming his original cabinet, Washington had offered Jay the post for foreign affairs that came to be called secretary of state. Instead, Jay requested and received appointment as chief justice of the Supreme Court.

As Madison had become increasingly estranged from Hamilton, his relationship with the third author of their *Federalist* papers was also strained. Madison's Republican faction in the House protested that it was improper to draft the head of the third branch of government to serve in the executive branch.

But the objections to Jay went deeper than his judgeship or his Federalist views. In the past, he had seemed a weak and hasty negotiator. At the conference to end the Revolutionary War, Benjamin Franklin had called on Britain to cede all of Canada to the United States. But Jay had been impatient to reach an accord and got Franklin's condition dropped. Jay explained that his country would not hold up the peace by haggling over what he termed a few acres of land.

Then, in his negotiations with Spain, Jay had appeared ready to sacrifice America's navigation rights on the Mississippi River in return for terms that favored East Coast shipping.

Madison worried that because Jay was known to admire the English, he might not be forceful enough during the new negotiations. And Madison expected France's recent military victories to compel the British Parliament to back away from their Order in Council. There would be no need for America to make concessions.

Washington received a draft of Jay's treaty on May 7, 1795, and kept it secret while he mulled over his options. Jay's terms seemed to justify Madison's misgivings about him. Although the British agreed to evacuate their posts along the Canadian frontier, they had made that same promise at the end of the Revolutionary War in 1783. True, several minor matters were resolved satisfactorily, but the treaty would impose a limit of seventy tons on the weight of American ships sailing to the British West Indies. When Madison got hold of a bootleg copy of the treaty, he complained that the restriction would force Americans to be "trading with canoes."

Jay also had agreed that the United States should pay British creditors for claims they had made before the Revolution, but he had not extracted compensation for slaves carried off by the British when the war ended. Britain's negotiators had argued successfully against returning to American captivity those men who had fought for England.

Other thorny issues, including where the Maine border between the United States and Canada lay, were deferred for future arbitration.

Bache's *Aurora* published the entire treaty, provoking an outcry on all sides. The Republicans believed Jay's most serious failing was that he agreed to waive America's claim of neutrality for her ships during the war between France and Britain. Nor had Jay won the battle over impressment. British naval commanders could go on stopping American ships to seize men they considered deserters. Madison branded the entire treaty "a ruinous bargain."

For their part, Federalists were unhappy with the treaty's unfavorable terms on tariffs and tonnage duties. As the debate continued throughout the summer, Washington withheld his signature. His Virginia crony, Edmund Randolph, who had replaced Jefferson as secretary of state, advised him against signing, but Randolph's reputation had become too badly tarnished for his voice to be persuasive. He had already raised doubts in Washington's mind by allying himself with Jefferson and Madison. Then Federalists in the cabinet intercepted messages from France's minister that suggested Randolph had been disloyal to Washington during the Whiskey Rebellion. The correspondence also could be read to imply that Randolph had asked for a bribe to influence his government.

Confronted with those charges, Randolph was appalled by Washington's willingness to believe them. He stumbled over his explanation and abruptly left the room. At that point, Washington made it clear to Randolph—former governor of Virginia, valuable delegate to the Constitutional Convention, America's first attorney general, close friend for twenty years—that he was expected to leave the government. Randolph dated his letter of resignation that same day and then prepared an unavailing 130-page defense of his conduct.

Hamilton had already left the cabinet, pleading, like Jefferson, the need to shore up his finances. But his influence remained strong, and he defended Washington when attacks on Jay's treaty became personal assaults on the president's honor.

The fury rose to a pitch that older men compared to the outcry provoked by Britain's Stamp Act. Protesting the treaty outside the president's house in Philadelphia, crowds shouted curses against Washington and his cabinet more vile than the vituperation against George III. Washington was charged with betraying his country, and there were dark hints that he deserved assassination. The Philadelphia cavalry had to be called out to protect him.

As for Jay, one Democratic Club announced that for kissing the hand of the queen of England, he deserved to have "his lips blistered to the bone." In Delaware, a chapter of the Cincinnati went on record as hoping that Jay might experience all the pleasures of purgatory.

At a tumultuous rally on Broad Street in New York, Hamilton was trying to defend the treaty when men started to throw stones. One struck him with a force that drew blood. "Those," Hamilton said, as he withdrew, "are arguments I cannot answer."

Washington was especially bitter about accusations from the Jefferson camp that he was behaving like a tyrant. Despite his best efforts, the president doubted now that he could ever reconcile the Republicans to his policies. As debate exploded in the House of Representatives, members broke with an annual tradition and voted 50 to 38 against adjourning for half an hour to pay compliments to Washington on his birthday.

"The cry over the treaty," Washington lamented to Hamilton in New York, "is like that against a mad dog."

Washington signed the treaty, and after deleting the restrictions on West Indian trade, the Senate narrowly approved it. But opponents were not ready to give up. They argued that the treaty's provisions about commerce required that it also be approved by the House of Representatives. Washington considered the treaty already to be the law, but he laid it before the House on March 1, 1796.

As vice president, John Adams stood aloof from the controversy, although he concluded that Jay had brought home the best terms available to him. Watching Madison's strenuous challenges, he wrote to his wife, "Mr. Madison looks worried to death. Pale, withered, haggard."

After more weeks of wrangling, Madison and his allies forced a vote demanding that the administration submit all documents that had led up to the treaty. George Washington refused in language that surprised Madison, who found his denial "improper and indelicate." When it looked as though the Republicans had the votes to scrap the treaty entirely, Federalist banks and insurance companies in New York and Philadelphia applied economic pressures. And Fisher Ames made a speech.

The young congressman who worshipped Washington at his inauguration had become the leading spokesman for the Essex Junto, a provincial but powerful group of merchant ship owners and admiralty lawyers who had moved to Boston from Essex County in Massachusetts. Even among Federalists, the Junto members were considered rigid conservatives, unwilling to compromise or acknowledge that politics had changed in the twenty years since America declared her independence. Albert Gallatin, now a Republican senator from Pennsylvania, granted that the Federalists had many clever spokesmen, but he considered only two of them to be brilliant—Ames and John Marshall.

The previous year, Ames had been stricken with a case of pneumonia so severe that he was not expected to live. The state of his lungs remained precarious, and his doctor had permitted him to attend the Fourth Congress only if he promised to take no part in the debates. Passively, Ames had endured the long argument over the Jay Treaty before he let it be known that on April 28 he would break his silence.

Both the Senate and the Supreme Court adjourned to hear him, and Vice President Adams and Justice James Iredell took places in the House gallery while men around them scrambled for seats. Getting to

his feet laboriously, Ames played to the drama of the occasion. "I enter-
tain the hope, perhaps a rash one," he began, "that my strength will
hold me to speak for a few minutes."

In lawyerly fashion, he rejected the Republican claim that the
House should play a role in approving treaties, but the heart of his
speech was a vision of what frontier life would become if the treaty
were scrapped and the British went on inciting hostile tribes along the
border.

"In the day time," Ames predicted, "your path through the woods
will be ambushed; the darkness of midnight will glitter with the blaze
of your dwellings. You are a father: the blood of your sons shall fatten
your cornfield! You are a mother: the war-whoop shall wake the sleep
of the cradle!"

Ames anticipated a cynical rejoinder from the Republicans. "Who
will say that I exaggerate?" he challenged them. "Who will argue, by a
sneer, that this is idle preaching?"

He concluded with a final reminder of his frailty. If the treaty were
rejected, "even I, slender and almost broken as my hold on life is, may
outlive the Government and the Constitution of my country."

John Adams wrote home, "Tears enough were shed. Not a dry eye,
I believe, except some of the Jackasses who had occasioned the necessity of the oratory."

When Ames took his seat, no one rose to rebut him. The treaty was
about to be put to a vote when an opposition leader saw the danger and
moved for a strategic adjournment. Given their current feelings, he
said, House members could not act wisely or safely.

Aspiring politicians—including Daniel Webster, a young congressman from New Hampshire—memorized Ames's speech as a
model of oratory. A friend told Ames that he should have died at the
moment he finished speaking since he could never make a more glorious exit. As it happened, Ames lived on in retirement for another
twelve years.

Before the final House vote, a new development proved even more
decisive than the speech: Washington's envoy to Spain, Thomas Pinckney, negotiated the free access to the Mississippi that was crucial to the
South and West. That gave Federalists a chance to argue that rejecting

one treaty meant rejecting both of them, and John Jay's treaty squeezed past the House, 51 to 48.

With Republican attacks growing more strident and wounding to the president, Jefferson wrote to assure him that he had no part in them. Washington used the occasion of that letter to unload his months of bitterness at what he saw as Jefferson's hypocrisy and betrayal.

It would not be "frank, candid or friendly," Washington wrote, to conceal the fact that he had heard how Jefferson was disparaging him. He added that it was only within the last one or two years that he had realized how far the two parties would go in their insidious misrepresentation. The exaggerated and indecent language denouncing every act of his administration "could scarcely be applied to a Nero, a notorious defaulter, or even a common pickpocket."

With that, Washington had spent his anger. "But enough of this," he wrote. "I have already gone farther in the expression of my feelings than I intended."

As Washington moved toward retirement, Jefferson watched with amusement when several clergymen decided that the president had not promoted religion ardently enough during his two terms. Washington had never avoided the word "God," either as an oath or a supplication. Conscious of his duty to set an example, he attended Episcopal services on Sundays — at least when the weather and roads permitted. Once in church, his calm demeanor could be read as devout.

The ministers wanted a more explicit acknowledgment. They sent a letter raising a number of doctrinal questions, which Washington answered courteously. But he passed over their central point about whether he was a Christian. Jefferson noted in his diary that "the old fox was too cunning for them" and recalled that Gouverneur Morris had often told him that Washington no more believed in Christianity than Morris did.

When the same issue arose during his own candidacy for president four years later, Jefferson was more forthright. A political ally urged him to write a statement on Christianity that would mollify the clergymen who were telling parishioners that if Jefferson won, they would have to hide their Bibles down their wells.

Jefferson replied that every church—particularly the Congrega-
tionalists and Episcopalians—already knew that he would never consent to naming an established church for the United States. "And they
believe truly. For I have sworn upon the altar of God eternal hostility
against every form of tyranny over the mind of man."

The harsh debate over the Jay Treaty had completed Washington's
alienation from Madison. Never again would Madison be consulted on
matters of state or be a guest at Mount Vernon on his ride to his own
estate. All the same, Washington retrieved farewell remarks that Madison had drafted for him four years earlier and passed them along to Jay
and to Hamilton for preparing the final draft. Washington intended to
publish his valedictory as his Eighth Annual Address on December 7,
1796, although his term would not end for another three months.
When the various versions were melded into one, Washington copied
it out himself.

With unchallengeable authority, Washington took the occasion to
warn against "the necessity of those overgrown military establishments,
which under any form of government, are inauspicious to liberty."
Love of their country was the Americans' best defense of that liberty.
Political factions tended to divide men "who ought to be bond together
by fraternal affection."

Washington said he was not opposed to rigorous debate, which was
"a fire not to be quenched." But "it demands a uniform vigilance lest,
instead of warming, it should consume."

America must treat all nations with good faith and justice, avoiding
both lasting hostility and passionate attachments for any of them. "Tis
our true policy to steer clear of permanent alliances with any portion of
the foreign world." Washington said that his own motive had been to
try "to gain time to our country to settle and mature its yet recent insti-
tutions."

He concluded, "In offering to you, my countrymen, these counsels
of an old affectionate friend, I dare not hope they will make the strong
and lasting impression I could wish . . . to moderate the fury of party
spirit, to warn against the mischief of foreign intrigue, to guard against
the impostures of pretended patriotism."

Abigail Adams   *John Adams*

Chapter Four

ADAMS
(1797–1801)

S ince Abigail Adams had been ailing and could not come to Philadelphia to watch her husband sworn in as president, he sent her a few
whimsical observations about the ceremony. Washington's face "was as
serene and unclouded as the day," Adams wrote. "He seemed to me to
enjoy a triumph over me. Methought I heard him say, 'Ay! I am fairly
out and you fairly in! See which of us will be the happiest!'"

Washington was not entirely free of responsibilities. As they prepared to depart from Philadelphia, his wife had entrusted to him the
transfer of the family dog and parrot to Mount Vernon. Washington
planned to obey, but he confided to a friend, "For my own part, I
should not pine much if both were forgot."

In November, Adams had gone to Philadelphia from his farm in Quincy, Massachusetts, to wait out the electoral vote. He was poised to accept defeat with a determined good grace since he knew that Hamilton had been intriguing on behalf of Thomas Pinckney, who had negotiated America's successful treaty with Spain. Hamilton explained that he was merely trying to cut into the vote for Jefferson, but Adams was suspicious.

With sixteen states now part of the union, the nine from the South and West were changing the presidential arithmetic. The Electoral College had grown to 136 voters, each casting a ballot for president and vice president. Electors in nine states were still selected by their legislatures, but in other states they were chosen by popular vote.

Election rules were also evolving. Six states had eliminated property qualifications, and others had lowered the amount of property required. But even for a taxpaying white man eligible to vote, exercising that right could be daunting. Counties in New Jersey averaged four polling places, and each parish in South Carolina only one.

Before the official announcement in February, Adams learned that he had won the electoral vote and that Jefferson was to be his vice president. His margin was unimpressive: Adams won 71 electors by carrying most of the eastern seaboard. Except for Pennsylvania, Jefferson's 68 came from the South and West. Pinckney took a scattered 59; Aaron Burr, 30. Samuel Adams, John Adams's fiery relative and his tutor in revolutionary tactics, received 11 of the 48 write-in votes.

It fell to Madison to inform Jefferson at Monticello that he should expect to serve under Adams. Jefferson claimed to be untroubled by the prospect. Adams was eight years older, he said, and "had always been my senior from the commencement of my public life." More than twenty years had passed since Adams had guaranteed Jefferson immortality by insisting that he draft the Declaration of Independence. Adams enjoyed telling how he had clinched his argument by saying to Jefferson, "You can write ten times better than I can."

Before leaving for Philadelphia, Jefferson wrote a generous letter of congratulation to Adams, assuring him of his respect and affection. But he sent it first to Madison, who objected that such effusiveness could embarrass Jefferson later if Adams were a failure in office, and the letter was not sent.

Arriving in town two days before the inaugural, Jefferson went immediately to pay a courtesy call at the house on Fourth Street where Adams had taken rooms. The next day Adams returned the call and asked that the two have a frank conversation.

Adams had made no secret of his hostility to the French Revolution. In its early days, he had told friends, "I'll tell you what, the French republic will not last three months." As the bloody drama unfolded in Paris, Adams wrote privately, "There is such a compilation of Tragedy, Comedy and Farce in all the accounts from France, that it is to me the last degree disgusting" to read about them.

As president, however, Adams wanted to pursue Washington's policy of avoiding an open rupture. Fencing with Jefferson over the situation, he said he wished that Jefferson would go to Paris and speak with the Directory. But he supposed that was out of the question?

Reading Jefferson's silence correctly, Adams drew back. In any case, he observed, it would not be appropriate to send abroad the man who might have to take his place as president. Nor, Adams continued, would it be decent to remove a political rival.

Adams seemed to be taking Jefferson's refusal in good spirit. He said that he would send to Paris instead a delegation consisting of Madison, Elbridge Gerry, and Charles Cotesworth Pinckney. Would Jefferson sound out Madison about serving? Jefferson was discouraging. Madison had retired from the Congress and had declined to replace Jefferson as secretary of state, even though Washington had brought pressure to bear. Adams replied that he would name Madison anyway "and leave the responsibility on him."

As Jefferson predicted, Madison declined the assignment. It was the last time Adams spoke with Jefferson on any matter of policy.

Nor would Washington in retirement be consulting with his former secretary of state. From the time that Washington let Jefferson know he doubted his denials about the newspaper attacks of the last year, their few letters were kept carefully to such safe topics as agriculture. But in April 1796, as Jefferson was emerging from a winter-long depression, he wrote a scathing and emotional letter to a distant friend, Philip Mazzei. An Italian wine grower, Mazzei had once lived at a plantation near Monticello before returning to his homeland.

"The aspect of our politics has wonderfully changed since you left us," Jefferson wrote ironically. In place of a noble love of liberty, he continued, a party had sprung up that favored the British model of monarch and aristocracy. Jefferson was pleased to report that most Americans remained true to their principles. But the executive and judicial branches of government were filled with "timid men who prefer the calm of despotism to the boisterous sea of liberty."

Perhaps Jefferson referred principally to Hamilton and Adams, but since he did not name the men he was denouncing, a reader might deduce that he included Washington among "the apostates who have gone over to these heresies, men who were Samsons in the field & Solomons in council, but who have had their heads shorn by the harlot England."

Jefferson might not have indulged his penchant for rhetorical excess had he known that a year later his letter would appear in the New York *Minerva*. It turned out that Mazzei had translated the letter into Italian. After publication in a Florence newspaper, an approximation of Jefferson's words was turned into French by a Parisian editor and then back into English by Noah Webster, who restored its sense, if not its precise language, before he published it. In Webster's version the word "harlot" became "whore."

The Mazzei episode seemed to end all further contact between the two most celebrated survivors of the American Revolution.

America's relations with France, which had been deteriorating since the Jay Treaty, got only worse with Adams in office. In place of Madison, Adams named John Marshall to join Gerry and Pinckney as his special envoys to the French Directory. Gerry and Adams were old friends, but Gerry was also a Republican and chosen to balance the delegation.

Arriving in Paris, the Americans were kept waiting for days and then granted an insulting fifteen minutes with Charles-Maurice de Talleyrand-Périgord, France's foreign minister. Three French officials acting on Tallyrand's behalf—their identities later shielded from the American public as X, Y, and Z—demanded a bribe of $250,000 to open negotiations. Even if such bribes were commonplace among European diplomats, Pinckney replied, "No! No! Not a sixpence!"

He and Marshall packed up and left Paris. Gerry stayed on and was heavily criticized for not leaving with them.

When Gerry sent home his further correspondence with Talleyrand, Adams was outraged by its tone. "I will never send another minister to France," he vowed publicly, "without assurance that he will be received respectfully and honored as the representation of a great, free, powerful and independent nation."

The X, Y, Z Affair had repercussions for both parties. Republicans charged that Adams had failed in his dealings with America's oldest ally. But in the South, the Federalists won recruits among men outraged by the French affront to the nation's honor.

The Congress of 1798 geared up for war, spurred on by a ferocious speech by Adams against France. The Federalists had sufficient votes to pass twenty bellicose measures, which broke off trade with France and allowed the seizure of French ships, setting off what was termed a "Quasi-War." Congress also overcame its long-standing resistance to a permanent military force and authorized arming merchant vessels and constructing twelve new ships to add to the existing six frigates. One bill provided for the immediate enlisting of twenty-five thousand recruits, with a goal for the army of fifty thousand men.

Adams strongly endorsed improving the navy, but the prospect of a large standing army disturbed him. Despite what the Republicans were charging and despite Adams's saber-rattling speech—which Jefferson called "insane"—he still hoped to avoid going to war with France.

The public mood was more martial, however, and fearful. The Reverend Timothy Dwight, Yale's Federalist president, predicted that if the French seized control, America's wives and daughters could become "the victims of legal prostitution." Rumors spread through Philadelphia that French residents and their American allies planned to burn down the city and massacre its citizens. Adams agreed to post a guard at his front door, and his wife fell under the influence of John Robinson, a Scot who claimed that a European conspiracy was working to destroy all religions and every government throughout the world.

Abigail Adams was also infuriated by the steady barrage of abuse against her husband from Benjamin Bache's *Aurora*, which summed him up as "old, querulous, bald, blind, crippled, toothless Adams." The president's wife wanted Congress to protect the nation against that sort of scurrility.

The prevailing hysteria spurred the Congress to pass four separate punitive acts within two weeks. The Federalists had observed that most recent immigrants gravitated to the more populist Republicans, and they made a Naturalization Act their first order of business. Before Madison retired from Congress at the end of the last session, he had submitted a bill that required a three-year notice of intent to become a citizen, followed by five years of residence. The applicant would then take an oath of allegiance and renounce all former loyalties.

The new legislation extended the waiting period to fourteen years before a foreigner could vote in U.S. elections.

Two other acts also took aim at foreigners. The Alien Friends Act gave the president authority to deport any alien he regarded as dangerous. The Alien Enemies Act allowed him to deport foreigners who had come from a country with which America was at war.

The crowning legislation of those two frenzied weeks was the Sedition Act. One Federalist congressman defended it as merely guaranteeing that newspapers reflect "pure sentiments and good principles." But the act was less benign than that. Conspiring against federal laws would lead to a maximum penalty of five years of incarceration and a five-thousand-dollar fine.

Other offenses included "false, scandalous and malicious statements" about the government, president, or Congress intended to bring them into disrepute or stir hatred against them. Punishment was a jail sentence up to two years and a fine of two thousand dollars.

The Sedition Act was written to expire in 1801, the year John Adams completed his first term as president. To Madison and Jefferson, the act was clearly designed to silence the press and intimidate Republican leaders through the elections of 1798 and 1800.

Even while the bill was moving through Congress, the administration began to round up newspaper editors with Republican sympathies. Bache's vehement denunciations of President Adams marked him for an early arrest, but he eluded further punishment by dying before he could come to trial. Another Republican editor who was arrested, John Daly Burk of the *New York Time Price*, was released after Aaron Burr paid his bail. Burk, who faced double jeopardy as an Irish immigrant as well as an editor, promptly disappeared among anti-Federalist sympathizers in Virginia.

Republicans could not stop the jingoistic onslaught. As vice president, Jefferson witnessed what he considered a scandalous scene in the House and conveyed his disgust in a letter to Madison:

Before a scheduled debate on the laws, the Federalists had held a caucus and agreed not to respond to anything their opponents might say. Albert Gallatin, who was a likely target for deportation given his Swiss birth, drew on his considerable powers of persuasion to oppose the bill. But as he spoke, the Federalists began to talk, cough, and laugh so loudly that, although Gallatin went on speaking, he was nearly impossible to hear.

During another challenge, Robert Livingston, who had become a Republican, scarcely began to speak when the Federalist Speaker ruled that whatever Livingston was saying was not germane and put the question to the House. Members approved the Sedition Act 52 to 48.

Once the legislation was passed, authorities rounded up Congressman Matthew Lyon, who represented Vermont but was also a Republican. Lyon had accused Adams of avarice and a lust for power and adulation. During the debate, he further outraged Federalists by spitting in the face of an opponent. Lyon was convicted of sedition, fined one thousand dollars, and sentenced to serve four months in an unheated jail cell usually occupied by runaway slaves.

Despite their victory in Congress, Federalists themselves were divided over the bill. Hamilton had warned against being "cruel or violent" toward foreigners. When he heard the terms of the Sedition Act, he objected: "Let us not establish a tyranny."

Hamilton also worried that this frontal assault on the Bill of Rights might backfire. From Mount Vernon, Washington agreed that public revulsion against the acts might give Jefferson's faction a potent weapon. But Washington added that there would always be something else for the Republicans to use "to disturb the public mind with their unfounded and ill favored forebodings."

Jefferson had left Philadelphia to avoid having to sign the Sedition Act. Presiding over the Senate, he had already felt compromised by adding his signature ceremonially to the alien acts. On his way home, Jefferson called on Madison at Montpelier to devise a campaign against the new laws. Without revealing their participation, Madison would draw up protests to come from the Virginia legislature, and Jefferson would write similar resolutions for North Carolina. But when Jefferson's were completed, his emissary diverted them instead to Kentucky.

At the time independence was declared in 1776, Kentucky had been a county of Virginia. Then, during the Washington years, the Commonwealth of Kentucky became the first state west of the Appalachians to be welcomed into the union. Jealous of their new status, Kentucky's legislators saw the federal government's sedition laws as a threat to their state's liberties.

Because he was vice president, Jefferson took pains not to be identified with the doctrine he was promoting—that states could nullify those federal laws they considered unconstitutional. Invoking the First Amendment's protection of freedom of the press, Jefferson urged individual states to consult together about the legality of the new laws and act accordingly. In Kentucky, however, Jefferson's radical defense of nullification was dropped, and the state's congressional delegation was instructed only to seek repeal of the "unconstitutional and obnoxious" acts during the next session.

Madison's draft of resolutions for Virginia was characteristically more temperate. When it was sent to Jefferson before going to the legislature, he did not consult Madison before adding a phrase that the acts were "null, void, and of no force, or effect." But that more aggressive phrase was also struck out, and Madison's initial language was restored before Virginia's approval.

Writing to Jefferson, Madison set out their basic disagreement on the resolutions: Madison was looking for a solution within the Constitution he had helped to draft rather than letting each state assert a "natural right" to declare federal laws void within its territory.

As the Kentucky and Virginia resolutions went to Congress and circulated among other state legislatures, George Washington held firm about not entering directly into the fray. But to bolster the Federalist argument, he urged Patrick Henry to come out of retirement from his home at Red Hill and run for the Virginia Assembly.

At sixty-three, Henry could barely stand up without support, and he claimed to be "too old and infirm" to reenter politics. But he bowed to Washington's insistence that he commit himself. Thirty-five years had passed since Henry's galvanizing cry, "Give me liberty or give me death!" Only ten years earlier, he had opposed the Constitution because of the threat he said it posed to freedom.

But in June 1799, when Patrick Henry died suddenly, he was firmly on record as supporting the Alien and Sedition Acts.

The rancorous debate had strained Jefferson's relations not only with President Adams but with Adams's wife as well. In London, Abigail Adams had been a loving guardian for Jefferson's younger daughter until the girl joined him in Paris with Sally Hemings. And, like many women, Mrs. Adams had found Jefferson himself an attractive friend to have in her life.

In marrying John Adams, Abigail Smith, a clergyman's daughter, had defied those members of her father's congregation who thought she could do better. Through the tumultuous years that followed, she had been an exemplary wife—raising their children, running the family farm, and, not least, easing Adams past his constant insecurities.

When the Republicans broke with the Federalists, there had been no question of her loyalties. To watch the gulf opening between Jefferson and her family gave Abigail Adams a pang, but she was unflinching. She agreed with Hamilton's recommendation that the army be kept on permanent alert and that the sedition legislation be enforced by sending federal justices of the peace to every court in America.

Her sole regret involved the way the alien and sedition laws had been softened as they proceeded through Congress. "The greater part of the abuse leveled at the Government is from foreigners," she complained to her sister. "What a disgrace to our Country." As for the French: "Was there ever a more basely designing and insidious people?"

A majority of the Congress was as militant as the president's wife and was making preparations for a war that looked inevitable. One sponsor of the Sedition Act had branded both the French government and the French people as enemies of the United States. He wanted any aid to them considered treason, a provision that was struck from the final bill.

Despite its bitter language, Congress adjourned without a formal declaration of war. Abigail Adams criticized the members for a lack of courage, but her husband, who still hoped to keep the peace, had not asked for a declaration.

Then, within the year, the war fever broke, and Americans saw that France was hardly a threat since its army was occupied elsewhere. Although Napoleon Bonaparte, a thirty-year-old Corsican artillery commander, had played no part in overthrowing the king, his inspired leadership of the French army in Italy persuaded the Directory to support his plan to cut off British trade through Egypt and the Levant. "In order to truly destroy England," Napoleon had proclaimed in August 1798, "we shall have to take Egypt."

But the British warships of Admiral Horatio Nelson destroyed the French fleet at Aboukir Bay, and the Turks of the Ottoman Empire were mowing down Napoleon's troops.

Before that reassuring news had reached America, Hamilton floated the idea of leading the expanded American army to conquer New Orleans and Mexico since Britain would now be America's ally against France. By joining together, they could subdue all of Spanish America. Adams put an end to that dream of empire when, in February 1799, he appointed an envoy to Paris to open fresh negotiations.

At the height of the national alarm, Washington had agreed to answer his country's call yet again. Adams appointed him to head America's new provisional army, which was being mustered to repel the French. Privately, however, Adams wrote that "there is no more chance of seeing a French army here than there is in Heaven."

Remarkably, Washington's latest assignment carried a promotion. Although he had been commander in chief during the Revolution, his official rank had never risen beyond major general. On July 2, 1798, Adams commissioned Washington as a lieutenant general. Washington set the condition, however, that Hamilton be named inspector general and given the actual command. Hamilton's promotion in rank would be even greater since during the Revolution he had been only a brigadier general in the reserves.

Despite his intense distrust of Hamilton, Adams reluctantly agreed. But events overtook that scheme, and Washington could gratefully devote himself again to overseeing Mount Vernon.

During the past thirty months of his retirement, Washington had often been ailing, but he refused to yield to his indispositions. As Jefferson knew, Washington had spoken for years about his physical decline. His pessimism was not unrealistic since Washington's grandfather had died at thirty-eight, his father at forty-nine, his brothers—Samuel and John Augustine—at forty-seven and fifty-one. But as 1799 drew to a close, Washington, at the age of sixty-seven, seemed hale and fit.

When dark clouds burst into a cold rain on the morning of December 12, Washington continued to ride to his outlying farmland. At half past three, he returned to the house, shivering and drenched with sleet. Tobias Lear, promoted to colonel, had followed Washington to Mount Vernon when he left the presidency. Seeing Washington with snowflakes in his hair, Lear said, "I am afraid you got wet."

"No," Washington replied, "my greatcoat has kept me dry." But when Lear showed him letters he had prepared, Washington said the weather had turned too bad to send a rider to the post office, and he went directly to the dinner table without changing clothes.

The blizzard continued throughout the night; by morning three inches of snow lay across the landscape. Washington felt that he had caught cold and spent the overcast day next to the fire, but as the sky cleared late in the afternoon, he went out to mark trees between the house and the river that he wanted cut down.

That evening, his voice, already hoarse, got worse, but he waved away any thought of medicine. "No, you know I never take anything for a cold. Let it go as it came."

Except for his raw throat, the evening passed normally. Washington talked with family members and browsed through newspapers, reading for them items he found entertaining. After his wife retired, Washington asked Lear to read aloud accounts of a debate in the Virginia Assembly and seemed annoyed with Madison's criticism of James Monroe.

As he lay in bed at 2 a.m., it became clear that this was no ordinary cold. Constant shivering was keeping Washington from sleep, and he woke Martha to say that his condition seemed serious. At sunrise, Washington allowed a messenger to be sent to Alexandria for his friend and doctor, James Craik. As they waited for Craik to appear, a plantation overseer bled Washington. Martha had misgivings. But Washington insisted, "More, more," until about twelve ounces of blood had been taken from his arm. Lear bathed Washington's neck with sal volatile, and Washington admitted that his throat was very sore.

By the time Craik arrived before noon, Washington was much worse. The doctor diagnosed "inflammatory quinsy" and immediately bled him again. Craik, who was seventy, decided to send for two consultants half his age. When one of them, Dr. Elisha Dick, reached Mount Vernon, he put a stop to any further bleeding. "He needs all his strength," Dick said. "Bleeding will diminish it."

Of the possibilities that presented themselves, Dick strongly recommended opening Washington's trachea below the infection to let him breathe. Craik weighed the suggestion but turned it down. He was supported by the last arrival, Dr. Gustavus Brown. Like Craik, Brown had studied medicine in Edinburgh.

Although the patient was clearly sinking, Lear tried to make him comfortable. At 4:30 p.m., Washington asked for Martha. When she came to his bedside, he sent her downstairs to get two wills from his desk. After inspecting them, Washington handed one back and asked that she burn it. He had made the earlier will when he took command of the Continental Army in 1775. The later document reflected the second lifetime he had lived during the next twenty-four years.

Lear took his hand. "I find I am going," Washington told him. "My breath cannot last long. I believed from the first attack it would be fatal." He asked that Lear arrange his military papers and letters since "you know more about them than anyone else."

As evening approached, Washington was helped to a chair but, after half an hour, asked to return to bed.

When Craik suggested that he sit up, Washington held out his hand as if to try, but he murmured, "Doctor, I die hard, but I am not afraid to go." When the other doctors came into the room, Washington said, "I thank you for your attention. You had better not take any more trouble about me, but let me go off quietly. I cannot last long."

Lear could barely hear as he leaned forward over the bed. "I am just going," Washington told him. "Have me decently buried, and do not let my body be put into the vault in less than two days after I am dead." Washington shared the prevailing fear that his coma might be mistaken for death and he would be buried alive. He looked into Lear's eyes. "Do you understand me?"

Overcome, Lear merely nodded.

Washington repeated, "Do you understand me?"

"Yes, sir."

Washington said, "'Tis well."

Before 11 p.m., Washington's breathing seemed to become easier. He removed his hand from Lear's and felt his own pulse. Lear called to Craik, who was sitting by the fire. When the doctor came to the bed, Washington's hand fell away from his wrist. Lear picked it up and pressed it to his own chest.

There was silence. Standing at the foot of the bed, Martha asked, "Is he gone?"

Lear could not speak. He nodded again.

"'Tis well," Martha Washington repeated numbly. Then, as though to herself, she added, "All is now over. I shall soon follow him. I have no trials to pass through." She would survive for another two and a half years, but at the moment life alone was impossible to contemplate.

In drawing up his will, Washington referred to a reason that he had not freed all of Mount Vernon's slaves. Martha Custis had brought many of them into marriage as her dowry, and his own slaves and hers had married among themselves. As a result, the estate's slaves were not Washington's alone. He could order them freed only upon her death.

Washington made an exception for his former valet, William Lee. Breaking his other knee had crippled Billy completely, and he had become a shoemaker at Mount Vernon, drinking heavily but with an eye out for military visitors. To them, he would send an invitation to visit him in his quarters, and those white veterans always came to listen respectfully as Billy reminisced:

"The new-time people don't know what we old soldiers did and suffered for the country in the old war. Was it not cold enough at Valley Forge? Yes, it was. And I'm sure you remember it was hot enough at Monmouth. Ah, Colonel, I am a poor cripple. Can't ride now, so I make shoes and think of the old times. The general often stops his horse here, to inquire if I want anything. I want for nothing, thank God, but the use of my limbs."

Washington's will gave Billy the choice of immediate freedom or, because he could no longer walk, of staying on at Mount Vernon. In either case, he was to receive, in addition to his usual food and clothing, an annuity of thirty dollars "as a testimony of my sense of his attachment to me, and for his faithful service during the Revolutionary War."

Washington's scruples about his wife's slaves prompted concern in the family that some of them might conspire to end her life. Martha Washington solved the problem by relinquishing her right of dower and setting them all free.

Jefferson's estrangement from Washington guaranteed that he was not asked to speak on December 26, the day that Adams and the Congress decreed for mourning. America's best-known writer was mortified by the intentional slight and remained at Monticello to avoid the ceremonies. Fifteen years later, when Jefferson's hurt feelings had eased, he could say of Washington, "He was, indeed, in every sense of the words, a wise, a good and a great man."

In Jefferson's place, his Federalist foe, Representative Henry Lee, delivered the official eulogy. Light Horse Harry Lee's summation—before repetition reduced it to a jingle—was simple and accurate:

"First in war, first in peace, first in the hearts of his countrymen."

Thomas Jefferson

Chapter Five

JEFFERSON
(1801–1804)

John Adams confided to his wife a premonition that he might not be elected to a second term. His own party was furious over his negotiations with France, and much of the country was troubled by the high taxes of the Adams administration and by the alien and sedition laws. Adams complained that it was unfair to blame him for laws that he had never sponsored. True, he had not vetoed them, either. But Adams pointed out that the vice president was also part of the government that approved the alien and sedition laws, despite Jefferson's lobbying later against them.

Even with Madison retired from the Congress, Adams expected that one day he would be a presidential candidate. For now, Jefferson

was his foremost opponent, although Hamilton's ambition was so fla-
grant that Adams wondered whether he would try to use his position as
the army's inspector general to launch a military coup.

Instead, Hamilton employed a different form of lethal attack. In
time to influence the electors, he sent a devastating assessment of
Adams to Federalist friends who might swing the 1800 election to
Thomas Pinckney. Aaron Burr got hold of the letter and passed it on to
a Republican editor who published it as a fifty-four-page pamphlet. In
vivid language, Hamilton pounced on Adams's every fault—his over-
weening vanity; his bitter jealousy that did not spare even his own cabinet; his weakness and vacillation; his uncontrollable temper.

"It is a fact," Hamilton wrote, "that he is often liable to paroxysms
of anger, which deprive him of self-command and produce very outrageous behavior."

No one in either party could fully explain Hamilton's motive, but
Madison summed up the prevailing sentiment when he rejoiced with
Jefferson that their Republican party "is likely to be *completely* tri-
umphant."

That was before an unexpected snag prevented Jefferson from sa-
voring an immediate victory. When the votes for president were
counted in February 1801, the result was 75 for Jefferson and a respectable 65 for Adams. The Adams faction pointed out that the Constitution's three-fifths clause concerning slaves had given Jefferson his
edge in the Electoral College. They mocked him as the "Negro president" and argued that the result was no fairer than counting the livestock on a New England farm as voters for Adams. Since the clause
was enshrined in the Constitution, however, it was not effectively challenged.

The greater surprise was the showing of Aaron Burr, who had offered Jefferson his strength with New York's Tammany Hall in exchange for the place of vice president on the Republican ticket.

In his negotiations with Jefferson, Burr had laid on flattery to a
shameless degree. He said he was becoming a candidate only to promote Jefferson's fame. He simply wanted to be close to Jefferson because he had always found his company and conversation to be
fascinating. Jefferson, who knew and distrusted Burr from his service in

Congress, wrote afterward, "Colonel Burr must have thought I could swallow strong things in my own favor."

Jefferson had noticed that whenever Washington or Adams had an important military or diplomatic appointment to make, Burr came instantly to Philadelphia. In fact, Jefferson added, he was always on the market.

To guarantee that Burr's total vote did not somehow outstrip Jefferson's, he had been scheduled to receive one less vote in Rhode Island and one other state. For some reason, that plan failed, and Burr tied Jefferson's 75 votes. At that moment, all of his past protestations of admiration evaporated. Since the election now had to go before the House of Representatives, Burr suggested that he be the nation's president. Jefferson could continue as his vice president.

The election results galled Adams despite his determination to be gracious in defeat. Because the House would have to be called back for a lame-duck session to decide the outcome, Adams began to float the idea of an interim president and suggested John Marshall, the Federalist whom Adams had recently elevated from secretary of state to chief justice.

Meeting privately with Jefferson, Adams made a ham-handed attempt to strike a bargain. He said Jefferson could guarantee his election by committing himself to several Federalist policies: He must pledge not to remove Adams's federal officeholders. He must not cut back the navy. And he must not increase the national debt. Infuriated, Jefferson noted in his journal only that he had "turned the conversation to something else."

Despite their own rupture, both Adams and Hamilton, who had feuded with Aaron Burr for years, found Jefferson, the nation's foremost Republican, a more palatable choice than Burr. Hamilton wrote to James Bayard, Delaware's sole representative, who was considered the deciding vote, and listed Jefferson's many liabilities. He concluded that Jefferson was "a contemptible hypocrite."

But, Hamilton continued, Burr was far worse: a profligate, an extreme voluptuary who would bankrupt the country. Burr "would try to change America's government in the manner of Bonaparte"—an odd criticism from a man who had once called Napoleon "that unequaled conqueror." In short, Hamilton concluded, Burr was "as unprincipled and dangerous a man as any country could boast."

On the day the congressional session opened to pick a president, a blizzard hit the capital. With the stakes so high, it kept only one of the 105 House members away from the chamber. Another, a seriously ill Jeffersonian from Maryland, had friends carry him on a stretcher two miles through the snow to cast his vote.

Jefferson presided over the session, maintaining his calm as repeated balloting left him one vote short of victory. On the sixth day, February 17, 1801, Delaware's Bayard made an announcement that provoked shouts of "Traitor!" from his fellow Federalists. Despite Hamilton's letter, he had held firm for Burr as the lesser evil. But before the thirty-sixth round of voting, he said that his next ballot would be blank. The result would reduce the number of states that were voting to fifteen. Jefferson would have his eight-state majority.

Burr and his allies charged that Jefferson had won over Bayard by agreeing to exactly the Federalist deal he had rejected when Adams proposed it. Unconvincingly, Jefferson called the accusations "absolutely false."

Entering office, Jefferson enjoyed new stature from the growing disenchantment with his opponents. Even Samuel Adams, John Adams's cousin and revolutionary comrade-in-arms, had preferred Jefferson. He had begun to desert from the Federalist ranks because the party supported the kind of standing army Sam Adams had been opposing for three decades. His final break came over the Alien and Sedition Acts. When a Boston bookkeeper was jailed for working at a newspaper that criticized the Massachusetts legislature, Adams paid a conspicuous visit to the man's cell.

Approaching eighty, Sam Adams was afflicted with palsy, but he took up his pen to congratulate the new president: "The storm is over," he wrote to Jefferson, "and we are in port."

Despite his resistance to creating an American navy, Jefferson also adopted a seafaring image in his letter to Lafayette: "The storm we have passed through proves our vessel indestructible."

＊   ＊   ＊

The recent deadlock had exposed a serious fault in the Constitution, and Hamilton was among those who proposed the remedy that was adopted in time for the next election. A twelfth amendment was added to the Constitution to instruct electors to cast separate ballots for president and vice president. With Federalist power increasingly limited to New England, that new procedure could prevent a stalemate that would let them broker another presidential election in the Congress.

Preparing for his inaugural morning, Jefferson neither powdered his hair nor strapped on a sword as Washington and Adams had done, and he walked to the ceremony rather than ride in a carriage—all symbols that a new and more democratic day had dawned.

As the first president to be installed in Federal City, Jefferson spoke in the Senate chamber of the new Capitol Building. Although he was taking over the presidency with his Republicans in firm control, he had written an inaugural address that was mild and conciliatory. Like Madison, Jefferson was no practiced orator, and his voice quavered as he reminded his countrymen that "every difference of opinion is not a difference of principle."

Jefferson went on to acknowledge the widening breach and tried to repair it. "We are all Republicans," he said, "we are all Federalists."

Past quarrels were not so easily set aside. Albert Gallatin, Jefferson's newly appointed secretary of the treasury, recommended a plan to reduce taxes while still paying off the national debt within the next seventeen years. To accomplish that would require severe cuts in America's military budget, no matter what the Federalists believed Jefferson had promised to win the election.

To Gallatin, the drain caused by the national debt presented a greater threat than any foreign enemy. The previous year, Adams and his Federalists had allocated $6 million to the army and the navy. After cutting taxes—including those on whiskey stills in his home state of Pennsylvania—Gallatin was left with $7.3 million to pay down the debt and only $2.65 million for all the rest of the government's expenses. He allocated $930,000 to the army and $670,000 to the navy.

Negotiations with Congress raised the total for both branches to $1.9 million, but that figure still reduced the army to three thousand men.

The effect on the navy was even more devastating. The number of warships commissioned during the Adams presidency was reduced from forty-two to thirteen, with many to be sold to private shipping firms. The drastic cuts meant that persuading a capable man to serve as secretary of the navy became all but impossible. Jefferson offered the job unsuccessfully to four potential candidates before settling on a nullity, Robert Smith of Maryland. His forceful brother, Senator Samuel Smith, was expected to make decisions for him.

When a veteran sea captain, Christopher Perry, was dismissed from service, he warned his young son, Oliver, that there was no future for him in the United States Navy. But Oliver had gone to sea with his father at the age of thirteen and now, only two years later, had been chosen as one of the 150 midshipmen to be retained out of the 3,500 men on active duty. The young man decided to gamble and stay on.

As a final act as president, Adams had appointed a number of Federalist judges who would hold office for life. Jefferson saw the move as Adams's way to thwart voters who had cast their ballots for his Republicans. The Federalists "have retired into the Judiciary as a stronghold," the new president complained. "There the remains of federalism are to be preserved and fed from the Treasury."

Jefferson was also angered by Adams's leaving the capital at 4 a.m. on Inauguration Day to avoid the swearing-in ceremony. Adams claimed later that he had been overwhelmed by grief at losing his young son. But for years hard-living Charles Adams had been a disappointment to his family—nothing like his brother, John Quincy Adams, who had begun serving as a diplomatic aide in Russia at the age of fourteen. When Charles died of alcoholism in late November, he had been estranged for more than a year from his father, who had denounced him as "a mere rake, buck, blood and beast."

Even though the alien and sedition laws had expired, Jefferson made an early priority of granting presidential pardons to their victims. He released David Brown of Dedham, Massachusetts, who had already served an eighteen-month sentence but was still in jail because he could not afford his fine. Brown had been convicted for holding up a sign directed at Adams: "Downfall to the tyrants of America, Peace and retirement to the President."

James Callender, Virginia's abrasive Republican propagandist, had already completed a nine-month term, paid a two-hundred-dollar fine, and was out of jail before the inauguration. Jefferson had originally welcomed Callender's attacks on the Federalists and doled out small amounts of money to him that he listed in his accounts as "charity."

During Washington's first term, Callender had printed charges about Hamilton's alleged embezzlement at the Treasury and his adultery with a married woman. Hamilton denied the financial accusations, but he confessed to a messy affair with a swindler's wife and rode out the scandal.

As Callender's attacks grew more vituperative, Jefferson had begun to distance himself. Now, however, as a matter of principle, he not only gave Callender a full presidential pardon but also ordered Richmond's federal marshal to repay the fine. When the money was slow in coming, Callender went to the capital to complain to Madison about Jefferson's indifference. He also demanded to be named the postmaster of Richmond. Denied the appointment, Callender began to collect information about the president's slaves at Monticello.

When Jefferson learned that Callender was threatening to be revenged for his ingratitude, he directed his secretary, Meriwether Lewis, to pay the journalist another fifty dollars and list the expense again as "charity."

In time, the full amount of Callender's fine was restored to him, and for the first year of Jefferson's presidency, nothing incriminating was published about Monticello. But on September 1, 1802, Callender produced his bombshell: The president "keeps and for many years has kept, as his concubine, one of his slaves. Her name is Sally. . . . By this wench Sally, our president has sired several children."

As the story spread throughout the country, Republican newspapers denied it and even Federalist editors demanded proof. Jefferson refused to comment. But the editor of the *Frederick-Town Herald* said he had conducted his own investigation and found that Sally Hemings enjoyed a room to herself at Monticello and that her son, Tom, "bears a strong likeness to Mr. Jefferson."

In retirement, John and Abigail Adams had different reactions to the charge. The former president went to his desk and wrote out an assurance that "no virgin or matron ever had cause to blush at the sight of me, or to regret her acquaintance with me."

Abigail Adams had resented Jefferson's attacks on the Sedition Act, and she was inclined to gloat. She wrote to him, "The serpent you cherished and warmed, bit the hand that nourished it."

But by the time of her reproaches, Callender had succumbed to his own frailties. Widely condemned, increasingly drunk, he staggered through Richmond one July night in 1803, fell into a river, and drowned.

Like Hamilton before him, Jefferson survived the scandal, although during the congressional election of 1802, he drew his acknowledged family closer to him. He invited his two daughters to come with their children to spend time in Washington, where the Jefferson women impressed local society as delicate and accomplished, if only "tolerably handsome."

Despite the published stories, Sally Hemings lived on at Monticello. At the time of Callender's exposé, she had given birth to five children, two of whom died in infancy. After the burst of notoriety, she bore two more sons, both conceived at times that Jefferson was at Monticello.

By December 15, 1802, Jefferson's message to Congress was a study in blandness: "Another year has come around," he began, "and finds us still blessed with peace and friendship abroad."

Even though Jefferson believed that the navy was a needless expense, he found one way to make adroit use of the ships he denigrated. For decades, the Barbary States—five principalities along the northwest coast of Africa—had been extorting bribes from the European ships that traded off their shores. At first, the newly formed United States had refused to pay that tribute. But by 1785, as Barbary pirates went on seizing American merchant ships, the Continental Congress struck a deal. In return for leaving the nation's ships unmolested, Congress agreed to send gifts amounting to ten thousand dollars to the state of Morocco.

Algiers, Tunis, and Tripoli continued their piracy, however, even after Congress authorized the construction of the six fighting frigates that would constitute the first U.S. Navy. That prospect of retaliation did not stop the looting of commercial ships and neither did a new round of bribes from Congress—$56,000 to Tunis, $107,000 to Tripoli, nearly $1 million to Algiers.

Payoffs were not always made in cash. When Tunis sent its ambassador, Sidi Suliman Mellimelli, to negotiate a new settlement in Washington, the diplomat brought along an entourage of eleven dignitaries and asked that concubines be supplied for all of them. As Jefferson's secretary of state, Madison accommodated the request. He rounded up women, including "Georgia, a Greek," and joked afterward with Jefferson that he had charged the expense to the State Department under the irrefutable heading "Appropriations to foreign intercourse."

The continuing bribes rankled Jefferson. He resolved to refuse any further demands from Tripoli and sent America's new warships to blockade its port. The president's firm stand won him popular support, and a defiant cry roused the nation: "Millions for defence, but not one cent for tribute."

Tobias Lear, Washington's former aide, was called from Virginia to travel to Algeria as consul general to the Barbary Coast, the highest rank ever bestowed on an American diplomat in Africa, and instructed to negotiate the best possible treaty for peace with Tripoli.

For Lear, the appointment was a godsend. Since Washington's death, he had been struggling financially despite the life tenancy that Washington had willed him in a property called Walnut Tree Farm. But Lear had spent a full year without pay working to get Washington's papers in shape so he could turn them over to John Marshall for a proposed biography.

Not only did his labor bring in no money, but just as Lear was sailing for the Mediterranean in July 1803, he learned that the Federalists were claiming that he got his appointment for a dishonorable reason. Rumors circulated that after Jefferson's Mazzei letter was published, Washington had written Monticello for an explanation and that angry letters were exchanged. Lear was accused of suppressing them to further Jefferson's ambitions; the appointment to the Barbary Coast was said to be his reward.

Unwittingly, Lear himself had contributed to the accusation. During the years he served Washington faithfully, Lear had also remained committed to Jefferson's ideals. And yet it was to Hamilton that Lear had confided that he was withholding several of Washington's letters from the public. Since Hamilton was hardly a man to protect Jefferson's reputation, that suggested none of the letters involved the Mazzei affair. And to Hamilton, Lear had added that because he considered all of Washington's documents "sacred," he had spoken with the president's nephew, Bushrod Washington, about those he was withdrawing.

No incriminating letters ever turned up. But the allegations followed Lear to Algiers as he waited impatiently for the royal court at Tripoli to open negotiations.

Then, in October, Lear's mission became more urgent. During the blockade of Tripoli's coastline, the USS *Philadelphia* hit a reef. Enemy gunboats shelled it into submission and took as prisoners its captain and his 330-man crew. The navy assigned Stephen Decatur, a lieutenant commander, the task of salvaging America's honor.

Like every navy man, Decatur knew of John Paul Jones's defiant cry during the Revolution from the deck of his sinking warship: "I have not yet begun to fight!" Decatur might create his own legend if he could set fire to the *Philadelphia* so it could no longer serve as a symbol of America's humiliation.

Leading a crew of sixty men in a ketch within Tripoli's harbor, Decatur sailed close to his target. Their Sicilian pilot called in Arabic to the guards aboard the *Philadelphia*, claiming that they had come from Malta to load cattle for a British garrison but the ketch had lost its anchor. Could they tie up to the *Philadelphia* until morning?

The guards threw down a line.

Slipping aboard with three-inch sperm candles saturated in turpentine, Decatur's men overwhelmed each guard with swords and knives rather than with noisy guns. But one twenty-year-old midshipman, Thomas Macdonough, had to break the silence. When his cutlass blade broke off during hand-to-hand fighting, he seized his opponent's pistol and killed him with his own gun.

Once the guards had been subdued, Decatur's men set fires along the length of the ship and jumped back to their ketch. The embarrassing ship was destroyed, and only one of their men had been wounded.

But Decatur's raid still left the *Philadelphia*'s crew held hostage in Tripoli. An American adventurer named William Eaton proposed to free them by marching an army across the Libyan desert and forcing Tripoli's ruler, the bashaw, to yield his throne to a more pliant brother. Eaton led six U.S. Marines, a patchy crew of Greek and Arab mercenaries, and 107 camels over five hundred miles to the town of Derma in Tripoli. As Eaton was marching, however, Lear negotiated a settlement with the bashaw that did not require him to abdicate.

Secretary of State Madison had authorized Lear to pay five hundred dollars per man to release the American prisoners. Lear bargained the price down to a flat sixty thousand dollars. In the process, he incurred the lifelong hatred of William Eaton, who wrote a five-thousand-word letter attacking him for paying the ransom when Tripoli was all but in American hands.

Federalists joined in the attacks, which did not let up until the day in 1816 that Tobias Lear, at the age of fifty-five, killed himself.

In 1803, well into his first term, Jefferson faced another unexpected dilemma: Either he could remain true to his principles about the constitutional limits of a president's power, or he could jettison them and accept one of history's greatest windfalls. For Jefferson and Madison, the choice was never in doubt. They had only to devise the philosophical contortions to justify it.

The issue concerned land the Americans called Louisiana. It had been home to Indians of the Fox tribe until the day in April 1682 when a French explorer reached the banks of the Mississippi. Bearing the title de La Salle, René-Robert Cavelier had claimed possession of the land in the name of Prince Louis the Great.

Within forty years, buildings were going up in New Orleans so rapidly that French developers predicted the settlement was destined to become a great port. First, though, nature had to be tamed. The town was built on land between the mouth of the Mississippi, the Gulf of Mexico, and a vast lake of three hundred square miles called Pontchartrain. Since the area lay below sea level, the likelihood of flooding was constant. In 1718, a French nobleman, Jean-Baptiste Le Moyne de Bienville, overruled warnings from his engineers and expanded the settlement, depending for protection on a network of levees and canals.

As New Orleans grew on its unstable base, settlers captured the Fox and sold them as slaves. The French noted that the number of Indians was already declining due to diseases the colonists had brought with them.

Other European leaders soon saw the value of a flourishing port at the mouth of a great river. In 1762, the French secretly transferred New Orleans to Spain as part of negotiations that led the following year to the Peace of Paris. After America won independence, those settlers who thronged to the Ohio Valley had to get Spain's permission to trade at New Orleans.

But when merchants from Kentucky and Tennessee sent shipments down the river by raft and flatboat, they were faced with arbitrary rules and prohibitive duties that could result in their leaving their goods to rot in the harbor. Outraged, the Americans presented their government with an ultimatum: If the United States did not seize New Orleans by force, they would secede from the union.

Thomas Pinckney's treaty with Spain during Washington's second term eased the crisis by guaranteeing free passage on the Mississippi. It also upheld America's right to transfer merchandise in New Orleans from river boats to oceangoing ships. For the next several years, the arrangement worked well.

By that time, however, the number of settlers in the Ohio Valley had reached 350,000. The port was dominated by Americans exporting sugar, cotton, tobacco, flour, apples, and cider. And in Paris, Napoleon was becoming jealous of Spain's holdings in North America. Through another secret treaty in 1800, he offered King Charles of Spain a duchy in northern Italy for Charles to bestow on a son-in-law. In return, France would regain Louisiana.

Since independence, Benjamin Franklin had worried that· Spain's holdings might hamper America's inevitable growth to the south and west. Before he died in 1790, Franklin warned that if Spain tried to buy more land on the American continent "a neighbor might as well ask me to sell my street door." The same fervor for expansion led John Adams to predict that the United States was "destined beyond a doubt to be the greatest power on earth, and that within the life of man."

Sharing those sentiments, President Jefferson had been alarmed to learn that France would once again own New Orleans. He put the issue starkly: Since nearly one-third of American goods had to pass through the port to market, whoever controlled it became America's enemy. If the French took possession, Jefferson vowed, "from that moment we must marry ourselves to the British fleet and nation."

Despite that clear statement, Federalists in Congress still considered Jefferson contaminated by his admiration for France and worried that he would be too accommodating to its emperor.

Early in 1803, as Napoleon prepared to assert ownership over Louisiana, a French general arrived there to congratulate its citizens on the prospect of living once again under his country's rule. His audience was inclined to agree, since the pious Spaniards had been harsh masters. For blaspheming against Jesus or Mary, a man could have his property confiscated and his tongue cut out.

To win over the surrounding tribes, the French had also struck two hundred medallions with Napoleon's image to distribute to prominent chieftains once the transfer took place.

So far, Jefferson's attempts at diplomacy had been discouraging. As his envoy, he had sent to Paris Robert Livingston, the New York chancellor who had presided over Washington's first inaugural. Livingston was instructed to prevent Napoleon from taking possession of New Orleans or—at the very least—to arrange free access to the Mississippi and the port. But Talleyrand, negotiating again for the French, remained unsympathetic to America. In any case, Napoleon was not listening to him or to anyone else.

Just then, pending the transfer to France, the Spanish abruptly closed New Orleans to American shipping.

Madison described the impact of Spain's action on people along the frontier: "The Mississippi is to them everything. It is the Hudson, the Delaware, the Potomac, and all the navigable rivers of the Atlantic States formed into one stream."

Jefferson prodded Livingston for progress. "Perhaps nothing since the revolutionary war," he wrote, "has produced more uneasy sensations through the body of the nation."

Given the emergency, Jefferson dispatched his friend James Monroe as minister extraordinary to France and Spain. When Monroe joined Livingston in Paris, they would be authorized to offer $10 million to buy New Orleans and the Floridas. Monroe would not be leaving for Paris until early March 1803, however, and with Napoleon's agent already headed for New Orleans to complete the transfer from Spain, Monroe's mission seemed aborted before he set sail.

But Napoleon, ever mercurial, was planning a historic surprise.

On April 6, 1803, Lucien Bonaparte planned to attend the premiere at the Theatre Françoise of the celebrated François Talma as Hamlet. Before he left for the evening, however, Lucien learned from another brother, Joseph, that Napoleon intended to sell Louisiana to the Americans.

The news disturbed Lucien, who had been the one to go to Madrid and arrange transfer of the territory back to France. The Corsican brothers shared a strong family bond, but Joseph could be hot-tempered, and Lucien, six years younger than Napoleon, had assumed the role of peacemaker. He canceled his theater plans and returned home to prepare his arguments against the sale.

Lucien intended to point out that the transaction would violate France's treaty with Spain, which remained Louisiana's official owner. The sale would also break French law.

The next morning, a Thursday, Lucien went to the Tuileries, where he found Napoleon in his bath. On days with no urgent reason to dress, the first consul enjoyed lingering in the scented water. Unlike Lucien, Napoleon had gone to the theater the previous night, and he praised Talma's performance. Better still had been the warm response of the audience when Napoleon arrived. He seemed to remember better than they did how he had once ended an insurrection by ordering the killing of a hundred royalists. "In fact," Napoleon said, still marveling at the memory, "I scarcely flattered myself they would ever become so sympathetic when I had to shoot them down on that October day in 1795."

Napoleon had already decided that France's average man retained no enthusiasm for the goals of the French Revolution. When he freed Lafayette from five years in captivity, the emperor had taunted him about his devotion to the concept of liberty.

The French, Napoleon said, "are thoroughly sick of it. Your Parisians — for instance, oh, the shopkeepers — don't want it anymore."

Lafayette had responded by opposing the legislation that made Napoleon France's first consul for life and then withdrawing from politics.

As Napoleon spoke with Lucien from his bath, an odd sound came at the door. Instead of knocking, visitors had been instructed recently to scratch at the door like a cat. Joseph Bonaparte entered and listened as Napoleon elaborated on his plans.

"Take note, Lucien, I have made up my mind to sell Louisiana to the Americans."

"Indeed." Lucien kept any hint of judgment out of his voice.

But Joseph vowed that he would lead the opposition in the Senate chamber. To that, Napoleon gave a loud, sarcastic laugh. He planned to allow no debate on the issue, he said. At that, he stood up from the tub so vehemently that water splashed Joseph's face and drenched his coat.

To calm his brothers, Lucien quoted in Latin a line from the *Aeneid* about quieting the disturbed waves. The gesture came too late. Napoleon's valet, who had been holding out a cloth to dry him, fainted from fright, and Napoleon slipped back into the water.

✻   ✻   ✻

Although Napoleon did not choose to discuss his reasons that morning, his brothers understood that events in French Santo Domingo had thwarted his aspirations for an empire in the New World. The island was rich in trade and strategically located for controlling the sea, but the natives had been rebelling for the past twelve years. Inspired by their Negro leader, Toussaint L'Ouverture, they had cut down thousands of French soldiers and blocked off their reinforcements.

General Charles Leclerc, married to Napoleon's sister Pauline, had tried to break the rebellion but died of the yellow fever that swept through his ranks. The French deceived Toussaint into surrendering and then shipped him to his death in a French Alpine prison. But with Napoleon's dreams for the New World thwarted, he needed to raise money for a likely war with Britain.

Livingston knew nothing of Napoleon's calculations. Still put off by Talleyrand, he wrote to Jefferson on March 12 that "nothing will be effected here." He was surprised soon afterward when Talleyrand obeyed Napoleon's instructions and suggested that America might be able to buy far more than the port of New Orleans. Although the cost would be considerably above the $10 million that Jefferson was prepared to spend, America could own the entire Louisiana Territory.

That grandiose offer staggered the conscientious Livingston. He protested that his country wanted only the port and West Florida and could not pay a higher price. Napoleon's treasury minister, François Barbé-Marbois, tried to spur him toward a compromise by complaining about the pressure he himself was under:

"You know the temper of a youthful conqueror," Marbois said ruefully. "Everything he does is rapid as lightning." Napoleon's advisers could only get his attention when the chance arose, and usually that meant being part of a crowd. If he could be alone with Napoleon, Marbois added, he could speak more freely, and Napoleon might listen. "But this opportunity seldom happens and is always accidental."

Given those circumstances, Livingston should try to meet the French price. "Consider the extent of the country," Marbois reminded him, "the exclusive navigation of the river, and the importance of having no neighbors to dispute you, no war to dread."

By the time Monroe arrived in Paris, the haggling had settled on a price of $15 million, an amount greater than the total annual income of the United States. But the Americans agreed to it.

Writing home, Monroe pointed out that the price of going to war over the territory would have been higher than what they had just paid. For his part, Livingston was exultant. Signing the purchase treaty on May 2, 1803, he assured Monroe, "We have lived long, but this is the noblest work of our whole lives."

The sale was completed by the time Monroe was finally received for the first time by Napoleon, and the first consul turned instead to more personal matters. Since he knew America's leaders only by name, he wanted intimate details. He asked Jefferson's age and whether he was married or single. Did he have children? America's new capital city had caught Napoleon's imagination, and he inquired about its size and whether Jefferson always resided there.

"Generally," Monroe answered, preferring not to confuse Napoleon with a description of Monticello.

"Are the public buildings there commodious—those for the Congress and President, especially?"

"They are."

"You—the Americans—did brilliant things in your war with England," Napoleon said. "You will do the same again."

The remark put Monroe on his guard. "We shall, I'm persuaded, always behave well when it should be our lot to be in war."

"You may probably be in war with them again."

Reporting to Jefferson, Monroe said that he had replied that he did not know, that it would be an important question to decide if the occasion should arise.

At home, Jefferson was having misgivings about the bargain struck in his name. Madison had hoped his Constitution would prevent high-handed actions by an American president. Now Jefferson would be burdening the country with a huge debt without any clear idea of what he had just bought. He had always appreciated the grandeur of the continent looming west of the original thirteen colonies and had envisioned enough room "for our descendants to the hundredth and thou-

sandth generation." But that same expanse might prove to be arid
wasteland.

A full ten years earlier, before Jefferson could imagine owning the
territory, he had sounded out the Revolutionary War hero George
Rogers Clark about exploring the continent from Mississippi to the Pacific Ocean. In their correspondence, Jefferson had given Clark full lee-
way in dealing with the local Indian tribes: "We must leave it to yourself.
The end proposed shall be their extermination or their removal," Jefferson wrote. "The same world would scarcely do for them and us."

Clark was retired by the time Jefferson could fulfill that dream, but
the president had engaged as his secretary Meriwether Lewis, a twenty-
nine-year-old protégé who hoped to explore the continent. During the
intervening decade, the British explorer Alexander Mackenzie had already crossed the Canadian Rockies and written about his travels.

Now, Jefferson explained to Lewis and William Clark, George
Rogers Clark's youngest brother, that they were to go west and learn
whether the Missouri River connected with the tributaries of the Pacific in ways that could provide a water route across the continent. Although Jefferson had cajoled twenty-five hundred dollars from the
Congress by stressing the commercial value of the enterprise, his personal interests remained scientific. He instructed the men to make
notes on the soil, vegetation, and animals they encountered. But Lewis
and Clark would not be leaving until the spring of 1804, and their report could be months, even years, in coming.

At the moment, the northeastern Federalists were attacking Jefferson for exceeding his powers in dealing with France. Some critics worried that the purchase would upset the current political balance as
easterners headed out for the new territory and uncouth westerners
claimed a share of power. Josiah Quincy saw no reason to be tactful.
Permitting Kentuckians into Congress had been calamitous enough,
but now "others like thick-skinned beasts will crowd around Congress
Hall—buffaloes from the head of the Missouri and alligators from the
Red River."

In New York, Hamilton favored the purchase, even as Madison was
expressing apprehension since he preferred to let Americans stay in the
East, rather than dilute the country's population.

Federalist newspapers jeered at the expense, pointing out that William Penn had paid a mere five thousand British pounds for all of Pennsylvania. They calculated that, piled in a stack, Jefferson's fifteen million dollars would reach three miles into the sky.

But the bargain was simply too good to pass up. Jefferson's cabinet urged him not to seek a constitutional amendment to approve the purchase; the process would mean an unnecessary delay. At that, the president overcame any scruples and asked Congress to approve the deal.

By a vote of 26 to 5, the United States annexed almost one million square miles of the North American continent at a cost of four cents an acre.

With Jefferson's reelection campaign approaching, he dropped the faithless Burr as his vice president and replaced him with another New Yorker, George Clinton, who had served seven terms as the state's governor. Burr announced that he would be returning home to run as a Federalist for the New York governorship. But he also seemed open to more devious ways to advance his career.

A group of New England senators had sounded out Hamilton about leading a secession movement that would join New York with their states and create a northern confederacy. Hamilton turned them down, but he heard that the cabal had next approached Aaron Burr. Over dinner in Washington, the dissident senators presented their proposal. Burr listened attentively but could not be pinned down.

On the basis of those rumors, Hamilton once again damned Burr as a dangerous man who should never be trusted with political power. In the New York vote for governor, Burr carried New York City, but only by one hundred votes, and lost statewide by more than eight thousand. His defeat destroyed Jefferson's only serious rival and guaranteed him a second term.

Two months later, Burr sent an emissary to Hamilton with a newspaper clipping from the *Albany Register* that quoted what Burr termed Hamilton's "despicable" attacks on him. Burr asked for an explanation. Hamilton waited two days before sending an evasive reply. Burr continued to demand the apology that Hamilton could not bring himself to make. At last, a duel was arranged.

A recent law had banned duels, but both men had already participated in them. Once, protesting charges that he took bribes, Burr had been shot but only through his coat. His opponent apologized before a second round.

During the Revolution, Hamilton had acted as the second to his good friend John Laurens, who had challenged General Charles Lee after the battle of Monmouth for slurs against George Washington. Lee took a shot in the right side but expressed his esteem for Washington before another round was fired.

But three years before Burr's challenge, a duel had proved more fatal. Hamilton's oldest son, Philip, died from dueling wounds, and his death had seemed to unbalance Philip's sister, Angelica. At least, it was blamed for the madness that blighted the rest of her life.

Early on the morning of July 11, 1804, the duelists were rowed across the Hudson to a field near Weehawken, New Jersey, where their seconds positioned them face-to-face. Hamilton supplied the pistols, borrowed from his brother-in-law. He squinted down the eleven-inch barrel and put on his spectacles. He had decided to miss on his first shot. Then, with honor satisfied, the pointless duel could end.

Hamilton fired twelve feet off the ground at a cedar tree to his right. Burr's shot hit Hamilton's liver and lodged in his back. When Burr went to assist the dying man, his second covered Burr's head in an inept attempt to shield his identity from any spectators before he could be spirited away.

Hamilton was too weak to be carried to the Grange, his house north of Manhattan. He was taken instead to a friend's home on Jane Street and given laudanum for his intense pain. The bishop of New York arrived and administered communion but only after Hamilton promised never again to engage in what the bishop termed "this barbarous custom."

Hamilton died thirty-one hours after Burr fired his shot.

*   *   *

In New York, mourners grieved for their brilliant adopted son. Throngs turned out to watch as Hamilton's body was buried with full military honors by an honor guard from the Cincinnati. Flags were furled in tribute and the city's bells muffled. The funeral oration set off intense weeping and recriminations against Burr, who fled to Perth Amboy, New Jersey. On his house were hung accusatory verses that began:

"O Burr, O Burr, what has thou done?

"Thou hast shooted dead great Hamilton!"

With Clinton replacing Burr on the ticket, Jefferson received 162 of the 176 electoral votes, losing only Connecticut and Delaware to Charles Pinckney, the South Carolina Federalist. Jefferson's Republican majorities in the new Congress were equally lopsided. The Federalists took only 7 of the 34 Senate seats and 25 of 141 in the House.

When grand juries in both New York and New Jersey indicted Burr for Hamilton's death, he traveled west of the Appalachians, where he got a raucous welcome from frontier settlers who had feared Hamilton's urban policies. In Nashville, Burr was introduced to a major-general in the Tennessee militia and claimed to find in him a kindred spirit. "A man of intelligence," Burr called Andrew Jackson, "and one of those prompt, frank, ardent souls whom I loved to meet."

Andrew Jackson   *Rachel Donelson Jackson*

Chapter Six

ANDREW JACKSON
(1805–1807)

Few men in public life had overcome greater obstacles to achieve eminence than Andrew Jackson. Jackson's father had brought his wife and two older sons from Ireland to the Carolinas in 1765. When he died two years later, he left behind a pregnant widow who gave birth to Andrew a few days afterward. Elizabeth Jackson took her sons to live with relatives in South Carolina, raising them to remember that the English had murdered their grandfather at Carrickfergus, a town on Ireland's northern coast. With the outbreak of the Revolution, her three boys enlisted to fight the Redcoats.

Hugh Jackson, the eldest, died in battle. Andrew and his brother Robert, both in their teens, were taken prisoner and sent to a British stockade at Camden. Andrew told later of the blows they received from a British officer when they refused to clean his boots. Robert took a gash in the head. Andrew, warding off the man's sword, was struck in the arm.

By the time they were freed, the boys were weak from hunger and suffering from smallpox. With one brother already killed and Robert and their mother both dying soon after his release, Andrew was left a fourteen-year-old orphan with three years of schooling. Undaunted, he found homes to live in and schools to attend. By seventeen, Andrew was studying law. By twenty, he was a licensed attorney in North Carolina but tending store to pay his bills.

Settling down in Jonesborough, Tennessee, Jackson adapted well to the rugged frontier life where, not so long ago, Kentucky and Tennessee had paid bounties for Indian scalps, including those of women and children. A popular game of the era was "snick-a-snack," with simple enough rules: Two players struck each other with their knives at the head, shoulders, and hands until one of them gave up. When fighting was in earnest, the knifings were fatal. Until dueling was outlawed, it had been considered the more civilized way of settling disputes.

But as families worked to clear the forests and till the land, the law was making inroads into their lives. They still amused themselves by drinking corn whiskey and dancing to fiddles and harmonicas, but they also came to look forward to criminal trials at the courthouse as an entertaining break from their harsh routine.

Jackson became a public prosecutor, working to resolve the constant quarrels that sprang from debt and drunkenness. Going about his rounds one day, he was faced with a drunkard named Russell Bean who had been indicted for cutting off the ears of his infant child in an alcoholic frenzy. The local sheriff refused to go near the wild man, but Jackson called out, "Stop and submit to the law," and Bean surrendered to that air of command. In his free time, Jackson developed an enduring love of horse racing, and he imported thoroughbreds from Virginia and North Carolina.

At twenty-one, Jackson fought his first duel against an opposing counsel; there were no casualties. But moving to Middle Tennessee, he always kept a pair of well-oiled pistols in a drawer of his desk in case he was compelled to defend his wife's honor.

Jackson had met Rachel Donelson Robards at a boardinghouse run by her mother. The unhappy wife of Lewis Robards, she had already separated from him twice before he accused her of having an affair with Jackson. When she ran off with Jackson downriver to Natchez, Robards threatened to "haunt" her. At the time, the region had no divorce law, but Robards successfully petitioned the legislature of Virginia to dissolve his marriage because of his wife's adultery.

Learning of the decree, Jackson married Rachel in Natchez, or so he claimed. Then, after a calm that lasted two years, Robards decided to make his divorce more binding and asked Kentucky's supreme court to hear his case before a jury. Once again, Robards was awarded his divorce, and Jackson undisputedly married Rachel in 1794.

Although whispering about their affair never entirely died, Jackson's reputation as an honest and able lawyer did not suffer. In 1796, he was elected to the U.S. House of Representatives by constituents who wanted him to press the government to pay claims from soldiers who had served in the Indian Wars of 1793. When Congress finally appropriated the $22,816, Jackson, who had spoken on no other issue, left Philadelphia before the second session.

Undeterred by his seeming indifference, Tennessee's governor appointed Jackson to fill a vacancy in the Senate. He traveled north again, was sworn in, and never cast a vote. When he was urged to yield his seat to a Revolutionary War general, Jackson agreed that the man would make a better senator and resigned.

Almost at once, he was named to the state supreme court. That post he relinquished without having written an opinion. Other candidates would make a more qualified judge, he said.

During his brief service in Philadelphia, Jackson had not impressed his more urbane colleagues. Albert Gallatin summed him up as "a rough backwoodsman," who was "tall, lank, uncouth-looking," with long strands of hair hanging across his face and the queue down his back tied in an eelskin.

*   *   *

At the time Jefferson bought the Louisiana Territory, Jackson had been quick to realize that the purchase would change the country. Pressed for money, he sold off fifty-six thousand pounds of cotton and a load of skins to get ready cash while he finagled for appointment as the territory's governor. He felt confident that Jefferson would name him and end his money worries.

Jackson got political allies to write on his behalf and sent his own message congratulating the president on the acquisition. It was "a golden moment," Jackson wrote—the entire Western Hemisphere was rejoicing.

But when Jackson went north on business, he did not ride out to see Jefferson at Monticello. He explained that "a call under present existing circumstances might be construed as the act of a courtier, cringing for office." As it turned out, renewing their personal contact might not have furthered Jackson's cause, since Jefferson remembered him vividly from his term in the Senate. "He could never speak on account of the rashness of his feelings," Jefferson recalled years later. "I have seen him attempt it repeatedly and as often choke with rage."

Jackson was in Philadelphia buying a stock of calico when he learned that Jefferson had appointed William Claiborne as governor. Since Claiborne was his friend, Jackson did not complain. His ambition would have to find another outlet.

Aaron Burr confided his grandiose plan to Jackson, who heartily endorsed Burr's vague scheme to force out the remaining Spaniards from America. Jackson lent Burr a boat to sail to a military post at the junction of the Ohio and the Mississippi. There, Burr met with General James Wilkinson, commander of troops in the Louisiana Territory. The men agreed that the northeastern Federalists would soon come to blows with Jefferson's Republicans. As anarchy overtook the nation, they would establish their own empire in Louisiana.

Burr had already contacted Anthony Merry, Britain's minister to the United States, who reported to the London Foreign Office that Burr had offered to assist Britain "to effect a separation of the Western part of the United States." But the British declined to underwrite the conspiracy, and Wilkinson's senior officers refused to join in. The general's own involvement was compromised by the secret payments of two thousand dollars he had been receiving annually for twenty years from the king of Spain. On Spain's books, Wilkinson was listed as "Agent Number 13."

Since he could not involve the British, Burr tried next to sell his services to Spain. He sent a friend to assure the Spanish minister to the United States that he had given up any plot against Spain's holdings on the continent and was proposing instead a daring coup d'etat.

Burr would infiltrate armed men into Washington. At his signal, they would kidnap Jefferson and other top officials, confiscate the money in local banks, and seize the weapons from the central arsenal. Burr would then try to make peace with America's state governments, but if that failed, he would escape with the loot from the banks and establish an independent New Orleans. The result would secure Spanish holdings in North America.

Could Burr have believed his fantasy? Although he approached other men, only the Spanish minister was gullible enough to give Burr a few thousand dollars and write to Madrid, unsuccessfully, for more.

Jefferson's friends, who picked up rumors of the plot and passed them along to him, considered the president foolhardy for dismissing them.

Awaiting further word from Burr, Andrew Jackson took part in his own fatal duel. His temper had already led him to draw his weapon once more—against Tennessee's governor at the time of the Louisiana Purchase. Friends broke up that fight, and Jackson's reputation had not suffered; in fact, his grit had been admired.

Three years later, the outcome was different. A man named Charles Dickinson had first antagonized Jackson by making lecherous remarks about Rachel Jackson. Dickinson claimed he had been drunk and apologized, but soon afterward a horse owned by Dickinson's father-in-law went lame before a race against one of Jackson's horses. A dispute arose over whether an eight-hundred-dollar forfeit was due Jackson, and an exchange of vituperative letters appeared in Nashville's only newspaper, the *Impartial Review and Cumberland Repository*.

After a few incidents of comic melodrama, Jackson finally challenged Charles Dickinson in earnest, and they agreed to duel on the banks of the Red River, just over the Tennessee state line.

Jackson's prominence and Dickinson's popularity with other young sportsmen ratcheted up the betting on the outcome. Odds favored the younger man, who was acknowledged to be the better shot. As he rode to the site, Dickinson fired at a string and cut it in half from twenty-four feet—the distance established for the duel.

Jackson had devised a defensive strategy. He would let Dickinson fire first and take a hit. Rather than return the shot quickly, since he might be reeling from the impact, he would take his time and fire with greater precision. That, of course, depended on whether he lived.

On the bright morning of May 30, 1806, Jackson and his seconds met Dickinson and his party in a grove of tall poplars. Dickinson fired and seemed to strike Jackson in the chest. When Jackson raised his left arm to fire back, Dickinson became frightened. "Great God!" he exclaimed. "Have I missed him?"

Jackson's shot struck just below Dickinson's ribs, and his friends caught him as he toppled forward. Crying out from pain, he bled throughout the day and died at nine o'clock that evening.

Leading Jackson from the field, his second saw that one of his shoes was filled with blood and asked, "General Jackson, are you hit?"

"Oh, I believe that he has pinked me a little," Jackson said. But he wanted nothing said in the presence of Dickinson's friends, and he revealed the degree of his determination: "I should have hit him if he had shot me through the brain."

Jackson was taken to an inn, where he asked for buttermilk. He downed the whole quart, then allowed a doctor to examine him. It turned out that the same indifference to his appearance that had repelled congressmen in Philadelphia might have saved Jackson's life. He had worn a frock coat that fitted so loosely it did not reveal the narrowness of his chest. Even so, Dickinson's bullet had shattered two ribs and lodged too close to his heart to be removed.

Fashionable Nashville mourners turned out for Dickinson's funeral while Jackson nursed his wound, which gave him a pain that never entirely subsided for the rest of his life. The editor of the *Impar-*

tial Review was among those who believed that Tennessee should never resort to "the barbarous and pernicious practice of dueling." His paper treated Dickinson as a victim, and the social leaders of Western Tennessee regarded Jackson as a lawless outcast.

When Burr returned to Nashville, he sought out Jackson and paid him thirty-five hundred dollars to oversee the building of five riverboats. Although Jackson was avid to attack Santa Fe, East and West Florida, and even Mexico, he differed from Wilkinson in his scruples over secession. He would joyfully invade Spain's holdings but would "die in the last ditch" before he would imperil America's union.

Jackson's concern was matched by that of Joseph Daveiss, the U.S. attorney in Kentucky, who tried again unsuccessfully to convey to Jefferson the urgency of coping with Burr. Jefferson remained curiously detached, perhaps because the warning came from Daveiss, a strong Federalist who was Chief Justice Marshall's brother-in-law. The president also seemed reluctant to prosecute a man who might have a sizeable following in the newer territories.

When the president refused to act, Daveiss charged that Burr's plan to invade Spanish territory violated the federal Neutrality Act. Burr appeared in court with a rising young Kentucky lawyer, Henry Clay, who had just been appointed to fill out a term in the U.S. Senate. Clay worried he might damage his career by taking the case, but Burr persuaded him that he had never intended to break up the union.

In the packed courtroom, Clay's language soared. "You have heard of inquisitions in Europe," he told the grand jury. "You have heard of the screws and tortures made use of in the dens of despotism to extort confession . . ." If the images hardly fit the case, they impressed Clay's audience. His oratory, combined with Burr's smooth denials, led the grand jury to find no wrongdoing. Cheers from the spectators drowned out disheartened protests from the prosecutor.

But by now, Andrew Jackson thought he had been duped, recruited for a plan that was not glorious conquest but despicable treason. He warned his friend, Governor Claiborne in New Orleans, to organize his militia and put the town on alert: "I fear treachery has become the order of the day."

Zebulon Pike

Chapter Seven

ZEBULON PIKE
(1805–1807)

Beguiled by Aaron Burr's vision, General Wilkinson wanted to learn more about uncharted territories where he might soon be fighting. To explore them, he settled on Zebulon Montgomery Pike, a twenty-six-year-old career soldier from New Jersey who had been named for his father, a veteran of the Revolution who was still on active duty.

The younger Pike had enlisted as a teenage cadet in his father's infantry unit and over the years had impressed Wilkinson, who instructed him to explore the headwaters of the Mississippi and remind Indian tribes and British traders that America now ruled the river and the land around it. Pike's party would be small—one sergeant, one corporal, and seventeen privates. He was not authorized a surgeon.

The expedition left St. Louis on August 8, 1805, on a seventy-foot keelboat laden with enough provisions to last four months. Pike's journal concluded each day with his progress—"Distance eight miles," "Distance 16 miles." On the day after Christmas, four of the sleds he was using to slide across the snow broke down and he managed only three miles.

Many times, his soldiers had to cram supplies into bundles of a hundred pounds each and transport them by land. The men were harnessed to sleds, two abreast, to pull four hundred pounds over thousands of yards. Sometimes Pike joined in, but usually he walked ahead, scouting for game and building fires against an unrelenting cold that could freeze a man's toes and fingers.

The monotony of the days presented Pike with a danger of a different sort. As he waited for the construction of a larger boat, he confessed to his journal that he was overcome with ennui and had begun to understand the attractions of the bottle. But rather than drink, Pike stirred himself and went in search of elk and buffalo.

In mid-February 1806, the expedition came upon Red Creek Lake in what is now Minnesota and assumed that it was the Mississippi's source. Since the lake split into channels, it was an easy error to make.

Returning to the outpost where he had left the bulk of his supplies, Pike found that his sergeant had eaten what Pike described as "all the elegant hams and saddles of venison" he had been saving to present to Wilkinson and his cronies. The sergeant had also consumed much of the camp whiskey, including a keg that Pike had set aside for his own use. As punishment, Pike reduced the man to private.

He waited until April for ice to break up on the river and finally returned to St. Louis on April 30, 1806. The expedition had taken eight months and twenty-two days, twice its scheduled time.

Delighted with his young explorer, Wilkinson sent him out again ten weeks later. This time, Pike was to escort a group of Indians to their home on the Grand Osage River. In the process, Pike was expected to broker a peace between the Osage and Kansas Indian nations, and he was directed to seek the headwaters of the Arkansas and Red rivers. Should his travels take him near the Spanish settlements in New Mexico, Pike was to reconnoiter without causing alarm. Pike told Wilkinson he would pretend that he was traveling to the American garrison at Natchitoches and had lost his way.

This second expedition, more ambitious than the first, included an interpreter and a civilian doctor, John Hamilton Robinson, who had volunteered to go along. There would also be Wilkinson's son, another lieutenant; a more trustworthy sergeant; two corporals; and sixteen privates; plus the fifty-one Osages and Pawnees in their charge.

On July 15, 1806, Zebulon Pike departed on the journey that would make his name immortal.

At first, Pike found the western landscape teeming with animals. Herds of wild horses ran along the Arkansas River, perhaps distant offspring of the Andalusians that Hernando Cortés had brought to the continent almost three hundred years before. One day, Pike spotted a surging sea of buffalo on the plains. He estimated three thousand in one sighting alone.

Then, on November 15, four months after his departure, Pike saw rising from the plains a mountain range capped with snow. It was Thanksgiving Day when he drew closer and observed that one peak soared above the others. No matter where he circled on the plains, it was never out of his sight. Pike resolved to get nearer still.

At the base of a less intimidating mountain some fifteen miles away, Pike and three companions stowed their blankets and supplies and began their ascent. He "found it very difficult," Pike wrote in his journal, "being obliged to climb up rocks, sometimes almost perpendicular; and after marching all day, we encamped in a cave without blanket, victuals or water."

His party had passed buffalo on the climb, and higher up they found deer and pheasants. The sky was clear around them, but Pike could see that it was snowing farther down a slope covered with yellow pine.

When Pike's journals were published two years later, some readers criticized his language as bare and uncompelling. But no one found fault with the entry for November 27, 1806:

"Arose hungry, dry and extremely sore from the inequality of the rocks on which we had lain all night, but were amply compensated for our toil by the sublimity of the prospects below. The unbounded prairie was overhung with clouds, which appeared like the ocean in a storm; waves piled on waves and foaming, whilst the sky was perfectly clear where we were."

Continuing to climb, Pike and his men reached the summit in about an hour. There they found deep snow and no trace of birds or animals. Pike looked across to the higher mountain that he thought of as Grand Peak and apologized to himself for not attempting to conquer it. His reasoning was persuasive:

Grand Peak was twice the height of the one they had just climbed. It would have taken a full day simply to reach its base. His men were wearing only light overalls with no stockings. There did not seem to be any game to shoot for food. And, finally, "I believe no human being could have ascended to its pinical."

Pike did not live to know that in the mid-1840s, General John C. Frémont would explore those same Rocky Mountains and on his map would label Grand Peak as "Pike's Peak." Or that other men would name the mountain that Pike had climbed "Mount Miller" for Theodore Miller, one of the soldiers who had joined Pike at its summit.

Scrambling down a deep ravine gave Pike and his men little trouble. They had not eaten for forty-eight hours and fell gratefully on a piece of deer rib "that the ravens had left us."

Although their climb was the literal high point of the expedition, further rigors awaited them. As Pike's men moved west, overcome by storms and cold, they found themselves wandering in a circle. Two men were stricken with frostbite so severe that they had to be left behind in a three-foot snowbank with one meal apiece. The rest of Pike's twenty men, each carrying a load of seventy pounds, struck out in search of buffalo that might have been driven off the plain by the January cold.

Pike had been adept at keeping morale high by sharing the burdens. For the first time, though, he overheard a complaint from a freezing and hungry soldier. At the moment, Pike ignored him, and Doctor Robinson saved them by killing a buffalo.

With their survival assured, Pike sought out the offender and warned him that another outburst would be punished by "instant death." But he did yield to the men's worries and delayed their departure until they had guaranteed their food supply by killing three more buffalo. When at last they moved on, they found, to Pike's chagrin, that their camp had been only two days' travel from the town of Santa Fe.

As they approached the settlement, Pike was arrested by Spanish dragoons and brought to the governor to explain his presence. In an era of uncertain boundaries, Pike could claim that he thought he was still within U.S. territory on the Red River, rather than being inside Mexico's border on the Rio de Norte. Nemesio Salcedo, commandant-general of the Internal Provinces of the New Spain, had no more accurate conception than Pike of the extent of the Louisiana Purchase. Salcedo considered it his duty to stop America's westward expansion, and he had also challenged Lewis and Clark on the Missouri.

Pike found that the forty-five hundred residents of Santa Fe treated his troupe decently. In town, he saw a Mexican newspaper's report on the activities of Aaron Burr and understood for the first time why his captors had been suspicious.

From Santa Fe, Pike and six of his men were sent south to appear before Spain's higher authorities in Chihuahua. Those officials accepted Pike's apology and his excuse that he had become lost. Sending him back to Texas under an armed guard, they imposed one restriction: Pike must write nothing further about his travels and particularly nothing about astronomy in the region that could be used for mapmaking. Pike thwarted the guards by taking notes in secret and jamming them down his men's gun barrels.

The trip itself provided a welcome thaw after the freezing temperatures they had endured. With the sun bearing down, they traveled from one hacienda to the next, feasting on the delicious native fruit. One host wrote a note to an aide: "Send this evening six or eight of your handsomest young girls to the village of St. Fernandez, where I propose giving a fandango for the entertainment of the American officers arrived this day."

The gesture was not lost on Pike, by now twenty-eight years old and away from his wife for almost a year. In his surreptitious notes, he wrote, "There was really a handsome display of beauty."

When his party arrived in Texas at Natchitoches at 4 p.m. on July 1, 1807, Pike wrote, "Language cannot express the gayety of my heart when I once more behold the standard of my country waved aloft."

Pike had returned with two grizzly cubs as a present for Jefferson, but homecoming also meant submitting an expense account. From the Arkansas River, Pike had sent Wilkinson a warning:

"The general will probably be surprised to find that the expense of the expedition will more than double the contemplated sum of our first calculations." Horses, for example, were costly—fifty to sixty dollars each. But Pike compared the expenses for his two expeditions to those of the single trip undertaken by Lewis and Clark: "I feel a consciousness that it is impossible for the most rigid to censure my accounts."

Pike was more distressed to learn that his countrymen shared General Salcedo's suspicions and were questioning whether he had been scouting on behalf of Aaron Burr. Since Wilkinson's authorization alone might not clear his name, Pike appealed to the secretary of war, and Henry Dearborn replied with a carefully crafted testimonial: Although Jefferson had not ordered Pike's explorations, "his services were held in high esteem by the President."

Sent to Congress and the newspapers, Dearborn's letter saved Pike's career.

In a final blow to Aaron Burr's conspiracy, James Wilkinson began to play another double game. The general wrote fervidly to Jefferson in mid-October 1806, although he did not use Burr's name:

"This is indeed a deep, dark and widespread conspiracy, embracing the young and the old, the Democrat and the Federalist, the native and the foreigners, the patriot of '76 and the exotic of yesterday, the opulent and the needy, the 'ins' and the 'outs,' and I fear it will receive strong support in New Orleans from a quarter little suspected."

Carried aloft by his own eloquence, Wilkinson concluded, "I gasconade not when I tell you that in such a case I shall glory to give my life in the service of my country."

He assured the administration that he would frustrate any plots hatched against either the United States or Spain, and he rewrote recent history to suggest that he had never wavered in his loyalty. As further proof, Wilkinson swore that if he caught Burr as a fugitive, he might very well have him court-martialed and shot. He did not mention that disposing of Burr would also protect him from exposure in the earlier plot.

Meantime, Burr was traveling on the Cumberland River with fewer than a hundred men, hoping to recruit more as he moved south. Jefferson had finally been moved to act, however, and had written to the western governors and district attorneys to watch Burr and arrest him if he committed an "overt act" of treason.

In January 1807, Burr surrendered to authorities in a town near Natchez, asking only for a chance to explain himself. Suave and gracious to his captors, he was feted by the local society until he was put on trial on February 2. Then, during the legal maneuvering, he fled into the woods.

Retaken within the month, Burr was sent to Richmond, a town of five thousand with a Capitol Building designed by Jefferson. Supreme Court justices sometimes rode on the circuit rather than wait in the capital for judicial appeals, and in Burr's case the judge would be the Federalist chief justice, John Marshall. Jefferson had already passed his own judgment. In a message to Congress, the president wrote that Burr's guilt was "beyond question."

Justice Marshall's opinion was less predictable. Like Hamilton, he was dedicated to the rights of property owners, and he was also determined to establish the powers of his Court. In *Marbury* v. *Madison*, Marshall's first notable ruling in 1803, he wrote that an Adams appointee who sued the Jefferson administration in the Supreme Court for not delivering his commission should have received it, but he struck down as unconstitutional the congressional statute that gave the Court jurisdiction over such cases.

In Burr's case, Marshall knew that the framers of the Constitution had taken pains to define treason carefully in Section 3 of Article III. Conviction required either a confession or testimony from two persons that the accused man had either urged war against the United States or aided and abetted its enemies. At the moment, America had no declared enemies. That meant that Burr—and a codefendant, an Irishman named Harman Blennerhassett—must be found guilty of "levying war" against the country itself. Blennerhassett had taken refuge in a secluded home on the Ohio River in Virginia after being ostracized for marrying his niece. He seemed to have been another of Burr's dupes. At least, he swore that he was "the last person in the world" to try to break up the union.

When Andrew Jackson was called to testify, his misgivings about Burr were outweighed by his contempt for Wilkinson. On the street, his denunciations of the general and of President Jefferson were so loud that Jackson was taken off the witness list. Wilkinson himself appeared in full uniform, with gold braid, plumed hat, and a sword that was immediately taken away from him on the grounds that it might intimidate the jury. Wilkinson assured Jefferson afterward that he had "darted a flash of indignation at the little traitor."

Washington Irving, who had become a writer of comic essays, was in court for the confrontation and described a different scene. He watched Burr look Wilkinson full in the face, eye him coolly up and down, and go back to a conversation with his lawyer. Irving was equally scornful of the planters and politicians who made up the grand jury. When the Court adjourned for a week, Irving wrote that the recess would give jurors time to "go home, see their wives, get their clothes washed and flog their negroes."

At one point, Burr's defense tried to embarrass Jefferson by asking that he be called to testify. Marshall ruled that the president of the United States could indeed be called, but he approved instead entering documents into the record without requiring that Jefferson come to Richmond.

Through the three months of arraignment and trial, Marshall had made a conspicuous effort to weigh the lengthy arguments impartially. At last he ruled against the prosecution on a key point and sent the case to the jury. Its members deliberated for twenty-five minutes before finding Burr not guilty of treason. But disposing of a second indictment—on charges of high misdemeanor—took another fifteen days.

Wilkinson retained his rank in the army but under a cloud. Virginia's scold John Randolph called him a rogue, a peculator, and a would-be murderer. Wilkinson threatened a duel, but Randolph sent back his challenge contemptuously. "I cannot descend to your level. This is my final answer."

Burr, despised throughout much of the country, sailed to England under the alias "H. E. Edwards." An unwelcome visitor, he was pressured to move on—to Sweden, Denmark, Germany, and finally to France.

The Chesapeake *and the* Leopard *battle near Hampton Roads*

Chapter Eight

EMBARGO
(1807–1808)

While Burr's trial was under way, Jefferson was beset by a new crisis involving the American navy. Ending North African piracy had not addressed the knotty issue of impressment and, like his predecessors, Jefferson had been feinting and ducking to avoid a confrontation with either Britain or France. Then, on June 22, 1807, the British challenged America's honor in a way no president could ignore.

An American frigate, the USS *Chesapeake*, had set sail that month from Norfolk, Virginia, and headed for Gibraltar. Unlike sloops, which carried guns only on their upper deck, frigates were fitted with guns on two decks. The *Chesapeake* also carried a crew of 329, plus 52 Marines, a handful of civilians, and several homesick Italian musicians who had resigned from America's Marine band. The ship's forty guns were tied down in case of rough weather, with lumber and civilian baggage stacked around them.

The ship's commodore, James Barron, was anticipating an uneventful cruise to the Mediterranean. All the same, it would be a momentous crossing for him. As the *Chesapeake* was being readied for duty at the Gosport Navy Yard, Captain Barron had been appointed its commander. The son of a distinguished naval officer, he had enlisted in Virginia's navy at age eleven, transferred to the merchant marine and finally to the fledgling U.S. Navy.

Barron sailed through the deep harbor known as Hampton Roads, unaware that a two-deck British ship, the *Leopard*, was lying in wait less than five miles away. At 3:27 p.m., Captain Salusbury Pryce Humphreys hailed the *Chesapeake* from the *Leopard* as Barron was clearing Cape Henry, claiming to have a dispatch for him. Barron hove to—adjusting the *Chesapeake*'s sails and heading its prow against the wind—and gave Humphreys's man permission to board his ship.

That messenger, Lieutenant John Meade of the King's Navy, asked to speak with the commodore privately, and Barron received him in his cabin. After Barron's officers left them, Meade handed Barron a demand for permission to allow a search of the *Chesapeake* for four British deserters suspected of being aboard.

To Barron, the idea was outrageous. Since the Revolution, American ships had been attracting British deserters by offering better pay and treatment, and Congress now authorized citizenship for foreigners who had lived in America for five years. Very reluctantly, the United States had agreed that its civilian merchant ships could be boarded to reclaim runaway British sailors. But the *Chesapeake* was a U.S. warship. Barron could not countenance such a search.

The war with France was leaving the British short of crew, and they held that a sailor's citizenship ran from birth to death and could not be altered without the consent of his native country. To underline Britain's assertion of rights, ministers in London had recently issued an Order in Council to retaliate against Napoleon's trade restrictions. The emperor was claiming as lawful prizes any ships that cleared a British port or allowed themselves to be searched by the British navy. For now, he was exempting American ships, but Britain's order permitted seizing those ships if they traded with France.

Britain did not fear retaliation from the United States since—in the words of George Canning, Britain's blustery foreign secretary—the upstart American fleet amounted to "a few fir-built things with bits of striped bunting at their mastheads." In contrast, Britain's victories over Napoleon were proving again that her fleet dominated the world's seas.

And yet, despite their overwhelming superiority, the British had no interest in provoking a confrontation with America. Captain Humphreys had sent along a conciliatory note, urging that Barron not let his demand disturb the harmony between their countries.

Barron assured Lieutenant Meade that an examination of their papers proved that those men the British sought had signed on legally with the *Chesapeake*. The standoff dragged on for more than half an hour until the *Leopard* flew a signal calling Meade back.

Barron braced for trouble. As Meade left, Barron told his second in command, "You had better get your gun deck clear, as their intentions appear serious."

He could see that the *Leopard*'s crew had removed the tampions that covered their guns and seemed to be training their sights on the *Chesapeake*. Barron ordered that his crew be sent quietly to their stations without the usual drum roll. If the *Leopard* saw his preparations, he would be accused of making the first hostile move.

But the drummer did not receive Barron's order and began to beat the signal. It hardly mattered. The British ship was close enough for its officers to observe Barron's every move.

In fact, the *Leopard* was so near that Humphreys could shout a threat to Barron across the water. Crew members on each ship reported a different version, but they agreed that Humphreys had told Barron that he must obey the British command.

Stepping into the gangway, Barron called back either "I do not understand what you say"—the American version—or, as a British sailor heard it, "You may do as you please."

Humphreys fired a warning shot across the *Chesapeake*'s bow. Barron ignored it. Two minutes later, the *Leopard*, now close enough for an exchange of pistol shots, fired a cannon amidship into the *Chesapeake*, driving wood splinters into Barron's right leg and thigh. To buy time for return fire, Barron offered to send a boat to the *Leopard* for further discussion.

But the rampant confusion aboard the *Chesapeake* was making retaliation impossible. Men had deserted several gun stations, and other stations lacked powder. One officer appealed to Barron, "For God's sake, fire one gun for the honor of the flag."

At last, Barron's third in command, W. H. Allen, grabbed a hot coal from the galley and discharged a solitary shot from one of the ship's eighteen-pounders. Even at close range, it missed its target. With that, Barron ordered his colors hauled down. Firing three broadsides in fifteen minutes, the *Leopard* had killed three American sailors outright; a fourth died later in Norfolk. Seven seamen were badly injured, Barron and nine others hurt less seriously.

The *Leopard* stopped firing and sent its boat again to board the *Chesapeake*. This time, the British mustered the American crew and seized the men they regarded as deserters. The one British sailor among them was summarily hanged at Halifax. The other three— native-born American black sailors who had deserted from a British ship—were told they would suffer the same fate if they did not return to the British navy.

At 8 p.m., the *Leopard* sailed off, leaving Barron to pump three feet of water from the hold of his crippled ship. He also prepared himself for the public outrage that was sure to follow. Barron knew better than most men the penalty for surrendering a ship. After the *Philadelphia* had been captured, Barron had presided over a court of inquiry into its captain's behavior. Although that man was cleared of cowardice and bad judgment, Barron could doubt whether his own judges would be as forgiving.

The denunciations that Barron had dreaded erupted immediately. In Hampton Roads, seething citizens stormed the British ship *Melampus* and destroyed two hundred of its water casks. Americans along the Atlantic coast debated whether the *Leopard*'s attack was the opening salvo in a second war with Britain, and one Revolutionary War general argued that keeping the British off American soil "can only be done by red-hot balls."

When Barron's officers urged that the secretary of the navy arrest him for "base and cowardly" behavior in surrendering so precipitously, Barron was grateful for support from one midshipman, Jesse Duncan Elliott, who did not join in the recriminations. America's other naval commanders agreed that President Jefferson should first demand an apology from Britain but, if that was not received, they called for "death before dishonor."

These days, Oliver Hazard Perry, the young sailor who had persevered through the years of naval budget cuts, was an ardent twenty-two-year-old and ready for war. To his father, who had found work as captain of a merchant ship, he wrote, "The British may laugh, but let them beware! . . . Our officers wait with impatience for the signal to be given to wipe away the stain which the misconduct of one has cast on our flag."

In the capital, Jefferson reflected that "never since the battle of Lexington have I seen the country in such a state of exasperation."

He yielded to the popular clamor by ordering British ships out of American waters and preparing to build more gunboats. For Jefferson, it was a cheap and expedient compromise; an armed frigate cost $300,000, a gunboat only $10,000 to $14,000. He also called Congress into session to cope with the attack, but skeptics wondered whether he had any intention of waging war, since he did not schedule that session for another three months. Until then, Jefferson planned to spend his summer at Monticello, where he said he worked even harder than in the capital.

At that moment, the nation's fury might have supported immediate war with Britain, but Jefferson preferred to follow the lead of Washington and Adams in not challenging a European power. At his writing table, Jefferson could spill blood with abandon. He had endorsed the concept of staging a revolution every twenty years, and he had written enthusiastically about watering democracy with the blood of tyrants. But once he was entrusted with power, a measured prudence had replaced his literary impulsiveness.

The *Leopard*'s assault brought a new urgency to Jefferson's negotiations with Britain over impressment. To strengthen his hand, Congress had already enacted a partial boycott of British imported goods, which Jefferson had not yet put it into effect. To a political ally, he wrote that so many bonds of friendship connected America and Britain that their rulers must be "great bunglers" ever to break them.

But what if the *Leopard* attack signified the beginning of war? Jefferson decided he must protect the nation's seamen by calling home all American ships and keeping their crews and cargo in port. He told Madison to draft a militant presidential proclamation. In August 1807—two months after the provocation—Jefferson released it.

Ruefully, the president noted that his belligerent statement marked the only time that the Federalists had approved of anything he said or did. "I confess," he confided to a friend, "I began strongly to apprehend I had done wrong and to exclaim with the Psalmist, 'Lord, what I have done, that the wicked should praise me!'"

Describing his policy as "peaceable coercion," Jefferson hoped to duplicate the successful nonimportation decrees that the colonies had levied against Britain in the edgy years before the Revolution. Economic pressure should be even more effective in 1807, since the previous year America's imports, largely from Britain, had run to about $15 million while exports stood at a record $101 million.

The British had already backed down slightly by returning the three Americans seized from the *Chesapeake*. But London remained adamant about its right to impress runaway seamen, and on the continent, Napoleon added to Jefferson's dilemma. He revoked his previous exemption for American ships from his restrictions on trade. Now if American vessels traded with the British, France could seize them as lawful prizes of war.

To show his nation's resolve, Jefferson persuaded Congress in December to pass an Embargo Act that prohibited American ships from sailing to any foreign port. To guarantee that they docked only at American piers, Jefferson required their owners to post a hefty bond.

Jefferson's embargo struck so hard throughout the nation that many countrymen concluded that he had declared war on them, not the British. Exports from New England dropped 75 percent, southern exports 10 percent more than that. Thirty thousand of America's forty thousand sailors were laid off, and they lined up to eat at local soup kitchens as their ships sat empty along the wharves. In New York alone, twelve hundred men were thrown into debtors prison.

American shipbuilding declined by two-thirds, farm prices went down 50 percent. Facing bankruptcy, merchants kept their ships away from American ports and traded only abroad or made illegal runs along the Canadian border.

To punish flouting of the law, Jefferson expanded the power of customs officials to conduct raids on ships and warehouses without a search warrant. The idealist who had lobbied for a Bill of Rights twenty years earlier found himself invalidating the safeguards of its Fourth Amendment.

Even as federal courts were ruling against Jefferson's violations of the Constitution, government troops were called out to enforce the raids. Unrepentant sailors who continued their illegal trade missions began to curse the "Dambargo."

Jefferson was slow to comprehend the misery overtaking the country, particularly in New England. To shame him, the guardian of a Boston orphan sent the president a bill for the one hundred dollars that the child's trust fund had lost because of his embargo. Massachusetts alone controlled about one-third of the tonnage that Americans shipped every year, and its merchants were talking openly about seceding from the union.

A prominent Federalist, Harrison Gray Otis, proposed a convention of the northern states to denounce the embargo and devise a strategy for ending it. Otis could claim strong family credentials for leadership. His uncle had been the brilliant, mad James Otis, who ranked with Samuel Adams as one of Boston's earliest rebels against British rule. Jefferson received warnings that the discontent had gone even further, that other Federalists had entered into secret negotiations with British agents about breaking away.

Jefferson confessed to his secretary of the treasury, "This embargo law is certainly the most embarrassing one we have ever had to execute."

But he blamed his countrymen, not his own misjudgment: "I did not expect a crop of so sudden and rank growth of fraud and open opposition by force could have grown up in the U. S."

The crisis was profound enough to challenge Jefferson's vision for America. With his bias for farming over trade, he had preferred a country that would flourish by selling to overseas markets its variety of crops, including tobacco. Now he was regretting his emphasis on shipping. Navigation, Jefferson wrote, "has kept us in hot water from the commencement of our government." With Europe in turmoil, he decided that Americans must become self-sufficient, even if that meant more manufacturing by small factories.

The country's distress made Jefferson eager for the time he could lay down the burdens of the presidency. Fifteen months before his second term was due to end, he reinforced George Washington's precedent by announcing that he would not be a candidate for another four years. Jefferson would be bequeathing to his successor a damaged economy, tense overseas relations, and, with a few exceptions like Albert Gallatin, a mediocre cabinet. At that, he continued to worry during his final months that open warfare might be inevitable.

"I think one war is enough for the life of one man," Jefferson wrote to John Langdon, who had turned down the post of secretary of the navy. Jefferson suggested that their shared experience in the Revolutionary War "at least may lessen our impatience to embark on another."

As a weary afterthought, he added, "Still, if it becomes necessary, we must meet it like men, old men indeed, yet good for something."

Oddly, the one notable political casualty of the furor was not from Jefferson's Republican Party. The victim was John Quincy Adams, his parents' treasure and a true son of the Revolution. As a child in Massachusetts, he had been taken by his kinsman Samuel Adams to witness the Redcoats parading on the Boston Common. Sam Adams wanted the boy to learn to detest the British from an early age. Later, John Quincy had heard the cannon fire during the battle of Bunker Hill and had looked on as British soldiers burned Charlestown.

At the age of eleven, he went to Europe when his father repre-

John Quincy Adams

sented America and spent most of his adolescence abroad, studying Latin, German, and French. To cap the fourteen-year-old's early education, Francis Dana, America's minister to the Russian court, invited him to become his private secretary in St. Petersburg.

John Quincy had seen the sacrifices his father made for the new nation and did not intend to follow his example. "My father has been all his lifetime occupied by the interests of the public," the young man wrote in his diary at seventeen. "His own future has suffered. His children must provide for themselves. I am determined to get my own living, and to be dependent on no one."

He resolved to study law, even though he expected to find it tedious, and entered Harvard as a junior in March 1786. As a fledgling lawyer, he was often as bored as he had predicted. Despite his earlier vow, John Quincy was grateful when President Washington appointed him as minister to the Netherlands on Adams's twenty-eighth birthday. During that service, he married the daughter of America's London consul and won high marks as a future stalwart in his country's foreign service.

As John Adams was about to assume the presidency, George Washington urged him not to withhold promotions from John Quincy—Washington called him "the most valuable public character we have abroad"—simply because the young man was his son. Washington said that would be "over-delicacy on your part."

But when Adams took that advice and named his son as minister to Berlin, John Quincy was reluctant. Even though he accepted, he asked his father never to nominate him again. Returning to Boston in 1801, he was rescued once more from practicing law by an appointment to the U.S. Senate. All outward signs suggested that he was as staunch a Federalist as his mother could wish. From the start of the French Revolution, he had denounced its philosophy and the actions of Citizen Genêt.

But John Quincy had inherited his father's streak of prickly independence. He opposed the philosophical contortions that let Jefferson buy Louisiana, then defied his fellow Federalists by voting the money to pay for it.

By the time of the *Chesapeake* affair, John Quincy Adams had served in four Senate sessions with little impact. Democrats remained hostile to him; Federalists seemed jealous. When he backed Jefferson's embargo wholeheartedly and praised the president's "firm and dispassionate course," John Quincy officially became a traitor to his party, to his northern constituents, and to his mother. He compounded his offense by attending the Republican caucus in January 1808. Abigail Adams wrote that she was "staggered" that he would violate his principles. Her son responded calmly, "I could wish to please my parents—but my duty I *must* do."

The Federalists took pains to guarantee that he would lose reelection and, rather than serve ineffectually for the rest of his term, Adams, by now almost forty, resigned. His father wrote a consoling letter explaining that John Quincy could never be a reliable party man because "you have too honest a heart, too independent a mind and too brilliant talents."

*   *   *

Madison, as Jefferson's choice to follow him into the presidency, had also supported the embargo enthusiastically but with little apparent damage to his political future. Madison believed that the measure could yet force both Napoleon and London to revoke their ultimatums. But Canning, the British foreign secretary, remained unmoved, and Madison was not wrong in suspecting that the Federalists had influenced London's policy. Canning was receiving reports that New England was on the verge of splitting away from the rest of America.

Those rumors did not alarm Madison, who considered the American people more resolute than Jefferson did. He observed that "the body of the people have borne the privations with a firmness" that guaranteed they would go on supporting the embargo. It was astonishing, Madison added, the zeal men had shown for buying homespun American cloth.

James Madison

Chapter Nine

MADISON
(1809–1812)

Three days before James Madison's inauguration as president on March 4, 1809, Congress bowed to the people's will and repealed the embargo. At the swearing-in ceremony, however, Madison demonstrated his loyalty to its memory by wearing a suit made entirely of American fabrics. Noting that fact, a friendly journalist went on to name the men who had presented the new president with gifts of a coat, vest, and knee britches.

In the recent election, Jefferson's vice president, George Clinton, had posed Madison's most serious challenge. Now seventy, Clinton had been jousting with Madison for two decades, first as a polemicist against the Constitution, then as a New Yorker resentful of Virginia's influence over the new nation.

After providing geographical balance for Jefferson's candidacy in 1804, Clinton had proved a genial presiding officer in the Senate, although serving with him there, John Quincy Adams complained to his father that the man was "totally ignorant of all of the most common forms of proceedings."

A widower, Clinton lived in a boardinghouse with his daughter and one servant. His defeat was assured early in January 1809, when a rump caucus of the Republican Party met in the capital without inviting either the New York delegation or allies of Virginia's bombastic dissenter, John Randolph. Looking ahead to the election, the caucus voted 83 for Madison, 3 for Clinton, 3 for James Monroe.

Monroe's challenge to Madison was largely personal and reflected the decline in Monroe's standing during the five years since the purchase of Louisiana. When Jefferson sent him to London to negotiate a stop to impressment, Monroe had disregarded his instructions and signed a treaty even less acceptable to Jefferson than John Jay's had been. The agreement not only did not end impressment, it added punishing new restrictions on American shipping.

Even as Jefferson was refusing to let Monroe's draft be published or submitted to Congress, his letters remained silky and reassuring. As a result Monroe blamed Secretary of State Madison for the damage to his reputation. When he announced his candidacy for the presidency, Jefferson tried to dissuade him, reminding him that he and Madison "have been very dear to each other, and equally to me."

Jefferson was now mediating between two young protégés, much as Washington had tried to keep peace between him and Hamilton, and with as little success. When Monroe persisted in his campaign, Jefferson wrote again to say, "I have ever viewed Mr. Madison and yourself as two principal pillars of my happiness." If either man left the Republican cause, "I should consider it as among the greatest calamities which could assail my future peace of mind."

At that, Monroe poured out his grievances; in return, Jefferson assured him of his own high personal regard. All the same, Monroe stayed in the race, attracting support from the Old Republicans and John Randolph, their most eccentric representative.

When the Electoral College votes were tallied, Madison took 122 to 6 for Clinton. Charles Pinckney, the South Carolina Federalist, carried all of New England but Vermont for a total of 47 votes. Monroe received none.

Although Madison took the oath of office in Federal City's new House of Representatives, his brief remarks made no attempt to reflect the chamber's splendor. Afterward, well-wishers followed his carriage to his house on "F" Street, with crowds along the way admiring Dolley Madison in her plain, low-cut gown with no handkerchief or silk panel to obscure the rise of her bosom.

According to local gossip, Madison had asked Dolley early in their marriage to give up plain Quaker dress for outfits that were more stylish and becoming. Since she had already been expelled from her church, Dolley could oblige him. She set off each new dress with ostrich plumes and feathery birds of paradise and topped those creations with matching headdresses from her collection of bright turbans and crimson caps.

People heard the story that Dolley had once teased a Quaker guest when he arrived for dinner not wearing the traditional Friend's hat. Raising a wine glass, she said, "Here's to thy absent broadbrim, Friend Hallowell!"

Hallowell bowed low, gazed into her décolleté gown, and replied, "And here's to thy absent handkerchief, Friend Dolley."

In her choice of dresses, Dolley Madison was only observing the current fashion. A first-time visitor to Washington noted that the men tended to dress alike in blue or black coats with vests and black breeches and stockings. But the women were remarkable for "the exposure of their swelling breasts and bare backs."

No one carried the fashion further than Elizabeth Patterson, who had married Napoleon's younger brother, Jérôme, during his stay in America. After the emperor had the marriage annulled, Elizabeth continued to call herself a Bonaparte for the sake of her small son. Beautiful and petite, Betsy Bonaparte wore gowns cut so low that a guest at one ball claimed she had attracted to the windows "mobs of boys to see what will not often be seen in this country, an almost naked woman."

The disparity between the statuesque Dolley and her husband—described even in his prime as "half a cake of soap"—led inevitably to speculation about the nature of their marriage. With her first husband, Dolley had given birth twice, but she and Madison had no children together. Their letters when apart revealed a warm and constant affection, however, and eventually Federalist innuendo to the contrary died away.

Madison's inauguration ceremonies ended with the first ball held since Washington's day. First dour John Adams and then Jefferson, as a widower, had forgone that public celebration, but a gala was held in Madison's honor at Long's Hotel. A crush of people surrounded Mrs. Madison, and, because the upper sashes of the windows were impossible to lower, guests broke the glass panes for relief from the fetid heat.

Jefferson had not yet vacated the President's House and did not stay long at the ball. A journalist's wife noticed, though, how broadly Jefferson beamed as he watched Madison being congratulated. But she thought Madison himself looked exhausted and spiritless. Commiserating, the woman told him she wished she had a chair to offer. Madison looked up woebegone and replied, "I wish so, too."

He went on doing his duty until supper ended. Then America's fourth president withdrew with his wife while their guests danced on until midnight.

John Quincy Adams had attended the inaugural ball that night but, he assured his wife, with no pleasure. "The crowd there was excessive; the room suffocating and the entertainment bad." He did have a brief conversation with Jefferson, who asked if he was still as fond of poetry as he had been as a boy. Yes, John Quincy answered, although he had lost interest in minor poets and love poems. Jefferson said he enjoyed Homer but no longer took much delight in Virgil.

Despite urging from John Quincy's allies, Jefferson had not consoled him with a federal appointment for giving up his Senate seat. Any offer would surely have been seen as a payoff by unforgiving Federalists, and John Quincy was resigned to practicing law again.

He was surprised, then, when two days after Madison's inauguration, a messenger from the new president summoned him for an urgent meeting.

At the President's House, Madison got immediately to the point: "I have sent for you, sir, to inform you that I propose to nominate you to the Senate as Minister Plenipotentiary to Russia."

Madison apologized for the short notice, but he wanted to send the nomination to the Senate in half an hour.

It took less time than that for John Quincy to accept. At first, the Senate balked, claiming that no representative was needed. But after some four months, the leadership relented and voted John Quincy nine thousand dollars in salary and expenses. Receiving his commission on July 4, 1809, a week before his forty-second birthday, he entrusted his two older sons to their grandparents and his brother, Thomas. He sent along instructions that the boys were not to expect a "life of indolence, and ease, and enjoyment."

With his wife and youngest son, two-year-old Charles Francis, Adams embarked on the seventy-five-day voyage to Russia.

During the Constitutional Convention those many years ago, Madison had shared Washington's fervent hope for an enduring spirit of national unity. But the party lines that emerged with John Adams's election in 1796 had only hardened. By the time of his own election, Madison found the country divided not only into two political parties but into splinters of those parties.

Wealthy merchants, professional men, and landlords continued to compose the Federalists of the northern states. Hamilton's enemies had attributed to him a remark that they claimed distilled the Federalist attitude toward democratic government into a single phrase. At a dinner in New York, Hamilton supposedly responded to a favorable remark about democracy by slapping his hand down on the table and exclaiming, "Your people, sir! Your people is a great *beast!*"

That canard, with its echoes of Hamilton's remarks at the Constitutional Convention, outlived him among Republican propagandists. But the Federalist party, including those southerners who shared

Hamilton's values, had a pat rebuttal to every Republican proposal: "Look at France!"

On the Federalist fringe was a faction called High Federalists, men like those of the Essex Junto, who were even less willing to compromise.

Madison's Republicans included a newer business class, the owners of large and small estates, and even tenant farmers. As far north as New York, workingmen were coming to share Jefferson's view of the Federalists as the party of speculators and property owners, men who cared only for protecting their economic interests.

Like Jefferson, those workers had come to distrust Hamilton and his financial schemes. To them, creating a national bank seemed aimed at delivering the country to its richest citizens. As president, however, Jefferson had been enough impressed with the bank's success to want to see its charter renewed.

John Randolph's bloc, the Quids, included the Old Republicans who resisted launching wars, running up debt, or maintaining a standing army. Randolph himself was as wedded to the past as the Essex Junto. He had named his plantation "Bizarre" and took pride in not having changed his views since Washington was president. Randolph challenged his critics to check the newspaper files for proof of his consistency.

But Randolph ignored the changes in Washington's own thinking during his eight years in office. He had come to see that the country could not be run like a Virginia plantation.

The most rambunctious of the current factions was the War Hawks, a cluster of young politicians from the South and West who often towered physically over their president; twenty-nine-year-old William Lowndes of South Carolina was a full twelve inches taller than Madison. The Hawks were led by Henry Clay of Kentucky, a state whose population had nearly doubled during the last ten years and now reached four hundred thousand. Since the time of Aaron Burr's trial, Clay had been cured of his belief in Burr's innocence by stopping in at the President's House, where he was shown documents that persuaded Clay he had been "much mistaken."

Clay had served out a brief appointment in the Senate — although at twenty-nine, he was a year younger than the constitutional requirement — before returning to Kentucky's general assembly. The *Chesapeake* affair brought him to new prominence when he denounced Britain as "our haughty and imperious foe."

Tall and wiry, Clay was another of the men who had tried his own hand at dueling. In a third exchange of shots against Humphrey Marshall, a cousin of the chief justice, Clay took a ball in the thigh. He limped home to recover while Kentucky's legislature censured both men for dueling.

By 1810, Clay's legal skill and profitable investments had made him wealthy enough to support a wife and five children. He accepted an invitation to finish out another Senate term, and from his first speech Clay derided both the earlier embargo and the nonimportation acts. "I am for resistance by the *sword*," Clay told the Senate. Great Britain's injuries and insults were "atrocious in character."

In Clay's view, Madison was not taking a strong lead in avenging those insults. But the president was gradually sounding like a wartime leader, although it would never be a natural role for a man whose temperament fitted him best for consultation and compromise. Madison had once denounced war as the worst of "all of the enemies to public liberty." But that was almost two decades earlier when he was a forty-four-year-old congressman supporting George Washington's policy of neutrality.

Early in his term, the British had reinforced his antipathy when they sent as their American representative the notorious Francis James Jackson. As ambassador to Denmark, Jackson had once demanded that the Danish prince royal abandon neutrality in Britain's war with France. When the prince refused, Jackson ordered a shelling of the capital by the British fleet that killed hundreds of Danes and destroyed the city. Now the Foreign Office chose "Copenhagen" Jackson to bring the American president to heel.

Madison's offense had been to rely too much on fuzzy assurances from Francis Jackson's predecessor that the Orders in Council might soon be withdrawn. Madison's misplaced trust had ignored London's prevailing fear that giving up impressment might bring down the

British government. When Great Britain rebuked its envoy, the misunderstanding embarrassed Madison, and then the British claimed to believe that his explanation had somehow insulted their king. Jackson was coming to make it clear that the gaffe had been entirely Madison's fault.

The Madisons tried to smooth over the rupture with a dinner at the White House. Jackson admitted that his reception had been extremely civil and attentive, although his Prussian wife described Dolley afterward as *"une bonne grosse femme de la classes bourgeoise."*

From that point, relations followed the downward spiral of Genêt's dealings with the first American president. After one too many public airings of their dispute, Madison wrote to inform Jackson "that no further communications will be received from you."

While Jackson became a hero to some northern Federalists, most of the nation rallied around the president.

The next irritant for Madison had been legislation known as Macon's Bill No. 2. In repealing the Embargo Act, intended to stop any U.S. ship from sailing to any foreign port, Congress had substituted a Non-Intercourse Act that forbade trade with Great Britain, France, and their colonies. The newest bill opened up free trade again and would only revive the Non-Intercourse Act against either Britain or France if they did not lift their own restrictions.

Madison complained to Jefferson about the wishful thinking behind the "botch of a bill" and predicted that British blockades and French raids at sea would continue.

For all his denunciations of the British, Henry Clay was mild about France's provocations: "I scarcely know of an injury France could do to us, short of an actual invasion of our territory, that would induce me to go to war with her."

Clay's remark reflected the success of Napoleon's deceptive diplomacy. The emperor seemed bent on provoking a war between Britain and America in order to ease the pressure on his own forces. Even though the French navy was seizing more American ships than the British were, Napoleon sent a letter from his foreign secretary, the Duc de Cadore, promising to revoke his maritime decrees if the United

Henry Clay

States imposed trade restrictions against the British. Since Macon's Bill No. 2 had given Madison that power, he took the emperor at his word and imposed the ban against Britain.

Along with defending France, Henry Clay also supported Madison's administration against Spain's accusation that America was occupying a region in West Florida not included in the Louisiana Purchase. Clay's rhetoric revealed his own vision of national expansion: He wanted, he said, "to see, ere long, the *new* United States (if you will allow me the expression) embracing not only the old thirteen states, but the entire country east of the Mississippi, including East Florida and some of the territories to the north of us also."

Given that attitude toward Canada, Clay derided the idea of America ever making conciliatory gestures to Britain. "I am not for stopping at Quebec or anywhere else," he declared, "but I would take the whole continent from them and ask no favors."

Such braggadocio confirmed British suspicion that the Americans' true reason for their trade restrictions was not simply to defend the national honor against impressment, since that practice was already being widely subverted. The British knew, for example, that the Massachusetts House of Representatives sold "certificates of origin" to any sailor who could afford one. And, despite the political bombast, only nineteen sailors who claimed American citizenship had been detained by the British navy during the entire previous year. Of that number, only two had been taken from their ships.

As the British Foreign Office saw it, if the Americans chose war, they might try to disguise their motive, but it would be their transparent lust for territory.

Clay had found that he preferred the rough-and-tumble of the House to the more sedate Senate. Winning a House seat in August 1810, he joined the Twelfth Congress, where his colleagues included a number of men in their late twenties and early thirties. Although they had been born since the Declaration of Independence, they shared Clay's hostility toward Britain and chose him as their Speaker.

Clay quickly asserted his authority when John Randolph showed up on the House floor with his bulky dog. In the past, another representative had complained that the dog had tripped him, and Randolph responded by striking the man with his cane. At the sight of the animal, Clay ordered the doorkeeper to remove it. When the dog did not reappear the next day, his party agreed that they had picked the right leader.

Among those who had voted for Clay was twenty-nine-year-old John Caldwell Calhoun from South Carolina. Calhoun's early schooling had been as sketchy as Andrew Jackson's. Yet, after his father died when John was thirteen, the boy not only took over management of the family farms but prepared himself well enough to enter Yale.

Calhoun had been twenty-five and just finished with his law studies when the *Leopard* fired on the *Chesapeake*. After leading a protest rally in his home town of Abbeville, he won election to the South Carolina legislature and then to the House of Representatives.

In Federal City, Clay, Calhoun, and their faction from America's

John C. Calhoun

South and West attracted the disapproval of Randolph, who was the first to label them "War Hawks" as he made a prophecy:

"They have entered this house with their eye on the Presidency," Randolph announced, "and mark my words, sir, we shall have war before the end of the session."

Sure that war with Britain was indeed inevitable, Calhoun mocked those who were urging a peaceful resolution to the crisis. "We are next told of the expenses of war, and the people will not pay taxes," he said. "If taxes become necessary, I do not hesitate to say the people will pay cheerfully."

In rebuttal, Randolph conjured up the specter of American slaves inspired by the French Revolution and rising up against their owners. Calhoun jeered that while Randolph "may alarm himself with the disorganizing effects of French principles, I cannot think our ignorant blacks have felt much of their baneful influence. I dare say more than one half of them never heard of the French Revolution."

Like Clay, Calhoun found Madison a weak leader and gravitated to James Monroe, who continued to nurse his past grievances. The result was a weakening of the president's influence over the Republicans and an increasing drumbeat for war. Too young to remember the blood and sacrifice of the Revolution, Clay, Calhoun, and their comrades-in-arms were ready to take on the world with a frontiersman's swagger.

With Madison's first term drawing to an end, the War Hawks succeeded in feeding the country's indignation over Great Britain's insulting behavior. By now, Madison did not absolve France of blame for his dilemma and deplored Napoleon's "crafty contrivance and insatiate cupidity." But he saw London's ministers as even more dangerous enemies.

All the same, reports from Britain encouraged Madison to hope that economic sanctions might still avert war. During the past year, his sanctions had cut British imports to the United States by more than 80 percent. Depression had struck England, shutting down factories and throwing workers into the streets. British manufacturers joined with the unemployed in petitioning Parliament to repeal the Orders in Council, but when the Foreign Ministry issued a carefully hedged set of conditions for repeal, Madison's administration accused Britain of arrogance and ignored them.

For all of their bellicose speeches, congressmen were resisting any increase in military funding. Men in both parties could not shed their habitual opposition to a standing navy, and the Senate killed a $450,000 House appropriation to repair six frigates, even though the work had been begun and half the allocation already spent.

Madison prepared for his reelection campaign by resolving two domestic irritants. When he had tried to appoint Albert Gallatin as secretary of state, he was blocked in Congress by other candidates for the job, including the Samuel Smith whose brother, Robert, had been foisted on Jefferson as secretary of the navy. Striking a deal, Madison had appointed Robert Smith as secretary of state as the price for retaining Gallatin at the Treasury. Now, however, Madison could finally shake himself free of Robert Smith and name as secretary of state his longtime friend and short-term foe, James Monroe.

Madison also moved to renew the twenty-year charter of the Bank of the United States. But members of his own party distrusted Gallatin as much as they had Hamilton. They reprinted Madison's original attacks on the bank's constitutionality and ignored Gallatin's warnings that if war lay ahead they were risking the country's economic stability. When the Senate divided equally on renewing the bank, Vice President Clinton cast the deciding negative vote and read to the chamber the speech Clay had written for him. Colleagues agreed that Clinton had never sounded better informed.

In March 1812, Secretary of State Monroe met with House Speaker Clay to plan the administration's next move against Britain. Although the War Hawks still regarded Madison as wavering and weak, the president had warned the British foreign minister that anything was better than the current state of indecision. Madison said that he continued to hope for a peaceful solution, but he would not bend on repealing the Orders in Council.

From Monticello, Jefferson questioned whether members of the House of Representatives would ever rise above their mania for talking: "That a body containing 100 lawyers in it should direct the measures of war, is, I fear, impossible." One New York Federalist put the economic issue baldly to the advocates of war: "Where are your armies? Your navy? Have you money?"

Avoiding those questions, Madison asked Congress for another general embargo, this one limited to sixty days. Although it was then lengthened to ninety days, Clay promised his more impatient colleagues that it was designed to lead directly to war.

Dolley Madison was getting that same signal from her husband. To a friend, she wrote, "You know of our embargo—to be followed by War!! Yes, that terrible event is at hand . . . Congress will remain in session perhaps, til July—If not, full powers to declare War will be vested in the President."

After Clay had satisfied his party's congressional caucus with assurances that Madison was fully committed to war, caucus members cast a unanimous 82 votes for Madison's reelection later in the year.

＊　　　＊　　　＊

In mid-May of 1812, Calhoun presented to Congress a recommendation for war drafted by James Monroe. The Committee on Foreign Relations followed up that resolution with a concise list of British wrongs:

The impressment of American seamen. And Britain's blockade of ports, which had plundered commerce of American merchants by cutting off their legitimate markets around the world. Tacked on was a final offense — "and the British Orders in Council."

By now, the *Chesapeake* affair was no longer inflaming the War Hawks. A year earlier, a forty-four-gun American frigate, the *President*, had devastated the *Little Belt*, a British corvette with only twenty guns. The Americans swore that they had mistaken the small vessel for a more lethal ship, but the unequal attack seemed to be a payback for the *Chesapeake*, and it was now the British who were claiming a grievance.

The congressional report concluded with a trumpet blast characteristic of the War Hawks but out of key with Jefferson's fastidious style and Madison's habitual moderation:

"Relying on the patriotism of the nation, and confidently trusting that the Lord of Hosts will go with us to battle in a righteous cause, and crown our efforts with success, your committee recommend an immediate appeal to *arms*."

In a secret vote on June 4, House members endorsed going to war, 79 to 49.

Convinced that war was his only option, Madison fretted as the Senate delayed its own vote. At Monticello, Jefferson had also accepted the inevitable. "We are to have war then?" he wrote. "I believe so, and that it is necessary." Jefferson added that he was being "forced from my hobby, peace."

The Senate vote finally came on June 17 and favored war, 19 to 13.

At her weekly receptions, Dolley Madison was scrupulous about never giving a sign which of her guests were her husband's allies and which his sworn opponents, but that night the triumphant mood of the War Hawks was impossible to miss. A Federalist reporter from New York called their enthusiasm for war "iniquitous" and observed that "the President was all life and spirits."

The setting for the celebration was opulent. During her four years in the President's House, Dolley had spent the twenty-six-thousand-dollar allocation from Congress to make the mansion fit for a head of state. Henry Latrobe, an admired architect, bought three large mirrors for Dolley to place strategically, and he paid $458 for the pianoforte she had her heart set on.

With gas lamps glowing, Dolley usually entered her drawing room carrying a book, which suggested how she had been occupied before her guests arrived. When she complained to one young admirer about the time that those official receptions took, he pointed to her book and said, "Still, you have time to read."

"Oh, no, not a word," Dolley said. She confessed that she carried her leather-bound copy of *Don Quixote* only for something to talk about if conversation lagged.

Sir August John Foster, Britain's current minister to the United States, had been sending back to London a series of misleading dispatches that reflected the bias of his Federalist contacts. After newspapers reported on a vast rally in Philadelphia supporting war with Britain, Foster assured his superiors that the event "amounted to but 2,000 persons principally composed of Irishmen or the lowest order, Negroes and boys."

Despite their political differences, Foster enjoyed the company of a number of Americans, even a Hawk like Henry Clay. He noted, though, that Clay and his friends "always talked to me of war as a duel." They seemed to think war was as necessary to their young nation as dueling was to a young man of honor. It prevented their "being bullied and elbowed."

And yet Clay concluded those belligerent remarks to Foster by predicting that when the present strife ended, it "would probably leave them both better friends than they had ever been before."

Clay's attitude confirmed for Foster an insecure aspect to the American character that he had noticed before. "A great many people here are afraid of being laughed at if they don't fight," he wrote home to his mother, the duchess of Devonshire. "It is really a curious state of things. They even refer to me occasionally to ask what we shall think of them."

As the Senate vote approached, Foster could no longer misread the likely result. He sent out an aide each day to be sure that one senator was kept drunk—"which was no difficult matter"—but by June 17, Foster was resigned to the outcome.

All the same, the evening of the Senate vote he attended Dolley's reception as usual. Foster thought Madison looked "ghastly pale," but they made the customary three bows to each other and chatted about Napoleon's recent reverses in Spain. Foster stayed nearly two hours, well aware that Americans around the room were already planning to bid on his string of race horses as soon as he was recalled to London.

The evening ended with neither Foster nor Madison aware that a lunatic in London had murdered Spencer Perceval, the British prime minister implacably opposed to repealing the Orders in Council.

Tecumseh

Chapter Ten

TECUMSEH
(1812)

As Madison prepared for war, a Shawnee chief called Tecumseh was holding tense meetings with Ohio's new Indian agent. Benjamin Stickney thought his visitor was either making a last-ditch effort to enlist with the Americans against the British or trying to lull him with insincere pledges of loyalty.

Tecumseh, in his mid-forties, looked ten years younger. White settlers encountering him for the first time were struck by his strong features and innate dignity. He spoke English but in meeting with British or American officials, he insisted on an interpreter. The honor of his people, he said, required him to speak the Shawnee language. The tribe's name came from fierce Algonquin forefathers, who believed that a different god ruled each of the four compass points. Shawan was the southernmost guardian spirit, and his people became known as Shawnee. Before his birth in 1768, the boy's mother had delivered three older children; after him, another baby was followed by the startling arrival of triplets. One of the three died at birth, but even twins were considered such a bad omen that they were sometimes put to death.

Tecumseh's brothers survived, however, and one grew up to complicate his life.

When Tecumseh's mother died, an adored older sister raised him and set a standard that neither of his two wives later could live up to. In each case, he seized on petty offenses as an excuse to send them away.

His own name had been bestowed during his initiation as a warrior in a painful rite. The aspiring teenager was suspended by skewers driven through the muscles of his back. During his ordeal, he was expected to reveal no sign of suffering. Next he was sent to the woods to fast and ask for guidance from the Great Spirit.

After days of hunger, a youth might see visions and hear voices. Tecumseh returned to say he had dreamed about a meteor that took the shape of a panther—the tribe's totem—and chased away a dragon. The elders embraced his vision as a good omen and named him Tecumseh—"Shooting Star."

His upbringing was marked by constant warfare. At the age of twelve, he watched an American colonel, George Rogers Clark, lead a thousand army riflemen in a reprisal for an Indian raid in Kentucky. Crossing the Ohio River, Clark's men razed Old Chillicothe and then the town of Piqua, where they destroyed the corn crop and shot down the Indian men defending their wigwams.

Tecumseh's oldest brother was killed fighting alongside the Cherokee against white settlers, and when Tecumseh was twenty-six, a second brother died in battle. By then, Tecumseh was protesting when other Indian leaders sold vast tracts of tribal territory to the Americans. In 1798, he refused to recognize one such sale even though the treaty had been signed on behalf of the Shawnee by an elder named Blue Jacket. Tecumseh argued that Indian land was the common property of all tribes and could not be sold by any one of them.

He was an early rebel, too, against the excesses of war. Stephen Ruddell, a young white child captured and raised by the Shawnee, recalled that the sixteen-year-old Tecumseh had denounced the burning alive of a white prisoner. Lecturing his elders against such brutality, Tecumseh swore that he would never take part in it. Nor would he allow the killing of women and children.

Meantime, one of the twins was becoming notorious throughout the territories. Laulewasika had been disfigured by losing an eye; he used a handkerchief to cover the socket. He had passed his youth drunken and dissolute until one day, as he smoked in his wigwam, the pipe dropped from his hand, and he fell into a trance so deep that the other tribesmen thought he was dead.

When he awoke, he told of having been carried away to a realm where he had spoken with the Great Spirit. After that, he took to calling himself Tenskwata and to preaching a radical gospel. His new disciples called him the Prophet.

Tenskwata assured the tribe that they were the first creations of the Master of Life and the greatest of all his children. But that distinction carried responsibilities. The Shawnee had to renounce all the habits they had picked up from the white man and were forbidden to take white wives. They must give up their rifles, which they called fire sticks, and return to the traditional bows and arrows. "Pay the white traders only half of what you owe because they have cheated you," the Prophet said.

Indians must abandon their linen and wool clothing for old-fashioned buckskin. They must eat no meat from sheep or cows, only from buffalo and deer. And they must shun the firewater that had brought such discord to the tribe.

The subject of whiskey raised the Prophet to his most sulphurous: "It is the drink of the Evil Spirit, made by the Americans," he announced. "It is poison. It makes you sick. It burns your insides."

The Americans themselves "grew from the scum of the great water, when it was troubled by the Evil Spirit. They are numerous, but I hate them. They are unjust. They have taken away your lands, which were not made for them."

Before his revelations, the Prophet had been considered stupid, but when tribal elders tried to discredit him, he invoked his new alliance with the Great Spirit, condemned them as sorcerers, and had them killed.

Tecumseh was enough influenced by his brother to revert to wearing outfits that had been out of style for more than fifty years. He gave up European shirts and trousers for tight-fitting suits of soft deerskin and moccasins decorated with dyed porcupine quills. For his part, the Prophet endorsed Tecumseh's call for a unity among the tribes that would stop further sale of their hunting grounds.

Stories of the Prophet's teachings had reached to Federal City while Jefferson was president. He viewed them tolerantly, concluding that the Prophet was "vainly trying to lead his brothers to the fancied beatitudes of their gold age."

Closer to the scene, however, the governor of the Indiana Territory, William Henry Harrison, became alarmed by reports that tribal elders had gathered at Greenville "for dark and bloody councils." In 1807, Harrison had ended a public message by urging the Indians to ignore "a fool, who speaks not the words of the Great Spirit, but those of the devil and of the British agents." Harrison called on the Indians to disperse and to take their impostor with them.

At that time, Harrison was thirty-seven, a tousle-haired Virginian with a long straight nose and delicate features. As a student in Prince Edward County, he had been drawn to the antislavery movement so strongly that his Episcopal father pulled him out from the contaminating company of Methodists and Quakers at Hampton Sidney College. The boy had intended, in his desultory way, to study medicine. But when his father died and money ran short, he signed on with the army. Harrison had always been fascinated by military history and happily left behind the comforts of life on a Virginia plantation.

The young man thrived on the frontier, serving as aide-de-camp to Major-General "Mad Anthony" Wayne in putting down rebellious tribes. In 1799, during the Adams presidency, the Ohio Territory was allowed to send a representative to Congress, and Harrison went to the capital, where he worked to expand white communities throughout the territory.

William Henry Harrison

Although his wife's father, John Cleves Symme, was a major land speculator, Harrison sponsored a law to survey the public land purchased from the Indians and give freeholders a chance to buy small lots with down payments of only one-twentieth of the land's price. Harrison eased the sting for his father-in-law with a measure that allowed Symme to extend the repayment deadline on his loans. But other speculators, who hoped to monopolize the new lands, convinced the Senate to scale back Harrison's original proposal.

He retired from Congress after one term and returned to the frontier as governor of the Indiana Territory. In that role, he held regular councils with the local tribes and came to know their culture.

From their first contact with natives of the New World, European settlers had found much to admire—beyond the valuable pelts they coveted. They heard the legends of Indians' bringing the corn and bread that saved the Jamestown colony from famine in 1607, and of Captain John Smith being spared execution when his captors took him to Chief Powhatan, the father of tender-hearted Pocahontas. That was about the time that the Dutch arrived on the Hudson River, ready to trade firearms and cloth for fur.

A hundred years later, John Lawson, a founder of the first settlement in North Carolina, made sympathetic notes about local tribes during his extensive travels among them. Lawson reported that the Indians thought of heaven as being on the other side of the sun. In that Country of Souls, a worthy brave would experience neither cold nor fatigue but enjoy beautiful young women and ample deer meat. Lazy or thieving Indians would experience a different afterlife—snakes, nasty food, old ugly women.

In the end, Lawson's warm feelings for the tribes could not protect him. During his third trip up the Neuse River, he was seized by warriors and sentenced to death. The companions who escaped did not witness his execution, but Lawson had already written that splinters were usually driven into the victim's body and set on fire.

Those practices had led Europeans to call Indians "savages." When the word was translated for them, tribes resented the insult. Scalping, after all, was practiced by whites as well as Indians, and American frontiersmen often raided Indian graves looking for plunder among the corpses.

Indians explained to Europeans that they scalped only dead enemies and then took a small portion of the scalp. Occasionally, a victim who proved not to be dead might even recover. Anticipating their own fate, warriors sometimes wove feathers into a convenient lock of their hair to make it more easily sheared.

An enemy's dried scalp was valued so highly that when a neighboring family suffered a death, a scalp with its spiritual powers might be offered as a gesture of sympathy. Seeing the regard in which the Indians held scalps, British and French traders began to pay for them.

William Harrison's own forays among the Indians led him to conclude that they were more hospitable to friends and visitors than the white race. He observed that they seemed to have few laws but depended instead on an internal sense of right and wrong. They were honorable, for example, about paying gambling debts. Indians who committed a crime that was not punishable by death were shunned and treated with contempt.

Harrison took special note of the hardihood of Indian women. On a journey, they were expected to give birth, wash the infant in a river, and, within two hours, be ready to set off again. Indian culture accepted polygamy, but young men were warned against sex with married women.

Harrison's most original insight contradicted the reputation of Indians as implacable warriors. Other white men had described Indians as stoics who embraced deprivation, but Harrison found them to be Epicureans, never passing up a chance to dance or drink. He claimed the pleasure-seeking side to their nature left them ready to abandon a military operation on a whim.

Harrison doubted the Indian capacity for sincerity. He was sure the British had been conniving with the tribes for years, and recent history gave him no reason to expect Indian loyalty to the American cause. Long before the Revolution, Chief Pontiac of the Ottawas had favored the French, who often got along better with the tribes than British traders did. When the French began to bring brandy to smooth over relations, the British retaliated with quantities of rum.

During America's Revolution, Joseph Brant, a celebrated Mohawk chieftain, had sided with the British. In Brant's boyhood, a titled Englishman took Brant's sister as his native wife and sent Joseph to a school for Indians in Lebanon, Connecticut. Brant stayed for two years, long enough to learn to read and write English, abilities that set him apart from his tribe. With no alphabet, other Indians depended on the picture-writing that their women wove into the elaborate belts and strings called wampum. Early wampum had been made from fragments of painted wood and shells, but tribes came to prefer beads, which the Europeans were pleased to trade for fur.

Brant had fought against Ethan Allen in Montreal, then traveled to England, where he sat for his portrait by George Romney and met Samuel Johnson's biographer, James Boswell. When Brant was presented to the king, he refused, as a chieftain, to kiss the king's hand but charmed the court by saying he was only too pleased to kiss the hand of Queen Charlotte.

After the British defeat, Brant led the Mohawks from their ancestral land on the west bank of the Niagara River to settle in Canada and go on living under British rule. By the time Brant died in 1807, Tecumseh had emerged as an Indian leader for the next generation. Brant had often said, "Without being united, we are nothing." Tecumseh was determined to make that dream of unity come true.

Harrison suspected that if the Indians ever achieved a federation, the British would provoke them into going to war against America. For the present, however, Britain seemed to want peace. Along with his usual gifts of food and weaponry, a British agent had passed this message to Tecumseh:

"My son, keep your eyes fixed on me. My tomahawk is now up. Be you ready, but do not strike until I give the signal."

In August 1810, Tecumseh paddled down the Wabash River to Vincennes to complain to Harrison about a recent land sale by the Miami tribe. Acting for the U.S. government, the governor had bought about three million acres—almost one hundred miles—on both sides of the Wabash.

Tecumseh arrived with four hundred warriors in eighty canoes painted with harsh colors and seemingly prepared for war. One U.S. Army officer on the scene admitted to being terrified by the sight, but he also described their leader as "perhaps one of the finest-looking men I ever saw."

Harrison had set out chairs for Tecumseh and his forty-man cadre on the portico of the governor's house, but the chief insisted that they talk instead in a nearby grove. Tecumseh said he did not mind the lack of seats since the earth was the most suitable place for his tribesmen, who loved to repose on the bosom of their mother.

Harrison yielded. Chairs and benches were moved to the woods for the American delegation while the Shawnee spread out on the ground. Tecumseh came quickly to the point: The Treaty of Fort Wayne must be repealed. The Americans had already forced the Indians from the seacoast and would soon be driving them into the Great Lakes. As he spoke, Tecumseh acknowledged that he had threatened to kill the chiefs who signed the treaty. Under the coalition he was forming, village chiefs had to turn over power to war chiefs.

As he recited the white man's crimes against the tribes from the beginning of the Revolution, Tecumseh's language was clearly inflaming his Shawnee. Harrison tried to temper the mood by pointing out that the Miamis were the owners of the property and could sell it if they wished. He went further: It was ridiculous to claim that red men constituted one nation. If that had been the Great Spirit's intention, they would all speak the same language.

When the interpreter began to convey Harrison's argument, Tecumseh leaped to his feet and launched an impassioned rebuttal. Harrison could not understand what he was saying, but Tecumseh's gestures looked violent. Out of sight of the Shawnee, a friendly chief named Winnemac showed Harrison that he was priming his pistol. An American army general on the scene understood enough Shawnee to tell his lieutenant, "These fellows intend mischief. You had better bring up the guard."

By now, the Indians were on their feet, brandishing tomahawks and war clubs. Everyone looked to Harrison, who was struggling to get up from his deep armchair as he drew a small sword at his side. Chief Winnemac cocked his pistol, and an army captain drew a dirk. The Americans on the scene outnumbered the Indians, but most were civilians and unarmed. The entire town's population was only a thousand, and Tecumseh's four hundred warriors could have murdered them all. A Methodist minister disappeared into the governor's house and emerged with a gun, ready to defend Harrison's family.

No one spoke.

But when the governor's guard came running up and looked ready to fire, Harrison stopped them and asked the interpreter what Tecumseh had been saying.

He learned that the chief had told his warriors that everything Harrison said was false.

At that, Harrison told Tecumseh angrily that he was a bad man and that Harrison would have no further dealings with him. Since the Indians had come under the protection of a council fire, they could return to their tribes safely. But they must leave the next day.

To enforce his ruling, Harrison called in two companies of militia from the countryside, who arrived during the night. The next morning, however, Tecumseh sent a request that he be allowed to explain his conduct. Harrison agreed, and Tecumseh appeared, dignified and respectful. He presented chiefs from the Wyandots, Kickapoos, Potawatamies, Ottawas, and Winnebagos, who all testified that they had entered into Tecumseh's confederacy.

Hearing them out, Harrison decided that if it weren't for the presence of the United States, Tecumseh might have founded an empire to rival those of Mexico or Peru. Although Harrison was unlikely to see a connection to the Constitutional Convention, Tecumseh was trying to forge the strong central union for his people that the Americans had achieved in Philadelphia.

Concluding his remarks, Tecumseh promised that, if the land was returned to the tribes, he would serve the Americans faithfully. Otherwise, he would join with the British. But he added that the British had never fooled him. He knew that they courted the Indians only to fight their wars for them.

Tecumseh clapped his hands and shouted like a man calling for his dog. That's the way the Redcoats behave with us, he said. All the same, he would be forced to fight Americans. If that should happen, Tecumseh promised to try to protect women and children. Harrison said he would pass along Tecumseh's ultimatum to President Madison but doubted the president would agree to his terms.

Even the stilted translation could not soften Tecumseh's reply:

"Well, as the Great Chief is to determine the matter, I hope the Great Spirit will put enough sense in his head to induce him to direct you to give up this land. It is true he is so far off he will not be injured by the war. He may sit still in his town and drink his wine, while you and I have to fight it out."

During the next year, tensions mounted when Indians murdered four white men on the Missouri River and when the Prophet's braves seized an entire boatload of salt, rather than the five barrels their government agreement entitled them to have. Summoned by Harrison once again, Tecumseh claimed the murderers had not been under his jurisdiction and dismissed the dispute over salt. To Harrison's repeated warnings against uniting the Indians, Tecumseh replied that, after all, he was only following the American example. To win independence from Britain, the colonists had once joined into a confederacy of Thirteen Fires—the Indian term for comparing American states to their tribal councils. In recent years, Tecumseh said, the Americans had added four more such councils—Vermont, Kentucky, Tennessee, and Ohio—until the United States now consisted of Seventeen Fires.

Drawing on that example, Tecumseh announced that he was taking twenty of his braves to recruit support from southern tribes throughout the Illinois and Michigan territories. In his absence, he was leaving the Prophet in charge of the Shawnee settlement at Tippecanoe. Tecumseh asked that any further action about the land sale be held off until his return.

Harrison was tempted to use Tecumseh's departure as his chance to drive the Indians from Tippecanoe. From his years as governor, however, he knew that Madison—like Jefferson before him—did not want to provoke war with the tribes.

In fact, in mid-July Harrison had received a direct order forwarded through Madison's secretary of war, William Eustis: "I have been particularly instructed by the President to communicate to Your Excellency his earnest desire that peace may, if possible, be preserved with the Indians."

Yet by early October 1811, Harrison thought he might be able to pressure the Shawnee to break up the concentration of warriors he found menacing. He would advance on the settlement peaceably but with an army so large that the Prophet would be intimidated into disbanding. Harrison informed Eustis that he intended to make his demand "in the most peremptory terms."

Harrison left the town of Vincennes with more than a thousand men and stopped long enough on the Wabash to build a fort that he named for himself. He stationed a hundred guards there before sailing down the east side of the river. After an exhausting month, his troops forded the river and set up camp ten miles from the headquarters that the Indians called Prophetstown.

On the morning of November 6, Harrison marched another five miles and sent out an officer and a few men to request a meeting with the Prophet. Although his troops bridled at Harrison's caution, he was trying to obey his instructions.

But when Indians attempted to seize his emissaries, Harrison advanced closer to the Shawnee camp. Ahead on the trail, the Prophet's ranking aide and two interpreters appeared and asked why the Americans were making such warlike moves. The Shawnee wanted only peace. They had even sent welcoming messengers at the first word of Harrison's approach, but those scouts had gone down the wrong path and missed making contact.

Harrison was suspicious, but he proposed a formal meeting and asked where his troops might camp until the next day.

The Indians were under orders from Tecumseh as strict as those binding Harrison. They pointed out a desirable campground close to a stream. But as he waited at Tippecanoe, the Prophet was chafing under Tecumseh's restrictions. He recalled bitterly Harrison's denunciation of him four years earlier as a fool and an impostor.

To take revenge, he persuaded his warriors that they must kill Harrison in his tent at the center of the American camp. As long as Harrison lived, the Long Knives—the Americans—could never be defeated. Once he was dead, his soldiers "would run and hide in the grass like young quails." They could be captured and turned over to the women of Prophetstown to use as slaves.

The Prophet had waived his earlier ban on rifles, and British agents had seen to it that the Shawnee were well supplied. Under a moon obscured by clouds, the Prophet conjured up an elixir that he claimed would protect his warriors by repelling the bullets from their bodies.

He put on a necklace of deer hooves and took up strings of beans that he said were sacred. Attack the enemy fearlessly, the Prophet exhorted his men. When the battle was done, the Americans would be dead or driven mad, and the Shawnee warriors would return unharmed.

Before 5 a.m. on November 7, Shawnee braves crept close to the American camp. The Prophet had chosen a hundred of his best men to slip past the northwestern perimeter and head directly to Harrison's tent for the kill. But a sentinel spotted them and fired a warning shot. At that, the Indians sprang up with the fearsome whooping that could chill an enemy's blood. Although the Shawnee preferred to fight from behind rocks and trees, they came out into the open and fell upon the Americans.

Harrison was pulling on his boots when he heard the first shot. In spite of promises for a peaceful meeting the next day, he had warned his men to stay on the alert. As they stamped out their campfires to make themselves less visible targets, Harrison called for his light gray mare. But the shots had sent the horse galloping away, and he took the dark stallion of one of his aides. Indians who expected to see him on the mare aimed for it, and Harrison eluded them. From a hillside on the sidelines, the Prophet was asking the Master of Life to kill his enemies.

With dawn, the Americans had overcome their initial surprise and mounted a charge that drove the Indians back. As their casualties mounted, the Prophet's warriors saw that he had lied to them. The Shawnee were not invincible. Bullets could kill. The surviving braves ran to the woods with Harrison's men in pursuit.

Coming upon thirty-six Indian corpses, the Americans scalped and mutilated them. When they reached Prophetstown, they spared the life of one old woman who had been too sick to flee with the rest. Otherwise, Harrison's troops confiscated everything valuable from the Indian households, burned five thousand bushels of corn and beans, and razed the settlement.

With Tippecanoe destroyed, Harrison's dispatches to Washington painted the encounter as an epic victory, even though the casualty figures did not justify his jubilant tone. Of the thousand American officers and men, at least 62 had been killed, another 120 wounded. The Indian forces, perhaps two-thirds that size, had lost more than 50 dead, with 70 to 80 wounded.

In the East, Henry Clay's War Hawks denounced British agents for provoking the Indians to break the peace. The battle at Tippecanoe became one more grievance against Great Britain.

*   *   *

Tecumseh rode home, gratified by his success in organizing the southern tribes. But when he reached the desolate battle scene, he learned that his orders had been ignored. The Prophet, a pariah now within the tribe, admitted that his magical brew had been somehow faulty. His wife was to blame, he said. She had not warned him that she was menstruating, and everyone knew that during a woman's period she was unclean. Had he known, he would never have allowed her to handle the sacred strings of beans.

Exasperated by his brother's excuses, Tecumseh grabbed him by the hair and shook him furiously. When he calmed down, he considered his next move. He decided to be conciliatory. Sending word to Harrison that he was back from his travels, Tecumseh asked permission to call on the president in Washington to reestablish peace. His request was granted, but nervous administration officials stipulated that he must travel without his usual cadre. At that point, since Tecumseh headed a coalition of five thousand warriors, the restriction offended him, and he refused to make the trip. But he took care to allay American fears about a retaliatory strike.

"General Harrison made war on my people in my absence," he told the grand council of chieftains he convened at the Wabash River. "It was the will of the Great Spirit that he should do so." Now he asked that the Great Spirit direct white people to let the Shawnee live in peace. "We will not disturb them."

Meeting with the British, Tecumseh was determined that they not judge Indian fighting spirit by the outcome at Tippecanoe. He repeated that he had not been on the scene and that "those I left at home were (I cannot call them men) a poor set of people, and this scuffle with the Long Knives I compare to a struggle between little children, who only scratch each other's faces."

Tecumseh still carried those vivid memories of Tippecanoe when he met with Stickney, the new Indian agent in Fort Wayne. Despite his public mildness, Tecumseh seethed over Harrison's attack and his refusal to return Indian land. Harrison returned his distrust, although he granted that Tecumseh probably possessed more integrity than any other chief. But weren't his constant travels aimed at uniting every dissident tribe for one concerted strike against the United States? A rumor had the Dakotas and Fox attacking Louisiana while warriors from northern tribes would come together at Britain's Fort Malden.

Tecumseh was being undercut as well by leaders of those tribes publicly committed to America. A few months earlier, Little Turtle, the Miami chieftain, had written to Harrison promising to keep an eye on Tecumseh and to send a warning if the Shawnee seemed to be gathering strength.

During his unprecedented four-day stay at Fort Wayne, Tecumseh seemed entirely at ease. He amused a fifteen-year-old white girl who was pledged to marry an Indian by trying to guess which tribe her groom came from. At dinner, he turned down most of the dishes except for potatoes. Only potatoes, he said, were a native food favored by the Great Spirit.

But his negotiations with Stickney took on a menacing edge. Even as messengers brought word that the Americans were marshaling troops along the Canadian border, Tecumseh claimed to be heading for Britain's Fort Malden only as part of his quest for peace among the Wyandots and the Ottawas of the Michigan Territory. But he said he needed weapons for self-defense and asked that Stickney provide them.

The American agent not only refused but warned Tecumseh that showing up at Fort Malden at such a tense time would be seen as hostile to the United States. Stickney reported afterward that when he turned down his request for arms, Tecumseh said, "My British father will not deny me. To him I will go." In parting, he refused to shake hands.

Hurrying toward Fort Malden, Tecumseh made an even sterner vow to a group of uncommitted Indians who were holding a council across the river from the British fort. They sent a runner to invite Tecumseh's men to join them and got back a sharp rebuff:

"I will suffer my bones to bleach upon the shore before I engage in any council of neutrality."

Brigadier General William Hull

Chapter Eleven

WILLIAM HULL
(1812)

To lead America's proposed invasion of Canada, Madison needed an experienced general, but his choices were limited. During three decades of independence, the reluctance of Congress to pay for an effective standing army meant he could pick either an aging Revolutionary War veteran or a younger officer who had never seen battle. Madison settled on fifty-nine-year-old William Hull, the governor of the Michigan Territory. If he could be persuaded to accept the commission, the Revolution's Lieutenant-Colonel Hull would leave Washington as Brigadier General Hull.

But Hull was proving to be a reluctant old soldier. He had fought vigorously against the British at Dorchester Heights, White Plains,

Trenton, and Princeton when he had been in his mid-twenties and not long out of Yale. Now, in February 1812, Hull was short, stout, and the survivor of a stroke. For the past seven sedentary years in the Michigan Territory, he had been dining well and drinking diligently. He seemed to have come to Washington in hopes that Madison would name him to replace William Eustis, the Boston surgeon who was proving incompetent as secretary of war.

Instead, the president called upon Hull to march troops north into enemy territory and capture Upper Canada from the British. Alarmed and disappointed, Hull tried to decline. He protested that for thirty years his sword had lain useless in its scabbard and his strength had become enfeebled. But he could not argue that his age alone was an impediment, since the seven other generals being commissioned by Madison and Eustis were also between fifty-eight and sixty-three.

Nor could he deny that he knew the northern territory well and had met often with the Indian chieftains whose neutrality would be crucial.

During his stay in Washington, Hull found the government deaf to any misgivings about the proposed Canadian adventure. Jefferson was on record as predicting that to conquer British North America would be "a mere matter of marching." Secretary Eustis went further still. He claimed that Canadians were so disgusted with their government that they would rally around any U.S. officers that America sent to them. "We can take Canada without soldiers," Eustis said.

Living in Michigan, Hull had not shared in the national outrage over the impressment of sailors—the chief reason Madison was giving for going to war. But Hull agreed that British agents along the Canadian frontier were encouraging local Indian tribes to harass and murder Americans.

As governor, Hull had proceeded gingerly in coping with tribal loyalties. His white constituents numbered only about five thousand— four-fifths of them French—and Indians of various tribes controlled the land that would become Ohio, Indiana, and the Michigan peninsula. Despite angry opposition from Indian leaders like Tecumseh, Hull had purchased for the American government four million to five million acres of Indian hunting grounds in east Michigan for less than a penny an acre. Hull hoped to pressure the chiefs to give up their traditional hunting and turn instead to farming on small reservations. Since he prided himself on being humane, Hull considered the transition to be in the Indians' best interest.

He wanted to believe assurances from the Shawnee that they remained friendly to the United States. But he had passed along to Washington the alarming rumors about Tecumseh and his goal of Indian unity.

By resisting a military command, Hull had been able to strike a strong bargain with the secretary of war. When at last he agreed to lead America's Northwestern Army, Hull was sure he had won several essential commitments: He could count on U.S. warships' being stationed on Lake Erie to guarantee open supply lines for his troops. And he could expect the number of his troops to be reinforced substantially before Madison declared war.

Hull did not believe he should be expected to subdue all of Upper Canada with only fifteen hundred men.

Hull reached Cincinnati on May 10, 1812, traveling with his wife, daughter, and son-in-law. Hull's scapegrace son, Abraham, was also making the trip to serve as the general's aide. They were greeted by the governor of the Ohio Territory, R. J. Meigs, whose given names carried a well-known romantic story.

Meigs's grandfather had been courting a reluctant young woman who kept putting him off until one evening he stomped away from her door in frustration. Watching him disappear down the lane, she called after him, "Return, Jonathan!" The couple was married soon afterward, and to commemorate that night they named their first-born son Return Jonathan Meigs. He passed on the name to the current governor.

Meigs announced that he had rounded up the twelve hundred militiamen President Madison had requested, but Hull was quickly reminded why most career officers scorned the militia. He watched men arriving in Dayton wearing tattered outfits and carrying an array of battered weapons. Hull could take heart only because some of the men also seemed to have brought a fighting spirit. At least, they had pinned to their caps the slogan "Conquer or Die."

The three hundred regular army troops who were marching to join him at Urbana came from the Fourth U.S. Regiment. Urbana was no more than a rough frontier town, and Hull soon ordered his men to leave its few comforts to begin hacking through nearly two hundred miles of wilderness. Their first destination was to be the Miami River, about seventy miles south of Detroit.

Learning of the rigors ahead, a number of the militia flatly refused to march. When Hull heard a clamor among the Ohio volunteers, a lieutenant explained that it was the sound of one company riding its officer out of camp on a rail.

On June 21, the remainder of Hull's men set out for Detroit amid swarms of black flies and mosquitoes and a heavy downpour that mired their wagons in mud. Abraham Hull provided the volunteers with their one laugh when he got drunk and was thrown from his horse into the Mad River. A respite of good weather allowed Hull to cover the next seventy-five miles more rapidly and reach the banks of the Miami.

Once there, he received a letter from Secretary of War Eustis. Written on June 18, it had been sent by special messenger and reached Hull on June 27. He found that Eustis was still couching his language tentatively about the coming war. "Circumstances have recently occurred," the secretary wrote, "which render it necessary you should pursue your march to Detroit with all possible expedition." Eustis added tactfully, "The highest confidence is reposed in your discretion, zeal and perseverance."

Hull had already sent back to Washington his own optimistic forecast: Despite desertions, he had now picked up a total of two thousand rank-and-file troops. "In the event of hostilities," Hull wrote, "I feel confidence that the force under my command will be superior to any which can be opposed to it."

At the Miami River, Hull came upon a schooner, the *Cuyahoga*, anchored along the bank. To lighten his load, he ordered that all hospital equipment and entrenching tools be carried on board and sailed to the fort at Detroit. Since war had not yet been declared, Abraham Hull decided that the *Cuyahoga* seemed a safe way to send the general's small trunk as well. He transferred to the ship the secret muster rolls of American troop strength and his father's private instructions from Washington.

As it happened, Secretary Eustis had sent two letters on June 18. Later that day, he wrote a second time to inform Hull that the war had officially begun. Enthusiastic congressmen were calling it "America's second war of independence," but the letter from Eustis was more subdued: "Sir," he wrote, "war is declared against Great Britain. You will be on your guard." Again, he urged a speedy trip to Detroit but added, "Wait for further orders."

One of the many complaints about Eustis was his foolish immersion in petty details—poring over newspaper advertisements for the cheapest price on army shoes or caps—but on this day one detail escaped him. Eustis neglected to engage a special messenger to inform Hull that his army was now at war. Instead, the letter was sent by public mail—first to Buffalo, then on to Cleveland and Sandusky. It reached Hull only on July 2. The British at their Canadian post near the town of Malden had heard about Madison's declaration of war three days earlier. On July 2, they seized the *Cuyahoga* and its trunk filled with Hull's military intelligence.

It was July 5 before Hull reached Detroit, across the river from British territory. Some eight hundred settlers lived in a ten-mile circle around Detroit's sturdy fort. Their farms were laid out to be narrow at the front to let them join together in repelling Indian attacks. Each farm then extended considerable distances to the rear.

The fort itself was a two-acre square built against an embankment and ringed with a double row of high posts. Hull knew the fort's chief weaknesses: It could not hold enough supplies to survive against a two-month siege. And it could be reinforced only by way of a sixty-mile road that was vulnerable to attack from hostile Indians or any British ship on Lake Erie.

Settlers had been drawn to the region around Detroit by the mildness of its seasons. Although the river froze over with ice thick enough to bear loaded sleighs, little snow fell each winter. In season, a profusion of apples, pears, plums, peaches, and grapes grew larger and sweeter than anywhere else in Upper Canada. One traveler described summer in Detroit as a forest of fragrant blossoms.

Hull directed the men to rest from the arduous trip and devote their free time to repairing and cleaning their weapons. Across the river, however, the British seemed to be building a fort of their own. Hull's young staff hectored him to cross to British territory and launch an immediate attack. To cool them down, he called together his field-grade officers and urged patience until he received express permission from Washington for an invasion.

But the insistence of his subordinates intimidated Hull into making a concession: If they could guarantee the discipline of their troops, he would storm Malden with bayonets. That bluff bought him time. The colonel in charge of the regular army contingent vouched for his men. But the three militia commanders refused to give the same assurance, and Hull could put off the attack on Malden.

Soon afterward, Hull got a packet from Eustis that included the text of Madison's proclamation of war and gave notice that "you are authorized to commence offensive operations accordingly." Eustis added that if Hull's troops could rise to challenge while also protecting their own posts, they should "take possession of Malden and extend your conquests as circumstances may justify."

The message left Hull with no excuse for further delay. Emboldened by the eagerness of his officers, he wrote back to the capital: "The British have established a post directly opposite this place. I have confidence in dislodging him and being in possession of the opposite bank."

Hull wanted to impress the administration with his diligence. "I have little time to write; everything will be done that is possible to do." But he also warned against unreasonable expectations: "I do not have the force here equal to command the water and the savages." Nor was the number of his troops sufficient to capture the British fort at Malden. Hull concluded, "You therefore must not be too sanguine."

For the next three days, Hull collected boats along the Detroit River. On July 12, he led his troops in a crossing to a settlement called Sandwich. The tranquil scene that greeted him on the Canadian bank seemed to bear out predictions of a bloodless victory. Without firing a shot, the British militiamen had withdrawn to the Canard River, twelve miles away. With them gone, many residents of Sandwich came out to welcome Hull's men warmly.

Just as Hull had hoped, his show of strength seemed to be intimidating the British and likely to prevent Indian tribes along the border from joining forces with them. In those heady moments of easy conquest, Hull issued a grandiose proclamation. He considered his words firm but conciliatory. If the tone was taken as somewhat threatening, Hull felt sure he was justified.

"Inhabitants of Canada," he began. "After 30 years of peace and prosperity, the U. States have been driven to arms." He explained that Great Britain had provoked the conflict through injuries and aggression, but he exempted the Canadians from blame since they were separated from Britain by wilderness and an immense ocean. Hull granted that his army had invaded their country and was flying its flag over Canadian territory. But "to the peaceable, unoffending inhabitants," his forces represented no danger: "I come to protect, not to injure you."

After more reassurances, Hull brandished a rhetorical sword. "Had I doubt of eventual success, I might ask your assistance; but I do not. I am prepared for every contingency—I have a force that will break down all opposition." He promised that more of his countrymen would soon be arriving and then turned to a topic that was never far from a settler's mind, although his threats about the Indians seemed to reflect Hull's own deep fear:

"If the barbarous and savage policy of Great Britain be pursued," he wrote, "and the savages are let loose to murder our citizens and butcher our women and children, this war will be a war of extermination. The first stroke of the tomahawk, the first attempt with the scalping knife, will be a signal of one indiscriminate scene of desolation. No white man, found fighting by the side of an Indian, will be taken prisoner—instead death will be his lot."

Hull's broadside was sent around the province, where the response seemed to justify his fierce language. Many residents did indeed favor the Americans, and the number of Canadians who accepted Hull's offer of protection quickly approached four hundred. Even fifty or sixty militiamen deserted to him from the British camp at Malden.

One week after his proclamation, Hull could convey his growing optimism in another dispatch to Eustis. He was mounting twenty-four-pounders for a siege of Malden and expected that in a day or two the entire British outpost would withdraw. After contacting a council of ten or twelve Indian nations, he was convinced they would remain neutral.

Hull had only one lingering worry. Was Eustis preparing the second strike force that he had promised and that Hull had invoked to intimidate the Canadians? If the American army had not yet moved troops to Niagara, then the entire British force in the province would be free to attack Hull's men. "It is all important that Niagara should be invested," Hull concluded. "All our success will depend on it."

While he waited for reassurance, Hull installed himself in the best and largest house in Sandwich, the residence of a British colonel away at the Canadian Parliament in York. From his comfortable headquarters, he sent out troops to scare up provisions, which meant demanding meat and grain from Canadian homesteaders. At times, it also meant roughing up or taking as prisoner those minor officials considered loyal to the British king. But the French farmers were the hardest hit. One lost 480 bushels of grain to the commandeering Americans, another 620 skins and all of his livestock.

Those inconveniences did not cloud General Hull's satisfaction. He had achieved victory in the opening gambit of America's new war with Britain.

Major General Isaac Brock

Chapter Twelve

ISAAC BROCK: DETROIT
(1812)

Secretary of War Eustis might be inept, but William Hull believed that at least he could count on backing from Henry Dearborn, another Revolutionary War veteran. Two years older than Hull and at least as corpulent, Dearborn had served as secretary of war under Jefferson, working obediently to maintain peace with the Indian tribes. At one point, he had fired Fort Wayne's bumptious Indian Agent, William Wells, because Tecumseh refused to deal with him. Now, as a major-general, Dearborn was commander in chief of America's forces.

When Dearborn and Hull conferred in Washington in April, they had seemed to agree on a strategy for the looming war with Britain, and Eustis had signed off on their vague plan: The main U.S. army would capture Montreal, going by way of Lake Champlain. Hull's men would march out of Detroit, to be joined by troops under two other commanders from Sackett's Harbor and the fort at Niagara.

So far, Hull had done his part. But an inexplicable lassitude seemed to have settled over Henry Dearborn. Leaving Washington, he had gone to Albany for a bit of desultory recruiting. Moving on to Boston and the towns of Springfield and Pittsfield, he complained that the people of Massachusetts resisted going to war with Britain.

Eight days after Madison's declaration, Eustis instructed Dearborn to finish his shoring up of defenses on the eastern seaboard and proceed to Albany for aggressive action. Eustis also told him, however, to "take his own time." Nearly two weeks later, with Hull poised to invade Canada, Eustis's next order to Dearborn took on more urgency. The secretary told him to get to Albany at once and organize his men for their own invasion.

By then, Dearborn seemed to have as dim a grasp as Eustis of the campaign he had planned with Hull in April. One week after Hull wrote that his success depended entirely on American troops' being massed at Niagara, Dearborn sent Eustis a befuddled and querulous note: "Who is to have the command of the operations in Upper Canada?" he asked. "I take it for granted that my command does not extend to that distant quarter."

The confusion might have seemed to mark a low point in the fortunes of William Hull, but far worse was in store for him.

Hull's first indication that Canada might not be his for the taking came when a British captain led a detachment of 46 regulars, 150 volunteers, and 400 Indians by boat and canoe to an American outpost in the straits between Lake Huron and Lake Michigan. Americans had shortened the post's unwieldy Indian name, Michilimackinac, to Mackinac and had entrusted its defense to 75 men led by an artillery lieutenant named Porter Hancks. In the four days since Hull crossed into Canada, Hancks had received no new orders, so when the enemy appeared suddenly at his gates, he surrendered.

In itself, the loss might have seemed minor, but its effect on General Hull was devastating. Sinking into gloom, he predicted that news of the defeat would travel quickly among uncommitted Indian tribes and bring them into the British camp. Although Tecumseh had not been a member of the raiding party, he sent runners throughout the region to report that the assault on Mackinac had been bloodless for the Indians and their plunder rich. Not only did the victors share in the fort's military supplies, but they also divided seven hundred packs of furs awaiting shipment to New York.

In the American camp, a major from the Ohio volunteers observed the demoralizing effect that delaying the attack on Fort Malden was having on Hull as he waited for reassurances about reinforcements: "Our general is losing all the confidence he had in the army. He holds a council of war every day, and nothing can be done—and councils again. The result is still the same."

Major-General Isaac Brock was too busy for endless councils of war. As Britain's acting lieutenant governor in Upper Canada, Brock was under the command of an older veteran soldier in Montreal, Sir George Prevost, whose father had fought with James Wolfe at Quebec. Sir George had suffered wounds in the Caribbean before being appointed governor-general and commander-in-chief of Canada's forces at the time the War Hawks in Washington began pressing Madison to stand up to Britain.

Despite Prevost's nominal authority, General Brock had a free hand in the town of York, which would later become Toronto. Hearing rumors of war, Brock called up his militia, ordering each man to arrive with his own short dark coat, dark trousers, and round hat. To avoid being conspicuous, officers were told to dress just as simply.

When the British sloop *General Hunter* captured the *Cuyahoga*, Hull's papers told Brock exactly how many men the Americans had at Detroit. The figure of two thousand was daunting, since Britain had fewer than five thousand regulars to defend the entire border from Quebec to St. Joseph on Lake Huron. For his militia, Brock would need every man from the ages of eighteen to forty-five, and he would permit no excuses or substitutions.

Brock's first order had directed the contingent at St. Joseph to seize Mackinac, and that raid had gone well. To counter Hull's earlier proclamation, Brock issued his own warning to Canadians against being tempted to defect to the Americans. Join the Yankees, he wrote, and you won't even participate in their boasted independence. You will be annexed again to the French. Brock claimed France had demanded that reward for aiding the colonies in their war for independence.

His officers wanted to attack the Americans immediately at Fort Niagara, but Brock resisted. "It can be demolished when found necessary in half an hour," he told them.

General Prevost had no appetite for this war. In the weeks before it was officially declared, he had hoped that the resistance movement in New England might still deter Madison and the War Hawks. Prevost warned Brock against any action that might unite America's northern and southern states, but he expressed confidence that Brock could hold Upper Canada. "All your wants shall be supplied as fast as possible," Prevost assured him, "except money, of which I have none."

Then Hull crossed into Canada, and Prevost alerted Brock that America's goal seemed to be capturing Malden. "I sincerely hope," he added dryly, "that you will disappoint them."

Brock responded with qualified bravado. "Whatever can be done to reserve it, or to delay its fall, your Excellency may rest assured will be done." To a friend, though, Brock confided his tactic: "Most of the people have lost all confidence," he wrote. "I, however, talk loud and look big."

In fact, it took no effort for Brock to look big since he stood an imposing six feet three. He was also more worldly than the society over which he presided at York. Brock read widely, danced gracefully at provincial balls, and, like Hull, enjoyed good food and wine. Although at the age of forty-two his waist might be expanding, he could describe himself accurately as "hard as nails."

On August 6, Brock took a small band of men from York to Burlington Bay and then overland to Long Point on Lake Erie. There he acquired 40 regulars and 260 volunteers, along with about 60 Mohawks from a nearby village who also agreed to follow him. Brock's men gathered up all the area's boats and prepared for the dangerous crossing against a pounding surf. Among his troops, Brock's philosophy was already well known:

"By the Lord Harry, sir!" he had once shouted at a young sergeant-major for not obeying an order. "Do not tell me it is impossible! Nothing should be impossible to a soldier! The word 'impossible' should not be found in a soldier's dictionary!"

Brock's blinkered willpower was tested often during the four days and nights of strenuous rowing through pitching rain that it took to reach Fort Malden. Gliding along the northern shore of Lake Erie, where cliffs of sand rose more than a hundred feet above the water, Brock's open bateau ran onto a sunken rock. When neither poles nor oars could dislodge it, Brock jumped overboard and his men followed him into the water. Relieved of their weight, the boat floated free. The crew of rookie militiamen climbed back aboard as Brock brought out his personal liquor.

Drink, he urged them. You need it because of those wet clothes.

While Brock was leading his spirited troops toward Malden, William Hull brooded over his isolated position at Sandwich. On August 5, he called yet another council of war and found that his officers were still pressing to begin the siege of Malden. They were sure that within three days, their troops could have in place their heavy artillery—their mortars and twenty-four-pounders.

His officers already held Hull in unmistakable contempt, even before he now proposed to retreat to Detroit. It would be better to go back on their own rather than wait for the British to reinforce Malden and drive them back.

In the hope of obtaining fresh provisions and picking up any official dispatches, Hull sent out army major Thomas Van Horne with two hundred regulars. Van Horne was to meet Captain Henry Brush at the Raisin River and escort him and his company of volunteers to Sandwich with their cargo. But an Indian scout reported the American movements, and Tecumseh led seventy braves to a wooded position at the side of the road that Major Van Horne was taking.

Not suspecting an ambush, Van Horne had neglected to send out advance scouts. He was overwhelmed by the Indians' assault and shaken by war whoops that made their numbers sound larger than they were. Before Van Horne's men escaped, one hundred Americans had been killed. Tecumseh's trophies included Hull's mailbag with a letter to Eustis dated August 4, in which Hull admitted that he was afraid of being besieged by thousands of Indians.

Hull's panic was hard for his officers to miss; they were now referring to him as the Old Lady. But on August 7, he took decisive action. Evacuating the town of Sandwich, Hull crossed the river again to reinforce the fort at Detroit.

America's invasion of Canada had ended one day short of four weeks.

Hull remained concerned with establishing contact with Captain Brush to open a supply line beyond Lake Erie, and he sent out Lieutenant Colonel James Miller with a force three times the size of the luckless Van Horne party. Once again, Tecumseh's scouts kept him informed of the Americans' progress, which was slowed by their dragging heavy artillery pieces over the rough roads.

This time, the Indians were joined by ten British regulars and by militia commanded by Major Adam Muir. The allies made a colorful contrast—the British bundled up in their red coats, the half-naked Indians painted almost as brilliantly. Both groups trudged down the muddy road, passing the carcasses of horses and men unburied since the last ambush.

At a slight rise in the field, Muir's men took their position while Tecumseh's warriors hid in the tall grass of a nearby meadow. Both ranks lay flat on the ground to wait for the Americans.

When Colonel Miller's troops, marching in two slow lines, came within sight, the Indians sprang up and sprayed gunfire across the plain. In fighting that lasted two and a half hours, the horses drawing the American artillery guns bolted, but Miller's soldiers fended off the enemy charge with bayonets. Muir's men in their red coats were easily singled out for attack, and they gradually gave ground.

Tecumseh did not. Nicked by a bullet to the neck, he fought on with his warriors. Their persistence discouraged Miller from pursuing the British as they scattered.

The American losses were eighteen men dead, sixty-four wounded.

Five British regulars and militia were killed and fourteen wounded; two were missing. Neither of the white commanders bothered to tally Indian casualties with much precision. By the best estimate, eleven braves had died and another six or seven were wounded. The count was complicated by the fact that during the hottest moments of battle, the Indians who tried to get behind the British line were mistaken in the confusion for American forces. Those Indians had been fired upon by the British and briefly returned fire.

Casualty figures alone could not convey the grave consequences of the ambush for the Americans. James Miller halted his march and waited for Hull's inevitable order to return to Detroit, where a petition was circulating throughout the camp to relieve the general of his command.

Tecumseh and his warriors were sleeping in an open field near Fort Malden when they were awakened by shouts and cannon fire. They discovered that the noise came from the deck of the *General Hunter* anchored on the river, where the crew was welcoming Isaac Brock to Malden. The Indians joined in firing muskets in their own salute until a British colonel rode up to say that they should preserve their low store of ammunition. He added that, although the hour was late, General Brock would be pleased to meet with Tecumseh and the other chiefs.

The Indians found Brock bent over a table with Hull's captured mail packet spread across it. As Brock absorbed the situation in the American camp, he was hatching a brash plan.

When they were introduced, Brock and Tecumseh took to each other at once. The British commander thanked the Indians for their salvo of welcome but repeated the admonition that bullets must be conserved. He praised what he had heard of Tecumseh's courage and then established his own credentials:

"I have fought against the enemies of our great father, the king beyond the Great Lake," Brock began, "and they have never seen my back. I am come here to fight his enemies on this side of the Great Lake and now desire with my soldiers to take lessons from you and your warriors so that I may learn how to make war in these great forests."

Heartened and flattered, Tecumseh turned to his cadre with an exuberant shout. The British translated it as, "This is a man!"

Having read Hull's despairing correspondence, Brock was considering an immediate attack on Detroit, even with the odds against him. The debate that followed was the reverse of the one in Hull's camp. Brock's officers said that his idea was premature, but Tecumseh spoke up for taking action. He unrolled a long peel of birch bark on the table, fastened its corners with stones, and drew a map of the area with the tip of his scalping knife. Brock watched with admiration as Tecumseh sketched in roads and streams, hills and ravines. When he finished, Brock suggested a council with the Indians the next day at noon. He retired to bed; Tecumseh's men returned to their camp.

The next morning, a thousand warriors from different tribes gathered at Fort Malden. The ceremonies of greeting and friendship took some time before Brock could speak and promise to drive the Americans from Fort Detroit. The Indians responded with loud shouts of approval, and Tecumseh pledged on their behalf that all of them "were ready to shed their last drop of blood" in service to the British king.

Brock grasped at once that Tecumseh embodied the bond that had brought the several tribes together. In a report to Prevost, he described the Shawnee leader as being admired by everyone who met him: "A more sagacious or more gallant warrior does not, I believe, exist."

Given Tecumseh's backing, Brock was determined to attack Hull, perhaps the next day. He reported to Prevost that some of his men were still warning that his plan was desperate, "but I answer that the state of the province admits only of desperate measures."

Among his officers, the militia's quartermaster was alone in endorsing Brock's plan wholeheartedly. I have lived in Detroit, the man said, and I know every feature of the town and the fort. Whatever point you choose for the attack, I can lead the men there.

Brock thanked him. "I have decided on crossing and now, gentlemen, instead of any further advice, I entreat of you to give me your cordial and hearty support."

With his own men, Tecumseh reminded them that the previous

British commander at Malden had said, "Tecumseh, *go* fight Yankee." Brock was different. "General Brock says, 'Tecumseh, *come* fight Yankee.'"

It was at that peak of exhilaration that developments in New York threatened to deny Brock his moment of glory and possibly rescue the unraveling William Hull.

Sir George Prevost, as Brock's superior officer, had watched with dismay as another American war came to look inevitable. He knew that Britain was in a deep economic depression and badly needed to revive trade with the United States. Prevost considered it certain that since Napoleon had rescinded his restrictions on shipping, Britain would do the same.

On June 16, 1812, his prediction was fulfilled. The Orders in Council were repealed in London. But delays in transmitting the news meant that Madison had already declared war before word of the repeal reached him.

After reading his proclamation of war on June 19, Madison had ridden over to the Navy and War departments. He was the first president to call at those offices, but he hardly made a commanding figure. At least one spectator was amused by Madison's round little hat, which was overwhelmed by a huge badge.

At the War Department, Madison urged Eustis and his staff to support measures that would lead to a "speedy, a just and an honorable peace." The War Department was manned by fewer than a dozen clerks, which was sufficient for the size of the army. Congress had finally authorized 35,600 men, but only 6,686 were serving. Besides its regular forces in North America, Britain had another 220,000 under arms in Europe.

Madison's audience at the Navy Department was also sparse. Secretary Paul Hamilton of South Carolina was on hand, although he was widely known to be drunk in his office most days. In the past, his behavior had hardly mattered, since his department oversaw only seventeen oceangoing ships. The British fleet numbered seven hundred.

*   *   *

Prevost shared the hope London had expressed—that eliminating the cause of discord with Washington would have "favorable effects." Elated by the repeal, he sent his adjutant general to Albany to ask that all hostilities be ended until both sides could see the result of jettisoning the Orders in Council. Prevost's aide reached Albany on August 9 and consulted with Henry Dearborn.

Two days earlier, Dearborn had written to Eustis that he was finally sending reinforcements to Niagara. "I trust they will move soon, but too late, I fear, to make the diversion in favor of General Hull, which is so desirable." Dearborn was still claiming not to know whether his command included Upper Canada. Now he used the proposed cease-fire to agree to suspend hostilities. Troops on both sides pledged to limit themselves to defensive operations.

But Dearborn specifically excluded Hull's army from the truce. He claimed that since Hull was under the direct command of the secretary of war, he should have the option of agreeing to the armistice or continuing with the war.

No one told Hull that he was being given that choice. News sent by express could have reached him in six or seven days, but once again no special messenger had been dispatched.

Even before Isaac Brock left York, Prevost had written to alert him to the possibility of a cease-fire. But after fighting in Lord Nelson's battle of Copenhagen in 1801, Brock had been rusticating in Canada for ten years, far from Britain's European wars. He intended to carry on his campaign despite the cease-fire since he knew now that Hull would not receive the reinforcements he was expecting. Brock could claim later that he had already set off for Malden before Prevost's messenger reached him.

On the morning of August 15, 1812, the British and Indians marched together to Sandwich, where Brock set up quarters in the same brick house Hull had just vacated. From there, he drafted a communiqué that reflected more his bravado than his troop strength. Brock's forces included about seven hundred British regulars and militia and the same number of Indians. From the American mailbags, he knew of the funk into which Hull and his men had fallen. Yet, in sheer numbers, Brock was badly outnumbered.

Detroit's fort was sturdily built in the shape of a parallelogram, buttressed strongly at each angle. The Americans had surrounded it with a moat twelve feet across and eight feet deep and ringed with ten-foot hardwood stocks, sharpened at the top and facing out at a forty-five-degree angle. The rampart itself rose twenty-two feet, with openings for cannon and a heavily reinforced entrance gate.

To that gate Brock sent two officers under a flag of truce and carrying a brazen message for General Hull:

"The force at my disposal authorizes me to require of you the surrender of Detroit." Brock then pronounced the one threat most likely to terrorize his American adversary. "It is far from my inclination to join in a war of extermination, but you must be aware that the numerous body of Indians who have attached themselves to my troops will be beyond my control the moment the contest commences."

Hull's family had remained in Detroit among the civilians huddling inside the fort for protection. He had just sent two Ohio regiments, totaling some 350 men, to make one last attempt to travel by back roads for the supplies still held up at the Raisin River. When he learned of Brock's arrival at Malden, he dispatched a rider to recall those troops. For now, he was left with about 1,000 functioning soldiers, far fewer than Brock had calculated.

And yet Hull's response was as ringing as his officers could wish. "I have no reply to make than to inform you that I am prepared to meet any force which may be at your disposal, and any consequences which may result from any exertion of it you may think proper to make."

Receiving that defiant answer, Brock ordered his batteries at Sandwich to open fire. Hull responded with his fort's twenty-four-pounders. Before nightfall, little damage had been done on either side. But when firing resumed the next morning, a British cannonball hit the fort's mess hall where it struck and killed a doctor from the Ohio volunteers and the same Lieutenant Hancks who had surrendered the American fort at Mackinac. To avoid guarding and feeding prisoners of war, both sides routinely paroled those men who gave their word not to join in more fighting until they were officially exchanged for an enemy soldier of the same rank. In recent days, Hancks had been allowed to go to Detroit for safety.

During the night, Tecumseh and his warriors paddled softly across the Detroit River and landed undetected two miles below the fort. Now they were moving up to join Brock's troops, who had crossed at Sandwich, where the river was about a quarter-mile wide.

During the crossing, Brock stood at the prow of the lead boat and, once landed, moved to the forefront of his men. The quartermaster who had backed the assault now pleaded with Brock to be more cautious. Let the troops be led by their own officers, he said. "If we lose you, we lose all."

Brock thanked him for his concern, but pointed out that "many here follow me from a feeling of personal regard, and I will never ask them to go where I do not lead them."

A scout located Brock and delivered an urgent warning: A large body of American soldiers was only a few miles to the rear and could trap Brock's troops before they reached the fort. They were the men Hull had sent for supplies at the Raisin River and then called back to assist in defending the fort. They had no idea that Brock's army lay between them and Detroit.

Brock had to move quickly. He formed his men into two columns and marched them within a mile of the fort. Halting there, he was joined by Tecumseh, and they climbed a slight hill to judge their position. As they were deciding on their next move, they saw the fort gates open and an American begin to gallop toward them. As the rider drew closer, they could make out that he was waving a stick with a white handkerchief.

They were not aware that the surrendering officer was General Hull's son. His father had ordered him to tell a major to carry the staff outside the fort, but that officer had said he would be damned if he'd disgrace his country. Abraham Hull then took out the flag himself.

Isaac Brock, primed for the battle of his life, could not believe what he was seeing. He sent forward an officer to ask what the flag meant. The man returned to say it was indeed the universal symbol of capitulation. The American general was surrendering his fort without firing another shot.

Hull asked two favors: A truce for three days to prepare the fort for evacuation; Brock gave him three hours. And Hull requested leniency for the Canadians who had deserted the British to join with him. Brock was equally unbending.

Riding through the open gates, Brock found American officers and their troops weeping from grief and humiliation. For hours, Hull had been sitting in a daze, spittle mixed with the tobacco juice that dribbled down his chin, over his beard and neck cloth, and onto his vest. But with his indecision ended, he seemed to recover his wits and promptly signed the articles of surrender. "I have done what my conscience dictated," Hull said, although he sensed that he had "sacrificed a reputation dearer to me than life."

Within an hour, the large party that Hull had sent to the Raisin River drew close to the fort. Surprised to find Brock's men already in command, most of them laid down their weapons reluctantly but peaceably. A few cursed Hull and broke their swords and destroyed their muskets rather than give them up. Their commander complained that if he had heard cannon fire, he would have joined the fray, fallen on the British rear ranks, and made a battle of it.

As the American troops filed out of the fort, the Stars and Stripes was hauled down. One of Brock's sailors had wrapped a Union Jack under his coat, and it was run up the pole to cheers and applause. From within the fort, Brock dated his report to Prevost "Detroit, August 16, 1812." In his elation, he may have inflated Hull's strength somewhat, but the gist of his account was accurate:

"I hasten to apprize your excellency of the capture of this very important post: 2,500 troops have this day surrendered prisoners of war, and about 25 pieces of ordnance have been taken without the sacrifice of a drop of British blood. I had not more than 700 troops, including militia, and about 600 Indians to accomplish this service."

Brock planned to send a step-by-step narrative of his triumph, but for now he concluded, "When I detail my good fortune, your excellency will be astonished."

Tecumseh had been amazed as well by Brock's daring. He told him that the Americans had been denigrating Britain's generals to the Indians, but now he viewed them differently. For his part, Brock intended to praise Tecumseh in his comprehensive dispatch and tell Prevost that once the fort had been taken, the Indians regarded the lives of their prisoners as sacred. There were no massacres, no scalpings.

For now, Brock gave Tecumseh a pair of pistols and removed the silk sash from his own uniform and put it across Tecumseh's shoulders.

The next morning, Brock's men celebrated their victory by firing a salute from the esplanade in front of Fort Detroit. They took delight in using a brass six-pounder that had been wrested away from the British at the battle of Saratoga, which they could identify by the brass plaque jubilant Americans had mounted to commemorate the date: "16 October 1777." The British salute was returned from the lake by the guns of the *Queen Charlotte*.

Observing his captors, an American colonel wrote down his impressions of the British officers with the same heightened admiration that Tecumseh inspired: Brock—six feet three, massive and large boned, apparently with immense muscular strength. His two chief aides—perhaps not quite six feet but elegant in their splendid uniforms. The contrast with William Hull was unavoidable.

At the traditional surrender ceremony, the Forty-seventh U.S. Regiment and the Ohio volunteers stacked their 1,900 muskets. The Michigan militia and other American units surrendered another 1,150. Surveying the 37 pieces of brass and iron ordnance, the 400 rounds of twenty-four-pound shot, the 100,000 cartridges, Hull's sullen officers resolved that he should never be allowed to claim a shortage of ammunition.

General Brock was eager to get back to his headquarters at York and prepare for guarding the frontier at Niagara. The men he left behind would share in the bounty seized from the fort—the equivalent of twenty weeks' pay for soldiers who usually earned about a dollar a week. Brock sent America's Michigan militia back to their homes, put other volunteers on parole, and arranged to transport William Hull and one thousand regular U.S. Army troops by boat to Fort Erie, then on foot from Kingston to Montreal as prisoners of war.

Before setting out, Hull entrusted his remaining papers and few valuables to his married daughter and asked that she take them to the Hull family home in Newton, Massachusetts. In his own mind, Hull could defend his decision to surrender: He had not known the size of Brock's army, and his supply lines had been cut. He had spared the women and children at the fort a hideous fate at the hands of Brock's Indian allies. Although here in Michigan he could not miss the contempt of his men, during the Revolutionary War his bravery had never been challenged. If his decision in Detroit were questioned, Hull had the documents to prove that Eustis and Dearborn had let him down.

But Hull's bad luck had not yet run out. His daughter sailed on a brig named for John Adams. It was set upon by the British, and when its American crew fought back, all of Hull's papers were destroyed in the ensuing fire.

As the American prisoners of war arrived in Montreal, William Hull became the object of intense curiosity. The local newspaper treated the arrival of the Americans as "an exhibition equally novel and interesting." A reporter noted jauntily, "It unfortunately proved rather late in the evening for the vast concourse of spectators assembled to experience that gratification they so anxiously looked for. This inconvenience was, however, in a great measure remedied by the illuminations of the streets through which the lines of march passed."

The parade began with a military band escorted by units of the conquering army. General Hull rode in a carriage with the British captain assigned to him. Wounded American officers followed in four other carriages and, on foot, the American troops—officers first, noncommissioned officers next, soldiers last. Hull was taken to General Prevost's residence until he could be returned to America. The officers were sent to a hotel, the soldiers to a British barracks.

Hull himself was received more cordially by the enemy than by his former comrades, who were already denouncing him to Washington as a traitor and a coward. Montreal newspaper readers learned that "the general appears to be about sixty years of age, and is a good looking man. . . . He is communicative, and seems to bear his misfortunes with

a degree of philosophical resignation that but few men in similar circumstances are gifted with."

In Washington, President Madison was still relying on Hull's optimistic
early reports when he learned of the truce arranged between Dearborn
and Prevost. Since he did not yet know how Britain would respond to
his declaration of war, Madison directed Dearborn to end the truce
and "proceed with the utmost vigor" to take the British post at Niagara
and preferably the British fort at Kingston as well.

Dearborn found a reason for delay. It wouldn't be expedient, he argued, to resume hostilities until the supplies arrived that he had ordered for the offensive.

At about the time that Tecumseh was meeting Isaac Brock, Madison was receiving a group of more compliant chieftains at the White
House. On August 6, some thirty Indians arrived with General William
Clark as their escort. Madison invited them to a state dinner, along
with five interpreters and his entire cabinet and their wives. The height
and bearing of those delegates from the Fox, the Sac, and three Osage
tribes awed everyone who met them.

During their visit, the president's wife made her own impression.
One evening, Dolley Madison looked into the mirror of her dressing
table to find an Indian chief staring back at her. Turning on her stool,
she greeted him calmly and waited a few moments before ringing for a
servant to escort the man gently from her bedchamber.

Madison was mustering an equal degree of tact to disengage the
tribes from any alliance they might have formed with the British.
Sioux leaders arrived on August 15 and were judged by their hosts to
be "terrific kings and princes." Once again Dolley Madison feted
them, describing her guests in the language of the day as "our red
children."

The tribes reciprocated with a feast of their own on nearby Greenleaf's Point, treating the audience to a war whoop and an Indian dance.
Madison used the occasion to remind the assemblage that white and
red people were made from the same clay and should be friends. My
Red Children, the president began, I had heard from General Clark
that your nations have shut your ears to the bad birds hovering around

them. Do not join the British, he implored them. "I warn all the red people to avoid the ruin this must bring upon them."

He spelled out the same vision for their future that Harrison and Hull had been promoting. No longer would Indians hunt on boundless lands. Instead, they would learn to do as the white man did—breeding sheep and cattle, spinning and weaving, plowing the earth. The result would be strong houses, warm clothes, ample food.

Few in Madison's audience seemed to share Tecumseh's rebellious spirit. The chief of the Big Osage tribe responded, "My great father, I feel newborn."

All his life, Madison had been aware of a small stature that required stretching to reach five feet five. Now a Sioux chief named Buffalo That Walks said fervently, "My father, I am a small man, but I am regarded as a man!"

Only one Sac warrior did not seem swept up in the night's emotion. "You have war," he told Madison. "It is very well—defend yourselves. We will do the same."

After the Indians left Washington, Madison began to receive reports that the war in Canada had soured. Never a sound sleeper, the president stayed up late, writing dispatches and troubled letters. In New England, what he termed "rancorous opposition" to the war was making it hard to defend the eastern seaboard. The governors of Connecticut and Massachusetts refused to call out the militia, a defiance that was bound to encourage the British. Although he had instructed his representative in London to drop America's demand about the impressment of sailors, Madison concluded that the British were ready to persist in the war.

News from Detroit was still vague on August 28 when Madison decided that he and his wife must leave Washington for a respite at his estate at Montpelier. "I find myself worn down," the president wrote to Dearborn. He explained that during August in Washington, he always accumulated bile.

By coach, the Madisons reached Dumfries Tavern, where a messenger caught up with them with a bulletin from Secretary Eustis: Hull had surrendered Fort Detroit and its twenty-five hundred men without firing a shot.

The next morning, Madison and Dolley returned to Washington, and he called the second full cabinet meeting of his presidency; the first had been to approve sending Hull to Detroit. Now Madison raised two questions: Should the United States finally create an effective navy on the Great Lakes? And should America try immediately to recapture Detroit? To both questions, cabinet members answered yes.

The president warned them that he did not want any public condemnation of Hull until they had all the facts. Dolley Madison wrote to a friend, "Do you not tremble with resentment at the treacherous act?" But dutifully she added, "Yet we must not judge the man until we are in possession of his reasons."

Madison directed his comptroller, Richard Rush, to write a judicious editorial about the debacle for the friendly *National Intelligencer.* But privately Rush showed less restraint. Although he considered Eustis a contemptible secretary of war, he didn't blame him for the disgrace at Fort Detroit. According to Rush, it was all William Hull's doing: "The nation had been deceived by a gasconading booby."

The United States frigate Constitution

Chapter Thirteen

ISAAC HULL
(1812)

Even before William Hull's ignominy, the Federalists were mounting strenuous opposition to America's new war. They had protested when Republicans doubled the taxes on imports and added a 10 percent surcharge on goods brought on foreign ships. The high taxes would penalize the northern states and were especially infuriating because Madison's party resisted imposing taxes within the United States that might anger Republican voters before the next election.

And yet many Federalists who considered the war an act of madness were resigned to supporting it now that the president had issued his declaration. A Massachusetts senator announced that "as the die is now cast, we must all hands play for our country." Any opposition should be mounted through open debate and by forming a coalition party committed to peace.

But those submissive Federalists found Republicans trying to stifle even their decorous dissent. One congressman declared that the only question was "are you for your country or against it." The *National Intelligencer* took the implied threat further: "He that is not for us must be considered as against us, and treated accordingly." The Baltimore *American* assured readers that once war was declared "there are but two parties, Citizen Soldiers and Enemies—Americans and Tories."

The newspaper spoke for the majority of Baltimore's forty-one thousand residents, who made up a Republican stronghold on the East Coast. So when a Federalist newspaper with the ambiguous name of the *Federal Republican* published antiwar articles, its editors knew they could expect trouble. One of them, Jacob Wagner, had been the State Department's chief clerk before he broke with Madison. Another, Alexander Contee Hanson, wrote that he would "hazard everything most dear" to fight against the "terror" that war would bring.

As Hanson predicted, he soon paid the price. A prowar mob pulled down his office building on Gay Street and threatened anyone rumored to have spoken against fighting Great Britain. As violence spread through the city, the mayor refused to call out the militia until he heard that a black church might be the next target.

Hanson lay low and plotted his response. On July 27, 1812, the *Federal Republican* reappeared, prominently featuring its new address on South Charles Street. Hanson announced that he would not allow vandals "to destroy the freedom of speech and of the press."

His defiance set off another riot outside the new offices. Inside the building, Light Horse Harry Lee was one of two dozen Federalists determined to resist the mob. When their door was broken down, shots were fired that killed a ringleader of the attackers and wounded several others. After hours of tension, Lee, Hanson, and their fellow Federalists surrendered to militia officers and were marched to the county jail.

The next day, a mob screaming for vengeance stormed the jail and seized Hanson and any other Federalist who had not escaped in the confusion. The prisoners were clubbed and stabbed with pen knives.

When they seemed dead, hot candle wax was spilled onto their eyelids to make sure.

Women cried, "Kill the Tories!" Children clapped their hands and gamboled among the bodies. James Lingan, a general from the Revolutionary War, begged in vain for his life. Amid shouts of "Tory!" he was stabbed to death. Harry Lee, who had eulogized George Washington only a dozen years earlier, was badly crippled by his beatings.

Arriving on the scene, Republican doctors managed to pry the victims from the rioters, carry them back to the jail, and treat their wounds. Rather than break up, the crowd drank throughout the night, shouting curses and threats that reminded witnesses of the French Revolution: "We'll drink their blood!" "We'll eat their hearts!"

Lingan was the one immediate fatality, but eleven others suffered broken bones, gashes to the head, and beatings that turned their skin black. Despite his many serious injuries, Hanson published again in early August and tried to mail his paper to Baltimore from Washington through the Georgetown post office. When the postmaster, a Federalist, asked the government for protection, Madison found reasons to refuse it.

Baltimore's mayor promised the latest mob that the *Federal Republican* would never again be published in his city, and after a few more troubled days, the crisis ended. Twenty-five-year-old Alexander Hanson never fully recovered, and died in his early thirties.

When news of the "Baltimore Massacre" reached the North, Federalists were confirmed in their opposition to the war. In Boston, citizens were warned to arm themselves, not against the British but against the excesses of a Republican mob.

Although America's foray into Canada had collapsed disastrously, Madison was soon able to take heart from a victory at sea. It was all the more unexpected because the victorious officer was another member of the Hull family.

On June 21, 1812, three days after Madison's declaration of war, the United States frigate *Constitution* left Washington with orders to sail to New York. Its captain was General William Hull's nephew, Isaac, as rotund as his uncle and, it first appeared, inheritor of the family bad luck. Writing to the secretary of the navy, Captain Hull complained about the 450 new men he was taking on at Annapolis. "The crew are as yet unacquainted with a ship of war, as many have but lately joined and have never been on an armed ship before."

The incentives for young men to go to sea lagged behind those Congress had voted for the army. A soldier got an enlistment bounty of sixteen dollars—half on enlisting, the other half on mustering out. He was also eligible for bonuses—a certificate of faithful service, the equivalent of three months' pay, and 160 acres of land. To reduce interservice rivalries, Secretary of the Navy Hamilton had recently raised the enlistment bounty for marines to twenty dollars.

Captain Hull had been instructed to join the five-ship squadron of John Rodgers in New York Harbor. Commodore Rodgers had been the victor in his unequal duel with the *Little Belt,* but before Hall reached him, Rodgers suffered a serious setback. With Captain Stephen Decatur as a squadron commander, he had sailed his frigate *President* to chase off several nearby British cruisers, especially an aggressive ship, the *Belvidera.* The British frigate was sighted, and from a distance Rodgers launched a barrage by firing the ship's starboard forecastle bow gun himself. More shots from the *President* hit the *Belvidera*'s stern, killing or wounding nine crewmen. Rodgers prepared for the next rounds that would have guaranteed success. But as his main-deck gun was fired a second time, it burst and the forecastle deck blew up, breaking Rodgers's leg and causing fifteen other American casualties.

Pandemonium spread throughout the American ship. As the *President* yawed and lost ground, Captain Richard Byron of the *Belvidera* pushed his crew to repair its earlier damage. For eight hours, he cut away fire-wracked boats and dumped fourteen tons from his barrels of fresh water. All the while, Byron continued to fire steadily from his stern guns. By midnight, the *Belvidera* had pulled away, heading for safe harbor at Halifax.

Although his American colleagues did not fault Rodgers's performance, they did praise Byron as a masterful commander.

While Isaac Hull was taking the *Constitution* north to New York, he was met at Barnegat Bay on the New Jersey coast by an imposing squadron coming south. They were too far off for him to make out their colors, but Hull thought they were Rodgers's ships. He sailed within six or eight miles to make contact with the nearest vessel. By then, it was 10 p.m. on July 17. For the next hour, Hull signaled the unidentified ship. When he got no answer, he concluded it must be the enemy and hauled off to lie low until daylight.

At dawn, Hull's suspicions were confirmed: An entire British squadron was bearing down on him. At that point, a fine breeze that had been propelling the closest British ship, the *Shannon*, dropped away, and it was all but becalmed, along with the *Constitution*.

Hull's crew pulled at their oars. The *Shannon*'s crew did the same, followed by the restored *Belvidera* and another frigate, the *Guerrière*. The *Shannon* was drawing close enough to experiment with firing its bow guns, but its few shots still fell short.

Hull's best hope was the maneuver called kedging. A lieutenant, Charles Morris, recalled that another crew had once used a kedge anchor to get the *President* out of harbor. Hull sent out two small boats half a mile ahead of the *Constitution* with light anchors and all the available length of rope. The crew then walked the capstan around to bring the ship up to the anchors. Lifting the anchors, they took them ahead and repeated the laborious process over and over again.

Some crew members slept fitfully on deck while others kept warping the ship forward. The British commander soon copied Hull's tactic and approached almost within firing range. But he had to move carefully. The *Constitution* was the heavier of the two ships, with forty-four guns to the *Shannon*'s thirty-eight. Blasts from its stern could sink the British ship.

The exhausting night passed with the ships maintaining their distance. At one point, Hull's men spotted an American merchant ship drawing close to the contested area between the two ships. To lure it closer, the British ran up false U.S. colors. Hull countered by running up a decoy English flag in order to alarm the merchant captain. His ploy worked. The American ship changed course and made her escape.

By the next daylight, after three days of tense sailing, Hull could see only three British ships, and they were some twelve miles off. His crew set to work on their sails and managed to race away at an unexpected speed of twelve and a half knots.

At 8:15 a.m., the British commanders realized that a chase was hopeless and made their way back to harass the harbor at New York.

Hull concluded that he should no longer obey his orders to join Rodgers there. Writing to Secretary Hamilton, he explained why he was proceeding instead to Boston and apologized for including so detailed an account. Circumstances, he wrote, "caused me to make this communication much longer than I would have wished."

Hull did not foresee that the account of his crew's skill and endurance in saving their ship was about to enter naval lore. Among the young sailors inspired by the story was David Glasgow Farragut, a thirteen-year-old midshipman on the thirty-two-gun *Essex*.

The people of Boston turned out to hail the *Constitution* and its captain. Federalists might oppose the war, but they had supported creation of a navy, and local shipyards had built many of the frigates that were now defending America's coast. Although Hull and his crew were widely praised, he found no word from Commodore Rodgers awaiting him, nor had Washington sent new orders.

Hull could guess that Secretary Hamilton intended to turn the *Constitution* over to a more senior officer. Before that happened, he wanted to test his luck for as long as the *Constitution* remained under his command. To cover any suggestion of insubordination, he wrote to Hamilton that he was sure the secretary wanted his ship to be at sea.

Hull stopped in Boston only long enough to accept accolades and to discharge twenty sick or disabled men. Then he sailed off to hunt down British ships along the eastern coast. When no enemy was sighted, Hull changed course and headed for Newfoundland.

By August 10, Hull's persistence was being rewarded. He boarded a British brig headed for England from Nova Scotia, seized its crew and a load of timber, burned the ship, and filed a laconic report about that engagement and a few other small successes. One target he had first considered promising turned out, on closer contact, to be the American privateer *Decatur*. Whatever Hull's disappointment that the ship was friendly, at least the *Decatur*'s crew could supply information about a real quarry—a British frigate only one day's sail away. On the afternoon of August 19, Captain Hull sighted the warship as it cruised alone south of Newfoundland.

For three hours, Hull chased the unidentified ship with his crew cheering the prospect of a real fight. When Hull drew closer, the frigate unfurled its Union Jacks and fired a broadside. The ship turned out to be the frigate *Guerrière* from the convoy that had pursued Hull the previous month. All of its shots fell comfortably far from the *Constitution*. The next volley did reach Hull's ship but caused no damage.

By 5:55 p.m., the other ship was less than a pistol shot away. Hull fired his own guns and within fifteen minutes, the *Guerrière* was listing badly from hits to its mizzenmast and its mainmast. Both broke off and fell over the side.

The British captain, James Dacres, tried to clear the wreckage, but the incoming broadsides hampered his ability to fight back.

Nightfall had made it too dark for Hull to see whether the *Guerrière* was flying a flag of surrender, and he sent a small boat to find out. If Dacres had, in fact, surrendered, Hull planned to offer his assistance because he could see that the British ship was sinking.

On board the *Guerrière*, Captain Dacres still hoped to jettison debris and resume the battle. But his main deck guns were under water, his crew was throwing dead bodies overboard, and those petty officers and seamen who had got into the ship's liquor supply were drunk. Dacres called together his remaining officers, who agreed that further resistance would mean a needless waste of lives. Reluctantly, Dacres struck his colors and fired a shot leeward as a sign of surrender.

The surviving British crew numbered 267 men; 15 had been killed, 64 wounded. The *Constitution*, carrying 456 officers and men, lost 7 dead, 7 wounded. Dacres accepted Hull's offer of help, and the two crews worked throughout the night to transfer the British survivors and their baggage to the *Constitution*. As soon as the last of the wounded had been evacuated, Hull's men set the foundering wreck on fire.

Writing from Boston to tell superiors in Halifax about his defeat, Dacres praised Hull and his officers for preventing the *Guerrière* crew from "losing the smallest trifle" and for their great attention to the British wounded.

When Dacres was court-martialed in October, he was acquitted of improper conduct in surrendering his ship. The court observed that the *Constitution* had been seventeen feet longer than the *Guerrière* and fitted with thirty twenty-four-pounders on her main deck, compared with the British ship's thirty eighteen-pounders.

That lenient judgment contrasted with the less forgiving penalty exacted from James Barron for his conduct five years earlier as captain of the *Chesapeake*. Judges at Barron's court-martial suspended him without pay for five years.

One yarn from its engagement with the *Guerrière* followed the *Constitution* into the history books. Seeing that a British shot had struck its side and fallen harmlessly into the sea, a sailor was said to have cried, "Hurray! Her sides are made of iron!" And the *Constitution* became Old Ironsides.

When Isaac Hull sailed into Boston Harbor for a second time with Dacres and his crew as prisoners, residents overcame their resistance to the war and celebrated the brief battle that seemed to raise America to the rank of a first-class naval power.

Hull's victory caused one British newspaper to observe that "a contest with the Americans is more worthy of our arms than we had at first sight imagined." Other papers still referred to the American frigates' being "manned by a handful of bastards and outlaws," but the London *Times* concluded that only a weak politician would not see how important a first triumph was in giving "a tone and character to the war."

In New York, the *Evening Post* praised Isaac Hull in order to take a swipe at President Madison: "Captain Hull, who has immortalized himself in the capture of the *Guerrière,* is a relative of General Hull, who has been sacrificed by an imbecile Administration on the borders of Canada."

But nothing could dampen spirits at the boisterous dinner given in honor of Hull and his officers at Boston's Faneuil Hall. Glasses were raised seventeen times, one in a toast that seemed slightly less forlorn these days:

"May danger from abroad insure union at home."

Hull traveled with Stephen Decatur to call on the venerable revolutionary Josiah Quincy. Over breakfast, Quincy's daughter granted that the bulky Hull was prepossessing but found Decatur "uncommonly handsome." Describing the battle, Hull explained to his companions what his reaction had been to the cannon fire:

"I do not mind the day of the battle," Hull said. "The excitement carries one through. But the day after is fearful. It is so dreadful to see my men wounded and suffering."

Hull went on to New York to receive further honors. Congress had voted him a gold medal, along with silver medals for his officers and fifty thousand dollars in prize money to be divided among officers and men. And Hull finally turned over the *Constitution* to the senior officer who had been ready to claim command since July. As consolation, Hull, a newly minted forty-year-old hero, married the daughter of a Connecticut merchant trader.

Chapter Fourteen

ISAAC BROCK: QUEENSTON
(1812)

In Canada, Isaac Brock had accepted being lionized with the proper show of public humility. An admirer who later became chief justice for Upper Canada wrote a typical letter congratulating Brock for his "fabulous" victory over William Hull. At York, Brock was received in triumph and turned the praise to his officers and men.

But writing to his brothers, Brock shared his true feelings. "I have received so many letters from people whose opinions I value, expressive of their admiration of the exploit, that I begin to attach to it more importance than I was first inclined." Brock predicted that if the English felt as strongly about his achievement as the Canadians did, "I cannot fail of meeting reward and escaping the honor of being placed on a high shelf never to be taken down."

Brock ascribed any criticism of his victory to envy among fellow officers of his own "discernment," his "cool calculation."

But as he left Detroit in mid-August, Brock learned that what he considered cool judgment had struck his commanding officer as risky and rash. Brock had ordered a subordinate to attack the American supply post at Fort Wayne, while he would strike at Sackett's Harbor, where U.S. ships were being readied to improve America's position on Lake Ontario. Instead, Brock was informed officially of General Prevost's armistice with Henry Dearborn but not of its quick repeal. Brock was forced to rescind his orders and proceed to Kingston.

Britain's Indian allies were under no such restraint. They attacked

Fort Dearborn—later renamed Chicago—massacred the garrison, and burned down the fort.

Brock had barely reached Kingston when Prevost wrote that Madison had rejected the armistice and hostilities would resume in four days. Exhilarated, Brock replied that "though landed only two hours, I must return immediately to Niagara." He called for a prompt attack on Sackett's Harbor to destroy the American arsenal at Kingston, thirty-five miles across the lake. Prevost refused permission. London was endorsing Prevost's attempt to keep the peace by waiting to see whether revoking the Orders in Council might yet lead Madison to call off the war.

Brock watched in frustration from across the river as the Americans prepared for battle. Their troops were arriving with a "prodigious quantity" of pork and flour, he noted, and he had heard that more Americans were marching up from Kentucky to join the fray. Not only did Prevost ignore those warnings but, citing a ten-week-old dispatch from London, instructed Brock to evacuate Detroit and the Michigan Territory immediately.

The prospect of having his glorious conquest snatched away provoked Brock to open defiance. "I shall suspend," he informed Prevost, "under the latitude left by the Excellency to my discretion the evacuation of Fort Detroit." Otherwise, he explained, the Indians would exterminate the population there.

Prevost tried to soothe his hard-charging commander while impressing on him that Canada did not figure greatly in London's thinking:

"I agree in opinion with you, that so wretched is the organization and discipline of the American army that at this moment much might be effected against them. But as the government at home could derive no substantial advantage from any disgrace we might inflict on them, whilst the more important concerns of the country are committed in Europe, I again request you will speedily pursue the policy which shall appear to you best calculated to promote the dwindling away of such a force by its own inefficient means."

But Brock was right about American intentions. The disgrace in

Canada had to be avenged. From Monticello, where Jefferson was enjoying his leisurely retirement, he sent to Madison the kind of advice he had been chary about offering:

"I fear that Hull's surrender has been more than the mere loss of a year to us," Jefferson wrote. "Besides bringing on us the whole mass of savage nations, who fear and not affection, had kept in quiet, there is a danger that in giving time to an enemy who can send reinforcements of regulars faster than we can raise them, they may strengthen Canada and Halifax beyond the assailment of our lax and divided powers."

Although Henry Dearborn continued to head the army, Stephen Van Rensselaer, a New York militia major-general, was put in charge of his state's militia. A Federalist politician from upstate New York, he had been chosen in hopes of winning support for the war from Madison's opposition. At first, Van Rensselaer's mission went well. He rounded up thousands of militia along the Niagara frontier and, together with the 1,360 regulars, had amassed more than 7,000 men along a border of thirty-six miles.

From his headquarters at Fort George, Brock calculated that his own combination of regulars, militia, and two or three hundred Indians totaled only 1,500.

Since he was limited to defensive measures, Brock felt helpless on October 9, when American seamen boarded two British ships. The insult was pronounced because one was the *Detroit*, the formerly American brig that had been christened the *Adams* before it was seized in the firefight that destroyed William Hull's papers. The other ship, the *Caledonia*, belonged to the North-West Company, and the Americans helped themselves to its cargo of valuable furs.

Brock lamented to Prevost about the "bold, and, I regret to say, successful attack by the enemy."

Brock's own plans were a puzzle to the Americans until one of their spies had drawn close enough to the British ranks to provide vital news. He reported that General Brock was heading for Detroit and depleting British defenses at Niagara so he could take with him the largest possible force.

*   *   *

Stephen Van Rensselaer, as heir to a great Dutch-American fortune, had always been more interested in education and public works than military affairs. He had funded the polytechnic institute named for him in Troy, New York, and had headed the commission that built canals at Erie and Champlain. Acknowledging his shortcomings as a soldier, Van Rensselaer appointed as his chief aide a militia officer, Colonel Solomon Van Rensselaer, who was also his nephew. Something of a martinet, the younger man had redeemed himself in his men's eyes by his evident concern for their horses.

But Solomon Van Rensselaer's appointment outraged regular army officers who objected to serving under a militia colonel. Lieutenant Colonel Winfield Scott flatly refused to take a subordinate role to Van Rensselaer. Another lieutenant colonel, John Chrystie, also balked but was won over by being given command of the regulars for the crossing.

The American informer with his tip about Isaac Brock had been either inept or a double agent. Brock had gone nowhere. He had been receiving reliable information about movements across the river from Americans who were deserting their own army to join him. In a letter to one of his brothers, Brock granted that those soldiers who remained loyal to the American cause were eager to fight but devoid of discipline. "They die very fast," he wrote.

As for his own men, Brock had 60 percent of the Forty-ninth Regiment with him; the rest were at Kingston. His evaluation of them was measured: "Although the regiment has been ten years in this country, drinking rum without bounds, it is still respectable and apparently ardent of an opportunity to acquire distinction."

Brock gave detailed instructions to his commanders along the Niagara about which posts Van Rensselaer might try to overrun. Particularly worrisome was the buildup across the river from Queenston, where the American post had been swelling for weeks. Henry Dearborn had explained his strategy to Van Rensselaer: "At all events, we must calculate on possessing Upper Canada before winter sets in."

The night of October 12 was marked by a bitingly cold storm.

Brock had warned Prevost again that an American attack was imminent, and he was trying to add two thousand militia to his regulars. But he fretted that he might not be able to fill that quota with "willing, well-disposed characters."

Soon after 4 a.m., Brock's premonition came true. He heard distant cannon fire and sent for the frisky ten-year-old horse he called "Alfred." Not waiting for his aide to join him, Brock mounted and galloped down the road to Queenston, seven miles away.

Stephen Van Rensselaer had intended to launch his attack two days earlier, but due to poor planning too few boats were available. As it was, he had rounded up only thirteen, although Henry Dearborn claimed afterward that eighty boats had been available.

Only two of Van Rensselaer's boats could carry eighty men. The rest would hold only twenty-five and were too small for cannon or caissons. Getting all six hundred men across the river would require many trips.

And now, after the forty-eight-hour delay, Van Rensselaer had run into this shattering storm, which would slow the crossing and push back his timetable. He intended that, once ashore, his men would shoot their way through the town of Queenston and seize a river bluff that rose almost 250 feet above the town. From that stronghold, American artillery would command the entire horizon.

Stephen Van Rensselaer's officers were competing for the honor of leading the charge, but he passed them over and entrusted the mission to his nephew.

The night storm had not abated when the thirteen American boats left Lewiston at 4 a.m. They expected to be shielded by a battery at nearby Fort Grey that included two eighteen-pounders and two sixteen-pounders. Shot from those cannon could reach any place on the riverbank where British soldiers might be firing muskets to prevent the landing.

The Americans were quickly spotted by a British militiaman, who ran to his guardhouse and sounded the alarm. At a site called Vrooman's Point on the steep cliff above the riverbank, the British had installed a gun that could be trained on the American boats. At the warning signal, it began firing and managed to turn back three of them, including the two largest.

About sixty of the three hundred British troops in Queenston raced toward the landing and opened fire. A skilled rifleman could load his single-shot musket two or three times in a minute with paper cartridges wrapped around powder and a ball. A good shot could bring down an enemy soldier at 150 yards. The American officer commanding the battery at Fort Grey respected the way British muskets were pumping out a solid sheet of fire.

The ten surviving boats unloaded their troops and went back across the river for reinforcements. Despite Fort Grey's cannon shot, the British drove the invading force back to the foot of the towering cliff. Solomon Van Rensselaer was wounded repeatedly—in his thigh, his calf, his heel—until his white trousers were red with blood. He borrowed a coat from his aide so that his men would not see the extent of his wounds. Then he put his men in formation and waited for reinforcements.

In another boat, Colonel Chrystie had also been wounded, and he lost a struggle with the helmsman, who insisted on turning his boat back to safety on the American side of the river. At the embarkation point, Chrystie found "a scene of confusion hardly to be described." No one seemed to be in charge, and the frightened militiamen wanted to go home. Their ringleaders were citing a rule that militia could not be required to fight on foreign soil.

After less than ninety minutes, the American assault was turning into a bloody rout. Then one American officer who had already made the crossing, a captain named John E. Wool, came forward with a plan that might avert disaster.

Dawn had barely begun to lighten the horizon when Isaac Brock reached the cliff overlooking the scene of the Americans landing below him. He paused briefly at the house of Captain John Powell, where the sound of artillery shells punctuated his conversation with Powell's twenty-year-old sister-in-law, Sophie Shaw, who brought Brock a cup of coffee. He did not dismount for it. He finished that stirrup cup on horseback and rode off toward the fighting.

On his way, Brock passed the York Company. Its commander had first suspected that the Americans might be staging a feint and intended to attack closer to his own location. But as the fighting wore on, he had decided to risk taking his men to the action. The militia from York were among Brock's favorites; they had been with him at the capture of Detroit. As Brock rode past, he waved at them to push on.

Reaching Vrooman's Point, Brock saw that the British long gun was placing its shells with deadly accuracy and had sunk one American boat with fifteen men aboard. Those who made it to shore were either mowed down at the river's edge or taken prisoner.

As Brock drew closer to Queenston, an officer informed him that most of the American boats had been sunk or captured. A final four were just casting off from Lewiston, and Brock rode forward to tell soldiers manning the V-shaped redan battery to increase the charge in its eighteen-inch mortar to prevent those Americans from landing.

Brock had barely dismounted and entered the British gun enclosure when shot began raining down from overhead.

Twenty-eight-year-old Captain Wool had done what British strategists considered impossible. Despite taking a flesh wound in the buttock, Wool led a band of sixty men along the riverbank with his lieutenant, John Gansevoort, who knew the terrain. Gansevoort spotted the merest outline of a path that fishermen had once used to get down to their boats. It was so narrow, steep, and overgrown that the British had not considered it worth guarding.

Wool's men made the torturous climb and hid in a thicket of maple trees to elude the few British regulars who were guarding their gun. They waited until 7 a.m., when the improving light let them overwhelm the small enemy force, commandeer the gun, and begin picking off targets on the riverbank below them.

Brock saw that his position had become a deathtrap. He told his men to spike their eighteen-pounder by breaking off a ramrod into its torchhole and then get themselves to safety as quickly as possible. As he rushed out of range of Wool's fire, he had no time to mount his horse.

But the crucial hill had to be retaken. Brock found shelter at the far end of the town and rounded up one hundred men from the Forty-ninth Regiment and another one hundred militia. He told them to follow him on foot and prepare to scramble up the steep incline. At its base, he shouted, "Take a breath, boys! You will need it in a few minutes!"

The men cheered and Brock began the climb. Leading his horse by the bridle, he had gone only a few steps when a deflected bullet struck the wrist of his sword arm. The wound was slight enough that he could wave his blade and shout to his troops to press forward.

But the next shot was deadly. An American scout from Ohio spotted Brock by his height and uniform and aimed directly at him, catching Brock in the right side of his chest. George Jarvis, a fifteen-year-old British volunteer, was the first to reach Brock as he lay next to a withered thorn bush. The boy asked, "Are you much hurt, sir?"

Brock could not answer. He put his hand on his chest and died. The men covered his body, carried it to a house at the base of the hill, and went back for a lieutenant who had been killed at Brock's side.

Two hours of inconclusive sniping passed until the British formed again at 9:30 a.m. for another charge up the hill. Despite American muskets and the field pieces that they had moved into place, fifty British troops succeeded in clambering up the hillside. The Americans took cover behind bushes and logs but did not move into any kind of formation. Firing from thirty yards, they shot down two British officers, whose troops returned only a few volleys before they skidded back down the bluff.

By 10 a.m., with the Americans still in control of the heights, rumors of Brock's death spread through the British ranks. One officer, pallid and mournful, walked in a daze amid musket balls that were kicking up the dirt around his feet. He said nothing until a soldier cried out, "For heaven's sake, tell us what you know!"

"General Brock is killed. The enemy has possession of Queenston Heights."

Hearing that news, the British battery stopped firing for a moment. In the silence, they heard a triumphant cheer from across the river and knew that the Americans somehow had also got the word.

Swearing, weeping, thrashing about in frustration, the British troops vowed revenge. But they had to wait until after noon before Major General Roger Sheaffe devised a way to make the Americans pay.

For years, Brock had deplored Sheaffe's rudeness and lack of insight into the troops he led. But he granted Sheaffe's zeal and professionalism and had sent for him at the first sound of cannon fire. By the time Sheaffe reached Queenston, Brock had been dead for more than an hour.

Sheaffe saw at once that another charge up the hill was sure to fail. Instead, he led 750 regulars and militia in a long doubling back through the woods. The trek brought them out to the rear of the Americans. Another 150 Mohawks also infiltrated the forest and boxed in the enemy.

At 3 p.m., Sheaffe was ready to move. By that time, the British troops were seething with fury. "Revenge the General!" they shouted, while the Mohawks gave their own resounding war whoop.

Not expecting an attack from the rear, the Americans panicked. Some scrambled down the cliffs into the British musket fire. Others jumped from the high banks and were smashed against the rocks.

Two American officers came forward with a white flag, but Sheaffe had a hard time putting a stop to the slaughter. His surprise attack had been a lightning flash; the mopping up took an hour.

In the end, one American general, sixty officers, and more than nine hundred men were taken prisoner. Ninety Americans had been killed, about one hundred wounded. The most telling loss involved the thousand American militia who heard of the defeat and deserted from their bases on the New York side of the border.

Brock was among the twenty British soldiers and five Mohawks to die at Queenston. Eighty-five soldiers had been wounded.

The week before he rode off to Queenston, Brock had celebrated his forty-third birthday. Not married, he had asked that when he died his sister be sent a token to remember him by. Now his body lay in state before he was buried at Fort George alongside Lieutenant Colonel John Macdonnell, his twenty-five-year-old aide-de-camp.

The Quebec *Gazette* called Brock's death "a public calamity." A newspaper in Montreal warned that the Americans "have created a hatred which panteth for revenge."

John Armstrong, Jr.

Chapter Fifteen

JOHN ARMSTRONG, JR.
(1813)

In Washington, the military disasters of recent months demanded a scapegoat. Instead of conquering Canada, the United States had been badly beaten on the ground, and so far the war's one result was the loss of the sweeping territory around Detroit. When Secretary of War Eustis offered his resignation in mid-December, Madison quickly accepted it.

Until he could find a replacement, Madison appointed Secretary of State Monroe as acting war secretary. In the chaos that followed William Hull's defeat, Monroe had entertained thoughts of leading his own campaign to retake Detroit. If successful, he would be a strong candidate to succeed Madison as president.

The idea of Monroe's reviving his military career was not far-fetched. At fifty-four, he was a decade younger than most men Madison had named as major generals, and his performance during the Revolutionary War, when he had risen to the rank of captain, matched that of Henry Dearborn.

Given that background, Monroe could be bitingly critical of Dearborn as a recruiter and a strategist. When he detailed his complaints in a letter to Jefferson, Monroe added that he was not surprised by Dearborn's shortcomings since he "was advanced in years, infirm and had given no proof of activity or military talent during the war."

Monroe's solution was to take on another title for himself. In addition to secretary of state and acting secretary of war, Monroe would become commander of the army.

That third appointment was too much for the New Englanders. They already suspected a plot to extend what they were calling Jefferson and Madison's "Virginia Dynasty." Congressman Josiah Quincy, the recent host to Isaac Hull, spoke for most Federalists when he rose in the House to protest.

Monroe would be taking command of "the greatest army this New World ever contained," Quincy said, "an army nearly twice as great as was at anytime the regular army of our Revolution." And its new commander would be a man "who is notoriously the selected candidate for the next Presidency."

Madison saw that he must go north for the appointment. Monroe was angry when the man who got the job was the extremely abrasive John Armstrong, Jr., although he could not deny Armstrong's military experience. During the Revolution, his father, a colonel in the Pennsylvania militia, had arranged a commission for his son when he graduated from Princeton shortly before his eighteenth birthday.

Armstrong, Jr., had served on the staff of General Horatio Gates at Saratoga, where he had written the notorious "Newburgh Addresses." Those leaflets, circulated among Continental Army officers at Newburgh, New York, urged them not to lay down their arms when the war ended until Congress compensated them fairly. George Washington had quashed that minor revolt by calling an open meeting where he

denounced the anonymous author of the leaflets and pledged to protect the officers' interests.

When Washington learned later that the complaints had been
drafted by the son of an old friend, he wrote an unsolicited letter ab-
solving young Armstrong of any dishonorable behavior. But Armstrong,
who had begun his military career commanding far older men, never
shed the air of belligerent superiority he had adopted as a teenager.

As America's minister to Paris in 1809, Armstrong recommended
that the United States annex the Floridas, as well as Canada and Nova
Scotia, by going to war against both France and England at the same
time. His idea was dismissed as absurd, and yet some men were arguing that once Britain was defeated, France should be America's next
target.

Despite his private views, Armstrong had been the envoy who forwarded to Madison the deceitful letter from Duc de Cadore that
helped to push the United States into war with Great Britain. But
Napoleon disliked Armstrong personally and told his own representative in the United States to inform the American government that "its
minister does not know French; is a morose man with whom one cannot treat," that all obstacles between the two countries would be eliminated "if they had here an envoy to be talked with."

Before he could be recalled, Armstrong decided to retire and
spend life as a farmer on the seven hundred acres he had purchased on
New York's Hudson River. But even retirement did not quench Armstrong's enthusiasm for war. He disapproved of Madison's hesitation
throughout 1811, and wrote, "We are a nation of Quakers, without either their morals or their motives."

When war came, Armstrong burnished his résumé by dashing off
in a few days a seventy-one-page book he called *Hints to Young Generals*. Armstrong signed it "By an Old Soldier," although his advice drew
heavily on a French military text.

Secretary Eustis appointed Armstrong a brigadier general in the
regular army and assigned him to the defense of New York Harbor.
With his new authority, Armstrong pained Gallatin by setting out to recruit five thousand volunteers solely to defend New York and promising to keep them on full pay.

After two other men declined to replace Eustis in the War Department, Armstrong was nominated as its secretary in early January 1813, and William Jones was named to replace Paul Hamilton as secretary of the navy. Monroe tried to overcome his distaste for Armstrong. At least he promised "to harmonize with him to support the Administration."

During Monroe's interim appointment, he had persuaded Congress to increase the number of senior generals, and in February, six new major generals were approved. Two nominees turned down the commission; among the remaining four was James Wilkinson, his murky behavior in Louisiana not disqualifying him. The round of promotions also moved Zebulon Pike up to the rank of brigadier general.

From Monticello, Jefferson sympathized with the inadequate pool of military leaders for Madison to draw from. Predicting which untried generals would distinguish themselves was always a gamble, he wrote. "Two of them have cost us a great many men. We can tell from his plumage whether a cock is dunghill or game. But with us, cowardice and courage wear the same plumes. Hull will, of course, be shot for cowardice and treachery. And will not Van Rensselaer be broken for cowardice and incapacity?"

Jefferson concluded that Dearborn and Harrison might do better. At least, they would have "no longer a Brock to encounter."

By the time of Madison's reelection campaign, the vote had become a referendum on the war. Madison chose Elbridge Gerry as his vice presidential candidate to replace George Clinton, who had died the previous April. On the national scene, Clinton's nephew, Dewitt Clinton, had taken over as New York's political boss, and he challenged Madison for the presidency. An aspiring politician named Martin Van Buren managed Dewitt Clinton's campaign, running him as a peace candidate who assailed "Mr. Madison's War."

Even though Dewitt Clinton was a Republican, the Federalists backed him as their best hope to defeat Madison. In New York, the Clinton campaign exploited the widespread dislike for Virginians and excoriated the president for appointing "the imbecile and inefficient" William Hull. In the South and West, Clinton supporters promised that their candidate's superior management skill would soon have the American flag flying over Quebec.

Madison won 128 votes in the Electoral College. Clinton took New York, New Jersey, Delaware, and three of the five New England states for a total of 89. But the president's margin of victory was only 39 votes, down sharply from four years ago. And in Congress, disillusionment with the war allowed Federalists to double their number of seats.

In his initial enthusiasm for Aaron Burr's wild scheme to conquer Spanish territory, Andrew Jackson had revealed an eagerness to take up arms. Then, during the months before Madison had decided on war, Jackson was already preparing himself. From the moment in February 1812 when Congress authorized recruiting fifty thousand men, he had cast his net aggressively for volunteers.

"Citizens!" began a Jackson broadside. "Your government has at last yielded to the impulse of the nation." He promised that the "hour of national vengeance is now at hand." To attract volunteers, Jackson singled out three world figures sure to arouse home-grown patriotism:

"Are we the titled Slaves of George the Third? The military conscripts of Napoleon the great? Or the frozen peasants of the Russian Czar? No—we are the free-born sons of America; the citizens of the only republick now existing in the world."

And should their government decide to occupy Canada, Jackson was sure the prospect would thrill his young volunteers since they were motivated "by an ambition to rival the exploits of Rome." Jackson may not have been speaking for his militia, but he was certainly defining his own soaring ambitions.

By January 1813, Jackson had collected twenty-five hundred men determined to repel an expected British attack on New Orleans. Speaking again on behalf of his men, Jackson assured the Madison administration that if he got the order, they would seize the towns of Mobile, Pensacola, and St. Augustine. They would not be held back by "constitutional scruples."

Jackson's pointed remark referred back ten years to the time Jefferson had to overcome his own misgivings to acquire Louisiana. Now Jackson awaited further orders in Natchez while his volunteers adjusted to their first exposure to military life. In the past, the militia had been mustered twice a year to hear a grandiose proclamation and then feast on barbecue. This time, away from home, the volunteers were tempted to explore their new freedom. Their carousing finally prompted Jackson to direct his aide, Colonel Thomas Hart Benton, to crack down on them.

Benton wrote that Major General Jackson was proud "to take for granted that every volunteer in his division is a gentleman at heart." But reports had reached his headquarters of certain conduct that, while not perhaps criminal, suggested "a disposition to heedless mischief, which causes the Commanding officer great regret. Such conduct might indeed be expected of hired soldiers, such as our enemies bring from the jails of Europe, but not of the Volunteer Gentlemen of Tennessee."

Not surprisingly, Jackson quarreled over his standing as a militia general with his old antagonist, James Wilkinson of the regular army. Their quarrel became irrelevant when Jackson received a curt message from Secretary Armstrong that the threat to New Orleans had passed and Jackson's corps was no longer needed: "You will on receipt of this letter, consider it as dismissed from public service."

Jackson apparently was expected to disband more than two thousand volunteers eight hundred miles from home and return to Tennessee without them. Written on February 7, the message was Jackson's first indication that Armstrong had replaced Eustis. The letter had taken thirty-six days to reach Natchez.

Armstrong's peremptory order aroused Jackson's formidable temper. Colonel Benton persuaded him not to send the War Department a letter that Benton found "violently insubordinate." But when Jackson called together his officers, he dropped the courtly language of his proclamation to the militia:

"Gentlemen, I cannot believe that the distinguished old gentleman and patriot who wrote and signed that order has the least idea of how we are situated here. To suppose that he has any idea of it would be to suppose that he is a damned old fool—which we all know that he is not!

"I met him in Philadelphia when I was a senator and know him to be a most sensible and practical man. There is only one thing to do. The order must be disregarded.

"We will go home. But we will not disband till we get there. We have nearly two hundred sick for whom transport must be provided. We have not more than four days' food on hand. More than that must be found."

Jackson concluded, "We have no money." But, he added, "I will obligate myself personally."

Several officers protested that his plan was impractical. Jackson offered makeshift solutions to their objections: "We can lie on our horses back to the Tennessee line, and the home people will take care of us."

But when the time came to move, Jackson gave personal drafts to the quartermaster in the amount of twelve thousand dollars and bought his men food for the march back to Nashville. In the years since his early financial distress, he had amassed a sizeable estate, including slaves, livestock, and the large house he called the Hermitage. All the same, the drafts strained Jackson's credit.

Armstrong's order particularly offended Jackson because he saw it as a transparent plot to force his volunteers into the regular army, and when Wilkinson sent recruiters into the militia camp, Jackson threw them out. By the time the Department of War agreed to authorize pay rations for his men, Jackson had proved his point. Even if the war was to be fought without the Tennessee volunteers, those men would remain devoted to their forty-five-year-old commander. For his reluctance to bend, they called him "Old Hickory."

Chapter Sixteen

YORK
(1813)

During his humdrum second inaugural address early in March 1813, Madison did not inform the nation that he had just received welcome news that his disastrous war might soon be ending. John Quincy Adams informed him from St. Petersburg that Czar Alexander had offered Russia's services in brokering a treaty between Britain and the United States.

The czar, kindly if condescending, had become friendly with Adams as they chatted during their daily strolls. Russia was Britain's ally against Napoleon, but here, so far from battle, civility outweighed jingoism. When Britain's new envoy, Lord Cathcart, arrived in the Russian capital, he left his card at the Adamses' residence.

Most conversations between Adams and the czar, who was ten years younger, were limited to pleasantries. But the high cost of maintaining the American mission was weighing on Adams, and sometimes he had to turn down social invitations because his wife could not afford a suitable gown. One day, as they spoke in French, the czar asked Adams if he would be taking a country house for the summer.

Adams said he would not.

Alexander smiled sympathetically. "Financial considerations, perhaps?"

"Well, yes, sire, in large part."

"Good enough," the czar replied. "You are quite right. One must always balance income and outgo."

Alexander raised his hand to his hat in something of a salute and went on his way, leaving Adams to reflect that he had just received excellent advice about managing money that few emperors in history had ever practiced.

As America's war proceeded, Russian officials engaged Adams in more substantial discussions. Secretary of State Monroe had assured Adams that, whatever happened in France's conflict with Russia, the United States would never forge close ties with Napoleon. That news delighted the czar's chancellor, Count Roumanzoff, who saw a way to end the hostilities between Russia's two English-speaking allies. Roumanzoff had already assured Adams that Russia's "obstinate attachment" to the United States was far greater than Adams could imagine. Now the count asked whether Adams would permit him to pass along Monroe's assurances to Lord Cathcart.

Sending to Washington for permission would take months. Adams exercised his best judgment and agreed. He told Roumanzoff that although he didn't have the authority to say so, he believed his country would welcome a Russian offer to mediate. "I lament the war," Adams added. The English were the ones prolonging it with their unreasonable policy of impressment.

When Madison received the Russian proposal, he immediately took heart, but he waited until Congress adjourned before he appointed two special plenipotentiaries to join Adams for any negotiations. Senator James A. Bayard of Delaware, as both a southerner and a Federalist, would have been confirmed easily despite his abstention thirteen years earlier that gave the presidency to Jefferson. But Madison's other choice, Treasury Secretary Gallatin, would have met with angry opposition.

For the Federalists, Gallatin was tarred by the Embargo Act, although he had warned Jefferson at the time that it would damage the economy. Gallatin had also pushed for renewing the charter of the Bank of the United States, but opposition from state banks defeated that measure. Despite Gallatin's shrewd finagling, he saw the country facing bankruptcy if the war continued.

Ship owners had defeated Gallatin's plan to fine them if they defied the nonimportation regulations and brought illegal cargo into America, and their successful lobbying had cost the Treasury $9 million the country could not afford to lose. Gallatin estimated that the war's cost would soon boost the budget to $36 million while the Treasury could expect to take in less than half of that—perhaps $17 million.

Congress had also resisted internal taxes, but Madison's Republicans managed to pass levies on land, on salt and sugar, and on bonds and other commodities. They had to stipulate, however, that the new taxes would not go into effect until the last day of 1812 and would continue for only one year afterward.

In asking Madison to be sent to Russia, Gallatin calculated that his greatest contribution to the economy would be to negotiate peace with Britain. But because Madison depended so heavily on Gallatin, he would agree only to his taking a leave of absence from the Treasury.

Before Gallatin sailed, he left two tax bills for his interim replacement, Secretary of the Navy Jones; at the appropriate time, Jones should simply sign them and submit them to Congress. Gallatin also arranged for $16 million in loans from three American investors, including his friend John Jacob Astor. But the nation's perilous finances meant that Gallatin had to offer the new bonds with such steep discounts that the Treasury would receive only eighty-eight cents on the dollar.

The nation's economic distress had been gleefully encouraged by New England bankers who opposed the war. Their "Peace Faction" hoped to compel an end to the fighting—or at least to discredit the Madison administration—first by opposing federal loans and then by imposing heavy interest on them. A prominent Boston newspaper objected to giving Washington even that much assistance. Its editor asked, "Will Federalists subscribe to the loan? Will they lend money to our national rulers? It is impossible, first, because of principle, and, secondly, because of *principal* and *interest.*"

The writer claimed that the money would not be safe and, more important, the bankers would be violating the Constitution. "Any

Federalist who lends money to the government will be called *infamous*."

Madison dispatched Gallatin and Bayard to join Adams with detailed instructions: They were to resolve the issues of the blockade and the impressment of sailors, but Madison let them know he was not inflexible on either point. He would also agree to a reciprocal return of any territory seized during the war. To date, that would not represent much of a concession for the United States.

Gallatin's European upbringing had given him a better instinct for world politics than most men in his adopted country. He urged that Madison's cabinet not try to annex the Floridas while he was away. Since both Russia and Great Britain denied that the Louisiana Purchase covered West Florida, any American action there would jeopardize the peace negotiations. Gallatin asked the administration to trust instead that the growing number of American settlers in Florida would lessen Spain's influence.

Ten weeks after the peace overture was received, Gallatin and Bayard sailed from New Castle, Delaware. Gallatin's sixteen-year-old son joined them as one of the mission's four secretaries, along with John Payne Todd, Dolley Madison's son from her first marriage. Todd, just turned twenty-one and towering over his step-father, was giving no evidence that eight years at a Catholic boarding school in Baltimore had been a steadying influence, and he was enjoying the round of Washington parties more than Madison considered suitable. After weighing a choice between Princeton College and St. Petersburg, the president shipped the young man off with Gallatin and a thousand dollars in spending money.

In making his careful preparations for the negotiations, Madison had not considered the one obstacle that could derail them: The British had not yet accepted Czar Alexander's offer to mediate.

At the Department of War, John Armstrong had drafted a plan for a new assault on Kingston, followed by a march along Lake Ontario to York, where the British were known to be building a formidable warship. Armstrong accurately estimated enemy forces at Kingston at about two thousand men. But Henry Dearborn, as senior major general, assured him that the British had concentrated at Kingston six thousand to seven thousand men—including three thousand regulars. Dearborn recommended marching directly to York, and Armstrong accepted his arithmetic and agreed. Given the general's history of evading combat, however, Armstrong insisted that Dearborn command the attack himself.

The town of York—which would become Toronto—was the capital of Upper Canada and Isaac Brock's former headquarters, but its military value was negligible. Only the residence of the province's lieutenant governor and the legislature's two brick buildings made it a target at all, and then largely a symbolic one.

When a winter attack on Kingston had seemed likely, Dearborn sent Zebulon Pike to Lake Champlain with twenty-five hundred men. Drawing on his experience with winter portages, Pike planned to move most of his troops by sleigh. He equipped the rest with snowshoes.

That ingenuity caught Dearborn's fancy. To demonstrate that normal close-order drill could continue even while wearing the cumbersome gear, he put on a pair himself. Dearborn was on the second floor of a local inn when he executed an "about face" by jumping a foot into the air and whirling into position. Since he weighed 250 pounds, the impact of his landing rattled china in a downstairs cabinet, but he had proved his point.

By the time the Americans set sail late in April, snow and ice had melted and the snowshoes were left behind. True to Armstrong's orders, Dearborn boarded one of the fourteen vessels ferrying troops to the offensive. Isaac Chauncey, a reliable forty-year-old seaman, commanded the flotilla; Dearborn turned the landing of troops over to Pike. Exhilarated by the challenge, Pike wrote to his father, "If success attends my steps, honor and glory await my name."

A heavy east wind on the night of April 26 forced the American boats to land near a thick woods three miles west of York. Sir Roger Sheaffe, the general whose troops had avenged Isaac Brock, appreciated the potential of the large ship being built at York; it could give Britain the control of Lake Ontario. But Sheaffe had not mounted enough guns to repel an invasion and had spread his men thinly across the area. Half were regulars, the rest militia and Indians.

The first Americans to land were riflemen led by an eccentric major, Benjamin Forsyth. In recruiting soldiers, Forsyth cared nothing for discipline and looked instead for a sharp eye and a steady hand. When not in battle, his men could do as they pleased so long as they ran instantly to Forsyth's tent whenever he blew the five-foot curved horn that he used as a bugle.

For this invasion, Forsyth had chosen a green coat with broad skirts. He wore it unbuttoned over a white vest across his considerable girth and topped off the outfit with a broad-brimmed black hat. His men were dressed more conventionally in simple green uniforms.

As the riflemen stormed ashore, they drove the Indian defenders back into the woods. Forsyth seemed ready to chase after them, but Pike was impatient to bring his own troops to the beachhead that Forsyth had created.

"By God," Pike shouted, "I can't stay here any longer!" To his officers, he called, "Come, jump into the boat!" With Forsyth's men providing cover, Pike's infantry units were taken ashore.

As he had demonstrated during his exploring days, Pike did not share Forsyth's permissive approach to command. He had trained his men methodically in the use of bayonets for close combat, but before they sailed, he had spoken sternly to them: The people of Canada were innocent victims of this war, Pike said. Any looting will be punishable with death.

Shoals along the lake front delayed Captain Chauncey's larger ships from joining the action, but accurate fire from his twelve schooners helped the Americans to land. By 10 a.m., Pike's troops were on the shore. He formed them in line to race up the low bank and join the battle in the woods.

Early resistance from Sheaffe's men forced them back temporarily before the Americans could resume a steady advance. Watching the British retreat, their Indian allies began to melt away.

In the melee, a British soldier who was holding a match to fire a gun allowed a spark to fall amid the ammunition pile and set off a huge explosion. The blast killed more than a dozen British grenadiers, badly wounded many more, and drained the spirit from the survivors. They ran for protection to Government House. Sheaffe convened his senior officers there, and they decided that their small numbers could not hold York.

Pike's men had drawn close to Government House. The British were still flying their flag, which suggested they were ready to go on fighting. Pike instructed his buglers to call his troops into formation. As fife and drum played "Yankee Doodle," the Americans advanced with their muskets unloaded, ready to fight with bayonets.

But by now Pike's troops were exhausted. As he waited for his artillery to be hauled up for the siege, Pike let his men sit down around York's ammunition dump while he questioned a British captive about the size of the enemy force he would be facing.

All at once, the stone structure blew up. Sheaffe claimed later that it had been an accident; Dearborn and Chauncey were convinced it was a low trick. In any case, the carnage was devastating, since the storehouse had held more than two hundred barrels of gunpowder. When they exploded, stones from the walls were sent flying high into the air. The Americans watched powerless as great slabs of wall seemed to hover for an instant and then come crashing down on them. Men within three hundred yards of the explosion were crushed to death.

Pike had bent forward to shield himself, when a boulder smashed his back. His body was first carried to the schooner *Pert*, then transferred to the flagship *Madison*. As soon as Dearborn heard the news, he left his boat, upset and angry, and put Colonel Cromwell Pearce in charge.

Sheaffe had already decided to withdraw his regulars. Preparing to leave, he told the militia to negotiate their surrender as best they could. Then he set fire to the warship that the British had been constructing to control the lakes.

* * *

Sluggishness settled over Dearborn's men as they tallied their losses from the explosion. By 4 p.m., the day's casualties stood at 52 Americans dead, 180 wounded.

Colonel Pearce did not attempt to pursue Sheaffe's troops, and Dearborn seemed in no hurry to accept a surrender. With Pike no longer there to stop them, American troops rampaged through the town looting homes and stores. York residents joined in the plundering.

What happened next would reverberate fatefully the following year in the United States. Americans retaliated for the explosion by setting fire to Government House. They carried off volumes from the library and stole gold and silver plate from the church.

York's bishop sought out Dearborn and protested that he was purposely delaying the surrender in order to give his men more time to steal. Dearborn claimed that he couldn't stop the troops. He said they were inflamed by finding a human scalp in Government House.

Throughout April 29, the sacking of York continued. When it ended, Dearborn denied that he had ordered the burning of the Parliament buildings. Captain Chauncey tried to make amends by sending back what books and gold plate he could wrest away from the looters.

The engagement had ended badly for all sides. Within four days, the Americans had withdrawn for a possible raid elsewhere, and the British had returned and built another blockhouse. Pike's remains were sent to Sackett's Harbor. The night before the battle, he had written to his wife, "My dear Clara . . . I have no new injunctions, no new charges to give you, nor new ideas to communicate; yet we love to communicate with those we love, more especially when we conceive it may be the last time in this world."

Prevost chastised Sheaffe for not concentrating his forces and launching an all-out attack at the landing site. Sheaffe was soon sidelined to a position with no troops to command.

Armstrong and Madison insisted that Henry Dearborn retire from the army.

Amid the loss and devastation, America could take one consolation. "Sir," Captain Chauncey had written to the secretary of the navy, "I have the satisfaction to inform you that the American flag is flying over the fort at York."

Minor and brief as the conquest of York had been, it was the American army's first victory in the war.

Oliver Hazard Perry

Chapter Seventeen

OLIVER PERRY
(1813)

William Harrison had been sent out to avenge the American loss of Detroit. As governor of the Indiana Territory, he had also been given command of the hard-bitten Kentucky militia, even though he was not a citizen of that state. But so far his campaign had not improved on the one waged by the despised William Hull.

Secretary Armstrong was unimpressed by state militias and persistently advocated a larger regular army. When he took over the Department of War, the army's strength had reached slightly fewer than 19,000 men, less than half the strength authorized by Congress when war was declared. In January, Congress agreed to another twenty regiments and tried to make enlistment more attractive by cutting the term of service to one year from the standard five years. But men continued to resist signing up, and Armstrong's forces did not reach 30,000.

The secretary wanted Congress to initiate a draft, but both Monroe at State and Jones at the Navy Department argued that conscription would be too politically unpopular. Madison permitted Armstrong to submit his plan to Congress, however, and the Federalists also balked. As a compromise, the army was allowed to offer larger enlistment bonuses and to recruit minors.

Although he had lost the debate over conscription, Armstrong still preferred that Harrison fight with regular troops. But recruits on the frontier were far more willing to join with neighbors and relatives in their state militia. Against his inclination, Armstrong agreed that Harrison could rely heavily on the Kentucky militia for his next campaign.

When Madison appointed Harrison brigadier general, he had added to his militia the ten thousand troops of the Northwestern Army so that Harrison's combined forces far outnumbered the fifteen hundred men granted to William Hull. But when Harrison deployed those troops along a two-hundred-mile front, heavy rains washed out his efforts to supply them.

Writing to Washington, Harrison restated the point Hull had made repeatedly: To take and hold Detroit, the Americans needed to dominate Lake Erie.

Harrison urged that the land campaign be delayed until late spring, but he recognized that Madison's reelection campaign might require retaking the Michigan Territory before that. By December 1812, Harrison was sending more of the same bad news that no one had wanted to hear from Hull: Detroit by itself could not be held.

Harrison further riled Madison's cabinet members by blaming his problems on the civilians he had to work with—"the imbecility, and inexperience of the public agents and the villainy of the contractors."

One of Harrison's commanders, sixty-one-year-old Brigadier General James Winchester from Tennessee, could boast of service going back to the Revolution. Winchester was convinced that it was only intrigue in Washington that had left him subordinate to a man twenty-two years younger, but he agreed to take charge of Harrison's left wing. Given their backgrounds, it was inevitable that the two commanders would clash over how to discipline their troops.

Harrison supported the ban on flogging that had been announced just before war was declared. Winchester recommended as a substitute ten or fifteen whacks "on the bare posterior well laid on with a paddle bored full of holes." When he was overruled, Winchester joined the chorus of regular army officers who considered Harrison too soft.

Harrison warned his men against dueling and barred selling liquor on army posts. Knowing the independent spirit and the physical stamina of his western recruits, Harrison considered public humiliation more effective than physical punishment. In his army, a captured deserter was unlikely to be shot. Instead, he might be displayed on a wooden sawhorse during morning parades with a sign pinned to his cap: "Deserter returning to camp on horseback." The man was then required to beg forgiveness from his sergeant while his regiment looked on.

A guard was found sleeping on duty and led before a firing squad. But at the command of "Ready," Harrison stepped forward and shouted, "As you were!" The private's life was spared, but he had to endure Harrison's lecture on the importance of sentinels' staying awake. Another man caught for the same offense was dunked two mornings in the Scioto River.

Winchester's more stringent approach to discipline guaranteed that his men looked for ways to humiliate him, especially at his latrine. During one encampment, they skinned a porcupine and stretched it across the log that Winchester sat on. As one soldier recalled, "He went and sat down on it, and it like to have ruined him."

Another time, his men sawed the log in half so that he fell into the muck in full uniform. His men sniggered the next day to see his regimental coat and trousers hanging out to air.

Winchester had the chance to demonstrate his brand of leadership when he provoked a battle at Frenchtown along the Raisin River. The action, which came shortly before the czar's offer to broker a peace treaty, ended with Winchester scoring an initial victory. But in the aftermath, he grew careless and left his right flank exposed. He sent out no scouts and dismissed as "only conjecture" a report that the British planned a counterattack.

That night, Winchester took over a nearby house, put on his night-shirt, and slept comfortably—at least, until two hours before dawn when he heard cannon shots. Throwing on his uniform over his night-shirt, he paced up and down outside the house while Indian sharp-shooters picked off about one hundred of his scattered troops. Only the Kentucky contingent held fast behind a split-log fence.

The British arrived and seized Winchester, his aide, and his sixteen-year-old son and took them to Chief Roundhead, who was in charge while Tecumseh was recruiting warriors among the Seminoles and southern Creeks. Roundhead ordered the American prisoners stripped of their uniforms, although Winchester was allowed to keep on his nightshirt.

Already embarrassed, the Americans found their humiliation com-plete when they were marched to the British commander. He turned out to be Henry Proctor, one of the British infantry officers at Malden who had argued with Isaac Brock about attacking Fort Detroit. Subse-quent months had proved Proctor no more daring. Rather than do bat-tle with the Kentucky holdouts, he ordered Winchester to force them to surrender.

While their fate was being discussed, the four hundred riflemen ate breakfast behind their fence, peering through its cracks for new devel-opments. With Winchester held prisoner, they decided that their rank-ing officer was Major George Madison, and when Winchester's order to surrender was read to them, they shouted their defiance. Major Madison had to pass through their ranks several times to calm the re-bellion. At last, trusting to British promises of safety for the prisoners and good treatment for the wounded, he agreed to give up. Around him, the Kentuckians wept and cursed.

When the last Kentucky rifleman had thrown down his rifle, British soldiers collecting the weapons agreed that they had never seen such a sorry crew. Their own uniforms, with two inches of ruffles at the chest and white trousers to scrub clean, could take three hours to pre-pare for inspection. Surveying the Kentucky volunteers, they were ap-palled by their filthy skin, their wearing cotton shirts in the depths of winter, their wrapping dirty blankets around their waists and fastening them with heavy belts that bristled with axes and knives.

With Harrison's men a two-day march to the rear, Proctor might have tried to trap them. Instead, he had retreated by noon to his camp at Malden, leaving behind about thirty wounded American prisoners. He had posted no British guards, and Tecumseh was hundreds of miles away.

That night, the Indians mourned their losses and drank steadily. Before dawn, they returned with tomahawks to the battle site at Frenchtown, scalped alive many of the wounded men, and burned others to death in their cabins. One surviving Kentuckian recorded that the road to the fort was "strewed with mangled bodies, and all of them were left for birds and beasts to tear in pieces and devour."

The Indians cut off the heads of several victims and stuck them on a picket fence near Detroit as a warning to the Americans. British soldiers at the fort did not want to offend their Indian allies by removing them, a reticence that kept the gory heads mounted for days, long after a winter frost had frozen their features with their eyes open. Some faces looked agonized, some scowled in defiance. Most disturbing were the grimaces that could look like smiles.

When Proctor's superior officers learned of the massacre, they did not condemn his negligence in failing to post guards; instead, they promoted him to major general. Americans, though, took up a new rallying cry, "Remember the Raisin!"

Harrison built a fortress on the Maumee River and named it for Return Jonathan Meigs. He brought up militia from the rear until he had amassed a force of four thousand men. He had planned a raid against Malden but when bad weather forced him to cancel it, militia from Ohio and Kentucky who had been called up for six months' service went home in February. Harrison was left with only enough men to defend Fort Meigs, and his appeals for replacements were attracting few recruits.

Because of his vaunted success at Tippecanoe, Harrison could weather those setbacks at a time Americans in the East were still belaboring the failure of his predecessor. William Hull was awaiting a military trial on charges that included treason, but since the men who would be judging him were needed for the war effort, the proceedings had been delayed for months.

As spring approached, Harrison's army was consuming supplies at an alarming rate with nothing to show for it. He sent a letter filled with excuses to Secretary Armstrong, who replied with a pragmatic directive that Harrison should appear to be threatening the British but in fact should delay any attack. Armstrong's priorities had shifted to the Great Lakes, where he hoped by mid-May to launch a decisive number of ships on Lake Erie. Harrison should settle in defensively at Fort Meigs until events on the Erie could guarantee him a secure supply line.

Harrison interpreted that strategy as a reproach. Outraged, he left the fort to be defended by only five hundred men while he set off on a recruitment drive in Chillicothe and Cincinnati. But as he traveled, he picked up indications that Henry Proctor might be marching against Fort Meigs. Harrison hurried back to the fort with a new contingent of three hundred men.

Proctor, forever indolent, did not reach the fort for another two weeks. He brought with him almost one thousand British regulars and Canadian militia, and this time he also had Tecumseh at his side with twelve hundred Indians.

Proctor's guns began to bombard Fort Meigs on May 1 and continued for four days. During that period, he did not detect the American relief column advancing from the rear—twelve hundred Kentucky riflemen led by Brigadier General Green Clay. The Americans might have revenged the Raisin River massacre if Clay's officers had not thrown away their advantage with bad strategy and worse discipline.

In the chaotic fighting that followed, the British and their Indian allies cut down many Kentuckians and took three hundred prisoners. From the battlements of Fort Meigs, Harrison watched in despair as American troops from another relief force were also wiped out or taken prisoner.

Proctor acted no more decisively to stop Indian reprisals among those captured men than he had done at Frenchtown. The Shawnee had already scalped twenty prisoners before Tecumseh rode up and cried indignantly, "Are there no men here?" He threatened to kill the next Indian who did not obey him.

Tecumseh sought out Proctor and demanded to know why he was permitting the outrages.

"Your Indians cannot be controlled," Proctor said.

"You are not fit to command," Tecumseh told him. "Go put on your petticoats."

Tecumseh's fury served Harrison better than he could know. Three days after the battle, many of the twelve hundred Indians stole away, along with half of the Canadian militia. Proctor made a halfhearted attempt to resume the siege, but his troops were drenched with rain and weak from dysentery.

On his side, Harrison had lost half his men—a thousand soldiers— and considered his own forces too debilitated to leave the fort again. From necessity, he accepted Armstrong's strategy of prudent delay while Henry Proctor executed his preferred military maneuver by retreating at full speed to Malden.

At George Prevost's explicit order, Proctor had to venture out one more time in an attempt to capture the provisions and ammunition that Prevost warned him he could not expect from him.

Proctor's assault against Fort Stephenson at Sandusky was a failure, and he sustained heavy losses. Writing to headquarters, Proctor blamed the Indians for not returning to his side but had to admit that he had lost the respect of his men: "I have also to observe that in this instance my judgment had not that weight with the troops I hope I might reasonably have expected."

If Proctor's behavior was being challenged, neither had Harrison's decision about Fort Stephenson enhanced his reputation. With the British advancing on the fort, he had ordered its twenty-one-year-old commander, Major George Croghan from Kentucky, to burn it down and retreat. Croghan defied both Harrison and the odds against him. He had 160 men, Proctor 500 regulars and about 800 Indians who had drifted back.

"We have determined to maintain this place," Croghan responded, "and by Heaven we will."

In the battle that followed, the Kentuckians held firm and could even afford the humane gesture of throwing down canteens of water to the Redcoats lying wounded outside their walls. When Croghan's obstinacy proved justified, it was Harrison's judgment that Washington questioned. He had to be grateful when Major Croghan, America's latest hero, spoke up in Harrison's defense.

Much later, Secretary Armstrong reflected on the behavior of both Proctor and Harrison during their standoff. "It is worthy of notice," he wrote, "that these two commanders were always in terror of each other."

Britain's strategists agreed with Armstrong that Lake Erie was the key to winning the war. They planned to destroy America's fleet on the lake and then proceed to defeat Harrison on the ground. By separating western land from the eastern seaboard, Britain might again establish a New World colony.

The American assigned to foil their plan was Isaac Chauncey, who had performed ably during the battle for York. His new mission was to build an effective fleet on Lake Erie, and Chauncey set about the challenge with considerable ingenuity. He established a base on the lake at Presque Isle—which would become Erie, Pennsylvania—to complement America's New York base on Lake Ontario at Sackett's Harbor.

Buying up merchant ships, Chauncey outfitted them for war, but lake schooners had not been designed for heavy weapons and were apt to capsize when their guns were fired. To build the brigs that America needed to challenge British control of the water, Chauncey sent out young Oliver Perry to undertake the task. America's belated demand for a larger fleet prompted jokes that the only victors in this war would be the shipbuilders.

Perry would have to depend on green timber for his ships. And with nails scarce along Lake Erie, they would be held together with wooden pegs.

*   *   *

From London, the British dispatched to the scene their own capable captain, Sir James Lucas Yeo, whose first attack at Sackett's Harbor came in late March 1813. Although he managed to destroy much of the ammunition that the Americans had carried off from York, Yeo's troops were routed by American regulars and militia. At Erie, Perry was excited to hear that the Americans might launch a counterstrike against the British base at St. George. He ordered a crew to row him to Niagara in an open boat, and after a rough night he reached Chauncey's side.

Perry's arrival was a happy surprise for Chauncey, who greeted the twenty-eight-year-old warmly: "No person on earth could at this time be more welcome." Together with General Winfield Scott, they consulted on a strategy for landing America's 4,500 troops to attack the 1,100 British regulars and militia from the rear of their fort.

The raid was an instant success. British casualties ran to 350 men, about 200 more than the Americans suffered. When Perry was not injured during the attack, superstitious sailors began to speak of "Perry's luck."

But the back-and-forth skirmishes that followed the raid reinforced the urgency of controlling Lake Erie. Perry returned to shipbuilding, taking with him the British brig *Caledonia*, three schooners, and a sloop that had been seized the previous year but penned up in the harbor by Fort George's guns.

By now, Perry's sense of urgency had become intense, especially after Harrison sent word that a large warship the British were building at Malden was almost ready to launch. That ship's name, the *Detroit*, was a deliberate taunt about William Hull's doomed invasion. But with their recent victory at St. George, the Americans could retaliate by calling one of their two large ships the *Niagara*.

Their second brig would be named the *Lawrence*, in honor of Captain James Lawrence, who had been killed in a sea battle. Perry and Lawrence had served together on gunboats before the war, and Perry admired his friend's fierce commitment to the U.S. Navy. Sailing against the British, Lawrence had flown a banner that read, "Free Trade and Sailors' Rights." But, as he was dying, he left behind a more stirring motto when he ordered his men not to give up their ship.

Although Lawrence's crew wanted to obey him, they had no choice. Their ruined ship was captured and sailed to England, where it was sawed up for timber.

Those last words of Lawrence, however, were proving indestructible. Perry ordered the phrase "Don't Give Up the Ship" to be sewn in white letters on a large blue flag that he intended to carry into battle.

While Perry pressed his carpenters to go on working through the night, the crew were being struck down so rapidly by a malarial fever that at any one time a fifth of them were confined to quarters. When the fever hit Perry, he was forced to lie in his berth for several days, but he kept demanding progress reports.

Spent from his illness, worn out by sleepless nights, Perry had become obsessed. Even though Chauncey had often demonstrated his high regard for him, Perry refused to see why Chauncey did not send all the men Perry wanted.

By July 20, bristling with impatience but still civil, Perry wrote again to Chauncey, "Think of my situation: the enemy within striking distance, my vessels ready, and I obliged to bite my fingers with vexation for want of men. I know you will send them as soon as possible, yet a day appears an age."

Three days later, seventy men arrived, but Perry was hardly grateful and complained instead about their quality—"a motley set of Negroes, soldiers and boys." Had Perry surveyed other ships sailing the lakes he would have learned that one sailor out of every ten was black and that they were serving harmoniously with the white sailors.

Chauncey's rebuke was quick and severe. He wrote that many of the men he had sent were among the best in the fleet, then added, "I have yet to learn that the color of the skin, or the cut or trimming of the coat, can affect a man's qualifications or usefulness. I have nearly fifty blacks on board of this ship, and many of them are among my best men."

Chauncey concluded with a more personal reproach. Perry had complained to Washington that the distance between Erie and Sackett's Harbor was too great for effective communication, and Chauncey thought Perry was angling for his own command. "Would it not have been as well," Chauncey asked pointedly, "to have made the complaint to me instead of to the secretary?"

Perry's nerves had been frayed for weeks. Chauncey's criticism struck him as a reflection on his honor, and he lost his last traces of self-control. The rebuke was the more irritating because of Perry's financial sacrifice. He had refused the "cut," a legal allowance that gave men who oversaw the building of ships a percentage of the money they spent. In turning it down, Perry had said the cut "might influence my judgment and cause people to question my faith." He knew that Chauncey had accepted it.

Perry forwarded Chauncey's letter to Navy Secretary Jones along with his resignation:

"Sir, I am under the disagreeable necessity of requesting a removal from this station." The Navy Department must certainly see that he could no longer serve under "an officer who has been so totally regardless of my feelings."

Jones seemed to recognize the symptoms of exhaustion. His long reply hinted discreetly that Perry was imagining his grievances. Replacing him would serve neither the navy's interests nor Perry's reputation. Complimenting Perry's skill and dedication, the secretary noted, "It is right you should reap the harvest you have sown."

That calming letter arrived before an earlier message from Jones that questioned Perry's request for $4,278 for lead ballast—stone could do the job equally well, Jones wrote—and chastised Perry for complaining about the shortcomings of his crew. Even if Perry's remarks were valid, they might become public, which would make the British bolder and demoralize Perry's current contingent of officers and men.

By that time, Perry had thought better of his hotheaded resignation. He answered calmly, and he reconciled with Chauncey, whose next letter was mild but carried one final sting: "You ought to consider that the first duty of an officer is to sacrifice all personal feelings to his public duties."

During the last ten days in July, Perry watched in frustration as six British ships sailed near his harbor. Their commander was Captain Robert Heriot Barclay, who had arrived to take charge of his country's naval forces. Eight years earlier, Barclay had fought at Trafalgar with Lord Nelson as a young officer and had also lost an arm in the king's service. Meeting him, Britain's Indian allies were impressed by his pluck; Tecumseh called him "our Father with One Arm."

By the end of the month, with Perry's fleet unwilling to accept his challenge, Barclay sailed to a small Canadian village on Ryason's Creek. His destination was just below Long Point at Port Dover, where residents had invited him and his crew to a public dinner. Welcoming the break, Barclay took his fleet to the town.

During the many rounds of toasting, Captain Barclay explained why he had felt confident enough to leave Erie unattended: "I expect to find the Yankee brigs hard and fast on the bar at Erie when I return," he said, "in which predicament it will be a small job to destroy them."

As Perry was discovering, Barclay was right that a sandbar could lock in his ships. One day after Barclay sailed off, Perry moved his fleet toward the lake. Another cadre of seventy men had arrived with a veteran sailing master, and Perry expected to set sail the next morning. From his past calculations, the sandbar that blocked the harbor entrance lay under enough water for his ships to sail over it.

But strong winds had changed the configuration. Now even his smaller ships required lightening their cargoes and then they could barely slip over the sand. But the two brigs, the *Lawrence* and the *Niagara*, at 480 tons each, required nine feet of water, and the deepest point now was only six feet. Perry had a solution, but it depended on his luck holding. He would require good weather and Barclay's continued absence.

To get his biggest ships onto the lake, Perry resorted to scows that were called "camels." He filled with water two of them, each fifty feet long, and positioned them on either side of the *Lawrence*. The crew fastened the scows with heavy timbers that they extended from the ship's portholes. During the next four nights, Perry once again drove his men to exhaustion as they pumped water from the scows to produce a buoyancy that gradually lifted the two brigs over the sandbar.

By the time Barclay sailed back from Port Dover, the *Niagara* was just clearing the bar and slipping onto the lake. With Perry's crew physically drained by their success, Barclay might have attacked the disorganized American flotilla, but from a distance he could not see that the guns were not tied down or that the crew was not prepared for battle. Since the Americans would not be the easy prey he had expected, Barclay chose to sail for Malden and await the completion of the *Detroit*, the new ship that would give him a decisive edge in battle.

For now, Perry commanded the lake. He put his flotilla in fighting order and welcomed Jesse Duncan Elliott, who had risen to captain in the six years since he served as James Barron's sympathetic midshipman on the *Chesapeake*. Elliott had brought one hundred more officers and men, and, although Perry still considered himself shorthanded, the new arrivals could man the *Niagara*.

After watching in vain for Barclay's ships to return, Perry set sail in mid-August for Put-in Bay, thirty-four miles from Malden and protected from seasonal thunderstorms by the lake's many islands.

Perry had signaled Harrison with gunfire that his ships were ready for combat, and he sailed to a peninsula off Sandusky Bay to send out boats for the general and his entourage. On August 19, Harrison braved heavy rains with two fellow officers and their staffs and boarded the *Lawrence* amid a salute from the ship's guns. Calculating that the sight of the fleet would impress his Indian allies, Harrison had brought along a chief named Tarhe—the Crane—and his band of Wyandots.

The Indians swarmed over the ship, poking into every corner, before breaking out in a war dance on the deck. When Tarhe was ferried back to land, he sent three runners to tribes around the British camp at Malden, urging them to clear out before the coming battle.

Harrison, now a seasoned forty-year-old commander, talked with Perry late into the night and slept on board. When he returned to camp, Harrison told his troops about Perry's need for crewmen and asked for volunteers. Three dozen Kentucky riflemen accepted the challenge, though they had never been aboard a ship.

When they arrived on the *Lawrence*, the riflemen inspected the ship as avidly as the Wyandots had done. For an hour, Perry gave them the run of the decks. Then he mustered them into ranks to listen to an officer instruct them in naval discipline and the etiquette of life at sea.

A little after five o'clock on the clear autumn morning of September 10, a lookout at the mast of Perry's *Lawrence* cried, "Sail ho!"

He had spotted British ships heading across Lake Erie. This would be their day for battle, although neither commander would have chosen it. Perry had barely recovered from his worst bout yet of a fever that left him weak from nausea and dysentery. For three days, Perry had seemed near death and could not leave his cabin. His younger brother and most of his officers, including the ship's three doctors, suffered along with him. One doctor speculated that lake water was making the men sick and insisted it be boiled before they drank.

Barclay's hopes rested on his lead ship, which had been fitted hastily with a collection of borrowed guns that had no locks; they had to be fired by snapping pistols over loose powder poured into their torchholes. And Barclay could complain as justly as Perry about the inexperience of his 440-man crews. Since no navy veterans were available on the lake, Barclay had staffed the *Detroit* with soldiers and novice Canadians.

But he could delay no longer. His men were already on half-rations, and back at Malden there was no flour at all and only meager provisions for his horde of Indian allies. The Indian dependents, combined with their own men, meant that the British had to feed thousands of people every day.

Sailing toward the Americans, Barclay knew that the wind at their back gave Perry a solid advantage in positioning his guns at their best range. After the full British fleet came into view at 7 a.m., another two hours passed while Perry tried to maintain that windward advantage. But the slight breeze died away before Perry finally gave the order to move out into open waters. When his sailing master objected, crew members remembered the way Perry had overruled him:

"I don't care. To windward or leeward—they shall fight today."

Then the wind shifted again and gave Perry the favored position, with Barclay's ships about eight miles away.

✻   ✻   ✻

By 10:30 a.m., Perry guessed that firing would not begin until noon. He ordered the midday meal served, together with a double order of grog to fortify the crew for battle. The cost of the rum would not draw another reproach from the Navy Department; grog sold in Erie for thirty cents a gallon. Perry ordered the crew to sand the decks and douse them with water because blood would soon be making the surfaces slick.

Since Perry knew he might not survive, he tied his instructions from Secretary Jones, Chauncey, and Harrison into a bundle loaded with shot. If he were killed, his aides were to drop the packet overboard. Perry also tore up letters from his wife and scattered the fragments through a porthole.

He had planned to let Elliott lead the fleet in the *Niagara*, but when Barclay seemed to be heading the British flotilla aboard the *Detroit*, Perry moved up his own *Lawrence*. By one calculation, Barclay had an edge—more ships, and a total of sixty-three guns to the American fifty-four. But the *Niagara* and the *Lawrence* were the strongest ships on the water, and in tonnage Perry's fleet outweighed the British.

Today would be the first head-to-head match-up between the navies of Britain and America. Chauncey had sent a stark admonition to remind Perry of the stakes: "You ought to use great caution, for the loss of a single vessel may decide the fate of a campaign." The looming battle would not merely determine control of the northern territory, it could spell victory or defeat in the entire war.

The ships sailed at each other in silence, with both crews flying their national flags. To loud cheers from the crew, Perry had also run up his blue banner, "Don't Give Up the Ship."

He moved the *Lawrence* forward aggressively, all sails flying. Elliott was not following behind him, but because Elliott had once been the senior officer on Lake Erie, Perry tended to defer to him and had let Elliott pick his own crew. So far, Elliott's demeanor had been entirely correct, but Perry knew that much of the crew believed that since Perry had no fighting background himself, he owed his superior command to political pressure from Rhode Island's senior senator.

At 11:45 a.m., the *Detroit* fired the first shot from a long gun. It fell short. At 11:50, a second shot smashed into the *Lawrence*. Perry shifted his position and returned fire five minutes later. Elliott's *Niagara*, carrying about one-third of the fleet's firepower, was still far from the action, and Elliott gave no indication of coming nearer. Perry saw that the reach of the *Detroit* guns would tear his ship to shreds if he did not move in closer for his return fire.

Over the next two hours, the *Lawrence* took a disastrous pummeling from the enemy ships. All the while, the *Niagara* and several lesser American ships kept their distance. Great Britain's *Queen Charlotte*, smaller than the *Lawrence* but better armed, sailed in to join the bombardment. Perry kept firing, even as much of his rigging was ripped away.

As thirty British guns poured shot into the *Lawrence*, Perry was left with only seven guns capable of covering the distance. Soon he was down to three. A lieutenant, J. J. Yarnell, his face bleeding from a bad wound, ran to Perry's side.

"The officers of my division have all been cut down," Yarnell reported. "Can I have others?"

Casting about, Perry called for three of his own aides to assist Yarnell. In less than fifteen minutes, the lieutenant was back, with a fresh wound in his shoulder. "Those officers have been cut down," Yarnell said.

"There are no more," Perry said. "Do your best without them."

Yarnell paused to be patched up and took up his station.

Perry ordered the surgeons' assistants to leave the injured to their wounds and come to fire guns instead. When those ranks were also depleted, Perry called down through the skylight, "Can any wounded men below there pull a rope?" Three men crawled up on deck and picked their way through the corpses to answer his call.

By now, Perry himself was manning the *Lawrence*'s last working gun, assisted by the ship's purser and its chaplain.

As the battle began, Tecumseh had paddled out in a canoe across the lake's glassy surface to see whether Henry Proctor's countrymen were braver at sea than Proctor was on land.

Tecumseh's own methodical preparations for battle were being undercut by the aggressive actions of an Indian faction of Southern Creeks called Red Sticks, and the failure to overrun Fort Meigs had weakened Tecumseh's standing among them. He had tried to minimize the siege's importance by calling the Americans "groundhogs" who would have to come out from the wooden shells of their forts sooner or later. When they did, the Indians would triumph as surely as they had over William Hull.

But the Red Sticks were unwilling to wait. An ambush by a band of whites and half-breeds at Burnt Corn Creek in southern Alabama had fired them up for revenge. A few weeks before this showdown on Lake Erie, the Red Sticks had attacked a settlement on the Alabama River named for a longtime settler, Samuel Mims.

The commander at Fort Mims, Major Daniel Beasley of the Missouri volunteers, was one of the men with Indian blood involved at Burnt Corn Creek. He was also another of those careless officers George Washington had deplored. Although cattle herders had reported seeing Indians in the vicinity, Beasley had dismissed their warnings. Sand had drifted against the fort's eastern gates, making them hard to close, and on August 30 Beasley allowed the fort's gates to stay open while he played cards.

All at once, several hundred Red Sticks poured inside, struck down Beasley with a tomahawk as he struggled with the gates, and massacred the white settlers, including as many as a hundred children.

Their assault marked the first time that Indians, without British leadership, had been able to overrun an American fort. In the bloodiest way, the Creek warriors had shown their scorn for Tecumseh's caution.

News from Fort Mims had not yet reached Lake Erie, but Tecumseh's thousands of Indians were already impatient for action and demanding that the British fleet drive the Americans from the lake. For weeks, Tecumseh had been assuring them that the British were not cowards; they were delaying because their big canoes were not quite ready.

Once the firing started on the lake, waters close to the shore grew choppy, and clouds of cannon smoke obscured Tecumseh's view. He could see nothing but black haze and bursts of orange flame around the top sails.

Aboard the *Lawrence*, every gun was now destroyed. Despite the best efforts of the sailing master, the ship was out of control. Forced to act, Perry made an unorthodox decision. He found a small boat that could still float and hauled down the blue banner with James Lawrence's mocking words.

Along with his brother and six other crewmen, Perry rowed back to the *Niagara*. They had to pass near enough to the *Detroit* that its guns could be trained on his boat. But Perry's luck held, and the British shots missed him. Behind him on the *Lawrence*, 80 percent of his 136 men had fallen; fewer than a dozen were left to tend the wounded. As Perry reached the *Niagara*, the wind fell away and the lake was calm.

Climbing aboard, he offered no recriminations beyond taking command of the ship. Elliott congratulated him on his daring in switching ships under fire. Once in a great while — the few instances dated back 140 years — the commander of a devastated ship had taken his flag to another ship and kept on fighting.

Perhaps to make amends for his unhappy performance, Elliott now volunteered — if Perry could spare him — to bring up the other lagging ships to the line of fire. Perry agreed, and Elliott got back into the boat and went to lead forward the fleet's smaller gunboats — the *Somers*, the *Porcupine*, the *Tigress*, and the *Trippe*.

For a moment, firing stopped. As the smoke cleared, Americans on the shore could make out the outlines of the ships but not which side was prevailing. Barclay and his crew had been relieved to see Perry hauling down his banner from the *Lawrence* but had read the wrong meaning into it.

Damaging as the engagement had been for the Americans, the British had barely survived. On his two largest ships, Barclay's captains and lieutenants were either dead or wounded, and he himself had been struck in five places. The severity of his injuries compelled Barclay to quit the deck and turn the *Detroit* over to a second lieutenant.

With the energy of the British crews depleted and their ships badly shot up, they were not prepared to respond when the undamaged *Nia-*

gara came to them with its guns blazing. At 2:45 p.m., Perry fired off broadsides into the bows of the *Detroit* and the *Queen Charlotte*. Neither ship had an experienced sailing master at its wheel, and the two nearly rammed each other. Their awkward position let Perry move in with the *Niagara* for more deadly raking fire.

During that assault, Elliott brought up the smaller boats ready to finish the job. The raw Kentucky volunteers had faced battle without flinching; the equally untested Canadians of the British ships had stood at their positions until they were shot down. On the *Lawrence*, a Narragansett Indian who manned a gun on the forward deck was praised after his death for gallantry, but the British claimed that their own Indian allies had panicked when the first shells burst and had cowered below decks.

After three and a quarter hours of frenzied battle, Barclay acknowledged the odds against him and surrendered his lead ships. The *Lady Prevost* and the *Hunter* followed suit. Captains of two other British ships, the *Little Belt* and the *Chippewa*, tried to escape but American commanders cut them off.

The American losses totaled 30 dead, 93 wounded; the British, 41 dead, 94 wounded.

Perry wanted to accept Barclay's surrender on his own ship even though the ruins of the *Lawrence* were floating aimlessly amid the wreckage of the other vessels. Carrying his blue banner, he was rowed again to the ship. The few surviving crewmen were too stunned by the masses of dead comrades and groans from the wounded to cheer his return.

Barclay's wounds prevented him from leaving the *Detroit*, but his ranking officer came aboard the *Lawrence* in full dress uniform to present his sword. Perry bowed ceremoniously and told him and his fellow officers to keep their weapons. They were impressed by Perry's obvious regret when he apologized for not having a surgeon to offer their wounded.

With the ritual of surrender completed, Perry called for his chief signal officer, Dulaney Forrest, to take word of his victory to William Harrison. During the height of battle, Forrest had been hit by

grapeshot that struck the ship's mast and ricocheted into his chest. He
assured Perry that he was not hurt, only winded, and stuck the dented
ball in his pocket for luck.

From his own pocket, Perry tore off the back of an envelope and
braced it against his hat to write a brief bulletin. He had admired
James Lawrence's inspirational last words. Now he composed another
terse message that would outlive its author.

At Camp Seneca, Harrison waited anxiously to hear whether Perry had
won. If his ships had cleared the way, Harrison intended to redeem
America's honor by moving promptly against Proctor at Malden.
When Dulaney Forrest came rushing up, his news was all that Harrison had wished.

Perry had written, "We have met the enemy, and they are ours."
The inventory that he added was something of an anticlimax: "two
ships, two brigs, one schooner and one sloop."

Tecumseh at the Battle of the Thames

Chapter Eighteen

WILLIAM HENRY HARRISON
(1813)

Before Harrison could chase down Henry Proctor, he had to send a detachment to the lake's shore to receive the 308 British prisoners that Perry's crews had taken. They were to be marched to a detention camp at Chillicothe by a band of Pennsylvania militiamen who had invoked their right not to be sent into Canada.

On board the ships, Perry ordered the dead enlisted men sewn into their hammocks with a thirty-two-pound shot and, at sunset, sent to the bottom of the lake. Bodies of fallen British and American officers were kept aboard while Perry took the fleet to Put-in Bay and then rowed ashore. Robert Barclay could barely stand, but he insisted on attending the memorial. Perry steadied him while the Episcopal service was read and muskets fired in tribute. He promised to parole Barclay as close as possible to the British lines on Lake Ontario.

Meantime, Perry had transferred his flag to the *Ariel* and was allowing himself less than a week to prepare to join Harrison in battle. In his official report, Perry tried halfheartedly to exonerate the behavior of his laggardly second in command: "Of Captain Elliott, already so well-known to the government, it would almost be superfluous to speak." He stretched a point and extolled Elliott's bravery and judgment. But Perry knew better, and Elliott never forgave him for that knowledge.

Perry was homesick enough to ask that Secretary Jones allow him to return to Rhode Island as soon as he could be spared. But first he had to carry the American troops into a climactic battle. He brought Harrison and his staff aboard the *Ariel* to plan strategy and by September 20 had moved the first contingent of soldiers to Put-in Bay. Bad weather and the small size of the ships slowed their progress. For the next three days, Perry ferried more troops, including Kentuckians led by their famous governor, Isaac Shelby.

His men called Shelby "Old King Mountain" because during the Revolution he had fought a battle at that site in western Virginia. His victory had come in 1780, the year Harrison was born. Now, at sixty-three, Shelby had signed up three thousand volunteers, many of them in their teens and new to any sort of discipline. Ohio had also raised a sizeable number of militia, but they were disappointed to be sent home because Harrison had no supplies for them. His expanded army totaled fifty-five hundred men.

For two days beginning on September 25, Perry transported the army to a forward position at Middle Sister Island. Merely the sight of American vessels on the lake could now panic the British since they had no ships of their own to protect them. As Perry sailed near Amherstburg and Fort Malden, Proctor's lieutenant colonel began preparing to evacuate the nearby town of Bare Point.

Despite recent defections, Tecumseh expected to supply the British with as many as two thousand warriors. But many of them had listened when Chief Tarhe's Wyandots returned from inspecting the American fleet and warned the Indians at Malden that Harrison's army would annihilate them; one chief promised Tarhe privately that his men would disappear as soon as the Americans arrived.

Chief Roundhead, however, was unyielding. He said his men were happy to learn that Harrison was "coming out of his hole." They would destroy him.

At his camp on Grosse Isle, Tecumseh received no information from Henry Proctor about the outcome of the naval battle on the lake, but forty-eight hours after the fighting ended, two Indians who had sailed out with Barclay's fleet still had not returned. Tecumseh deplored their absence and then experienced an even greater loss when loyal Roundhead fell sick and died.

It was September 14 before Tecumseh heard from Malden, and then only indirectly. A band of Indians raced to tell him that the British appeared to be tearing down the fort's walls. Proctor had hoped that no scouts would observe the dismantling and had warned his chief engineer to proceed discreetly enough not to alert the Indians.

Proctor's situation was desperate. Only the day before, he had imposed martial law over the western district of Upper Canada in order to ration out his dwindling provisions. Even then, he did not consult with Tecumseh about his obvious intention to retreat up the Thames River.

Sluggish mail delivery prevented Proctor from getting guidance from his superiors; they underestimated his shortage of food and assumed that he was being candid with Tecumseh and the Indians. When news of Barclay's defeat on Lake Erie reached George Prevost, he admitted that Malden could no longer be held. But he assured Proctor that a large supply of gifts—"of the very first quality"—had arrived from England to placate his Indian allies. Those presents would be forwarded as soon as shipping them was considered safe.

By that time, no gifts, however desirable, could undo the effect of Proctor's duplicity. Tecumseh sent runners to assemble his forces at Amherstburg for a council that would confront Proctor about his planned withdrawal.

On September 18, Tecumseh appeared in the large council room in a fitted leather suit and with a plume of white ostrich feathers in his hair. He carried wampum of many-colored beads arranged to tell the story of his people. His eyes were fierce, his voice both angry and plaintive.

"Father! Listen to your children," he began, as he traced the history of his dealings with the British. Two summers ago, they had counseled patience. Then war was declared, and the British told the Indians to bring their families to the fort. They were assured they would want for nothing while the British reclaimed for the Indians the land that the Americans had taken from them.

"Father, listen! Our fleet has gone out. We know that they have fought. We have heard the great guns but know nothing of what has happened to our Father with One Arm."

Now he and his Indians were "much astonished to see our Father tying up everything and preparing to run . . . without letting his red children know what his intentions are."

Tecumseh understood the power of ridicule. Speaking in Shawnee, he conjured up an image of a frightened dog that made his Indian cohorts chuckle. When the English interpreter translated it, members of Proctor's staff joined in the laughter:

"You always told us that you would never lift your foot from the British soil. But now, Father, we see you drawing back, and we are sorry to see our Father doing so, without seeing the enemy. We must compare our Father's conduct to a fat animal that carries its tail upon its back; but when affrighted, it drops it between its legs and runs off."

Tecumseh fingered the wampum beads to refresh his memory of instances that the British had shown bad faith, including the time in 1794 when gates of a British fort had been shut against defeated Indian warriors. If Proctor now considered abandoning his garrison, he should leave behind his arms and ammunition for the Indians to use. "Our lives are in the hands of the Great Spirit. We are determined to defend our land, and if it is His will, we wish to leave our bones upon it."

At that, the Indians in the hall stood up and shouted and shook their tomahawks. Alarmed, Proctor asked for another council in two days, at which time he would respond. The public insults had impressed on him just how far from Malden he could withdraw without destroying his alliance with the Indians. He would return to his base at

Sandwich and plan a retreat to the north and east along the Thames River. Once again, Proctor did not confide that strategy either to the Indians or to his own subordinates.

When Proctor returned for the second council meeting, the atmosphere was poisonous. The Indians had brought their great wampum belt with a figure of a heart woven into its center that symbolized their pact with the British. They intended to cut the belt in two and deliver half to Proctor as proof that their alliance was forever ended.

Proctor asked that Tecumseh be brought to the outer court of the hall, where he spread a map across a table. When Tecumseh appeared, Proctor seemed ready to be forthright for the first time and told his briefing colonel to be frank about the dilemma the British faced.

Here's Amherstburg, the officer began, and here's Detroit and the surrounding country. The American gunboats can now intercept all communication and supplies. Or they can go up the River Thames and cut off any retreat. That is our situation.

Tecumseh listened intently. The British officers found his many questions pointed and shrewd but not unsympathetic. Now that Tecumseh seemed more receptive to some form of retreat, Proctor set out terms that he hoped would be acceptable. British forces would occupy the banks of the Thames near Chatham, he promised, although he had not sent scouts to determine whether that location could be held. His new fort would be away from Lake Erie and yet not too far from Sandwich. He would be moving his two twenty-four-pound guns onto the high ground for defense, and, as an incentive, Proctor promised that gifts for the Indians would be distributed there.

By the time the second council convened, Tecumseh had persuaded the other chiefs to drop their opposition. Now it was Proctor who was vowing to fight to the death. We will mix our bones with your bones, he told the assembled Indians. They remained skeptical. The British seemed willing to fight only because Tecumseh had shamed them into it.

While Proctor was preparing to move up the Thames, Harrison was integrating his troops from Camp Seneca with Shelby's Kentuckians for their march on Detroit. He was also awaiting Colonel Richard Mentor

Johnson, who was riding up from Fort Meigs with the one thousand cavalrymen the Americans needed to pursue Proctor. On their way, Johnson's men had passed the Raisin River, where they found that the Indians had dug up the bleached skeletons of the Kentucky riflemen who had died there in January. The piles of bones, stretching for three miles, fed the fury of Johnson's troops.

Their commander did not need reminders to stoke his own desire for revenge. A prominent War Hawk, Johnson had represented Kentucky in Congress since December 1810. Not formally educated but admired for his direct good manners, he had accused Britain of breaking her promises and inciting the Indians in ways that justified retaliation. The constant atrocities along the Wabash were proof that "the war has already commenced," Johnson had told the House. "I shall never die contented until I see England's expulsion from North America and her territories incorporated with the United States."

Now Colonel Johnson would back up those words by leading two battalions into battle.

As the attack grew nearer, Harrison was tightening discipline. He ordered one man shot after he had deserted three times, and he warned new recruits that they could use the memory of the Raisin River massacre as a spur to battle only until they had achieved victory. "The revenge of a soldier," he said, "cannot be gratified upon a fallen enemy."

Oliver Perry was equally firm in lecturing the crew that would be ferrying the soldiers to the battle site and then supporting them with their ships' guns. "You will not allow a seaman, marine or another person under your command to plunder any articles from any person at this place." He promised that offenders would be severely punished; by that, he meant that they would be hanged.

At 3 a.m. on September 27, Harrison loaded his troops onto Perry's ships. Twelve hours later, he sent his infantry ashore in small boats to a landing about three miles below Malden called Hartley's Point. The American army was now back on Canadian soil. To mark the significance, fifes and drums played "Yankee Doodle" as they marched.

But the troops heard neither cannon nor muskets being fired against them. Their advance party came upon a farm woman who told them that just one day earlier Proctor's army had burned the public buildings and retreated up the river.

If Harrison was relieved to be spared a battle, no sign of it appeared in his truculent dispatches to Governor Meigs. Proctor had upward of three thousand Indians, and with his regulars and militia, he came close to matching Harrison's force of forty-five hundred men. But, Harrison concluded, Proctor had committed "a series of continued blunders."

And yet, Harrison himself seemed in no hurry to catch up with the British army. Entering Amherstburg, he found the charred ruins of Fort Malden, and a resident of the town told the Americans that Tecumseh had just left. He had sat on his horse on a hilltop watching the Americans enter the town and then turned to join the British retreat.

Despite Harrison's warning, many Kentucky riflemen took what they could carry away from the town. He promised that those men would be punished, but he confiscated gratefully the limited stores of green corn and potatoes the British had left behind. From Malden to Sandwich was only a distance of eighteen miles; Harrison's army took two days to reach it. Then Harrison paused for another three days to let Colonel Johnson's mounted Kentucky infantry join him.

When they arrived, Johnson vetoed Harrison's plan to use boats to land his men on Erie's north shore and cut off Proctor's troops with a rapid march to the Thames. Johnson said that his Kentuckians were poor sailors, and Perry agreed that open boats would be hard to navigate through the autumn storms.

Harrison took over the sturdy home of Colonel James Baby, already past headquarters for William Hull and Isaac Brock. By September 30, the British were reported to be gone from Detroit after burning down two hundred buildings. Indians who had deserted from the British had been looting in Detroit, but now they sent emissaries to make peace with the Americans.

Harrison wrote to Secretary Armstrong that he would be leaving a third of his forces to guard Malden and Detroit while he set off after Proctor. Since his ranking officers had also voted against the lake route, Harrison needed to bolster morale for the slog that faced his troops. It would be a hard march, he told the men. But until the British were caught and defeated, "let no man grumble or complain or even think of his wife or sweetheart."

The rain that had begun to fall on the day that the Americans occupied Sandwich showed no sign of letting up. For both armies, with their uniforms soaked through, the roads were troughs of mud. Proctor had been traveling at the rear of his troops, but when they reached the Thames River, he rode in his light carriage to the front and ordered his second in command to set up camp only thirty miles from Sandwich. Later, he claimed that the Indians and their families might have become even more suspicious if the British moved ahead too fast. Because Harrison's men were not in hot pursuit, the British could also take a three-day hiatus.

Proctor's continued absence from his troops troubled Tecumseh. He asked Lieutenant Colonel Matthew Elliott, who headed the British Indian Department, what had taken Proctor away. Elliott's answer was not reassuring: "We do not know what he is gone for."

Once again, Proctor was confiding in neither Tecumseh nor his own officers. He may have been attempting to gather intelligence about the situation upriver, but it was also true that his wife and children had gone with the other civilian evacuees to a settlement another thirty miles away. Although everyone called that village Moraviantown, its official name was Fairfield; it was home to a small group of Indian missionaries who grew corn and worshipped at a chapel set among the sixty or seventy houses on land parallel to the Thames.

With Proctor away from his troops, no progress was made in fortifying Chatham, the site at which he had promised the Indians he would be mixing his bones with theirs.

On October 2, Harrison began to make up for lost time. The mounted Kentucky regiment tore through the sodden countryside as infantrymen ran and slid behind them on roads with little solid footing. By covering twenty-five miles in one day, the Americans at sundown were only nine miles from the Thames. Despite the weather, Oliver Perry had succeeded in bringing the *Ariel* and the *Caledonia* close enough offshore to offer valuable support. But Perry himself was attracted by the excitement of the overland pursuit and had borrowed a white horse to join Harrison.

Their advance party was headed for McGregor's Creek when a local woman warned them that Tecumseh's Indians were planning an ambush. Harrison formed his troops into columns and ordered them to move forward slowly. They easily dispatched the few Indians they came upon, and several Kentuckians returned with scalps.

The Americans were buoyed by the chase. Harrison had set the example by traveling with only one valise and a blanket strapped to his saddle. After covering sixty rough miles in the past three days, he rested at a farmhouse and told his troops to slaughter what cattle they had been tending and to prepare fresh beef for another accelerated march. He would leave all other provisions at the farm, along with those men too sick to go further. He would also detach enough guards to protect Perry's ships, which could travel no farther up the narrow, fast-running river.

As the rest of the army moved forward, Richard Johnson's mounted troops fired practice shots in the air to keep their horses from bolting at the first sound of gunfire. Twenty men rode at the very front of the column. They had volunteered for service in a squad they called the "Forlorn Hope." Their assignment was to charge into the enemy ranks to draw the first fire, and they did not expect to come out alive.

News of the Americans' approach found Henry Proctor away again from his men. His deputy, Lieutenant Colonel Augustus Warburton, had been assuming that Chatham was to be defended, but in any case Harrison's men were now too close, and the British entrenching tools were seven miles away with no wagons to transport them.

Warburton moved his men farther upriver to a position with banks high enough for a possible defense. He sent a messenger to Tecumseh to post his warriors across the river.

Tecumseh would not move. Proctor had promised a stand at the river forks at Chatham, and Tecumseh had been infuriated to arrive there and find no fortifications in place. Chatham had proved to be merely a single hut on a small plantation. The fork in the river was no more than this stream called McGregor's Creek, which ran west into the Thames.

When Warburton rode back to calm him, he found Tecumseh across the river, violently haranguing his Indians. Colonel Elliott came to Warburton in tears and said that something must be done. He would not, by God, stay to be sacrificed to their outraged allies.

The night of October 3 passed fretfully with the British on their bank sleeping with their muskets. Early the next morning, Tecumseh sent Elliott to say that he was taking his warriors to Moraviantown, since that was where Proctor seemed to be headed.

Henry Proctor had reached Moraviantown at nightfall on October 3. When he heard that his rear guard had been set upon and its officer captured, he seemed numbed. His only response was, "Very well." Proctor inspected the town, judged that it could be defended, and went to bed.

His sleep was disturbed by a messenger from Warburton, who insisted on his being awakened to hear that the British were retreating in his direction, accompanied by hundreds of enraged Indians. Proctor protested that he had never authorized such a movement. But then he had sent no instructions at all.

He told the messenger to assure Warburton that he would be rejoining him later in the morning.

In that much, Proctor kept his word. He oversaw the destruction of ammunition and equipment the British could no longer use and then returned to Moraviantown to spend another night with his wife.

Harrison's men were able to salvage some of the arms that Proctor ordered destroyed, including one thousand muskets in a storehouse that the British had tried to burn down. While Proctor was sleeping, Harrison was checking the trenches and barricades he had thrown up at a clearing called by old-time settlers either the Bowles Farm or the Traxler Place. Before dawn on the morning of October 5, Harrison gave the order for the Forlorn Hope to ride out and court fire from Indian hiding places.

As the Americans pressed on in his direction, Proctor had his decision forced on him. He would fight where he stood. His troops were only a few miles downriver from Moraviantown on a road between a woods and the north bank of the Thames. If he did not make a stand, Richard Johnson's mounted men could quickly overtake his troops, encumbered as they were by the wounded and by women and children. But Proctor's formations were badly under strength, each perhaps fewer than 370 men. Those troops left off grousing about how hungry they were to complain instead about the battle site. One officer said it would be "downright murder" to try to fight at such a vulnerable spot.

All the same, the two hundred men from the British Forty-first Regiment took cover in the woods, and the Indians, keyed up for battle, waded into the swamp. One observer described Proctor's deployment as all bustle and confusion.

Once again, Tecumseh was keeping a close watch on the American advance. He and a few chiefs had spent the night downriver at the house of a friendly mill owner so that they could see whether their enemy was marching toward Moraviantown. Tecumseh went galloping out to his troops only after he saw the Forlorn Hope riding ahead of Johnson's mounted regiment. He crossed the Thames by the ford that Harrison's men intended to use and arrived among his braves about noon.

To know how many warriors he could count on, Tecumseh had given each man a stick. When the sticks were collected from the swamp, there were only five hundred. During the past month, Tecumseh had lost one thousand braves. But he and his men considered themselves better fighters than the Americans, and they could take cover behind trees with thick trunks. They could not rely, however, on the cannon that was pointing down the road toward their enemy. Proctor had started in September with an overwhelming array of artillery, but through losses and bad management, he was down to that one six-pounder and no ammunition for it.

After inspecting his own men, Tecumseh went down the British line, shaking the hand of each officer and murmuring in Shawnee some words they took to be encouragement. His remark to Proctor was translated as "Father! Have a big heart!" Later, men would recall Tecumseh's air of melancholy, but at the moment he seemed exuberant about the showdown ahead.

✳   ✳   ✳

The first casualties of the day were predictable. The twenty men of the
Forlorn Hope did their duty too well, riding out to attract an enemy response that proved deadly. Before the engagement had even begun, fifteen were killed outright and four wounded.

When Harrison discovered how Proctor had arrayed his troops,
with gaps in their customary close order, he changed his own tactic.
Consulting with Richard Johnson, he said, "Form your regiment on
the left to fight against the Indians, and I will bring up the infantry and
attack the British."

Johnson sent lieutenants to inspect the swamp, and when Harrison
returned to ask whether he was ready, Johnson said, "I have examined
the swamp and find it impassable."

Clearly dismayed, Harrison thought for a moment. Then he ordered Johnson to pull back his men and act as a reserve.

Johnson answered him with firmness that was not a request. "General Harrison, permit me to charge the enemy, and the battle will be
won in thirty minutes."

The colonel's response bordered on insubordination, and there was
a long silence. Then Harrison said, "Damn them! Charge them!" He
would go to inform Shelby that he had changed the order of battle.

As Harrison rode off, an aide brought news that he had found a
place to cross into the swamp, after all. Richard Johnson made a quick
unauthorized decision. To his brother, James, he said, "Brother, take
my place at the head of the first battalion and charge the British. I will
cross the swamp and fight the Indians with the second battalion."

Officers from both battalions could not miss the exchange—
Richard Johnson had a booming voice—and they listened proudly.
They knew that he was assigning himself the greater risk.

"Brother," Richard Johnson added, to cinch the point, "you have a
family and I have none."

At 2:30 p.m., James Johnson instructed his men to charge through
the British opening fire and engage the enemy at close range. A trumpet sounded. Oliver Perry was riding at his side when Harrison shouted
the charge. In the years to come, Harrison would convey the impression that the strategy had been his, telling listeners that he could not

recall a precedent for what he had been doing but that he'd had faith in Kentuckians on horseback: "The American backwoodsmen ride better in the woods than any other people."

The first Kentucky riders broke Proctor's thin line of regulars and rode on to assail his reserves. As the British fell into small isolated bands, they began to surrender even before they fired another volley. Except for a few Indians and British dragoons, James Johnson had rounded up the entire enemy force on the road without an American fatality.

The skirmish with the British had taken ten minutes—one-third the time that Richard Johnson had estimated. But the Indians kept firing from the swamp. Richard Johnson was hit five times, and his pony ensnared by branches from a fallen tree. Johnson was carrying two pistols and managed to shoot an Indian who was aiming directly for him. After his horse broke free and hauled him out of range, Johnson did not have the strength to dismount. He was pulled from his horse, laid out on the ground, and treated for his wounds.

With his army disintegrating, Henry Proctor gathered together forty dragoons from the rear to race for Moraviantown. Harrison sent a major dashing after him, but with an unorthodox order: Harrison wanted Proctor protected from the wrath of his Indian allies.

When they rushed through Moraviantown, the Americans found that Proctor had not spared time for his baggage. The Kentuckians confiscated his possessions and collected his dispatches so that Harrison could forward them to Washington. As they gathered up the documents, the unschooled Kentuckians marveled at the elegance of Proctor's handwriting.

General Proctor had bolted into the woods and then taken refuge in the swamp. Among the casualties that day were several Indian babies drowned by their mothers because they had heard stories about the way the Kentuckians butchered infants. In fact, the Americans did kill and scalp Indian stragglers, and they looted the missionary houses. They also wolfed down raw vegetables dug up from the back gardens.

Because the battle had been brief, the Americans lost only twenty-four dead, and they counted thirty-five British bodies on the battlefield. The figure for the wounded was twice as high. The Indians took substantial casualties but removed most of their fallen tribesmen.

To both sides, however, only one dead Indian mattered.

When the battle was first joined, Tecumseh's shouts exhorting his warriors could be heard above the tumult. As the gunfire died away and the British began to surrender, there was silence from the swamp. The Indians at last accepted defeat and started to slip away.

What had become of Tecumseh? That he had been killed was the only unarguable fact. The one chieftain with the vision and skill to unite the continent's Indians against American expansion was lost, and irreplaceable. His enemies had feared and hated Tecumseh, but they never doubted that he was a worthy adversary.

One corpse splendidly decked out in plumes and war paint had been left behind. Kentuckians who took him for Tecumseh cut strips of flesh from his back and thighs for souvenirs. But they probably flayed the wrong body; for battle, Tecumseh always dressed simply. When Harrison was shown the mutilated remains the next day, he said its features had been smashed beyond recognition.

As for how Tecumseh died, versions of his final hour began to circulate that day and were still being embellished years afterward. One popular version cast him as the Indian who was advancing on Richard Johnson while his pony struggled to free itself. According to that account, Johnson shot him as Tecumseh was raising his tomahawk. Other men told different stories.

Whatever the truth, triumphing over North America's most celebrated chieftain provided the two commanders with campaign slogans to last a lifetime. When Harrison won a seat in the House of Representatives three years after the battle, he became "Old Tippecanoe." Four years after that, Richard Johnson won an election in Kentucky for the U.S. Senate, and by 1836, his successful campaign for vice president was still being propelled by a bouncy chant from his supporters:

"Rumpsey dumpsey, rumpsey dumpsey! Colonel Johnson killed Tecumseh!"

Jackson faces down the militia

Chapter Nineteen

CREEK WARS
(1813–1814)

S o far, Albert Gallatin's appointment to the peace delegation in Russia had produced only frustration and political embarrassment. The czar had been away from St. Petersburg when the American party arrived, offering the excuse that he was needed with his troops nine hundred miles away in Bohemia. After the Americans had been waiting for two months, however, the true reason for Alexander's absence became clear: The British had rejected his offer to mediate.

Lord Ashburton wrote to Gallatin from London to explain why: Since the dispute between Great Britain and the United States was "a sort of family quarrel," no foreigner could judge it fairly.

Ashburton's patronizing letter added that Russia might be trying to make "a tool of America" and proposed instead direct negotiations in either London or the Swedish city of Gothenburg. Gallatin rejected the slur on the czar's motives and pointed out that ending the war with America would free thousands of British troops to meet the latest threat in Europe.

As he waited for London's next move, Gallatin learned that his opponents in the Senate, by a vote of 18 to 17, had blocked his appointment to the peace delegation even though he was already in Russia. In naming him while Congress was in recess, Madison had hoped that the negotiations would have progressed before Gallatin's nomination came up for a vote. Instead, the Federalists pointed out that Gallatin had been absent as secretary of the treasury since June and could not continue with both assignments.

After much contentious debate, Madison named a new treasury secretary, and the Senate confirmed Gallatin as a minister plenipotentiary and extraordinary, along with an expanded peace delegation that included not only John Quincy Adams and James Bayard, but also Speaker of the House Henry Clay and Jonathan Russell, a veteran negotiator nominated by Madison as ambassador to Sweden.

Gallatin preferred to hold the talks in London in order to prevent the British delegates from claiming that they could not get instructions from their foreign secretary, Lord Castlereagh. But after Russell and Clay stopped over in Gothenburg, Clay opposed leaving that town because the Swedes might be somehow offended. Castlereagh's deputy resolved the stalemate by proposing the city of Ghent in Belgium.

As a private citizen, Gallatin had already made a fact-finding trip to England that convinced him negotiations were not likely to run smoothly. In early June, Czar Alexander showed up in London and confessed to Gallatin that he had made three attempts to intervene with the British, all of which had come to nothing.

Gallatin found, however, that the war seemed unpopular among wealthy Britons. Ship owners suffered from high insurance rates because American privateers were seizing their vessels, and the owners of Britain's large estates were protesting the steep war taxes. But the British ministers seemed to be listening to rumors that the United States was near financial collapse, even on the verge of a slave revolt.

Certainly the popular mood in London favored the jingoes. On stage, hugely successful entertainments featured mock battles between Redcoats and trembling, cowardly American militia. *Gentleman's Magazine* was among the publications that favored taking a hard line in negotiations: "Our forbearance has been despised as weakness," its editor wrote. "If we cannot gain their gratitude for our patience," it was time "to awake in them something like respect for our power."

It seemed inevitable that when the British delegates arrived in Ghent, they would try to drag out the talks as long as possible, convinced that Britain's superior strength must prevail.

Embarrassing proof of that superiority had been resurrected in Albany, New York, when William Hull finally faced a court-martial for his behavior at Fort Detroit.

On January 17, 1814, Hull pleaded not guilty to a charge of treason. He was allowed to cross-examine his officers, who testified to his trembling voice as the British approached and the tobacco-colored spittle running from his mouth. Hull lamented the loss of the documents he said would have exonerated him but acknowledged that he had received "a fair, candid and patient hearing."

The twelve-member court did not agree that Hull had committed treason but found him guilty of neglect of duty and unofficerlike conduct. Two-thirds of the panel concurred in sentencing him to be shot to death.

On April 25, President Madison reviewed Hull's service to the nation during the Revolution and wrote, "The sentence of the court is approved, and the execution of it remitted." Hull was sent home to Massachusetts.

In central Alabama, the heart of the Creek Nation lay near the junction of the Tallapoosa and Coosa rivers and was called "Hickory Ground." The tribes believed that the gods protected the sacred site so powerfully that any white man who dared to enter upon it would die.

In their surrounding villages, however, the Creeks traditionally had been affable to strangers. As early as 1540, one explorer had been welcomed warmly and given the chance to observe daily life. He noted that Creek houses were kept very clean and that each family maintained a second house—a winter retreat with only a small covered entrance so that fires kept the inside as hot as an oven.

British explorers were usually credited with naming the Creeks for the many streams and rivers of their tribal land. When the British began to arrive in greater numbers, they found that the Creeks enjoyed the sport of trading, ready to sign a treaty and then seal the pact with toasts of rum.

Only after the American Revolution had some Creek elders come to doubt whether the British could enforce their treaties. Those tribes chose to throw in their fortunes with the Americans, but when Jefferson's purchase of Louisiana sent more white settlers south, both the Creeks and the neighboring Chocktaws found their lands threatened.

Ten years later, Madison's administration invited favored chieftains to Washington to sign a pact that would allow federal troops to open a horse trail through Creek territory from the Ocmulgee River to the Alabama. But when the secretary of war asked permission for Tennessee settlers to sell their goods in Mobile by sailing down the Coosa River, the Creeks resisted adamantly.

Their spokesman said, "When friends ask for property, we must tell them straight words. If he asks for the waters of Coosa or by land, my chiefs and warriors now present will never say yes. I hope it will never be mentioned to us again."

Tecumseh had paid a visit to the larger Creek towns late in 1812 and whipped up passions with his oratory and by teaching them the hypnotic ceremonial rhythms of the Dance of the Lakes. He also capitalized on nature's phenomena by claiming that a meteor shower and an earthquake were proofs that the gods had endorsed his crusade.

The result of Tecumseh's agitation was not tribal unity but instead a civil war among the Creeks. An early skirmish at Burnt Corn Creek in August 1813 had been followed by the massacre at Fort Mims, and white settlers sent riders to New York to warn of the threat that hostile Creeks now posed throughout Alabama. But the journey took thirty-one days. By the time the messengers arrived, the North was caught up in celebrating Perry's victory on Lake Erie.

The governor of Tennessee was closer to the danger, and he promised aid. But Andrew Jackson, the likeliest general to launch a counter-strike, was still recovering from near-fatal wounds inflicted in a free-for-all with one of his most trusted colleagues.

When his militia was left stranded in Natchez, Jackson had sent Colonel Thomas Hart Benton to Washington to plead for money to get the men home. Benton made that case successfully to the War Department, but back in Nashville his brother, Jesse Benton, became caught up in a feud with a veteran named William Carroll. A native of Pittsburgh, Carroll had come to Nashville to open a hardware store. When his past military service led to his being named inspector in the militia, he claimed that his rapid promotion had made him unpopular.

A remarkably poor shot, Carroll had turned away two earlier challenges to duel on the grounds that his opponents were not gentlemen. Since that excuse did not deter Jesse Benton, Carroll had to accept his challenge. Finding no one to serve as his second, he turned to Jackson.

At first, Jackson declined on the grounds that he was too old. Then he tried to patch up the quarrel. But Jesse Benton refused to withdraw his challenge, and the duel went forward on June 14, 1813. Firing first, Benton inflicted a negligible wound on Carroll's thumb. As he turned and crouched to avoid the return fire, Benton took a shot in the buttocks.

The only serious injury that day was to Jesse Benton's pride. The frontier jokes were raw and unceasing, and when Thomas Benton returned to Nashville, he was chagrined to hear that Jackson had taken part in the debacle. After Benton did not make his usual courtesy call at the Hermitage, he and Jackson exchanged angry notes until Jackson swore to friends that he would horsewhip Tom Benton the next time he saw him.

Early in September 1813, the Benton brothers rode into Nashville, avoiding Jackson's usual haunts and booking rooms instead at the City Hotel. Their paths crossed, however, and Jackson outdrew Thomas Benton and backed him up through a tavern at gunpoint. Jesse Benton slipped behind Jackson and fired. Jackson fell forward but got off a shot that burned the sleeve of Thomas Benton's coat.

In the melee that followed, one gun jammed and a swordcane

broke off, but the only grave wounds were Jackson's. He was carried to the Nashville Inn, where his blood soaked through two mattresses. At first, the Bentons lingered in front of the hotel shouting curses until the crowd's rage sent them escaping from Nashville.

Jackson's doctors pronounced him near death. One of Jesse Benton's slugs had shattered his left shoulder. Another ball had lodged in his left arm, and the doctors wanted to amputate. Fending them off, Jackson muttered, "I'll keep my arm."

Although he gradually recovered strength, when the legislature authorized recruiting more militia to challenge the Creeks, Jackson could not leave his bed for more than an hour or two at a time. But he could write. To volunteers who had followed him the previous year to Natchez, Jackson issued a new call to arms: The victims at Fort Mims "are our brothers in distress, and we must not await the slow and tardy orders of the General Government." Despite his wounds, Jackson announced that he would be joining them.

Arm in a sling, gritting his teeth against the pain, Jackson rode the eighty miles south from Nashville to Fayetteville. After a week preparing his men, Jackson learned on October 11 that the Indians were on the march. He led his men on an all-day, thirty-six-mile trek to Huntsville only to discover that the rumor was false. Jackson combined his troops with a regiment of five hundred cavalry commanded by an able former business partner, John Coffee, and took the twenty-five hundred men to camp at the edge of the hostile wilderness.

Jackson had brought enough provisions for only six days, and dry autumn weather had lowered the Tennessee River until no loaded boats could float downstream. Jackson's men were surviving on a dwindling supply of biscuits and unseasoned tripe. At one point, he had to face down mutinous troops by drawing on a gift for swearing that was widely celebrated. Even when he was feigning a greater fury than he felt, his curses were so inventive and were delivered with such ferocity that few men could withstand them. Now his indignant bombast helped to keep the rebels in camp.

Desperate for supplies, Jackson marched his men to the upper Coosa in late October, pausing to attack an Indian village simply for the cattle and corn that could last them another three days. Even with that short-term relief, his men remained on the verge of defecting. Since he could not give them food, Jackson ordered twenty extra rounds of ammunition for each man and hoped that fighting the Creeks would distract them.

On the morning of November 2, Jackson conferred at Fort Strother with John Coffee, who had been promoted lately to brigadier general. They planned a major attack on the Alabama town of Tallushatchee, thirteen miles from the fort. Jackson intended to destroy the Indian settlement with a force that included friendly Creeks and Cherokees. White soldiers might deride the war paint of their Indian enemies, but among their allies they welcomed the white feathers and deer tails.

One of the Tennessee volunteers preparing to attack was a twenty-seven-year-old sharpshooter named David Crockett. Crockett's grandfather had come over the Blue Ridge from North Carolina and was killed in a raid led by a sworn enemy of white settlers, a Cherokee called Dragging Canoe. Crockett's father, a former constable who ran an inn for wagonmasters, drank heavily and made a practice of beating his sons. When David was twelve, John Crockett hired him out to an abusive Dutchman. The boy managed to sneak home, but after a ferocious schoolyard fight during his first week back, he ran away and spent three rough years as a teamster and farmhand. At nineteen, Davy Crockett had taken a wife — "I was plaguy well pleased with her from the word go" — and settled down with the former Polly Finley and their two sons and a daughter.

Settlers who were streaming into the valleys along branches of the Mississippi insisted that getting rid of the Indian tribes was vital to their security. If it could not be done by treaty, they were demanding force.

Crockett was as outraged as his neighbors by the Red Sticks' massacre at Fort Mims and determined to avenge it. Polly begged him not to leave his family, but he said that if there were no retaliation, the Indians would go on scalping women and children.

He clinched his argument by telling her indulgently, "If every man would wait until his wife got willing to go to war, there would be no fighting done until we would all be killed in our own houses." Crockett signed up for sixty days, which he expected to be plenty of time to punish the Creeks.

But military discipline did not rest easy on him. Crockett admitted that, when provoked, he was inclined to get "wrathy." One commanding officer vetoed a young man Crockett had chosen to join him on a scouting expedition because the recruit did not have enough beard. He wanted men, the officer said, not boys. Nettled, Crockett answered that courage shouldn't be measured by the beard; otherwise, "a goat could have preference over a man."

The tendency of officers to belittle the rank-and-file volunteers—"I was no great man but just a poor soldier"—bred in Crockett a hatred of the regular army.

When his first sighting of Indian movements was discounted until an officer could confirm it, Crockett struggled to contain his indignation. "I kept it all to myself," he recalled, "though I was so mad that I was burning inside like a tar-kiln, and I wonder that the smoke hadn't been pouring out of me at all points."

As Crockett's first battle unfolded, the hostile Creeks were severely outnumbered and driven into a nearby river too deep to cross. Seeing their dilemma, many Indians offered themselves as prisoners. But Crockett counted another forty-six Indians who ran for safety into a house with an Indian woman guarding the doorway. As the Americans approached, she raised a bow, braced her feet against it, drew with all her strength, and sent an arrow into the chest of an American lieutenant. Enraged, his men fired back. Crockett estimated that twenty musket balls blew through her.

Then true retaliation began. "We shot men like dogs," Crockett wrote afterward, "and then set the house on fire and burned it up with the forty-six warriors in it."

Crockett watched with awed admiration as an Indian boy, no more than twelve years old, was shot so near the burning house that "the grease was streaming out of him." The boy's arm and thigh were broken, and yet he was making no sound as he tried to crawl away. "So sullen is the Indian when his dander is up," Crockett wrote, "that he had sooner die than make a noise, or ask for quarters."

Jackson's men killed 186 of the enemy. In desperation, other Indian women had taken up rifles, and 16 of them were among the dead. The Americans lost 5 killed, 14 badly wounded.

Looking over the surviving children, Andrew Jackson came upon a child clutched in the arms of his dead mother. He named the boy Lincoya and sent him back to the Hermitage to live with Rachel and their family. To look after him, Jackson seized a Creek woman as a slave.

Among the Tennesseans, victory could not appease their hunger. They went back to the Indian village the next day, and even though they were repelled by the sight of half-burned corpses, they scavenged through the ruins. Crockett described his fellow volunteers as "hungry as wolves," and when they discovered a potato cellar, they devoured the contents even though the potatoes were covered with charred flesh until they "looked like they had been stewed with fat meat."

Back at Fort Strother, the men learned that the contractors who were paid to send provisions still had not delivered them. They were cut back to a ration every two days of one pound of bacon or dried venison and a quart of corn meal. With the season turning to winter, there was no shortage of cold water.

A new crisis developed when a lone Indian stood outside the fort and shouted Jackson's name. He had come to warn of a threat from eleven hundred of the best Creek warriors, who were poised to strike. Their target was Fort Talladega, which was manned by Creeks friendly to the Americans. When a contingent of Tennesseans rode up to the fort, men called from inside to alert them that the Indians were waiting in ambush.

In the fighting that followed, American firepower carried the day. Jackson could report on November 15 that his men had left 299 Indians dead on the ground, compared with the 15 Americans killed. The result confirmed the Indians' name for Jackson—"Sharp Knife."

Three days later, a failure in coordination resulted in a needless assault against a Hillabee faction of Creeks. General James White, commanding the offensive, overran the astonished tribe and inflicted heavy casualties. Hillabee emissaries had been seeking peace with Jackson, and to them the raid looked like a double-cross. White's victory was further tarnished when other officers learned that many of the Indians his men killed had already been badly wounded at Talladega and elsewhere. Some were shot or bayoneted as they lay on their sickbeds.

From Washington, Armstrong demanded to know why Jackson had not followed up his victory at Talladega. Jackson blamed both White and his own lack of supplies. By now, Crockett and his fellow volunteers were alarmed that the weather had turned harshly cold, and their horses had grown so feeble they seemed about to die. Jackson's officers reminded him that their enlistment period had long since expired. They wanted to go home for fresh horses and warmer clothes before the next campaign.

When Jackson refused, Crockett joined the men ready to disobey him. As they moved toward the first bridge on their route home, they found that Jackson had installed a cannon in their path, flanked by his army regulars.

The rebellious men were equally determined. They had their guns primed and their flints ready. They vowed that if they were fired on, they would shoot their way through the barricade or all die together. As they drew closer to the bridge, Crockett saw Jackson and heard the sound of his men cocking their guns. Crockett did the same.

Jackson knew he did not have troops enough to stave off the mutiny. But with his left arm still in a sling, he grabbed up a musket in his right hand and rode to the front of the angry men. Facing them down, he swore that he would shoot the first man who took another step forward.

As the confused volunteers debated what to do next, two more companies of men loyal to Jackson appeared at the bridge. Amid loud curses and grumbling, Crockett's group returned to duty. But they had made their point. After one more showdown, Jackson agreed to release those men who still insisted on returning home, and they left in droves.

For the next weeks, Jackson stayed on at Fort Strother with the idle and dispirited remnant of his troops. Crockett, who went home for a new horse, headed back to rejoin the fight, but most of the other volunteers, including their officers, claimed that they had already served out their term of enlistment and stayed home.

Crockett was going back, but it wasn't for the eight dollars a month or the forty-cents-a-day allowance he was paid for his horse. Not only did he feel it was his duty to report back to Jackson, he knew himself well enough to admit that he "always delighted to be in the very thickest of danger."

As Jackson fretted at Fort Strother, other militia units from Georgia invaded Creek country from the east and scored notable successes. Jackson himself could do little more than ride out regularly across the rough country between the Coosa and the Tennessee rivers, hoping to hurry along supplies for the fifteen hundred new troops the governor was said to be sending his way.

When the first nine hundred arrived, they were not only inexperienced but again had signed up for only sixty days. Jackson led them immediately to the former battlefield at Talladega, where they were joined by two hundred friendly Creeks and Cherokees.

Setting out in mid-January 1814, they came upon a heavily traveled path that indicated a huge number of hostile Indians had recently passed by. Jackson paused to send out scouts, who reported that a large contingent of Indians was three miles away. They had sent off their women and children and were staging a war dance.

Jackson prepared his troops to expect an attack, which broke over them at 6 a.m. on January 22. With rifles blazing, the hostile Creeks charged a circle of brush fires that Jackson had set. The Indians thought that the flames marked the perimeters of the American position, but Jackson had ordered them built half a rifle shot in front of his position. Their flames illuminated the Indians' silhouettes and allowed the Tennesseans to pick them off from a safe distance of fifty yards.

The tactic led to the killing of about 40 Indians, which caused the others to run off. With daylight, Jackson followed along to their camp and shot down another 160 braves.

Despite being untested, the newest Tennessee volunteers had stood their ground. Jackson wanted to follow up their victory with an attack on the Indian encampment at Emucfau, but he found the position too strongly fortified to overrun. Although fighting outside the settlement had gone well for the Americans, Jackson was impressed again by the courage of the Creek defenders.

Along the march back to Fort Strother, the Tennessee troops ran into a second assault by Creeks who had taken the American retreat as a sign of weakness. Jackson's situation looked desperate until his men dragged their single six-pound cannon to the top of a hill. There, the one regular army officer among them used it to turn the battle. Several of Jackson's officers were killed or wounded, but Indian casualties ran far higher.

After twelve days away from Fort Strother, Jackson returned to camp in a mood to celebrate. To Major General Thomas Pinckney, commander of the Southern Department, Jackson's self-satisfaction was justified. Pinckney reported to the War Department that without Jackson's "personal firmness, popularity and exertions," the Indian War in Tennessee might have been abandoned.

On the same day that Jackson reached Fort Strother, William Weatherford struck at Camp Defiance, a fort near the town of Chattahoochee. A respected chieftain of mixed Scots and French Creek ancestry, Weatherford stood just under six feet, his skin almost white, his features clear-cut, including a sharply beaked nose. His brother John had chosen to pass as white, but William took the name Red Eagle and lived as a Creek. He had remained friendly to settlers until the battle at Burnt Corn Creek provoked him to join the attack on Fort Mims.

Weatherford deplored the massacre that followed. After that day, his naturally solemn manner seemed to deepen into a depressed awareness of the pain that might await his people.

The Creeks had one hope for reversing their losses. A British colonel had promised that if they would just hang on against the Tennesseans, his army would soon be coming to their aid. It was a conscious lie. No British troops were heading their way, but the colonel hoped to keep the Americans tied up while Britain struck elsewhere.

With the Creeks committed to fight, Jackson was equally set on a stroke that would defeat them decisively. In the spring of 1814, tightening discipline in his camp for the campaign ahead, he decided to make an example of a recent recruit, a seventeen-year-old farm boy named John Woods. Woods's local commander had promised his light infantry regiment that their three-month service would allow them to return home in plenty of time to tend their crops.

During a stint on guard duty, Woods got permission to leave his post briefly to pick up a ration of food and a blanket against the cold. As he finished eating, Woods dropped bones in the dirt. When an officer ordered him to pick them up, Woods refused. The confrontation escalated until Woods took up his rifle and threatened to shoot anyone who tried to arrest him.

Jackson was still smarting from the earlier threat of desertions. He ordered Woods put on trial, and on March 14 saw him convicted of mutiny and sentenced to death. As a militia general, Jackson was not expected to invoke the death penalty, and he was inclined to commute the sentence to flogging Woods, branding him with the letter D, and drumming him out of the corps.

But Jackson wondered whether he had been too lenient. He was hearing taunts that it took half his army to make the other half obey him. Afterward, he said that he paced his tent for two sleepless nights.

On the morning of Woods's execution, Jackson ordered the army to watch as the boy was surrounded by a squad of regulars with .70-caliber rifles. Then, after Jackson had ridden beyond the sound of their gunfire, Woods was shot to death, the first militiaman to be executed since the Revolution. Jackson hoped it was a lesson the men would not forget.

Less than two days later, he launched his new campaign against the Creeks.

Jackson sent three thousand recruits south along the bank of the Coosa while he waited for another fifteen hundred men coming with provisions. Leaving guards behind to protect those supplies, Jackson led the rest of his men on a march through sixty miles of forest to the point where William Weatherford and his Creeks were understood to have massed for a desperate final stand.

On the morning of March 27, Jackson reached the Tallapoosa River and a sharp bend in the shape of a horseshoe. Within the bend, the Indians had surrounded one hundred acres of land with a wall of pine logs. Rising to heights of eight feet, the wall was designed to let the Indians fire on their enemies from two directions.

Davy Crockett was not among the Americans poised that day outside the Creek fortress. With a crippled horse on his hands, he had waited for the reinforcements to arrive and then applied for a furlough and gone home again: "I began to feel as though I had done Indian fighting enough for one time."

Another young man, who did fight for Jackson at Horseshoe Bend, had grown up loving the Indian life, but his heart lay with the Cherokees, not with the Creeks. Samuel Houston had run away at sixteen from his family's large brood of children to be adopted into the household of an amiable Cherokee named Chief Oolooteka. White settlers called him "John Jolly."

When his older brothers came looking for him, young Houston — already six feet tall, with fair skin and blue eyes — told them that he liked "the wild liberty of the Red Men better than the tyranny" of his family. When he finally returned after a year away, his mother bought him a new suit, but she could not tame his spirit. Among other offenses, Houston was fined five dollars for playing a drum so loudly that he disrupted a militia meeting.

After another row with his brothers, Houston went back to Chief Oolooteka, whose Cherokee name happened to translate as "He Puts the Drum Away." Oolooteka gave Houston the name of Colonneh — "the Raven." With the other adolescent braves, Houston learned the tribe's sports, its theology, and its erotic Green Corn Dance. The Cherokees, who practiced polygamy, did not consider chastity a virtue.

Houston never forgot his days of "wandering along the bank of streams, side by side with some Indian maiden, sheltered by the deep woods . . . making love and reading Homer's *Iliad*." Cherokee wooing involved an appeal to the gods as well as to the maiden herself. In the last stage of courtship, a suitor was required to declaim, "Your soul has come into the very center of my soul, never to turn away."

Only a need for money could compel Houston to leave that idyllic life. He had gone occasionally to the Tennessee town of Maryville to buy powder and shot for his Indian friends and trinkets for his sweethearts. There he had run up a debt of a hundred dollars with no way to pay it.

Lacking any discernible qualifications except his constant but untutored reading, Houston opened a school and took good-naturedly the jibes that he had earned his degree from "Indian University." When the Creek War came, Sam was barely twenty. He asked his mother's blessing, and she gave him a gold ring and the family musket. Sam then went to collect the recruiting bonus of one silver dollar.

He felt no pang about the fighting in store for him since his Cherokee family had remained loyal to the United States. He would be fighting the British and their treacherous Creek allies.

Jackson planned to trap those Creeks inside their fortress while his two six-pound cannon, reinforced with a new four-pounder, fired into the encampment from a hill eighty yards away. He sent word that Weatherford should send his women and children to safety across the river and waited until that had been done.

At 10:30 a.m., Jackson ordered his cannon to fire, but over the next two hours they did little damage. As a distraction, Coffee's friendly Creeks swam across the Tallapoosa and burned the canoes of the besieged Indians.

At that, the American infantry and the east Tennessee militia stormed the walls. Their major, Lemuel P. Montgomery, was instantly picked off, but Sam Houston leaped down, flashing his sword to keep the Creeks at bay. An arrow struck his thigh, and Houston called to a nearby lieutenant to pull it out. The barb was deeply lodged, and when it came free, Houston was left with a bleeding slash that sent him to a surgeon. Hastily patched up, he was lying on the ground when Jackson rode past and ordered him to stay out of further combat. But Houston had vowed that the town of Maryville would hear of his exploits, and he limped back to the line.

Inside the barricade, the Americans were fighting hand-to-hand with the Creeks, who resisted with the same tenacity that had impressed Jackson during each earlier engagement. Even with a sword at his heart, a Creek warrior would refuse to surrender.

At three o'clock, Jackson called a halt and offered clemency for any Indian who accepted his truce. But as his announcement was being translated, a cloud passed overhead. Since Creek medicine men had promised that the Great Spirit would send a sign from heaven that their enemies would be swept away, the favorable omen emboldened them for another furious but doomed assault. Looking on, Houston called the American response a slaughter. The tally counted 560 Creek bodies behind their barricade or immediately outside. A hundred badly wounded warriors were burned to death as fires swept the site, and another hundred were killed at the river. Apparently, only forty Creeks had escaped. Another sixty were too seriously wounded to run, and they were taken prisoner with 370 women and children.

At dusk, rain was falling when the last resisters holed up in a covered stronghold deep within a ravine. Jackson asked for men to overrun the position. At first, no one volunteered. Then Houston ordered his company to charge. Five yards from the redoubt, he took a ball in the right arm and another that shattered his right shoulder. As his musket fell from his hand, he urged his men forward.

They had seen enough carnage for the day and refused. Houston climbed back out of the ravine and collapsed on the ground. That last Creek resistance ended when Jackson ordered the stronghold set on fire with flaming arrows.

Doctors were sure that Houston had lost too much blood to be saved and turned their attention to wounded men with a better chance of surviving. Left alone, not expecting to last the night, Houston said afterward that he had passed the darkest hours of his life.

But in the morning, his eyes opened to the desolation around him. He was carried sixty miles by litter to a fort where he could begin his slow recovery. After two months, he was jostled in another horse-drawn litter and deposited near Maryville with his family. By then, Houston was barely more than bones. His mother said she recognized him only by the trace of a familiar expression in his eyes.

With Weatherford's defeat, the Creeks had to accept the ruin of their nation. A thousand Indians fled to Florida for refuge on land under Spanish control. But a dozen chiefs came to a new American base named Fort Jackson and purposely built near the sacred Hickory Ground. The Creeks were met with rigid demands. They could either move their tribes to a northern part of the territory that was covered by a long-standing treaty or they could migrate north of a boundary where Cedar Creek met the Coosa River.

Jackson asked the other chiefs whether Weatherford had gone to Florida. They said he was only thirty miles away. They expected him to show up at Fort Jackson in the next few days to surrender.

Jackson assured them that he would prefer to take him prisoner. Weatherford was to blame for the massacre at Fort Mims, Jackson said. He wanted to punish him.

After the chiefs passed along that threat, Weatherford decided to surrender immediately and trust to Jackson's mercy. He set out on horseback that same night and reached the fort the next morning. Thrown across his saddle was an impressive buck he had killed along the way.

Weatherford assured the sentries that he was only another Creek chieftain come to surrender and bring Jackson a peace offering. But when he identified himself at Jackson's tent, the general launched into a furious harangue:

"How dare you, with the blood of women and children murdered at Fort Mims upon your head, ride up to my door?"

Weatherford was braced for the invective and replied calmly. "As to that, General, let me say that I did all I could to prevent the killing at Fort Mims. But you know how hard it is to restrain Indians at such a time."

Jackson was unmoved. "You were their leader and ought to be held responsible for their acts. You richly deserve hanging!"

Weatherford looked over to Major John Reid, who was writing

down the exchange. "General Jackson," he said in a low voice, "I am not afraid of you or of any man. I ask nothing for myself. You can kill me if you like, now or at any other time. I am in your power."

He had come instead to beg for the Creek women and children who were starving in the woods. He asked that Jackson send search parties to bring them back to camp. He would tell Jackson where they were hiding.

"I am done fighting," Weatherford concluded. "The Red Sticks are almost all killed. If I could fight any longer, I would not be here. But please send for the women and children. They never did you any harm.

"Now you can kill me if you like, or if the white people want it done."

A crowd of officers and men had gathered at the tent, and some called out, "Kill him!" To Weatherford, Jackson said, "Come into my quarters," and told the crowd to disperse: "You are not needed just now."

Inside, Jackson offered the terms he had extended to the other chiefs. If he refused them, Jackson said, Weatherford would be given safe conduct beyond the lines. But afterward he would be hunted down and, if captured, killed.

Weatherford accepted the amnesty. He said he would see to it that his people agreed to the conditions; Jackson promised to send out search parties with food for the Creek women and children.

As Weatherford moved to leave, Jackson offered him a whiskey.

"General," the chief said, smiling ruefully, "I am one of the very few Indians who do not drink liquor. But I would thank you for a little tobacco, if you have it."

Jackson gave him a bag of tobacco with an ornamental pipe. Then he pointed to the rifle Weatherford had left leaning in a corner. "Take it along," Jackson said. "You will need it to hunt with."

Before the summer was out, Weatherford proved better than his word. Jackson, who had been rewarded with a commission as major general in the regular army, spent six weeks at home at the Hermitage before being ordered by Washington to return to Alabama immediately and negotiate a lasting treaty. He found Weatherford and the other ranking chiefs waiting for him at Fort Jackson.

The treaty terms, which had been sent south by Secretary Armstrong, were especially punishing for the Creeks who had remained friendly to America during the conflict. Those chiefs resented being penalized for the Red Sticks' rebellion, and they were vocal now in opposing permanent banishment from their traditional hunting grounds.

During the early negotiations, Weatherford sat by silently, calculating the disastrous effect of the uprising upon his people. When the war began, the Creeks were among the richest tribes on the continent. Now, after losing three-fourths of their braves, they were the poorest.

During a recess in the talks, he lectured his fellow chieftains:

"You people can no longer fight," he reminded them. "How foolish it must be, then, for you to keep on talking." Weatherford said he was ready to accept Jackson's orders. "All of our talk is like wind whistling through the tops of tall trees."

Despite that burst of realism, it took intense pressure before the Creeks agreed to give up twenty-three million acres of land across Georgia and central and southern Alabama. The swath amounted to more than one-half of the original Creek Nation.

The treaty, as signed on August 10, 1814, called for the Creeks to accept a reservation bounded by the Coosa River to the west and the Chattahoochee to the east. The northern boundary would adjoin traditional Cherokee territory; a southern line was drawn through Fort Jackson.

Jackson was candid with the chiefs about his reason for sending them north. He wanted to keep them away from British agents, he said, and from the Seminole tribes in Florida.

The friendly faction of Creeks was granted partial compensation for their immense loss of property. Federal agents estimated their damage at $195,417.90, but Congress did not approve the first $85,000 until three years after the treaty; appropriating the remainder took another thirty-six years.

After Jackson's initial outrage, Weatherford's character had come to impress him. To shield him from families of the massacre victims at Fort Mims who were demanding vengeance, Jackson arranged a special exemption that allowed Weatherford to take his family and slaves to property that the chief owned near the junction of the Alabama and Little rivers.

In time, Weatherford began to call on Jackson at the Hermitage and to train his own high-spirited horses alongside those of the general who had vanquished his people.

Dolley Madison

Chapter Twenty

DOLLEY MADISON
(1814)

Throughout the Revolution, state militias had held a romantic place in the American heart. Instead of a professional force modeled on the arrogant Redcoats and posing the same risk to democracy, the United States would rely on the nation's farmers, sailors, and shopkeepers to step forward in time of danger and volunteer to protect their country.

In the fall of 1813, William Harrison had endorsed that view at a dinner given in his honor. He denounced the growing sentiment for increasing the size of the regular army and offered instead a ringing toast to the militia of the United States.

In the following months, however, Harrison's reputation was becoming tarnished and his victory on the Thames was looking less decisive. He made his base at Amherstburg and sent the majority of his
men to join an attack on Montreal. But Armstrong and James Wilkinson, brought north and promoted to major general, bickered constantly over tactics and the proposed campaign fell apart. Instead, the
British, under an aggressive new commander, Lieutenant General
Gordon Drummond, surprised Fort Niagara on the night of December
19, 1813, and went on to set fire to small settlements along the American side of the Niagara River.

More damaging personally to Harrison was the way he was undercut by Armstrong, who disliked both him and his style of warfare.
When Armstrong provoked the Senate into investigating Harrison's lax
accounting practices in the spring of 1814, he became enraged by the
"most malicious insinuations" against his honor and resigned his commission.

Andrew Jackson had displayed his own preference for the militia at
Natchez by refusing to enlist his volunteers in Wilkinson's regular
army. His antagonism to regulars had surfaced again during the early
days of the Creek campaign, but after the militia's threats of mutiny
and desertion, Jackson was coming to value the regular army for its fidelity and professional training.

In Washington, since Madison had been swayed by James
Monroe's misgivings and had not backed Armstrong's call for conscription, enlistment in the regular army ran far below the authorized
strength, even though direct threats to the president himself were growing closer to home.

Commanders like Oliver Perry could testify that the presence of a
professional crew might be the decisive factor at sea. The *Chesapeake*
had been captured in June 1813, when its raw recruits could not
match sailors from Britain's *Shannon*, who boarded the ship and won a
bloody hand-to-hand battle. In the contest for merchant vessels, statistics told the story: The U.S. Navy captured 254 British ships, but American privateers took another 1,345.

Locked in its crucial war with Napoleon, Britain had spared only a token force of some twenty ships to harass America's eastern seaboard. To fan the dissatisfaction with Madison's policies, they spared the New England states at first from their blockade and concentrated instead on the coast around the Delaware and Chesapeake bays, punishing local support for the war. By May 1814, however, Britain had defeated Napoleon and could send more than one hundred ships to extend its blockade along the entire Atlantic coast.

The effect was as disastrous as Jefferson's embargo. American imports and exports dropped from a peacetime high of $114 million to $20 million. At a time when the war was demanding a rise in expenditures, customs revenue fell by more than half. With the 1814 congressional elections looming, the Federalists seemed to be gaining strength.

On April 1, 1814, Madison astounded his party by calling for a repeal of his latest embargo. Critics said he was making too great a concession before peace talks had even begun. They worried that he was giving the Federalists proof that his administration was vacillating and inconsistent. But John Calhoun was able to overcome last-ditch opposition from a bloc of his own Republicans and carry the repeal for Madison.

For Britain, the time had come to use her navy for a decisive blow. Survivors of the triumphant army that had defeated Napoleon in France were summoned to Bordeaux and loaded aboard ships headed for America. Some of the older enlisted men chafed at the prospect of another campaign. They had looked forward to going home or at least to idling in conquered French towns.

Others, like Lieutenant George Gleig, a veteran of the battle for Bayonne, welcomed the prospect of more warfare. Gleig's father, an Anglican bishop, had been pleased when the boy won a place at Oxford in Balliol College, but George had soon dropped out to enlist as an ensign in the Eighty-fifth Regiment and sail for Spain. Now, after a year in the service, Gleig was only eighteen, and his regiment had not suffered the same degree of casualties as other units. He knew that if he was not sent into battle again his pay would be cut in half and his prospects for promotion would be slight.

Beyond those practical considerations, Gleig and his comrades had heard about the Americans' burning government buildings in York. They agreed that no enemy "had ever proved more vindictive or more ungenerous." They intended to fight so gallantly that London could dictate the terms of a peace treaty.

Sailing from Bordeaux to Bermuda took almost seven weeks. Gleig was able to avoid boredom because he and his good friend, Captain Charles Grey, were assigned to the *Diadem,* a smaller ship but one stocked with a good library. Gleig and Grey shared an ambition to write a book about their adventures and carried at all times a small notebook with a pencil attached.

Throughout the fleet, officers' wives had come along to share in the inevitable victory, and they planned regular diversions at sea. A high point came on the night of July 19, when the commander of the flagship *Royal Oak* invited all of the officers to a gala. Arriving in his best uniform, Gleig found the ship's cannon removed from their portholes to make more room for guests. The deck had been hung with flags to mark off a stage and lights were suspended from the rigging. Gleig was dazzled by the brilliance.

The ship's officers then performed a comedy, *The Apprentice,* and a farce, *The Mayor of Garrett.* Gleig marveled that a warship deck, which had seen so much tragedy, should be the scene of light-hearted laughter. When the performance ended, seats were removed and dancing began. With the women aboard outnumbered, most men danced with each other.

The music continued past midnight. Then the *Royal Oak* hoisted a blue light as the signal for the other ships to reclaim their officers.

In Bermuda, the fleet took on fresh water, food, and ammunition. It sailed for America on August 3 and reached the coast eleven days later. Sir Alexander Cochrane, who had taken command, gave his junior officers and crew no hint of their destination.

For months before the British navy was due to arrive in force, Rear Admiral Sir George Cockburn had been conducting raids along the eastern seaboard with a ruthlessness and glee that disturbed even his fellow officers. When Cockburn—whose name was pronounced "Coburn" by the British and as it was spelled by the Americans—led one typical assault, another officer wrote a bitter account:

British troops entered a Maryland village, accompanied by Cockburn and Sir Peter Parker, a first cousin of the poet Byron and considered to be the handsomest man in the British navy. Most residents, who were civilian workers in the local factory, had escaped, but Cockburn came upon three young women who had stayed behind to protect their home.

He told them that he already knew that their father was a colonel in the state militia. In exactly ten minutes, Cockburn said, he intended to burn down their house. Until then, they could remove what they most wanted to save.

Cockburn laid his watch on a table.

While the sixteen-year-old threw herself at Cockburn's feet and the other sisters appealed to Parker, the admiral stared at the minute hand of his watch.

When the time was up, Cockburn cut short Parker's protests and ordered his men to bring in fireballs. Parker was weeping along with the women as their house went up in flames.

Similar scenes had been repeated up and down the coast—British sailors hurrying ashore only long enough to plunder a town and set it on fire before returning to their ships. Disgusted British officers regarded Cockburn's tactic as ancient barbarism rather than modern warfare between civilized nations.

The British command often used the American destruction of York to justify their behavior. But even before that battle, Cockburn had been boasting that he would burn down the President's House. After presiding over a harsh raid north of Annapolis in the town of Havre de Grace, Cockburn announced that the next time he went ashore he planned to bow to Dolley Madison in her drawing room and then set fire to her home.

When that was relayed to her, Dolley wrote to a friend that she was not trembling at the prospect but did resent Cockburn making his threat personal. Since the British had neither land troops nor artillery positioned around the capital, however, Secretary Armstrong dismissed any danger from their fleet.

In June, Armstrong had overridden Major General John Van Ness, commander of the District of Columbia's militia, when Van Ness pointed out the peril that British ships would pose on the Patuxent River. "What the devil will they do here?" Armstrong demanded. "No! No! Baltimore is the place, sir. That is of much more consequence."

Monroe and Secretary of the Navy Jones agreed that an attack on Washington was highly unlikely.

Now, with Cochrane's fleet approaching, Britain would be able to make good on Cockburn's threat. An American sea captain claimed that British ships were on their way to devastate Washington, but Madison seemed alone in taking his warning seriously. At a meeting of cabinet officers, Armstrong led the derision.

Madison ignored them and acted on his intuition. He asked Maryland's Federalist governor, Levin Winder, to add fifteen hundred militia to the defense of Fort McHenry outside Baltimore and to send two regiments from the regular army to Norfolk. Madison created a new military command to include the District of Columbia, Maryland, and northern Virginia. To guarantee the governor's support he put in charge Levin Winder's nephew, thirty-nine-year-old Brigadier General William Winder.

In making the appointment, the president overlooked the fact that the previous year General Winder had been captured and paroled by the British during one of the frontier battles near Niagara that followed Harrison's victory over Tecumseh and Henry Proctor.

Amid his forebodings, Madison was momentarily heartened when Richard Rush, now his attorney general, showed him a letter from an old political foe. John Adams wrote that he did not know who could prevent the President's House and the Capitol Building from becoming British headquarters, but nonetheless the time had come for winnowing—"the real military genius and experience have been neglected and chaff, froth and ignorance have been promoted."

Even so, the former president reminded Rush that times had been "infinitely more difficult and dangerous" during the Revolution. Madison chose to focus on that somberly consoling thought. He told Rush that "opinions from such a quarter had the smack of rich and old wine."

* * *

Armstrong was coming to understand that if he were wrong about an attack on Washington, he could expect a torrent of blame. His relations with Madison were frayed, however, and he had opposed the appointment of Winder. James Monroe had recently agreed that Washington must be protected, but Armstrong regarded that change of heart as being dictated solely by politics. For months, Monroe had been pushing for Armstrong's dismissal and, in fact, had written to Madison the previous December that Armstrong did not have the skills or energy the times required. "My advice to you therefore is to remove him at once."

The role of America's militia again became urgent. Winder wanted four thousand men called up for as long as three months, but Armstrong resisted paying them when they were not fighting. Citing a recent small victory when the Americans had faced down the British on the Patuxent, Armstrong decided that he could count on the militia being rounded up on "the spur of the occasion" and then sent into immediate battle. On July 12, the secretary told Winder to avoid unnecessary call-ups and to request men only "in case of actual or menaced invasion of the District."

Armstrong's direct order left Winder reluctant to defy him. When the British sailed again on the Patuxent, Winder called for three companies of militia but sent them home before he could be sure about the enemy's intentions. Winder now claimed to agree that turning out troops rapidly was as effective as keeping them in the field. Besides, by being home, they could attend to their private affairs.

Winder settled on the town of Bladensburg, four miles northeast of Washington, as the gathering point for Maryland's militia. He sent their arms and supplies there and late in July inspected regular army detachments from the Thirty-sixth and Thirty-eighth regiments. On August 1, Winder set up his own headquarters with a staff consisting of one aide and a topographer. He had been promised one thousand regulars and four thousand militia, but they were not yet on hand. Secretary Armstrong was offering no advice and had not issued a call for more cavalry or riflemen.

* * *

On August 16, 1814, more than twenty British ships entered the two hundred miles of Chesapeake Bay, carrying several thousand land troops. The fleet separated, half sailing up the Chesapeake toward Baltimore, the other headed to the Potomac.

Joshua Barney, an American commodore, described the enemy's movement to the Navy Department, along with reports that the British were bragging that they would destroy America's ships in time to dine in Washington the following Sunday.

The Navy Department ordered Winder to summon Maryland's third militia division and directed General Van Ness to set up camp near Alexandria with two brigades from the District of Columbia militia. But Van Ness, angered by Winder's claiming authority over the militia, resigned his commission rather than comply. Yet, when Winder instructed all other Maryland militia to send half of their men, his call was answered smartly. On paper at least, Winder now had seven thousand men to resist a British landing force estimated at forty-five hundred. But Winder had no talent for organizing them, and they were drifting aimlessly around Bladensburg.

Of Winder's defending army, only nine hundred were regular army enlistees. Another four hundred were cavalry. And almost all of his twenty-six cannon were small six-pounders.

As the Americans struggled to form into effective ranks, the British made their most threatening advance up the Patuxent, this time with launches and barges. Captain Barney was ordered to destroy the American flotilla rather than let its ships fall into British hands.

George Gleig stepped ashore the afternoon of August 19 and met no resistance as he marched his men through small towns along the Patuxent River. At Nottingham, he found its four short streets entirely deserted but with bread still baking in the ovens. His men came upon a store of rich tobacco in a nearby barn instead of the maize and wheat they expected. Gleig authorized them to seize the crop in the name of His Majesty, King George III.

Rumors spread that American gunboats were about to attack, but Gleig heard instead the heavy explosions of Barney's men blowing up their own squadron.

The British marched ten miles down good roads from Nottingham to the village of Marlborough, where they stayed the night and enjoyed delicious peaches from the many family orchards. The following afternoon, they met the first determined opposition, but after a heated exchange the American riflemen gave way.

The British column moved to a fork in the road, with one branch that led to Alexandria and the other to Washington. The troops themselves now understood that Washington was their destination, but they were marched down the other path until the American scouts who had been watching turned their horses to alert the people of Alexandria.

At Bladensburg, Winder was trying to compensate for his lack of planning with bursts of feverish activity. He spent a sleepless night reconnoitering with a cavalry unit, then led a contingent of troops to monitor British progress up the river. While their destination was still in doubt, their advance was inexorable. Winder turned back his men to avoid an unequal contest.

General Robert Ross, the British commander, had been reluctant to attack Washington and thought a reprieve had come when Admiral Cochrane ordered the troops back to their ships. Since Barney's fleet was now destroyed, Cochrane disapproved of carrying through with a raid.

Primed for glory, Cockburn persuaded Ross that to back down now would be a stain on their honor. The American militia could never stand up to the British regulars. Ross brooded throughout the night before he said, "Well, be it so. We will proceed."

During the recent anxious weeks, Dolley Madison had confided to Gallatin's wife, Hannah, that knowing the enemy was within twenty miles of Washington made her long to have her family safe in Philadelphia. But she was determined to stay with her husband. By late July, she could still take comfort in the small number of the British marauders.

Meantime, Dolley was grateful for any news of her son—her "precious boy"—who remained with the peace delegation in Europe. His mother preferred to consider his long silences as proof that he was "engrossed by a variety of objects in Europe, which are to enlighten & benefit you for the rest of your life." To spare Payne worry, his mother assured him that "nothing has occurred either public or private worth writing since my last"—although she did admit that not far away British soldiers were stealing and destroying private property.

As Dolley chose to keep calm, Madison received bad news from the Niagara frontier. Fifteen thousand British troops had landed in Montreal and seemed poised to take control of the region around Lake Ontario. And riding out of Washington, Monroe had been scouting enemy positions around the city and returning with reports that were equally gloomy. Yet, with Ross and Cockburn moving so slowly, Madison could believe that the British might not be headed his way, after all.

Then British intentions became unmistakable. Even as their troops proceeded toward the capital, however, the Americans were not firing on them. One British soldier compared their progress to strolling through open fields on a summer picnic.

Madison ordered most government records moved out of Washington. He assured Monroe that nothing more could be done to help Winder and that the crisis would be "of short duration."

To raise morale among the defending troops, Madison decided he should tour their ranks. British soldiers liked to believe later that he had abandoned his capital out of fear. But Madison, while no battlefield hero, knew where his place was during a military crisis and was riding to the front lines as commander-in-chief.

Dolley sensed Madison's concern for her. She assured him that she was not afraid to stay alone in the president's mansion and that her only fear was for him and for their army's success. As Madison left, he told her to take care of herself and to protect his official documents.

British agents had already tried to infiltrate the administration in order to make off with any useful papers. At the first word of danger to the capital, a number of linen bags had been filled with government correspondence, and carts and wagons were loaded to haul them the thirty-five miles from Washington to an empty house in Leesburg.

*   *   *

With Secretary Jones, Attorney General Rush, and three aides, Madison rode to the east branch of the Potomac. Their party crossed the river and traveled southwest of the President's House to the Maryland encampment, where they met with Winder and Armstrong. Madison spent the night of August 22 in a nearby house.

The next morning, he wrote a note in pencil to reassure Dolley that he was among troops "who are in high spirits & make a good appearance." Since the British lacked both cavalry and artillery, he and Winder expected them to be retreating soon to their ships as they had done before.

Later that same morning, however, Madison spoke with two British deserters who told him that General Ross might have more ambitious plans. The British ranks were stronger than they had first appeared, and they could be coming to destroy Washington. Madison sent Dolley a more urgent note, instructing her to be ready at a moment's notice to call for her carriage and drive out of the city.

That night, Madison slipped home to spend a few hours with her before riding back to Winder's camp. Dolley was hearing that residents of Washington were complaining bitterly that Madison's lack of planning had left them vulnerable. She resolved not to leave the President's House until her husband came back and they could travel together.

At an early hour the next morning, the British marched in the coolness of dawn through woods and under boughs that protected them from the rising summer sun. But when they left that leafy shade, the boiling heat became overwhelming and dust from their path flew up to choke them, and many soldiers began to lag behind. Lieutenant Gleig, who could barely breathe, felt he was suffering more in those few miles than at any other time in the army.

To let stragglers catch up, their officers called a halt by a stream and told the men to wash themselves down. They knew a battle was looming because they were passing fields with smoking ashes and scraps of food, and the road bore fresh marks of hooves and army boots. If the Americans had just bivouacked there, there was sure to be a battle before dark. Gleig thought every British soldier was holding his breath.

After another hour's march under the harsh sun, even some of the most physically fit British soldiers were prostrate from heat and dust. As noon approached, a stir of activity in the distance announced the presence of their enemy two or three miles ahead. Turning a corner in the road, the British spotted the American army for the first time. Gleig's reaction reflected the relief they all felt:

"Country people who would have been much more appropriately employed in attending to their agricultural occupations, than in standing with their muskets in their hands."

But Gleig admitted that the Americans had chosen a commanding position, with their left flank at a branch of the Potomac and their right flank among a thick growth of willows and larch beside a deep ravine. Gleig judged the river to be about as wide as the Isis at Oxford. It flowed between the Americans on a hillside and the town of Bladensburg. They had posted riflemen at the front of their infantry, and on the nearest slopes twenty pieces of artillery were aimed at the advancing British.

The Americans now slightly outnumbered their enemy. Winder estimated his strength at five thousand; the British were attacking with about forty-five hundred.

In positioning his troops, Winder had tried to anticipate the British targets and yet take into account the local political sensibilities. He knew, for example, that the people of Baltimore would not tolerate his stripping their city of its defenses in order to protect Bladensburg. Instead, Winder had called out a brigade of militia from the District of Columbia and another five hundred or six hundred from Alexandria. But when five hundred more Virginians arrived, they came with neither weapons nor equipment.

Confusion was still rife. Men from one unit left their posts at Bladensburg before Winder could call them back to defend the town. An aide informed Madison that Armstrong was not consulting with Winder and that the secretary of war was predicting the American militia could never stand up to British regulars. Madison gave Armstrong explicit orders to assist Winder in any way he could, adding that he had ridden out especially to remove any question of authority.

Exhausted and aching from his fall into a ditch, Winder had started on the one-hour ride to the bridge at Bladensburg. Armstrong followed, but when Madison joined them, he learned that Armstrong still had not met with Winder, who seemed on the verge of collapsing. Armstrong said he would confer with the commander if Madison gave him a direct order. Madison issued that order, but because he was riding a balky and unfamiliar horse, he could not draw near enough to hear what Armstrong and Winder were saying.

All the while, dubious intelligence and questionable advice were pouring into the American camp. When Francis Key, a popular Georgetown lawyer, showed up to suggest where Winder should be posting his troops, the general fobbed him off on a subordinate.

As the morning ended, Winder felt he had done all he could. Watching the British creep forward from behind houses and trees, he waited for the moment when enough of them were massed in one place to provide a target for his artillery.

So far, the British scouts were still encountering no resistance. As Winder surmised, their officers told the men to break ranks as they entered Bladensburg and take shelter behind trees and houses. But the only way to advance further would be to cross a bridge that ran from the center of town directly into the middle of the American position. Speculating among themselves, the British soldiers expected a prolonged halt that would give their exhausted comrades at the rear a chance to catch up.

Instead, they were ordered to jog forward in double-time toward the head of the bridge.

The first Redcoats were met only by scattered gunfire. But when the bridge was swarming with them, the nearest American two-gun battery opened up. Its first rounds swept through an entire British company, and American riflemen picked off others from their hiding places in the woods. Rather than retreat, British soldiers pushed forward, trampling over the fallen bodies of their comrades to get to the other side of the stream.

The Americans had not expected that daring infantry charge. Much of their own front line broke and ran, abandoning the two cannon in the road. Seeing the Americans running away pumped up the courage of the British light brigade. The men threw off their knapsacks and broke formation to rush what remained of the American front line. At that, Winder's troops unleashed volleys from their other cannon so intense that the British were driven back to the riverbank.

But in the end, America's militia were no match for British regulars. Once their line was broken, the militia could not be rallied again, and another British regiment joined the chase behind Americans dashing for the woods. Robert Ross was left with possession of the battlefield and ten of the twenty American artillery pieces. Watching the Americans vanish, he thought it would be madness to follow them.

Fighting that afternoon had lasted the three hours from 1 to 4 p.m. The Americans lost 26 dead and 51 wounded. General Ross reported 64 dead, 185 wounded. But the outcome had laid open the road to Washington.

Despite the disparity in casualties, the battle did nothing to raise Lieutenant Gleig's opinion of the enemy. He admitted that the Yankees did seem to be fine marksmen. After all, they had grown up with rifles on their farms. But their skill had counted for little because a militia could never stand up to regular troops. Gleig had learned that success in battle depended on acting together, quickly and with full confidence in one's fellow soldiers. Serving in a militia could never instill that essential discipline.

Dolley Madison had risen with the sun on Wednesday morning to stand at the window with her spyglass, watching for her husband and his aides. She became increasingly anxious as she glimpsed instead only gangs of American soldiers wandering about aimlessly. Dolley thought that the men seemed to have neither the weapons nor the spirit to defend their homes.

Most of her friends had left Washington the previous night, and an army colonel who had been stationed with one hundred men to guard the President's House departed with them. Yet, despite the chaotic scene outside her window, Dolley was sure the Americans would prevail.

Jean Pierre Sioussat, the butler they all called "French John," had remained behind with her. Born in Paris, Sioussat had cast up in America during the Jefferson years and worked for the British minister before hiring on with the Madisons. He came now to ask Dolley's permission to disable the cannon at the front gate and to lay a train of gunpowder that would blow up any British soldiers who entered the mansion.

After she turned down his suggestion, Dolley worried that she had not made French John understand why, even in war, certain tactics were not permissible. She may have owed her scruple to her Quaker upbringing, although Dolley had once assured a cousin, "I have always been an advocate of fighting when assailed." That philosophy explained why she kept an old Tunisian saber within reach.

By 3 p.m., the sound of cannon fire told Dolley that there had been fighting near Bladensburg. She jotted down her swirling thoughts for her sister, Lucy:

"Mr. Madison comes not; may God protect him! Two messengers, covered with dust, came bid me to fly."

One of them was James Smith, a free Negro, riding fresh from Bladensburg. Waving his hat, Smith was shouting, "Clear out! Clear out! General Armstrong has ordered a retreat!"

But Dolley would wait for the president. In the meantime, she ordered another wagon filled with the mansion's silver and other valuables and sent it off to the Bank of Maryland for safekeeping. With the British so near, though, she knew the wagon might fall into their hands.

A family friend, Charles Carroll from Georgetown, rode up to insist that Dolley leave. Still, she delayed, on the chance Madison might yet arrive. She asked Carroll to remove the front seats from his carriage to make room for her piano. As for her closets filled with gowns and turbans, Dolley was resigned to leaving them behind.

As Carroll fidgeted, Dolley insisted on waiting even longer so that she could protect a large portrait of George Washington attributed to Gilbert Stuart; Dolley was determined that the British not be allowed to defile Washington's image. But she knew Carroll was getting annoyed with her as minutes passed and it became clear that the picture's frame was so tightly mounted that it would have to be unscrewed from the wall. Dolley admitted that time was too short for that slow process and ordered the frame broken and the canvas lifted out.

The portrait had been hung high enough on the wall that the servants needed a ladder to reach it. When French John cut the canvas from its outer frame with his pocket knife, he found it nailed to a light wooden outline called a stretcher.

"The precious portrait," Dolley assured Lucy, "was placed in the hands of two gentlemen of New York for safekeeping." One of the men, a banker and family friend named Jacob Barker, worked with his companion to free the painting from the tacks holding it to the stretcher. They rode off with it to a nearby farmhouse.

Dolley could stall no longer. She concluded her letter in a rush. "And now, dear sister, I must leave this house, or the retreating army will make me a prisoner in it, by filling up the road I am directed to take. When I shall again write you, or where I shall be tomorrow, I cannot tell."

General Ross had left on the battlefield the two brigades that suffered the greatest casualties, and he was leading the third brigade, his reserve unit, on a leisurely march to Washington. As he crossed the Eastern Branch Bridge, Ross satisfied himself that the Americans had retreated past Georgetown and ordered most of his men to pitch camp a mile and a half from the capital.

Instructions from George Prevost in Canada had called for revenging York by razing all public property. Ross protested that his service in France had never required destroying property, but when his orders from Canada proved inflexible, he agreed to take a company of men to burn down the President's House and the Capitol Building.

That would be a last resort. Ross sent out an aide to locate a ranking American official with whom he might negotiate a cash payment in return for sparing the city. His emissary found no one, and had Madison been available, he would have spurned the offer.

It was 8 p.m. by the time Ross, Cockburn, and two hundred guards rode into Washington. From a house along their route, a sniper picked off Ross's horse. In retaliation, the British fired rockets into the house and burned it down.

But a greater blaze on the horizon was the handiwork of the Americans themselves. Captain Thomas Tingey, who had run the U.S. Navy Yard for the past fourteen years, sorrowfully gave the order to set fire to its every structure, down to the paint shops. Tingey completed the sacrifice by torching the *Argus,* a sloop ready for battle, and the nearly finished frigate *Columbia.*

Rowing to a safe berth in Alexandria, he could see more flames from the direction of the Capitol Building.

When squads of British soldiers converged on the Capitol, they formed a line, raised their rifles, and fired into its eastern windows to discourage any sharpshooters lurking there. Breaking down the doors, a search party ransacked the building for souvenirs; Cockburn pocketed a small Treasury report.

Groups of three men chopped up the woodwork, strewed gunpowder over the floors, and set off small fires. To speed the destruction, they fired rockets into the Hall of Representatives and shattered the hundred squares of imported English glass-plate at the roof. Ross watched with regret as flames consumed the 740 books that had been bought during Jefferson's administration as the core of a congressional library.

Razing the Treasury followed, then the city's arsenal and a barracks built for three thousand troops. Discovering a frigate and several smaller brigs and armed schooners that had been left behind, the British soldiers reduced them to ashes and dumped their shot and grenades into the river. The ball of one small-caliber cannon was fired into the mouth of a larger artillery piece to blast out its breechings.

By now, flames reached so high they could be seen in Baltimore thirty-four miles away. Marching by that flickering light, the two brigades that Ross had kept behind now moved unchallenged toward Washington, down a road that glowed red from the reflection of the fires. But they spotted American soldiers on distant hills and understood they might have defeated their enemy's troops but they had not annihilated them.

*   *   *

The British raiding party moved toward the President's House, speculating over the whereabouts of its residents. As they rode by, a man named William Gardner watched with his family from an upstairs window of their house on Pennsylvania Avenue.

Spotting them, Ross and Cockburn doffed their hats. "I hope, sir," Gardner called to Cockburn, "that individuals and private property will be respected."

"Yes, sir," Cockburn replied. "We pledge our sacred honor that the citizens and private property shall be respected." But he advised Gardner to stay in his house and then asked, "Where is your president, Mister Madison?"

Gardner said he did not know but guessed that he was far away. Cockburn told him that the British held Commodore Barney prisoner.

"So I have heard, sir," Gardner said. "And that he is badly wounded."

Yes, Cockburn agreed, badly wounded. "But I am happy to inform you, not mortally. He is a brave man, and depend upon it, he shall be treated with the greatest humanity and kindness."

Ross spoke up to agree, "Yes, sir, he shall be taken good care of."

But now they must be off to pay a visit to the president. They bowed to Gardner and said good night.

Because Dolley Madison's appealing qualities were known to the British commanders, Ross swore later that if she had stayed behind, he would have shielded her. "I would rather protect, than burn, a house which sheltered so excellent a lady," he said.

But as they entered the mansion, Cockburn took particular relish in sitting down at Dolley's table, where forty places had been laid out when Madison had thought his cabinet and military staff might be coming to supper. Wine, ale, and cider were waiting in coolers.

Pouring himself a glass of wine, Cockburn drank to "Jemmy's health." For more than a year, Cockburn had taunted citizens around the Chesapeake Bay that they had Jemmy Madison to thank for the war's destruction. "It is he who has got you into this scrape," the admiral would say. "We want to catch him and carry him to England for a curiosity."

Admiral George Cockburn

After the other British officers had drunk freely of Madison's wine—which they pronounced very good—they discovered a minia-ture painting of Dolley and carried it off as a prize of war. Cockburn took for himself one of the cushions on which Dolley had sat and made a ribald joke about it.

When their amusement was ended, the troops lighted rags soaked in oil and hurled them through the mansion's windows. The building became enveloped in smoke, and flames shot up toward the gathering storm clouds.

On that first night of the invasion, a rain extinguished many of the fires. The next morning, the mayor of Georgetown sent out a flag of

truce and won assurances that the British would spare his city. Cockburn taunted him by promising to give them the protection their president had failed to provide.

Nine hundred of Ross's troops marched to the State and War departments and set them on fire. Most documents had been removed
from those offices, but it took a personal plea from the superintendent
of the Patent Office to spare his files.

The previous night, with his own scores to settle, Cockburn had
asked directions to the offices of the *National Intelligencer*. Its editor,
Joseph Gales, Jr., was known for printing what Cockburn called "tough
stories" about him. As he prepared to burn down the building, two
neighborhood women prevailed on him not to risk setting their own
houses on fire. Cockburn listened jovially and agreed to return the
next morning and wreck the offices instead.

True to his word, the admiral appeared after dawn with a gang of
British soldiers who threw the printing presses and type galleys into the
street. "Be sure that all the 'c's are destroyed," Cockburn told his men,
"so the rascal can't abuse my name any more."

Nightfall on August 25 brought one of the worst storms in Washington
history. As gales uprooted trees and blew the roofs from houses, thirty
British soldiers were buried in rubble. The winds were strong enough
to lift British cannon off the ground and carry them several yards.
Civilians had to tie their horses to their largest trees. When the torrents
of water beat down, they were more like cataracts than showers of rain.

The British deputy adjutant general urged Ross not to evacuate the
city on such a night, but Ross wanted to move out before the Americans could regroup. He sent soldiers through the storm to enforce a
curfew that had begun at 8 p.m. and kept residents inside until sunrise
under penalty of death. Ross did not want to alert the remnants of the
American army to what he was planning.

With the streets cleared, Ross's troops retraced their march to
Bladensburg, not speaking above a whisper until they were out of the
city. The storm passed after another brutal two hours, and their way
was illuminated by a bright moon. When the British passed the battle
site again, they did not pause to bury their dead. Nor had Ross found a

way to transport his wounded men out of Washington. He left them behind in hopes that the Americans, even with their capital a blackened shell, would be merciful.

His faith was rewarded. Commodore Barney, having been received respectfully by Ross and Cockburn while in their custody, insisted on humane treatment for the British prisoners.

Ross's men were so exhausted by the last two days that whenever their column halted, they sprawled down on the road for a moment's sleep. By 7 a.m., Ross could be sure no Americans were chasing after them and let the men stop until noon to rest and eat breakfast. They covered the next thirty-five miles at such an easy pace that it took them three days to come in sight of their ships.

Along the Potomac, the only impediment to the British fleet was Fort Washington on the Maryland side of the river. Armstrong had refused to fortify it, since he had never believed the British would attack the capital. Now when the British approached the fort with two frigates and five other gunships, its commander, a captain named Charles Dyson, blew up its 3,346 pounds of gunpowder and abandoned his post without a fight. Dyson was dismissed from the service later for making no effort to use Fort Washington's heavy cannon to repel the fleet.

In any case, residents of Alexandria had never trusted the fort to protect them. They sent a delegation to ask what the British would demand to spare their city, and the terms they were offered were steep: The town must surrender all armaments, all available food and drink, and the merchandise from every shop. They were given one hour to make their decision.

The Alexandrians felt they had no choice. After three days of lading, the British sailed off with 16,000 pounds of flour, 1,000 hogsheads of tobacco, and 100 bales of cotton. The wines and cigars they took were valued at $5,000. Alexandria's mayor consoled himself with the enemy's good manners. He wrote to his wife, "It is impossible that men could behave better than the British behaved."

News of Alexandria's capitulation provoked an angry reaction throughout the neighboring region. Secretary Jones summoned naval officers from Baltimore, including John Rodgers and Oliver Perry, and told them to gather all sailors they could find. They were to head for the Potomac and stop the British fleet from reaching Chesapeake Bay.

The British outgunned the American ships, however, and sailed to safety. They intended to combine their scattered forces to produce an armada of fifty British ships. Then they would move the ten miles to the Patapsco River and make Baltimore their next target.

As the nation's third-largest city, Baltimore would be a prize worth capturing, even though its wealthier citizens had disappeared into the countryside with their valuables. All that stood in Britain's way was a small fort built on a narrow inlet at the city's harbor.

The fort had been named for a secretary of war under President Adams before Adams fired James McHenry for his political ties to Hamilton.

After leaving the presidential mansion, Dolley Madison had expected to meet her husband at Charles Carroll's house in Georgetown. Because the American militia had charged off in every direction, she was sent instead to a safer spot near the Great Falls called Wiley's Tavern.

When the night's rain caught Dolley's carriage in its downpour, a servant went ahead with a lantern to light the road while Dolley remained inside and indulged in vengeful thoughts far removed from her Quaker upbringing. She told herself that if only she could have had a cannon mounted in every window, she would have set them all blazing and never left the premises. Alas, soldiers who should have stood their ground had run away even before she did. Dolley acknowledged that being free of fear was probably "unfeminine." But instead she was furious, and she grieved for her country.

Dolley was also exhausted. Rather than push on to the tavern, she stopped to spend that first night at a friend's plantation called Rokeby. Madison had been riding through Falls Church toward Wiley's before he also stopped at midnight at a clergyman's house about a mile away from Rokeby.

The next morning, with the British troops in full retreat, Dolley and her servant, Sukey, rode on to the tavern and spent an anxious day waiting for Madison. At Wiley's, the mood was rude and boisterous, which gave rise later to highly embellished stories about Dolley being reviled and blamed for the ruin that Madison's war had visited on the neighborhood. A local woman confirmed that there had been jeers, but she said that, when Dolley seemed even more miserable than the others were, "our bitterness relented."

Madison arrived at dusk and left again at midnight to join in rounding up the scattered troops. He promised to send a message when it was safe for Dolley to return home. Reaching the Potomac, Madison found that the storm had left the river too treacherous to risk crossing. He waited on the bank with his companions until morning before moving into Maryland. Madison traced Winder to fifteen miles northwest of Washington; arriving there, he learned that the general had already left to join in defending Baltimore. By that time, Madison had been riding for eighteen hours, but he pushed on another ten miles to a Quaker pacifist who was opening his house to refugees and wounded soldiers.

The presence of the president of the United States brought villagers from nearby Brookville to gape at the sight of Madison and his small retinue getting ready to sleep on beds spread across the parlor. They found the president grave but tranquil and not dispirited.

With word the next morning that the British had returned to their ships, Madison wrote to Dolley that he was going back to Washington and presumed that she would do the same. About 5 p.m., he headed out to the capital to see what damage the invasion had done.

Even before the British raid, the city had been a contrast of squalid huts among the magnificent public buildings. Workmen had competed for jobs that might give them a good wage for a short time but left them afterward in sickness and poverty. Now even the capital's few enclaves of splendor were destroyed.

Picking his way past dead horses on Capitol Hill, Madison grieved for the building itself. The pillars of Representatives Hall were broken and cracked, the dome Madison had admired for its beauty and artful carvings had crashed through to the basement.

Cockburn had tried to keep his pledge to William Gardner about private property. One British soldier caught stealing was shot and two others were flogged with one hundred lashes. But Americans had scrambled through the ruins of the public buildings to carry off what they could and had broken into deserted private homes looking for plunder.

On the charred and vacant buildings, other citizens were painting bitter graffiti about their leaders. One pointed out that George Washington had founded the city after a seven-year war with England; "James Madison lost it after a two-year war."

With looting rampant, the invasion had sent prices soaring. The cost of household necessities had tripled overnight, firewood going up to twenty-five dollars a cord and hay to fifty dollars a ton. Madison ordered cannon installed along the Potomac in case the British intended to return. He was dismayed to hear that the explosion on Saturday night had come from Captain Dyson's blowing up Fort Washington.

But at least his wife was safe. When Madison stopped at her sister's house on F Street in Georgetown, he found that Dolley had borrowed a carriage and got there before him. The sight of her coming back to town had heartened the residents who had heard rumors that the British were planning a second invasion, and they cheered Dolley's progress along her route. Monroe said afterward that if the Madisons had delayed their return even as little as twenty-four hours, Washingtonians might have been inclined to surrender as abjectly as the people of Alexandria had done.

Armstrong's return provoked a different reaction. His effigy had been hanged from a gallows with a note, "Armstrong the Traitor," and one tactless remark attributed to him was widely circulated. Armstrong was quoted as saying that despite the recent damage, Washington would still "make as good a sheep walk as before, and was never fit for anything else." Armstrong had never bothered with tact, and his insult was taken as proof that he wanted to move the capital north again.

A delegation from the army complained about the secretary to Madison and swore that "every officer would tear off his epaulets if Armstrong resumed their command." They added that Monroe would be an acceptable replacement. The president assured them that Armstrong would be issuing no further orders.

That evening, Madison braced for the sort of showdown he dreaded. In their meeting, he repeated to Armstrong the threat the officers had made. Armstrong called the uprising in the ranks "altogether artificial" and suggested it had been orchestrated by his enemies. But he acknowledged that he probably had to leave town and offered Madison a choice: Either Armstrong would resign outright, or he would depart from Washington on the pretext of visiting his family in New York.

Madison felt he could not accept his resignation in the middle of a crisis. But he did respond sharply when Armstrong continued to justify his strategy about Washington. The president reminded him that Armstrong had never suggested a single precaution and that whatever defensive steps had been taken Madison himself had recommended.

Armstrong left for Baltimore, where he immediately published a defensive and sarcastic rebuttal to the accusations against him, concluding that the poor performance of the American troops at Bladensburg had caused the burning of Washington. On September 4, the day after his letter appeared in the Baltimore *Patriot*, Armstrong sent Madison his resignation. He remained convinced that Monroe and his allies had undercut him. To a friend, Armstrong wrote, "With men of such imbecility, I can no longer connect myself."

No one came to his defense. Navy Secretary Jones described Armstrong to his wife as someone "whose nature and habits forbid him to speak well of any man." But now that Armstrong was out of office, Jones added, "he is full of venom but without a sting."

Jones himself came under fire, however, for his order that the Navy Yard be burned, and he resigned a week after Armstrong.

Monroe took over the War Department temporarily and persuaded Madison to make the appointment permanent. In political exile, Armstrong was counting on a congressional investigation to clear his name. But the eventual report merely described the invasion of Washington in detail without assessing blame for it.

The day the British first menaced Washington, Frank Key, the Georgetown lawyer, had ridden forty-five miles out of the city before he could find two wagons that were not commandeered by the army or hired by other panic-stricken residents. Key loaded up the wagons with his documents and personal property; his wife was already at an inn some distance away, and their children were in Fredericksburg with his parents.

When he rode out to assess the situation at Bladensburg, Key discovered that Ross and his men were following only ten minutes behind him, and he joined the American retreat. After the battle, however, as the British fleet sailed past Annapolis, Key sought out John Skinner, the United States agent assigned to arrange prisoner exchanges. Key was pressing for the release of a good friend, Dr. William Beanes, a Federalist who claimed to be opposed to the war.

When the British had stopped at Beanes's house before Bladensburg to chart their course of action, he had offered them tea and accepted money for the supplies and horses they requested. But after the battle, General Ross recalled the episode and decided that Beanes and several other Americans had betrayed his trust by pretending to be neutral. When Ross ordered the men seized, Beanes was given hardly the time to change out of his nightclothes.

His companions were quickly released after Maryland's governor appealed on their behalf. But Ross could not forgive what he took to be Beanes's treachery. The sixty-five-year-old doctor was kept in custody in a ship's forecastle for two weeks, guarded by contemptuous sailors who did not let him change his clothes.

Now, with Madison's permission, Key had come to make another plea. He and Skinner sailed up to the British fleet in a sloop flying a white flag and were received by Admiral Cochrane and his officers aboard the HMS *Tonnant*. Ross and Cockburn were still incensed by Beanes's behavior, but Key had brought letters from wounded British prisoners testifying to the doctor's skill and kindness after the fighting at Bladensburg.

It took persuading before Ross granted that only Beanes's admirable compassion justified his release, "not from any opinion of his own merit." Ross then informed Key and Skinner that they could not return Beanes to American soil until the planned attack on Baltimore was under way. They had seen too much of the British fleet's munitions, and Ross would not risk another betrayal of his plans. He ordered them transferred to the frigate *Surprize*, commanded by the admiral's son, Sir Thomas Cochrane.

The British had taken advantage of balmy days in early September to prepare their assault on Baltimore. On Sunday evening, September 11, the day that Jones resigned as navy secretary, the British fleet was observed at North Point, fifteen miles overland from Baltimore.

The next morning Ross was taken ashore, where he and his officers commandeered an early breakfast from a nervous American farmer. When their host asked if he should prepare supper for their return, Ross said, "No, I shall sup in Baltimore tonight—or in hell."

By 7 a.m., Ross and Cockburn were back at the head of nearly five thousand army troops, including two thousand marines and an equal number of sailors. They had landed at daylight on North Point, each man carrying eighty rounds of ammunition and enough cooked meat to last three days.

By now, Baltimoreans had snatched up anything they could carry and hurried to fill every inn north of the city. The American command, the Maryland militia, and the Pennsylvania volunteers had all moved toward North Point and set up three lines of battle. After Bladensburg, they had some idea of Ross's tactics.

They also knew how to spot him. They had passed the word among the ranks, "Remember, boys, General Ross rides a white horse today." Two sharpshooters, Daniel Wells and Henry McComas, vowed that instead of retreating with their comrades they would bring him down. They expected to lose their own lives but at least, they said, they would be selling them dearly.

Ross's tactics did not disappoint them. He sent out light companies from three regiments and his entire Eighty-fifth, along with a company of marines and a battalion described as "disciplined negroes." Behind those 1,100 men, his horses pulled six field pieces and two howitzers. Ross's second line comprised 1,400 men, the third another 1,450.

The British were halfway to Baltimore before they encountered an American militia force about three-fourths their size. When the gunsmoke cleared, the British had held the field at North Point but had lost 340 men to the Americans' 250 dead.

Among the British bodies was their commander—killed by two bullets from Wells and McComas. As they had predicted, they paid with their own lives when Ross's men took particular aim at them.

Ross lived long enough to murmur, "My dear wife," as he was being carried by litter toward the beach. Grieving troops prepared his body to be sent to Halifax with a rum cask as his coffin. One of his men lamented, "It is impossible to conceive the effect which this melancholy spectacle produced throughout the army."

When Colonel Arthur Brooke assumed Ross's command that afternoon, Admiral Cochrane forwarded instructions that the Canadian administration expected severe retaliation for "disgraceful outrages" by the Americans along the Niagara frontier. Cochrane said that if Ross had lived to receive that note "he would have destroyed Washington and Georgetown." But he added that Ross's replacement could use his own judgment about accepting a "contribution" to spare Baltimore's property.

Brooke pressed forward in two hours of fighting that ended when the Americans fell back. The British consolidated their forces and seemed to bivouac on the battlefield, but they intended to slip away before dawn.

By 3 a.m. they were gone. The jubilant Americans made no serious attempt to pursue them.

As the British fleet sailed toward Baltimore, Frank Key had been dining nightly with officers of the *Surprize* and found them ignorant and vulgar. But he granted that the circumstances might explain their violent prejudice against everything American.

The day before the battle of North Point that took Ross's life, Cochrane had declined, again with a smile, to free his three captives, but he did let them return to the sloop that had brought them so they could watch the assault against Fort McHenry under their own flag.

Francis Scott Key

He sent along British sailors and marines to guard against their making signals to the shore.

The Americans had sunk enough vessels to block the narrow channel into Baltimore and hold the British fleet at bay. Cochrane was positioning his ships to send bombs and rockets against the fort, where several companies of the American army and volunteer artillerymen were waiting for the barrage to begin.

Flying over McHenry was an immense flag commissioned by its commander, Major George Armistead. He had insisted that its size be thirty by forty-two feet, in the same defiant spirit that John Hancock had once signed his name in bold letters to the Declaration of Independence.

"It is my desire," Armistead said, "to have a flag so large that the

British will have no difficulty seeing it from a distance." A Baltimore widow sewed the flag to his specifications and charged the army $405.90.

The British launched their attack at about 7 a.m. on September 13. The fort fired back, but its shells fell short. Then a British bombshell destroyed a twenty-four-pounder at the fort's southwest corner, killing the second in command and wounding several of his men.

Cochrane could see the consternation that his hit had caused and ordered three bomb ships to move closer. His aggressive maneuver turned out to be a godsend to Armistead. Ordering his cannon fired from every position in the fort, he had driven the British back to their previous moorings within half an hour. The British rocket ship *Erebus* was so damaged it had to be towed out of range.

Cochrane had a back-up plan. He sent 1,250 men in barges and equipped them with scaling ladders to assault the fort from the rear. For the next two hours, nearby houses were shaken to their foundations from gunfire as the American cannon from nearby Fort Covington drove the attackers back to the fleet.

The British bombardment went on until the morning of September 14, when their guns fell silent. The siege had lasted twenty-five hours. Armistead estimated that as many as 1,800 shells had been fired at his fort. A fraction of them had fallen short. More had burst in midair, showering the Americans with shrapnel. About 400 bombs—weighing 210 and 220 pounds—fell inside the garrison itself. Yet only four men had been killed, and the twenty-four wounded were all expected to recover.

Aboard the *Minden*, Frank Key had watched through the night as explosives lighted the sky. Going through his head was a well-known drinking song, "To Anacreon in Heaven." Years earlier, Key had already composed words to that tune to celebrate the American victory at Tripoli. Now he took out a letter he was carrying and on its back scratched out the opening stanzas of a new poem of jubilation.

He had seen the red glare of British rockets and bombs exploding above Fort McHenry. In the morning, he had been relieved and proud to see his nation's immense flag still flying above the fort.

"O say!" Key wrote, "can you see by the dawn's early light

"What so proudly we hail'd at the twilight's last gleaming

"Whose broad stripes and bright stars, through the clouds of the fight,

"O'er the ramparts we watch'd were so gallantly streaming?"

Signing of the treaty of Ghent

Chapter Twenty-one

GHENT
(1814)

On July 11, 1814, John Quincy Adams celebrated his forty-seventh birthday with a self-flagellating entry in his diary. "Two third of the period allotted to the life of man are gone by for me," he wrote. "I have not improved them as I ought to have done." Adams prayed that the rest of his life would not be wasted.

Adams was even less tolerant of his fellow peace delegates and made little effort to ingratiate himself with them as they waited for the British commissioners to arrive. Albert Gallatin he could respect, despite their political differences. But James Bayard was annoying, Jonathan Russell a nullity, and roistering Henry Clay a breed apart from the sort of men Adams had grown up admiring. Yet Adams knew himself well enough to acknowledge certain traits that he shared with the Kentuckian, who was twelve years his junior. Adams confessed to his wife that he and Clay had in common "that same dogmatical, overbearing manner, the same harshness of look and expression, and the same forgetfulness of the courtesies of society."

Even so, Adams had remained his parents' dutiful son while Clay seemed to glory in his own recklessness. He referred to luck in card games as "the fickle goddess" and boasted about his devotion to her. Clay's favorite game was "brag," a variation of poker, with three cards in the hand and one card face up on the table. Friends had looked on aghast when a run of losses seemed to sting Clay to madness as he went on raising his bets. He had lost as much as eight thousand dollars in a single night.

Adams's discomfort with his colleagues was intensified by their close quarters. In renting the home of a baron de Lovendeghem, they were condemned to each other's constant company, and sleeping in adjoining rooms meant that Adams regularly heard Clay returning at 4 a.m. from a night of cards just as Adams was rising to await the dawn.

He tried to maintain his distance by taking meals at a table apart from the four other commissioners. To his diary, Adams justified his aloofness:

"They sit after dinner and drink bad wine and smoke cigars, which suits neither my habits nor my health, and absorbs time which I cannot spare."

When Clay lightly chided Adams for his absence from their table, however, he felt compelled to join them. At night, Clay and the others enjoyed excursions around the town, but their pastimes bored Adams. On the one occasion he was enticed into a game of cards, he lost and never played again.

The three members of Britain's peace commission finally arrived in Ghent at about the time that America's troops were preparing to defend Bladensburg. Expecting victory, the London ministry had sent off the delegates with instructions that reflected that triumphant mood. Lord Castlereagh was counting on Cochrane and Ross to take Washington and Baltimore, while George Prevost with an unconquerable force would sweep down from Canada to invade New York.

In the South, with Napoleon exiled on Elba, Sir Edward Pakenham would match the glory of his brother-in-law, the duke of Wellington, by capturing New Orleans. For the time being, however, Castlereagh wanted simply to initiate the talks, and he expected his commissioners to display discretion and finesse.

That his delegates might not posses those qualities soon became apparent when, on their arrival, the British commissioners summoned the Americans to their quarters. Adams warned his delegation that accepting that peremptory invitation would establish British superiority. At his insistence, the Americans replied that they would meet any place except where the British were residing. Both parties settled on the Hotel des Pays-Bas at 1 p.m. on August 8.

With America's honor upheld, the teams could then agree to alternate future sessions between their lodgings.

Whatever their pretensions in Ghent, Britain's three delegates had given scant evidence at home of any superiority. Five years earlier, James Gambier, an admiral in the British navy, had been court-martialed for incompetence; his acquittal did not improve Baron Gambier's disposition. Gallatin's son compared him to a firecracker that was always spluttering.

The second delegate, Dr. William Adams, was said to be versed in maritime law. When he tried to be witty, however, John Quincy Adams, whose own sense of humor was imperceptible, found the results decidedly unfunny. The two men compared branches of their Adams families and seemed equally relieved to discover that they were not related.

The best-prepared delegate was also the youngest. At thirty, Henry Goulburn, undersecretary of state for war and colonies, was a rising man in his party. Goulburn appreciated Clay's open-handed hospitality, and the fine Spanish cigars that he imported from Amsterdam. But he sized up Swiss-born Gallatin as the least like an American in the opposing delegation, which made him the most congenial.

Albert Gallatin

*   *   *

The Americans came to the first session primed to take up the issue of impressment. It had been, after all, Madison's stated reason for declaring war, and long before the negotiations began, Monroe had reminded the delegates of its importance.

"If this encroachment of Great Britain is not provided against," the secretary of state had written sixteen months earlier, "the United States will have appealed to arms in vain. If your efforts to accomplish it should fail, all further negotiation will cease, and you will return home without further delay."

The Americans were astounded and outraged, then, when the British opened instead with sweeping demands that they had not anticipated. Particularly infuriating was a proposal to create a vast neutral zone of Indian territory around the Great Lakes. Tribes would be forbidden to sell that land to either America or Britain but could offer it to a third party.

Gallatin asked William Adams what he proposed to do with the one hundred thousand or so U.S. citizens who had already settled in the sections of Michigan, Illinois, and Ohio that would comprise this new Indian sanctuary. The Briton said blithely that those people "must shift for themselves."

Great Britain's delegates also wanted to reverse Oliver Perry's naval victory by insisting that the United States abandon its military positions along the Great Lakes. Gallatin asked whether Britain intended to maintain its own posts there. Certainly, the British delegates replied. There need be no restrictions against their nation because Britain had no ambitions for conquest.

The British were also calling for the United States to cede, without compensation, a portion of Maine that would allow Britain to run a road from Halifax to Quebec. And they wanted formal acknowledgment of the rights of Englishmen to navigate on the Mississippi River.

By the time the exploratory talks ended on August 19, the Americans found the British increasingly presumptuous and overbearing. Since John Quincy Adams was the nominal head of their delegation, his colleagues expected him to prepare their rebuttal, and he labored diligently to come up with a draft. For the next four days, each delegate then picked it apart, paragraph by paragraph.

Because Gallatin hoped to salvage the talks, he struck out phrases that might offend the British, and Clay objected to any figures of speech, at all. He wanted language that could not be misinterpreted.

Jonathan Russell limited himself to minor points of grammar and to pointing out that "until" was spelled with only one "l." But Bayard exasperated Adams the most by insisting that they couch in Bayard's words exactly the same points Adams had made.

Adams noted in his diary that the one thing everyone agreed upon was "that what I had written was too long and with too much argument about the Indians."

The committee's final language about an Indian zone exposed the arrogance of the British position: "To surrender both the rights of sovereignty and of soil over nearly one-third of the territorial dominions of the United States to a number of Indians, not probably exceeding twenty thousand, the undersigned are so far from being instructed or authorized that they assure the British plenipotentiaries that any arrangement for that purpose would be instantaneously rejected by their government."

Although Adams was prepared to break off negotiations over that demand, his fellow delegates would not go along with him. To move the troublesome issue off the table, Adams went to talk with Goulburn, who quickly agreed that it was a secondary concern. Since the Indians were British allies, however, Britain had to protect them.

Goulburn assured Adams that there was nothing humiliating about the provision. Canada could never attack the United States, since the disparity of their armies was too great. But Canada needed the protection of a buffer zone.

At another time, Adams had described America's expansion into those western territories as "destined by Divine Providence." Now he detected a British attempt to hem in the United States while Britain maneuvered its way back onto land south of the Canadian border.

Adams told Goulburn that if the British meant to preclude the people of the United States from settling in the West, they must be prepared to exterminate them. That, he added, would be a formidable task. Four years ago, the population of the United States had passed seven million. As they spoke, the figure had undoubtedly passed eight million.

"What!" Goulburn exclaimed. "Is it then in the inevitable nature of things that the United States must conquer Canada?"

"No," Adams replied tersely.

"But what security, then, can Great Britain have for her possession of it?"

The best security for Canada, Adams assured him, would be a liberal and amiable policy toward America.

As delegates debated among themselves, London and Washington were already retracting their original hard lines. Looking around the world, Madison's administration had more cause than ever to sue for peace. All of Europe was now siding with England, and Czar Alexander could offer no further help. Ferdinand VII was back on the Spanish throne and pressing Britain for help in reclaiming West Florida and

Louisiana. After America's failure to conquer Canada, even the War Hawks in Congress were not ready to take on Spain.

With the war going badly and the country near bankruptcy, James Monroe acted on a recommendation from Gallatin and withdrew his ultimatum about impressment. He authorized the delegates to postpone the issue or even to drop it altogether.

On the British side, Lord Liverpool, the prime minister, had staked his government on achieving a satisfactory peace at Ghent. Castlereagh had passed along to the British delegates his stringent bargaining terms without expecting to rupture the negotiations over them. Passing through Ghent on his way to an international conference in Vienna, Castlereagh urged his delegates to adopt a less belligerent tone.

But they were not easily restrained. After James Bayard had warned the British that their conditions would prolong the fighting, Goulburn boasted to London that the American threat had not "made the least impression on me and my colleagues." It had impressed Castlereagh, however, and he wrote to instruct the delegation to await his further orders.

Amid that uncertainty, the British delegation invited the Americans to dinner in late August. Although Adams was expecting the talks to be broken off at any moment, the event took place as scheduled but with no great show of camaraderie. After another three weeks, the Americans reciprocated with a dinner of their own. As they chatted, Gambier asked Adams whether he was intending to return immediately to St. Petersburg.

"Yes," Adams said. Then, to avoid any blame if the talks failed, he added, "That is, if you send us away."

The American delegates first heard about the burning of Washington when Goulburn sent Clay a packet of newspapers accompanied by a polite note with no hint of gloating.

Everyone, even the usually optimistic Clay, was cast down by the news. Gallatin's house had been destroyed, although his wife and children were in Philadelphia and their furniture and silver plate

stored for safekeeping. Adams tried to reassure his wife in St. Petersburg:

"In itself," he wrote, "the misfortune at Washington is a trifle. The
loss of lives amounts scarcely to the numbers every day sacrificed in a
skirmish between two regiments of soldiers. The loss of property cannot exceed the expenses of one month of war."

News of the occupation of Washington reached London before
word came about Ross's death and the failure to take Baltimore. The
prime minister sent Castlereagh a jubilant message that British troops
were creating "the greatest degree of alarm" and making Madison's administration very unpopular.

Lord Liverpool pointed out that the Americans had taken more
than a week to answer the last British note. "We need not, therefore, be
in any great haste about our reply. Let them feast upon Washington."

The British had every reason to believe they would soon provide new
humiliations for the Americans to digest. Until now, Britain had assigned no troops to attack Lake Champlain, and the Americans had
made no move to secure it. As a result, Chauncey and Yeo had indulged in only fleeting skirmishes, with neither trying to control
Champlain as Perry dominated Lake Erie. Now, reinforced by infantrymen newly arrived from Wellington's grizzled army, George Prevost
was ready to change the course of the war and force America's capitulation at Ghent.

Commanding thirty thousand veteran troops in Montreal by mid-
August, Prevost was eager to move deep into United States territory, to
the town of Plattsburgh, New York. His army was the largest and most
lethal force Britain had ever sent to North America—greater even than
the armies of Burgoyne and Cornwallis during the Revolution. Prevost
intended to march his troops on foot across the Canadian border,
where misjudgments by the Madison administration had reduced the
defending forces at Plattsburgh to four infantry companies and three
companies of artillery.

On September 1, Prevost took one-third of his army over the border at the town of Champlain. When Wellington's veterans had been
divided up in Bermuda, the regiments not sent to Admiral Cochrane

were shipped to Prevost in Canada. Wellington's men disliked the prospect of fighting in a war that promised so little glory, and they resented being led by a commander who could not compare with their Iron Duke.

Prevost's new arrivals recalled that Wellington had never cared what his officers wore into battle so long as they showed up with their men equipped with sixty rounds of good ammunition. Prevost had other ideas. He issued an order denouncing the uniforms of the Wellington men for "a fanciful variety inconsistent with the rules of the Service" and ordering them into "the established uniforms of their Corps."

Wellington's men also grumbled about Prevost's lack of planning and his indifference to gathering intelligence. But on September 6, the British marched coolly and efficiently against Plattsburgh and drove Brigadier General Alexander Macomb to retreat across the Saranac River with troops that amounted to fewer than two thousand.

Prevost was headed toward Albany as one part of the three-pronged strategy—along with the attacks against Baltimore and New Orleans—that would dictate the peace terms at Ghent. But just as Harrison had paused until Oliver Perry could clear the banks of the Erie, Prevost depended on controlling Lake Champlain. He waited impatiently for Captain George Downie to drive America's ships from the lake.

Downie expressed no doubt that he could meet the challenge, even though he would be sailing aboard a ship that was still being hastily outfitted. He pronounced the thirty-nine-gun *Confiance* the equal of all the local American vessels combined. Against that behemoth, the United States would have as its lead ship the twenty-six-gun *Saratoga*. Its commander, Thomas Macdonough, had risen steadily in the navy from the day he had fought hand-to-hand at Stephen Decatur's side on the Barbary Coast. Not yet thirty, he devised a strategy to neutralize Downie's advantage in the number and thrust of their guns.

Macdonough anchored his four largest ships across Plattsburgh Bay close to the promontory of Cumberland Head and extending down the bay to Crab Island. To approach his fleet, Downie would

Thomas Macdonough

have to round Cumberland Head in a narrow line facing winds off the lake.

On September 10, those winds kept Downie from sailing to battle and left Prevost furious at the further delay. But overnight, the wind changed, and at dawn Downie had himself rowed around Cumberland Head to inspect the American position.

He found the *Saratoga* and three other imposing vessels lined up to face his own largest ships. Both commanders had ten or twelve gunboats in support. Aboard his ship, Macdonough gathered his officers and made a brief appeal for the help of Almighty God. His prayer seemed answered when the wind failed Downie just as he was bringing the *Confiance* into the bay. It was badly hit by the Americans awaiting him, but Downie proved unflappable. Anchoring his stricken ship, he opened fire at a range of five hundred yards. The *Saratoga* shuddered under that blast, and Macdonough lost a fifth of the ship's crew.

But within fifteen minutes, a freak hit blasted one of the *Confiance* guns off its carriage and into Downie's chest. He was killed instantly. The British crews fought on for the next two hours without their commander. They disabled the *Eagle*, a brig with twenty guns, and ran ashore an American sloop, the *Preble*. Aboard the *Saratoga*, Macdonough was knocked unconscious by a chunk of heavy spar, but he came to and went on firing until the *Confiance* smashed all of the *Saratoga*'s guns that faced it. When none could fire, the British seemed to have won, and they waited for Macdonough to surrender.

But he had used his days before the battle to protect against such a reversal. He had laid out kedge anchors that allowed his crew to pull on cable that wheeled the *Saratoga* around until the side with its guns intact faced the *Confiance*. From his new position, he opened fire with devastating fresh broadsides.

Under that barrage, the British officers refused to stand at their positions, and the *Confiance* struck its colors. The smaller ships also surrendered. After trading volleys for most of the morning, Macdonough had won the fight in its final thirty minutes.

Of nearly 900 men, Macdonough lost 56 killed and 58 wounded. From a total British crew that was about 50 men larger, 57 sailors were killed, but 72 were wounded. Comparing the engagement with the last great battle on the lakes, Oliver Perry had lost one man in six, Macdonough one man in eight.

Early the next day, George Prevost marched his men back to the town of Champlain, leaving behind vast amounts of food and arms for the grateful Americans. Hundreds of Prevost's demoralized troops deserted him rather than return to their base. He argued to his superiors that the "unfortunate occurences" of his campaign would have been far worse for Britain if he had persisted in his attack without controlling Lake Champlain.

From his headquarters in Paris, the duke of Wellington was one of the few observers to sympathize with Prevost. Wellington said he did not see how he had any choice so long as the Americans held the lake. But Wellington also observed that Prevost had at his disposal a contingent of men who represented Britain's finest troops; they simply needed to be led with an iron fist.

When Liverpool offered Wellington the chance to go to America and take command of the British troops, he turned it down. He was remarking privately that Britain was unlikely to prevail on the American continent.

The *Times* of London judged Prevost's retreat more harshly. Commenting on his recall from Canada, the newspaper called Prevost's failure "a defeat still more disastrous" for England than Perry's success on Lake Erie.

At home at the Hermitage, Andrew Jackson had been considering ways to consolidate his victory over the Creeks. He estimated that his hard-driving negotiations had brought into the Union "20 million acres of the cream of the Creek country" and recommended that Congress settle that land as quickly as possible by selling it to his militia troops at two dollars an acre.

Jackson also worried about a threat from those Red Sticks who had fled south to join the Spanish in eastern Florida.

When Madison named him commander of the Seventh District, Jackson used that authority to write a threatening letter to the Spanish governor of Pensacola that concluded with a blunt statement of Jackson's creed: "An Eye for an Eye, Toothe for Toothe and Scalp for Scalp."

The letter rattled the governor, Don Matteo Gonzalez Manrique, enough to violate his nation's official neutrality and invite British troops to land at Pensacola. Admiral Cochrane welcomed the opening, since he proposed to invade the United States from the mouth of the Mississippi. Cochrane's initial strategy involved seizing the town of Mobile and then marching troops to capture New Orleans.

With the Spanish as his allies—along with the refugee Creeks and other tribes—Cochrane estimated that Britain would need only a few thousand troops. Adopting his plan, the London Admiralty committed the troops from the Chesapeake area, plus another two thousand that would be sent by November from Europe to Jamaica.

By mid-August, Jackson was fretting over a possible assault on Mobile. Marching over four hundred miles of rough terrain in eleven days, he led his men from Fort Jackson and reached Mobile on August 22. When he learned of the British violation of neutrality at Pensacola, Jackson complained to Washington that he should have been given permission to invade the Spanish territory. Had that been done, he wrote, the American eagle would now be soaring high above the fangs of the British lion. Instead, Jackson warned that the British and Spanish would soon try to take Mobile. He promised that "there will be bloody noses before that happens."

Jefferson had not heard the details of Macdonough's victory when he wrote to console Madison for the burning of Washington. He assured his friend that even George Washington himself had been let down by his field commanders, and no one should blame Madison for the calamity. Britain's successes in the land war, according to Jefferson, had been due only to America's traitors and inexperienced officers.

Jefferson concluded with heartening news for Madison. Because of the destruction of the small congressional library, Jefferson had offered to sell to Congress his own collection of some sixty-five hundred volumes.

Even before Jefferson's encouraging letter, Madison had been plunging forward with new determination. He might look haggard, but he and Dolley had accepted an offer from Colonel John Tayloe to live at his property, the Octagon House, until their nearby mansion could be restored, and Dolley was already planning to hold an open house in those temporary quarters by early November.

In less than four weeks after Washington was burned, Madison sent his sixth State of the Union report to Congress. He had called the session two months early, warning that Britain might yet threaten the nation's very existence. But his message ended on a conciliatory note: America wanted no more than "peace and friendship on honorable terms."

*   *   *

The Americans in Ghent were still coping with the shock of Cochrane's assault on Washington, and they had bought time by asking that the British clarify every point they considered essential to achieving a treaty.

On October 18, the answer came. Stripped to its essence, the British dispatch called for barring American fishermen from the Grand Banks of Newfoundland and insisting on navigation rights on the Mississippi. The British also wanted to consider their holdings in North America as *uti possidetis*—the Latin phrase for letting each country keep any territory it had won in the war.

Despite Prevost's spectacular failure, a smaller British amphibian force had invaded Maine and seized Bangor and Machias. To avoid forfeiting that territory permanently, the Americans were forced to press for *status quo ante bellum*, which would restore the boundaries to where they had been before the war began. London was likely to give way on that point because worrisome tensions had developed in Vienna between Britain and Russia.

Even Britain's relaxed terms were again dividing the American delegation, however, and pitting New England against the western frontier. The Treaty of 1783, which ended the Revolutionary War, had granted the British rights on the Mississippi. But at that time, the United States had not controlled the river's western bank. After the Louisiana Purchase, America possessed both banks, as well as the river's mouth. Clay was ready to break off the talks rather than extend the British rights.

To Adams, that issue was negligible. He pointed out that during the past three decades, the British claim had never damaged American shipping in the slightest degree. As he spoke, though, he could foresee the reaction: "Mr. Clay lost his temper," Adams wrote in his diary, "as he generally does whenever this right of the British to navigate the Mississippi is discussed."

Clay retaliated by taking an equally cavalier attitude toward the Atlantic fisheries. Travel on the Mississippi was "much too important to be conceded for the mere liberty of drying fish upon a desert," Clay said.

John Quincy Adams remembered better than anyone that his father had risked the peace of 1783 to guarantee inland fishing and curing privileges for American fisheries off the banks of Newfoundland. He wrote to John Adams in Massachusetts, "The situation in which I am placed often brings to mind that in which you were situated in the year 1782," since the son was being "called upon to support the same interests, and in many respects, the same identical points and questions." Negotiating with Britain was always about "the boundaries, the fisheries, and the Indian savages."

The former president forwarded that letter to Madison, asking him to order John Quincy to hold firm on the fisheries. The senior Adams also wanted the impressment issue resolved before a treaty was signed; he did not know that demand had already been scrapped.

With France defeated, the British no longer had the same urgent need to bolster their crews by seizing sailors from American ships. As for Madison's other reasons to fight, the Orders in Council had been rescinded when the war was barely under way. And lately any question of national honor had been resolved on Lake Champlain.

Just as a settlement was beginning to seem possible in Ghent, tensions between New England and Washington had flared up with renewed bitterness. As acting secretary of war, Monroe was determined to infuse new spirit in the United States Army; the unequal battle at Bladensburg had pointed up again the weaknesses of the state militias. But volunteering for the regular army had slowed down dangerously, with only ten thousand men signing up during the past year. If Britain was determined to drag out the war, Monroe would command only half of the men Congress had authorized.

To make up the difference, he broke with his party's long-standing opposition to conscription and proposed drafting enough men to bring the army's strength to one hundred thousand. To make his plan more palatable, Monroe offered several modifications and compromises, but Congress rejected all of them.

Another solution would be to put state militias under federal commanders; that would crack down on units in New England and New York known to be riddled with cheaters—men who served only a few days to collect their pay before returning home.

Massachusetts governor Caleb Strong flatly refused the changes Monroe proposed. From the beginning, Strong had denounced the war, and his legislature had issued a statement calling it unjust.

Given that background, Madison ordered its military appropriation withheld from Massachusetts. When he took the same action against Connecticut, the Peace Faction complained loudly that, despite the taxes they paid, they were being left to defend themselves.

A committee of the Massachusetts legislature recommended convening a conference of northern states to discuss their common defense and to recommend radical changes in the U.S. Constitution. Harrison Gray Otis would finally get the regional convention he had first proposed during the embargo crisis six years earlier.

At a Boston town meeting on September 3 in Faneuil Hall, Otis set out an agenda. He promised that "we shall not be turned aside from our course, which we believe to be the path of duty, by any fear of rulers at Washington, on the one hand, nor by that of apostasy on the other."

With that last phrase, he gestured toward Samuel Dexter, who had deserted the Federalists to support the war.

Starting to get up from his seat, Dexter shouted, "If he does not retract those words, I'll wring his nose, in spite of his popularity!"

A friend pulled Dexter back into his chair to hear Otis make a quick and florid apology. Otis said that he would as soon think of doubting the existence of his God as he would of questioning Dexter's patriotism.

For those few Republicans left in the Massachusetts legislature, the idea of a conference reminded them of the radical changes that had been made by the Constitutional Convention in Philadelphia. And if British troops ever threatened the city of Boston, they predicted the Federalists would want to pay a ransom, as the citizens of Annapolis had done. They could even foresee New England breaking away from the United States and rejoining Great Britain.

The Peace Faction had enough votes to overcome that opposition, and the conference was scheduled for mid-December.

Twenty-six delegates from Massachusetts, Connecticut, Rhode Island, Vermont, and New Hampshire agreed to meet in Hartford, Connecticut.

In Ghent, Clay had suggested early in the negotiations that the British were bluffing and might back down. At the time, John Quincy Adams had called it an "inconceivable idea."

Now Clay taunted Adams by asking if he knew how to play brag. Adams said he had forgotten.

The art of beating your adversary, Clay told him, is to hold your hand with a solemn and confident face and outbluff him. He turned to James Bayard and asked if that wasn't the winning strategy.

Bayard gave his qualified support. "Ay," he said. "but you may lose the game if the adversary sees the weakness of your hand."

To Adams, Bayard added, "Mr. Clay is bragging for a million against a cent."

Clay repeated his optimism in a private letter to Secretary Monroe. The British had given up their original demand for an Indian buffer state and for the withdrawing of American forts from the Great Lakes. Now they would probably settle for the prewar borders if they were beaten at New Orleans. But Clay and his fellow delegates did not expect a settlement until that battle had been fought.

Among the American delegates, sentiment had swung against making a critical issue out of British rights to the Mississippi. But Clay said he would not sign any treaty that gave Britain access to the river again. Gallatin, who had become the delegation's cool, commanding voice, began to work on bringing him around.

On November 18, Lord Liverpool wrote to Castlereagh that he did not want to prolong the fighting in the hope of gaining more territory. The war had already cost Britain more than 10 million pounds, and the prime minister was not prepared to wait for Admiral Cochrane's fleet to reach the Mississippi Delta and stage a climactic battle at New Orleans.

In a final compromise, the Mississippi and the fisheries were excluded from the treaty and left to joint commissions once peace was restored. And borders were to be restored to *status quo ante*. Clay acknowledged to Monroe that those latest terms were "not very unfavorable" since America had lost no territory and no honor.

When the renegade New England delegates assembled in Hartford, Connecticut, on December 15, they found that a federal army major had stationed his regiment outside their opening session. His excuse was that he was recruiting for the regular army, but everyone had heard rumors that the convention could be headed toward a treasonous secession from Washington.

How the Hartford delegates were viewed depended on who was describing them. Jefferson invoked Marat, Danton, and Robespierre — radicals who had doomed the French Revolution. But Boston's leading Federalist newspaper hailed them as "wise and manly" for their willingness to end a wasteful war and seek peace with Britain. In retirement, John Adams said he respected many of the delegates, but he could not endorse any threat to the Union to which he had devoted his life. He called them "intelligent and honest men who had lost touch with reality."

At least some of those elderly and conservative men seemed to be resisting the cry for desperate action. When George Cabot of Massachusetts was asked what he intended to do in Hartford, he replied, "We are going to keep you young hotheads from getting into mischief."

The hotheads included John Lowell, called "the Boston Rebel," who had been urging for a year that New England draft a new constitution to protect its shipping and business interests. He wanted that revised document presented only to the original thirteen states.

Timothy Pickering, another member of the Peace Faction, expected that General Pakenham's British expeditionary force would take Louisiana easily. "From the moment that the British possess New Orleans," Pickering predicted, "the union is severed."

And Governor Strong had dispatched an emissary in mid-November to sound out what the British would offer if his state broke entirely with Madison. The ministers in London knew better than Strong did what progress was being made in Ghent. But if Madison did not accept the emerging peace treaty, they gave the British command in Halifax authority to sign a separate pact with New England.

Canada could also offer aid—although not British troops—to Massachusetts for defending itself against Washington.

George Cabot's calm approach suited the majority of the Hartford delegates, who elected him their president. But because the conference voted to keep their deliberations secret—as Madison and his colleagues had done in Philadelphia—rumors of secession continued to circulate.

Accusations of sabotage had also arisen. Stephen Decatur claimed that he had been driven back the previous year as he tried to slip away from Connecticut's New London harbor when someone on the shore flashed blue lights to alert the British fleet. The phrase "Blue-Light Federalist" became a damning epithet.

Whatever their intentions, however, the delegates were at the mercy again of sluggish communications. As far as they knew, peace negotiations had broken down in Ghent and the country faced a protracted war. On their second day in Hartford, delegates castigated the Madison administration for failing to defend the northeastern states.

The final recommendations presented on December 24 allowed states to retain a portion of their federal taxes for self-defense. They also proposed an amendment to the Constitution that would restrict the power of Congress to declare and wage war. Several parochial amendments also put forward on that Christmas Eve underscored the delegates' resentment that their states had become politically irrelevant.

America had declared in 1776 that it had outgrown England. In 1814, had America outgrown New England?

To answer that question, the Hartford delegates wanted to restrict the power of Congress to create new states and admit them to the Union; to curtail the right to impose embargoes and restrict trade; and to stipulate that a president from the same state could not be elected for two consecutive terms.

And delegates proposed an amendment on taxation and slave representation that linked New England's economic self-interest to its traditional opposition to slavery. Members of the Peace Faction also went on record urging that Madison serve his country by resigning the presidency.

Although the final resolutions were couched in drastic language — "the time for a change is at hand" — nothing submitted to the convention mentioned breaking away from the United States. The Federalist delegates were arguing instead that states' rights extended to matters of defense. They were making the expansive case that Jefferson had made in 1798 with the Virginia Resolutions.

The moderate outcome in Hartford dismayed the more radical voices, and they denounced Harrison Gray Otis, chairman of the final report, for a timidity they said he had shown after an anonymous warning threatened him with physical harm.

Even as Otis prepared to take the convention's message to Washington, developments in Ghent and Louisiana had raced far ahead of the debates in Hartford.

On that same Christmas Eve, as the delegates voted in Connecticut, the Americans in Ghent paid a call on the British delegation to sign copies of a peace treaty. One last-minute flutter arose when the U.S. copy was found to refer to the earlier treaty as being signed in "seventeen hundred and eighty-three" while the British version gave the year as "one thousand seven hundred and eighty-three." The two teams decided that the discrepancy, while unfortunate, was not serious enough to delay their signatures.

As delegates exchanged copies, Adams told Gambier that he hoped it would be the last treaty of peace ever required between Great Britain and the United States.

The Battle of New Orleans

Chapter Twenty-two

NEW ORLEANS
(1814–1815)

The Creeks who had fled south knew how implacable Andrew Jackson could be in war. When British ships failed to capture America's Fort Bowyer on the Gulf of Mexico, their Indian allies sensed disaster and scattered into the wooded countryside.

Outside Pensacola, Jackson decided he could not wait for authorization from Washington and called for reinforcements from Tennessee. The afternoon of November 6, 1814, with three thousand men in camp, he sent a flag of truce to Governor Gonzalez Manrique, along with an explanation that he had not come to attack a neutral power or to damage Pensacola but simply to prevent the British from using the town as a haven. Jackson called for the surrender of two nearby forts where British and Spanish flags had been flying together.

As Jackson's emissary approached with his flag of truce, he was driven back by cannon shot. When Jackson demanded an explanation, Gonzalez Manrique apologized and assured him that a second flag would be respected.

It was midnight before the governor finally received Jackson's terms: He must open Fort St. Michael and Fort Barancas to the Americans, who would hold them until enough Spanish troops arrived to protect their neutrality from the British.

Gonzalez Manrique consulted with his officers and rejected the proposal.

Before dawn, Jackson marched his men along a beach east of Pensacola, but sand made dragging their cannon impossible. After a brief skirmish, the terrified governor appeared with his own white flag and surrendered the town. The British remained in command of Fort Barancas six miles away.

Jackson planned his attack for the next morning. On his way to the fort, however, a deafening explosion told him that the British had blown up Barancas before abandoning it.

Although Jackson wrote a bitter note to the governor accusing him of bad faith, his progress so far left him buoyant. "The steady firmness of my troops has drew a just respect from our enemies," he wrote. "It has confirmed the Red Sticks that they have no stronghold or protections, only in the friendship of the United States."

Best of all, the good behavior of Jackson's Indian allies had impressed the Spanish residents of Pensacola. During their time ashore, Britain's troops had plundered the town and carried off most of its slaves. Jackson was gratified that the Spanish now believed "that our Choctaws are more civilized than the British."

All the same, Jackson had invaded a neutral territory. After he had already succeeded, he received Secretary Monroe's letter instructing him to do nothing to provoke a war with Spain. He could be certain, however, that Monroe was not unhappy with him. Jackson's exploit had further demoralized the hostile Indians, and newspapers back home were filled with extravagant praise.

✻   ✻   ✻

Jackson still suspected that the British might attack Mobile, but the pirate Jean Lafitte, a tall and elegant former blacksmith from Haiti, was telling the Americans otherwise. Lafitte had commandeered a port on Barataria Bay outside New Orleans as headquarters for his flotilla of outlaw ships. His men, called Baratarians, had struck lucrative alliances with the local businessmen for disposing of their contraband. Slaves who brought six hundred dollars or seven hundred dollars in legal trading could be purchased from smugglers for less than two hundred dollars.

Congress appreciated the damage being inflicted on British commerce by America's privateers, who had seized almost fourteen hundred British ships since the war began. Daring commanders were able to dart into a merchant fleet with their lightly armed ships and take over a British vessel before its guardian frigate could give chase. The American ship names reflected the spirit of their crews—*True Blooded Yankee, Rattlesnake, Scourge, Catch Me If You Can.*

In July 1812, Congress had taxed the privateers 2 percent of their bounty to provide for widows and orphans created by the war. Lately that levy had been lifted, but any legislation out of Washington hardly concerned Lafitte. He scoffed at neutrality laws and evaded all U.S. taxes, even though he considered himself an American patriot and claimed, "I have never ceased to be a good citizen."

Lafitte made good on that boast when the British invited him to regain respectability for himself and his gang by joining the Royal Navy. He would receive a naval commission and thirty thousand dollars; his men would be allotted sizeable tracts of the land the British intended to occupy.

In rejecting the offer, Lafitte turned over the British correspondence to Louisiana's governor Claiborne. He made the gesture in hopes of obtaining the release of eighty of his men, including his brother Pierre, who had been imprisoned after a recent government raid on their base.

With the letters he forwarded, Lafitte did not include his earlier draft in which he accepted Britain's offer. Given his change of heart, Lafitte wanted to impress on Claiborne that while America might see him as a criminal, he would never miss the chance to serve her.

Jackson also received copies of Britain's overtures. They underscored the urgent message he had received from Secretary Monroe
that Admiral Cochrane was sailing in his direction with a formidable
invasion force—as many as fourteen thousand troops in at least sixty
ships.

Arriving in New Orleans on December 1, Jackson understood why the
British might feel confident. The local defenders were in disarray, with
few ships on the water and only two small militia units for protection.
Despite rumors of the impending danger, residents remained divided
by politics and nationality into squabbling factions.

At the last census, New Orleans' total population had been less
than twenty-five thousand. Most residents had been born into French-
speaking families, and those of English heritage accounted for only
one-eighth of the city. "Creole" had first been the name given to descendants of French settlers; now it also could apply to the Spanish and
Portuguese. Cajuns, originally landing from Nova Scotia when the
British drove them out in 1755, had settled along bayous that emptied
into the Gulf of Mexico.

Despite their quarreling, all of the communities seemed to take
heart from the general's arrival and were passing the word: "Jackson's
come!"

The man they hailed as their savior had been weakened by his constant exertion and was near collapse. When Jackson had been rewarded with his commission in the U.S. Army, he shed his touchy
preference for a volunteer militia, and his letter to Rachel had glowed
with pride:

"You are now a Major Generals lady," he had written, and must appear "elegant and plain, not extravagant" in the style expected of her.

But urging his wife now to join him in New Orleans, Jackson was
less concerned with her wardrobe than with the beds and bedsteads he
wanted her to bring to his camp. He explained that before leaving Pensacola, he had been taken very ill. Purging him with two herbs—jalap
and calomel—the doctors had helped to restore his health. But there
had followed "eight days on the march that I never broke bread."

Although Jackson looked cadaverous and older than his forty-seven

years, he willed himself to stand erect in his uniform of blue homespun, yellow buckskin, and scuffed boots, and to ride with his usual
energy.

He set about blocking the mouths of the many bayous that extended into the city. Jackson posted a guard at each of them and
brought forward five gunboats to Lake Borgne. They were to act as de-
coys and attempt to draw the British ships into range of the guns at Fort
Petites Coquilles, a small base built on a channel of land connecting
Borgne and Lake Pontchartrain.

Next, Jackson had to decide what use to make of Jean Lafitte. In
the past, he had cursed the pirates as "hellish banditti." But he might
need their skill and daring. As his go-between, Jackson could depend
on his new aide-de-camp, Edward Livingston, a brother of the Robert
Livingston who had negotiated the Louisiana Purchase. After a financial scandal forced Edward to resign as mayor of New York, he had
moved south, married the sister of a prominent Creole, and embraced
the unfettered life of the frontier. His law clients these days included
pirates forced to appear in court, and when Livingston suggested that
Jackson recruit them, his motive was not entirely civic-minded. The
imprisoned pirates had promised him twenty thousand dollars if he
could get them acquitted on charges of violating U.S. trade laws. Livingston had recommended that their best strategy would be to join the
American army.

At first, Jackson refused to deal with the outlaws. When they finally
met at Jackson's headquarters on Royal Street, however, Jean Lafitte argued compellingly in English—he also spoke French, Spanish, and
Italian—that his men should be allowed to join in defending the city.
Looking past Lafitte's courtly manners and expensive tailoring, Jackson
recognized, as he had with William Weatherford, a kindred fighting
spirit. A federal judge released the pirates from jail on the condition
that they enlist, and Jackson sent Lafitte to run two batteries below
New Orleans and assigned others from his crew to a company of
marines.

Even before he arrived in New Orleans, Jackson had resolved the question of whether to recruit the town's six hundred free black men. In the

past, many had fought for Spain, but Claiborne interviewed their leaders, including Major Pierre Lacoste, and satisfied himself that they
were committed to America. The governor had written to Jackson in
August and got back the general's exuberant approval.

"Our country has been invaded and threatened with destruction,"
Jackson wrote. "She wants soldiers to fight her battles. The free men of
color in your city are inured to the Southern climate and would make
excellent soldiers. They will not remain quiet spectators of the interesting contest. They must be either for, or against, us."

Jackson also sent a proclamation to speak directly to black recruits:

"Through a mistaken policy, you have heretofore been deprived of
a participation in the glorious struggle for national rights in which your
country is engaged. This no longer shall exist. As sons of freedom you
are now called upon to defend your most inestimable blessing."

Volunteers were to receive the standard inducements—160 acres
of land and $124 in cash, along with rations, uniforms, and regular
pay. They would be commanded by black noncommissioned or militia
officers; their commissioned officers would be white.

The district's assistant paymaster was among those white men who
opposed putting guns in the hands of black men. Questioning
Jackson's authority, he got a quick comeuppance:

"Be pleased to keep to yourself your Opinions upon the policy of
making payments to particular Corps," Jackson wrote. "It is enough for
you to receive my order for the payment of the troops with the necessary muster rolls without inquiring whether the troops are White, Black
or Tea."

In outlining to London his original plan for invading New Orleans,
Cochrane had argued that since slaves and freemen alike would welcome the liberation of Louisiana, the British would need only three
thousand regular troops to take New Orleans and then continue up the
Mississippi Valley to Canada. When the campaign was over, the
United States would be wedged between Britain to the west and Spain
to the south. Further American expansion on the continent would be
halted.

Cochrane's superiors considered his estimate too optimistic and tripled the force he suggested. Not only would the troops of the late Robert Ross be sent from the failed Baltimore campaign, but soldiers would come from Ireland and France, and black regiments shipped from the West Indies because they were accustomed to the Louisiana climate.

Sir Edward Pakenham was hurrying to the scene to replace Ross but had not arrived when Cochrane's fleet moved toward Cat Island. From there, he planned to send small boats onto Lake Borgne. Jackson had anticipated that strategy when he sent out his five gunboats for Cochrane to pursue. But the winds died before the Americans could lure the British ships near enough for the guns of Fort Petites Coquilles to fire on them.

Two days later, on December 14, Thomas Ap Catesby Jones, the American naval commander, fought for forty-five minutes until overwhelming salvos from Cochrane's barges blasted his flotilla and Jones's ships were taken. But the guns at Fort Petites Coquilles did prevent Cochrane from heading toward the best route into the city, and his men landed instead at the westerly end of Lake Borgne. They intended to travel along Bayou Bienvenu, which drained into Borgne, and mount a surprise attack from the east.

At first, Jackson took the news from Cat Island as a feint by the British, but by December 15, he could no longer doubt that the invasion had begun. He sent at once for John Coffee at his camp above Baton Rouge. Coffee was now his most trusted general, and Jackson ordered him to march day and night to reach him. Coffee was also to summon from further up the Mississippi other commanders, who included William Carroll, last year's winner of his duel with Jesse Benton.

With bands in the streets alternating between "Yankee Doodle" and the "Marseillaise," Jackson was convinced that the citizens of New Orleans backed him even if the legislature and the larger property owners might have less confidence in his ability. Jackson admitted, though, that the local government appeared to be supporting his measures. Along with five hundred volunteers, the state had drafted its full quota of one thousand militia and had them equipped and ready when Jackson arrived in New Orleans. Legislators had also voted funds for uniforms for the Tennessee militia and had committed crews of slaves to work on fortifications.

But Jackson suspected that their resolve would falter at the first sign of British success, and like the residents of Annapolis, they would try to buy protection for their property. To guarantee his control, Jackson declared martial law on December 16 and drafted all able-bodied men for service. Suspending the right of habeas corpus, he also required written permission for persons or ships to leave the city. Street lamps were to be extinguished by 9 p.m. After that hour, anyone found in the street without authorization was to be arrested as a spy.

Two days later, still waiting for reinforcements, Jackson reviewed the troops he had on hand. Throngs turned out to watch as he inspected his soldiers in front of the Cathedral of St. Louis and then congratulated his audience for rising above "the differences of language and the prejudices of national pride."

Early on the morning of December 20, Coffee arrived with 800 troops and another 450 on the way. Carroll got to town a day later, then a major in the dragoons brought 100 of his men. The newcomers represented about 4,000 militia from Tennessee and Mississippi.

Meantime, Jackson was astride his horse, trying to guess the route the British would choose. Most likely, he thought, they would leave Lake Borgne by way of Bayou Sauvage and an area known as Chef Menteur. That option would require wading through ten miles of marsh until the land grew solid again five miles east of the city at an expanse called the Plains of Gentilly.

Jackson sent many of his troops, including Major Lacoste's free black soldiers, to build redoubts and prepare a line of defense for the battle he expected to fight on that open field. Even if the British appeared to be heading elsewhere, it would be only another trick. Jackson was counting on his forceful instructions' being carried out, and he expected that trees had been cut down to block every major bayou. By now, he felt he was more familiar with the treacherous New Orleans landscape than the British could possibly be. He had outguessed them and now had only to wait.

*   *   *

Jackson would soon find that because of an oversight Bayou Bien-venu had not been blocked, but the narrow straits and a spate of foul weather helped to compensate for that negligence. The distance from Cat Island to the bayou was sixty-two miles and would take the British thirty-six hours of strenuous rowing. As they set out on the morning of December 19, an icy gale swept over the British troops and froze the tops of their water tanks. During the rowing, Lieu-tenant Gleig was determined not to complain. But, cold and wet to the skin, he did admit in his notebook that the trek was "the reverse of agreeable."

After two days and a night of weather as severe as any at home in England, they reached their destination with their uniforms stiff from morning frost. Gleig's commanding officer, Colonel Thornton, had re-covered from a wound at Bladensburg, and he led a British advance party of eighteen hundred in open boats to the mouth of Bayou Bien-venu. Thornton had agreed with Admiral Cochrane in rejecting a landing near Chef Menteur as too predictable.

Cochrane left a schooner on the lake and came ashore to watch his barges rowing past alligators and snakes to reach the landing site. The admiral was assuring his crew that he would be eating Christmas din-ner in New Orleans. And, if he chose to do it, he might stay on for Mardi Gras.

Nearing a rough collection of huts called Fisherman's Village, the British troops could congratulate themselves that so far their landing had gone undetected.

At the head of Bayou Bienvenu lay the sugar plantation of General Jacques Villeré, commander of the first division of Louisiana's militia. Jackson had ordered the general's son to post a guard, and Major Gabriel Villeré had sent out an eleven-man militia detachment. They had gone to the village to check on the Portuguese and Spanish fisher-men there but found the area all but deserted. The Americans did not suspect that the fishermen had recently defected to the British.

Reassured by the quiet scene, the American sentries relaxed. By the following night, they were stationing only one man to keep watch while the others slept. After midnight, that sentinel heard a noise and woke the others in time to see five barges filled with British soldiers rowing up the bayou.

Realistic about the odds, the Americans hid until the barges had passed, but in their eagerness to escape they made enough noise that most of them were immediately captured. The others, defeated by the terrain, soon surrendered. One lone man survived in the swamp for three days before he reached an American camp.

When the prisoners were questioned, they proved to be skillful propagandists or inveterate optimists. Inflating America's strength by more than fourfold, they assured their captors that Jackson commanded eighteen thousand men.

Distressing as Colonel Thornton found their estimate, he felt he had no choice but to push forward more rapidly. On the night of December 22, he ordered his men to row their boats carrying his main force to another bayou called Mazant. The way proved so shallow that they had to push their barges forward from the stern with long poles. When scouts jumped out and found a solid path, the men stepped from their boats and moved in a single file beside the swamp until they reached the wide expanse of Jacques Villeré's plantation.

Seeing the farmhouses, Thornton rushed his men to surround them. Since Gabriel Villeré had received no warning from his sentries, he and his brother were smoking cigars as they lounged on the front porch of their house. Too late, Villeré caught sight of Thornton's troops trotting through his orange grove. He jumped up and ran through a back door into Thornton's arms. The brothers were taken inside under guard while Thornton awaited further orders.

Desperate to warn Jackson of the threat, Gabriel Villeré broke free, jumped out an open window, and ran across the lawn. Thornton shouted futilely to his men, "Catch him or kill him!"

Struggling through the swamp ahead of his captors, Villeré reached the house of his nearest neighbor. Together they rowed across the Mississippi to reach stables, where they were given horses. Throughout the morning of December 23, they rode up the levee on the west bank and crossed the river again at New Orleans.

Augustus Rousseau, a young Creole, had come to American headquarters when British ships were first sighted and had arrived only minutes before Villeré rode in at 1:30 p.m. to verify Rousseau's report.

Because Villeré spoke in French, his words had to be translated. When he finished, Jackson was furious at having been outmaneuvered. Pounding on the table, he swore, "By the Eternal, they shall not sleep on our soil!"

To his aides, Jackson said more calmly, "Gentlemen, the British are below. We must fight them tonight."

Brave words were not enough to reassure the nervous residents of New Orleans. A Creole militia colonel sought out Magloire Guichard, Speaker of the Louisiana House, to ask what would happen if Jackson were defeated. He took away the impression that the legislature would sue for an independent peace with the British and rode to inform Jackson's cadre what he had learned.

By the time Jackson got the message, it was third-hand and garbled, but he sent another aide with instructions for Governor Claiborne:

"Major General Jackson has received the information that the legislature is on the point of assembling to give up the country. His orders are that the governor should immediately close the doors of the State House, surround it with guards, and fire on the members should they persist in assembling."

Claiborne did as he was told. Two days later, with the rumors laid to rest, the legislators returned to their seats. Furious and humiliated, they ordered an immediate inquiry to exonerate themselves from accusations of treason.

Until Pakenham arrived, the British troops were being commanded by Major General John Keane, who caught up with Thornton's advance column, formed his troops into battalions, and marched them to the northern boundary of the Villeré estate. There he called a halt to wait for his main force to join them.

Thornton protested Keane's decision. Given the element of surprise, they could march on New Orleans now with the men they had and take the city with a minimum of resistance. But Keane, only the

interim commander, displayed an interim's caution. Wary because of
the inflated estimates of the American forces, he preferred to hold off
for another day. Better to forgo a chance at glory than to risk a cata-
strophic blunder. Keane made Villeré's house his headquarters and ordered his men to set up camp.

That afternoon, he and Cochrane approved a proclamation to be
distributed in town. "Louisianians!" it began, "remain quietly in your
homes; your slaves shall be preserved to you, and your property respected. We make war only against Americans."

That pledge would be difficult to honor. New Orleans was reputed
to be irresistibly rich, and the watchword among the British troops was
that "beauty and booty" awaited them in the city. George Gleig observed that the prospect of reaping lavish rewards had inflamed everyone from the general down to the youngest drummer boy.

Moving his ground troops into position, Jackson told the resourceful
New Orleans commodore, Daniel Patterson, to send all available ships
down the Mississippi. Patterson hurried to bring his schooner *Carolina*
to the far side of the river out of sight of the British camp. He would
fire his guns when the American troops were ready to attack.

Jackson led fourteen hundred soldiers with two cannon down a
narrow road along Rodriguez's Canal toward Keane's men. Coffee took
another 732 riflemen, including a black battalion, behind the British
positions to cut off communication between Keane and his troops still
on Lake Borgne.

Jackson sent General David Morgan south of the Villeré estate to
create a diversion. He left behind the Louisiana militia and William
Carroll's Tennessee troops because he could not quite give up his initial certainty about the British strategy, and he still wondered whether
the landing was a ruse. Claiborne tried to dissuade him, and even
some of Jackson's officers privately ridiculed their general's obsession.

All the same, Jackson would guard against a trick; he sent Carroll
and the others to patrol Chef Menteur.

At the Villeré plantation, Keane's men had lighted fires for cooking the
hams and chickens they had confiscated from neighboring houses.

Others of the exhausted troops had already stretched out on the ground for the night. Lieutenant Gleig and his friend Captain Grey had fashioned a cone-shaped hut from fence stakes torn up around the Villeré perimeter and rested there with Gleig's dog at their feet. Their enlisted men brought them a couple of hens for roasting and a few bottles of an excellent claret.

Since British soldiers had been warned against looting, Gleig preferred to regard the wine as "borrowed" from a nearby cellar. As they relaxed and reminisced in the glow of six or eight wax candles, they agreed they were ready now to return to England. Gleig had hoped to write a book about his adventures, but so far he felt he had not seen enough action to make a compelling story.

Through the late December darkness, their regiment had watched the *Carolina* approaching with no sense of alarm. It must be either one of their own or a harmless American merchant ship.

From his deck, Patterson checked the time and passed word to his captain. He had orders to begin firing at 7:30 p.m., and the *Carolina* was now directly in front of the British camp. A shout from American Captain John Henley cut through the night air to where Gleig and Grey were sitting:

"Now, boys, give it to them for the honor of America!"

The *Carolina* fired its starboard guns, and the British troops jumped up in confusion and ran to get out of its range. Their artillery tried to answer back, but the shots only allowed the *Carolina* to home in more effectively on their position.

Hearing the guns, Jackson marched his men to overrun the British guard posts. Musket fire coming from the direction of the British sentinels convinced Keane that the estimates of Jackson's superior numbers had been accurate. Shaken by the crisis, he gave Colonel Thornton full authority to repel the Americans any way he could.

Heavy clouds obscured a crescent moon. In the blackness, Gleig and Grey rushed to their right to beat back the American attack. The two young officers waded across a pond in the direction of the firing, collecting strays from their regiment until they had about thirty men.

Gleig was moving blindly forward, trying to avoid the plantation's ditches, when he dimly made out a band of men coming toward them. In the gloom, he could not tell whether they were friendly or hostile.

Gleig called to them. When there was no answer, he and Grey led the British soldiers forward until they were about twenty or thirty yards from the strangers. A burst of fire proved to Gleig that they were Americans, but Grey worried that if they returned the fire they might be shooting at their own troops. And, despite their friendship, Grey was the ranking officer.

The two of them directed their men to take cover behind a stack of cane stubble while Gleig crept forward alone. Under the protective darkness, he got even closer to the opposing line. Convinced more than ever that they were Americans, he scuttled back to Grey. But for reasons Gleig never understood Grey could not be moved. He insisted that it was impossible for the Americans to have penetrated past the British outposts. That meant that the men standing before them had to be members of Britain's Ninety-fifth Rifle Corps.

They agreed on a compromise. Grey would remain where he was with half of their men while Gleig tried to circle around the other soldiers with a dozen or fourteen of the rest.

As he reconnoitered, Gleig joined forces with a British squad also stumbling through the darkness toward the Americans. Climbing over a fence, the British squad moved across a field and found themselves on the left flank of John Coffee's men. With no time for strategy, the British could fire only one round before the two sides charged each other with bayonets, musket butts, sabers, and then fists. They fought, Gleig thought afterward, with the savage ferocity of bulldogs.

The exertion was too strenuous to last long. When the Americans gave way and ran, Gleig's men took after them briefly until he called a halt. Looking around for his friend Grey, Gleig was surprised not to find him.

Meantime, Jackson was marching up Levee Road with his artillerymen when they ran into a British squad that fought fiercely to wrest away their cannon. Jackson raced to the forefront and called, "Save the guns, my boys, at any price."

A British squad arrived from Bayou Bienvenu but broke off its attacks for fear the men were getting too far from their ships on the lake. As the British withdrew to the comparative safety of Villeré's plantation, Jackson and his officers decided that a deepening fog made it too dangerous to pursue them.

The Americans camped on the grounds of Villeré's neighbor, Pierre Lacoste, and by 9:30 p.m. the battle seemed ended. Two hours later, both sides were awakened by musket fire coming from below the Villeré estate. It turned out that recently drafted militiamen from Louisiana had heard the *Carolina*'s guns and insisted on joining the fray. After trading a few shots with British sentinels, they retreated at dawn to their own post.

When quiet descended again over the fields and swamps, the British officers were claiming victory. The night's battle had lasted from 8 o'clock until three in the morning, and an early count found at least two hundred of their men killed or wounded, and another sixty-four missing. But they had escaped the trap Jackson had tried to spring.

George Gleig was standing with two swords in his hands—his own and one that an American had surrendered to him—when a British officer stepped forward and told him that Charles Grey had been killed.

Gleig's jubilant mood vanished, and he ran to the cane stack where he had last seen Grey. Gleig found his body with a shot that had torn through his head and left him in a pool of blood thickening in the night air. It looked as though Grey had been struck almost as soon as they had parted.

Numb and exhausted, Gleig was standing over the body when a bugle called him back to duty. To avoid shots from the *Carolina*, the British troops passed the rest of the night and most of the next day lying low on the riverbank without fires and shivering in the cold air.

When the threat seemed to be easing, Gleig rounded up three enlisted men and went to recover Grey's body. He passed dozens of the dead. Those struck down by bullets seemed to be sleeping. But men slashed with bayonets or sabers lay in grotesque formations of four or six, one Englishman and an American still joined by blades in each other's belly.

Locating Grey's pale and bloody corpse once again, Gleig threw himself down beside it and sobbed like a child. The other men wept along with him as they loaded Grey onto a cart and dug a shallow grave for him in the Villeré garden.

The British had turned the mansion itself into a field hospital. As Gleig walked its halls, he heard the wounded enlisted men cursing and shrieking from pain. In a small room, he recognized the officers who had been separated because of their rank. One, shot in the head and barely alive, gasped for breath. Another, a musket ball lodged deep in his backbone, was biting down on his blanket to stop himself from screaming.

Andrew Jackson also regarded his first joust with the British as, if not a victory, certainly no defeat. His killed, wounded, and missing men totaled 213, somewhat less than those of the enemy. America's regular army had taken the heaviest casualties.

The next day, Jackson was more ebullient as he relayed the results to John Coffee. They had halted the British advance and could dig in for the defense of New Orleans that lay ahead. Morale was running high, with many of yesterday's green recruits more confident now that they had stood up to the best soldiers Britain could field.

And Admiral Cochrane had learned—as General Ross had been taught outside Baltimore—never to announce his dinner plans in advance.

Whatever their commanders might be saying, British soldiers hurrying from their ships on the lake found their advance party subdued, even downcast. By working through the night, the entire army had arrived at the campground before dark on December 24. But two more U.S. ships were now pointing their guns at the British position, and General Keane's new arrivals were penned in until he could withdraw them from the riverbank, company by company.

The soldiers had no idea how long they would have to remain pinned down. Because their local guides had been either inept or treacherous in not alerting them to the American raid, the British now paid no attention to their rumors and treated them as spies.

Gleig reflected bitterly that every one of their expectations had been shattered. Instead of an easy march to a city whose residents would flock to welcome them, they had been mauled in their own camp. Around them, they saw deserted houses and the cattle and horses that had been driven away by outraged citizens. The men had already accepted that this expedition would not add to their glory but might at least fill their pockets. Instead, the new year promised only fierce resistance against men fighting to defend their homes.

A moment of hope arose when Pakenham arrived to the customary cheers from his new troops. But it was Christmas Day, and melancholy settled again over the camp. Eating in a barn with too few plates and forks, his officers reminisced about happier holidays, spoke of fallen comrades, and tried to ignore the salvos from the American ships. Most guns were far enough away to be harmless, but a few shells shook the barn walls. Then one shell hit an enlisted man and cut him in half. As they looked on, he took an hour to die.

The spectacle reminded Gleig of the difference between honorable European soldiers and ruthless Americans like Jackson's men. In France, British sentries could stand twenty yards apart from the French guards and, if neither army planned an advance, they might face each other throughout the night with no shots exchanged. That was civilized warfare.

The Americans acted as though any man they could kill was one less enemy. Tennessee riflemen were creeping through the brush to take potshots at the British sentries, and when they killed them, they scrambled out to strip their bodies of weapons and valuables. At one post, three replacements had been picked off before the British stopped posting guards and abandoned the area.

To Gleig and his fellow officers, those cold-blooded murders exposed the Americans not as soldiers but as simple assassins.

Jackson had drawn most of his men back two miles to dig entrenchments along the left bank of Rodriguez's Canal from the river to a swamp thick with cypress trees. Their new position was several miles southeast of New Orleans.

Jackson worried that a larger enemy force would soon be charging his meager defenses. He was somewhat relieved to learn at 4 p.m. on Christmas Eve that the British troops were being held in camp. The reprieve made Jackson redouble his efforts. He sent to the city for shovels and pickaxes and for slaves to fashion a rampart from mud and salvaged scrap; the slaves would free his soldiers for the battle ahead. When digging too deep sent up geysers of water that washed out their efforts, they cut down cypress logs and laid them in a way that kept the mud stable.

Jackson made his headquarters in a plantation house one hundred yards behind the fortified ditch and then rode up and down the line to urge speed. By sunset, a breastwork rose from three to four feet and stretching three-fifths of a mile.

Jackson was still sickly and weary from the battle, but he would not pause to sleep. He was determined, he said, either to halt the enemy there or to bury himself in the ruins of his defensive wall.

As Jackson was raising that bulwark, Major Latour cut a levee in front of a neighboring plantation, trying to flood the open plain between the two armies. Then the river dropped so low that Latour's effort made little difference, and the Americans put two six-pounders at the head of the road as added protection. The crew of a converted merchant sloop, the *Louisiana*, brought their ship downriver to two miles below Jackson's army; the *Carolina* remained anchored opposite the British camp.

Even with their nonstop exertion, the Americans were celebrating a merrier Christmas than the British, who had expected to mount an attack at any moment. But Pakenham, although a veteran of the battle of Salamanca during the Peninsular War, was also a cautious thirty-eight-year-old. His rewards from a victory would be great—an earldom and possibly the governorship of Louisiana. But failure would be ignominious.

At home, his brother-in-law Wellington was suggesting that Pakenham commanded enough troops to assure victory—some eight thousand well-equipped and disciplined men.

Pakenham seemed to agree. At least, his reproaches were scathing when he learned about the British decision not to move from the Villeré plantation and attack New Orleans instead of letting the troops be bottled up in this cul de sac.

Resenting the slur against his strategy, Cochrane protested that it had been Keane who refused to move his men. Cochrane vowed that if the army were to shrink again from launching an assault, his sailors and marines would do the job.

"We will storm the American lines and march into the city," the admiral said. "Then the soldiers can bring up the baggage."

For all his criticism, Pakenham himself would not commit his land troops until he could end the harassment from the American ships on the river. He would wait a few more days for the heaviest guns of his fleet.

On the night of December 26, Lieutenant Gleig was sent to an outpost at his army's left flank. With his dog trotting ahead of him, he checked on his sentinels every half hour. Even when they had become separated during the last battle, Gleig knew he could count on his dog to find him.

About 1 a.m., the animal stopped a few paces in front of a small woods and began barking fiercely. Gleig froze. A moment later, half a dozen muskets fired at him from only several feet away. He pulled out his pistol and fired back, and his attackers ran off.

As a clear but chilly dawn broke and the sun burned off the mists, Gleig was relieved to find that these inconclusive nights were over at last. At camp, he found his senior officers forming the men into ranks, with horses commandeered from nearby plantations lined up to create a makeshift cavalry unit.

At 7 a.m., Pakenham gave the order to open sustained fire against the *Carolina*. British nine-pounders threw shot that had been heating for five hours, their six-pounders hurled shrapnel, and their howitzers fired cold shell and shot. Within fifteen minutes, the American schooner was in flames and its crew jumping from the decks.

When the *Carolina* blew up an hour later, the British guns turned on the *Louisiana*. As America's largest armed vessel on the river, the ship was too valuable to lose. The winds were not strong enough to move it to safety, but 150 sailors rowed under a barrage of shot and pulled the *Louisiana* out of range.

Now that the British were on the move, their spirits were rising. Gleig enjoyed hearing his men shouting out coarse jokes to each other

as they marched toward the Americans. He had concluded that living
with death left soldiers as immune to its terror as animals were, and
hunger and exhaustion were less disagreeable because they experienced them so often. Truly, Gleig told himself, a soldier was the man
most free from care, which made him the happiest of men.

Gleig's musing ended abruptly when the British ran into a concealed
American position and were cut down by extremely accurate artillery
fire. The cheerful mood gave way to panic and cries from the
wounded. The left flank broke to cower behind high reeds in the knee-
deep water. Men of the right flank took fewer hits but were stopped by
the salvos at the marsh's edge.

The British retreated to settle onto a new campground at the Bienvenu and Chalmette plantations. Gleig worried that they were not
much better protected there than at the Villeré estate—no woods or
other cover, only open spaces visible to the American scouts. Nor over
the next three days could he understand why Pakenham was keeping
them there with no attempt to fortify the camp or even to send out riflemen to harass the Americans.

The British had already sprung their one surprise, a new weapon
called the Congreve rocket. Pakenham had hoped that its novelty and
the noise it made would terrorize the Americans. But William Carroll's
troops had adjusted quickly to the device, and it turned out to be more
effective at frightening the horses.

By the end of December 28, deciding that the British charge had been
only a feint or reconnaissance, the Americans went back to digging in
for the real battle. They had no idea what preparations the British were
making, but on New Year's Eve, they heard a hammering and clamor
that suggested the British were creating a battery for mounting their
cannon.

In their haste, the British soldiers were rolling out the hogsheads of
sugar they found in local barns and building the gun mounts from
sugar instead of dirt. Gleig and his fellow junior officers calculated
sadly that the sugar they were destroying would have fetched them
many thousands of English pounds sterling.

On January 1, Pakenham waited for a heavy fog to lift at 8 a.m. before he tried again to carry the fight to the Americans. He opened fire from his new batteries, confident that the odds would now favor him. He could draw on ten of the eighteen-pounders the British sailors had labored strenuously to haul from their ships, plus four twenty-four-pound carronades and ten field artillery pieces and howitzers. Against those twenty-four guns, the Americans had fifteen, and those guns had been mounted on higher and more vulnerable platforms than the British had built.

Pakenham seemed to expect his superior firepower to open up a gap in the American defenses that would let his infantry pour through. He did not take into account how skillfully the Americans fired what guns they had.

The first British salvos were aimed at Jackson's headquarters in the Macarty farmhouse. Jackson had passed the night fitfully on a couch in his rumpled uniform, with a guard on duty in the hallway and aides sleeping on the floor, their sword belts and pistols at their sides. They sprang up as a hundred hot balls, shells, and Congreve rockets hit the building. The barrage splintered furniture in every room, but Jackson and his men were unhurt as they evacuated the house.

Those first shots had scattered the American ranks in confusion. Gleig watched the frightened troops being coaxed back into formation and wished Pakenham had taken advantage of those minutes for his charge.

By noon, despite hits on American artillery caissons that had the British troops cheering, the battle was turning. Pakenham's fire remained intense, but answering shots from the American side were more precise and damaging. On the river, British batteries firing from the Chalmette and Bienvenu camps were trained ineffectually on Commodore Patterson; he lost not a man. Under his steady return barrage, British gunners began deserting their positions.

Jackson's troops remained far back, out of range of the shells. He kept them ready to leap forward and repel a British infantry charge. But that charge never came.

When the shelling died away, the British had lost forty-four killed and fifty-five wounded. Eleven Americans had died. The twenty-three American wounded included civilian visitors who would have been safe behind Jackson's lines if the British firing had been less erratic.

In retreat, Gleig pretended not to hear the mutterings and curses of his frustrated men. He admitted that they were justified. These soldiers had cheerfully endured hardship and exhaustion because they had expected to be led to victory. Instead, they were furious. Their swearing reminded their lieutenant of "the growling of a chained dog when he sees his adversary and cannot reach him."

But the preamble was ending. Commodore Patterson had spent hours studying the British position through his telescope and could give Jackson a clear idea of British strategy. Pakenham's troops would first assault the American position from the west bank of the river. They would try to capture Jackson's cannon and turn them against him while another British attack from the other bank would trap the Americans in their crossfire.

When Jackson was reluctant to split up his men to meet both charges, New Orleans' unstable geography worked in his favor. Pakenham demanded that Cochrane move another fourteen hundred men and their artillery by barge over the two miles from their bayou to the west bank of the Mississippi. The admiral's officers complained that the barges would require digging a canal, but Cochrane had made a proud boast to Pakenham and would not back down.

The British crews were split into four teams, working day and night, to cut a channel across the entire neck of land to the river. Gleig watched admiringly as the men worked past the limits of their fatigue and got the job done by January 6. But when transporting of the new troops began, the banks of their canal crumbled. The soil was too soft, and collapsing earth stopped larger boats from moving up the passage. Of the 1,400 men Pakenham was expecting, only 340, plus 100 sailors and marines, made it into position.

As he reviewed his troops on the night of January 7, Pakenham discovered a setback even worse. The men were properly arrayed in battle gear, but the Forty-fourth Regiment seemed to have misunderstood his

Sir Edward Pakenham

orders. Its troops had neglected to bring the ladders and fascines needed for crossing the Americans' ditch and scaling their walls.

Furious, Pakenham galloped up to Lieutenant Colonel Thomas Mullens, a regimental commander widely scorned for his incompetence. He ordered Mullens to return to camp for the ladders. But the sun rose during the delay, and Jackson's men had a clear view of the British soldiers lined up as they awaited orders. The Americans opened fire and began to strike them down by the hundreds.

Pakenham still did not have the essential ladders. He lacked support from soldiers and seamen who should already have seized the American guns on the west bank. But he had no choice. Pakenham gave the order to charge.

In those first moments, a British detachment overran one American battery and captured its three guns. They were expecting more troops to arrive soon. When none came, the Americans retook their position with punishing losses for the British.

Down the line, other men braved the American fire in an attempt to cross the ditch between them and storm the American parapets. But without ladders, they could only boost each other up on their shoulders. They were instantly cut down by Americans who pointed their muskets over the wall and fired directly into the tops of their heads. British soldiers were being killed without ever seeing an enemy face.

Mullens's Forty-fourth Regiment had returned to battle, but its ranks were disorganized and ineffectual. Sending orders to advance, Pakenham learned that Mullens had disappeared. When he could not be found, Pakenham rode to the head of the regiment to lead the troops himself.

A musket ball merely nicked his knee but killed his horse. Pakenham had barely called for a replacement when a burst of grapeshot dropped his body into the arms of his aide-de-camp. General Keane and the leader of the British third column were also wounded and carried from the field.

The Redcoats were left with no leaders and no plan. They stopped their charge, drew back from the American bombardment, and began to run for their lives. In a matter of minutes, Andrew Jackson had scored a stunning victory.

It seemed too easy. Major Thomas Hinds of the Mississippi Volunteers asked Jackson's permission to pursue the British with his cavalry. But when Jackson called together his generals, they all opposed the idea. John Adair, who had led a reserve force of one thousand Kentuckians, warned Jackson that his troops fought well behind breastworks or in the woods, but their officers were inexperienced and their soldiers undisciplined. If Hinds provoked a fight on an open plain, Adair's men could not be relied upon.

Edward Livingston agreed. As an adopted son of New Orleans, he worried about his friends. "What more do you want?" Livingston asked. "Your object is gained. The city is saved. The British have retired." For the pleasure of a blow or two, he added, Jackson would be risking the city's leading citizens and depriving many children of their fathers.

Jackson was easily convinced. He denied Hinds's request and

adopted Livingston's reasoning in his later justification for keeping his men secure behind their battlements.

With the last sporadic firing over, Jackson walked from battery to battery, congratulating the men as they cheered and the military band played "Hail Columbia."

He was surveying the bodies fallen in front of him when the smoke cleared and Jackson saw hundreds of British soldiers seeming to rise up from the dead. They were the men, terrified by the first barrage, who had fallen without a scratch and lay among the dying and wounded until the battle was over. Now they were coming forward to surrender as prisoners of war.

Along the American defenses, soldiers were jumping down to tend to the enemy wounded. New Orleans hospitals were already filled with Americans from the earlier engagements, but residents had begun to hear of the victory and were collecting mattresses and linen for binding up wounds. Local women were volunteering as nurses.

Less compassionate men picked their way among the carnage, collecting souvenirs or valuables that could be sold—swords, money, telescopes, and the uniform caps they clamped on their heads.

A sudden outbreak of gunfire seemed to make the American self-congratulations premature; it also revealed a weakness in Jackson's single-minded approach to strategy.

Just as he had neglected New Orleans while driving the British from Pensacola, he had concentrated his formidable energies on the east bank of the river for his showdown with Pakenham. For more than two weeks, he had not inspected the west bank's defenses. At the last minute, Jackson had sent another 500 Kentuckians to reinforce that flank, but only 170 of them were carrying weapons.

Earlier in the morning, William Thornton's reduced number of British troops had landed from their boats after long delays and had rushed double-time to the west bank. Scattering the Kentucky defenses, they charged General David Morgan's position and seized his cannon, one inscribed like Isaac Brock's Canadian trophy, "Taken at the surrender of Yorktown, 1781." But the spiked guns were useless.

Lieutenant Gleig was among Thornton's officers, all of them con-

vinced that the entire battle was going well for the British. They chased
the Kentuckians for more than two miles before they were ordered to
halt. It was then that they learned how disastrously Pakenham's attack
across the river had failed. Thornton, severely wounded, was told to
march his men back to their boats and join the rest of the army in its
retreat. Gleig set fire to a plantation house and withdrew under the
cover of its smoke.

Infuriated by the Kentuckians' fleeing, Jackson directed a French general, Jean Humbert, to cross the river and retake the American position. Humbert, who had fought under Napoleon and always appeared
on the streets of New Orleans in his old uniform, was delighted to accept the assignment. But in the U.S. ranks, he was serving as a volunteer private. Since Jackson neglected to give him written authority,
American officers on the west bank refused to take orders from a man
who was not a citizen, and Humbert returned angrily to Jackson's
headquarters.

By noon, the British sent a flag of truce with a letter asking for a two-
day armistice to bury their dead. Tough as ever in negotiations, Jackson
agreed only if the truce did not involve the west bank and if neither
side reinforced their troops there. He was demanding surrender.

John Lambert accepted those terms for the British. In his note,
Lambert included only his rank of major general but not his new au-
thority over the army. He did not want Jackson to know yet that the
British had lost the three generals who outranked him.

The next morning, after Lambert had brought the remainder of his
troops over to the east bank, they began to collect the dead and any
wounded men who had been left overnight where they had fallen.
Carried off the battlefield, the corpses of Pakenham and three other
generals were gutted, according to military practice, and their remains
nailed into barrels of rum to be shipped back to England.

Young Gleig was curious enough to ride out to the front, where
he found the scene even more shocking and humiliating than he had
expected. Within the narrow passage in front of the American defenses lay a thousand or more corpses. He knew they were all British

because they were in full uniform, with not an American body to be seen.

The dead were being thrown by the dozens into shallow holes with barely enough dirt to cover them. Gleig rode through the solemn scene recalling the laughter and high spirits—above all, the confidence—of these same men only twenty hours ago.

Gleig estimated his army's loss at two thousand men; he was only thirty-six short of the final tally. As he surveyed the scene, Gleig came upon an American officer who was smoking a cigar as he made his own count. To everyone who passed, he repeated exultantly that his side had suffered only eight men killed and fourteen wounded! Only eight killed and fourteen wounded!

The man's insufferable bragging cut through Gleig's sorrow. He wanted to fight. But with an armistice in effect, he had to choke back his anger. Gleig rode back to the British camp and found the defeated regiments quarreling among themselves and seething for one more chance at revenge.

Although Thornton's attack had not affected the day's outcome, Jackson sent word to David Morgan to improve his defenses and posted men to warn if the British were regrouping for another attack. Over the next days, he kept up incessant artillery fire to trouble the sleep of the British survivors.

Jackson and Lambert sent representatives to work out an exchange of prisoners. Admiral Cochrane would give up the Americans being held by his fleet and receive the same number of British prisoners of an equal rank.

"Peace of Ghent 1814 and Triumph of America"

Chapter Twenty-three

PEACE
(1815)

Because the Tennessee River was flooded, President Madison had received no news from Louisiana for two weeks. A Federalist newspaper was speculating that his administration already knew that the British had captured New Orleans.

On January 20, a courier reached Washington with a report that the fighting so far was indecisive and that General Jackson had retreated to a stronger position.

The next night, Madison was called away from dinner to receive the New Orleans mail. He returned to the table to tell his guests that there was still no news. A young Harvard professor dining with the president recalled that no one knew what to say and a silence lingered.

371

Later, when the young man had a chance to talk with the president, he found Madison surprisingly droll but looking serious even as he joked. Their talk turned to religion. During the war, congressmen had requested that Madison issue the usual proclamation setting a day of prayer and fasting for America's success. He had refused. The people, Madison said, could pray on their own if they were disposed to do so. On this night, he confided to the professor that among religions, he favored the Unitarians.

When Jackson's next letter arrived at the end of the month, the outlook seemed no better. One leading opposition newspaper renewed its call for Madison's impeachment.

Outside New Orleans, General Lambert weighed his options as commander of the British forces and found none of them satisfactory. His army had launched its most promising plan of attack and had been beaten decisively. If he tried and failed again, his army would lack the men to make a successful retreat.

If he did decide to withdraw, however, Lambert had only enough small craft to evacuate half of his men at a time. And yet splitting into two groups meant that both might be destroyed. One alternative would be to wade through miles of swampland to get to the water.

Lambert sent men to strap together bundles of reeds they could lay across the marshes to form a slippery path. At the broader ditches, men were to build bridges, even though they would be equally fragile.

Constructing that tenuous getaway took nine days. During that time, Jackson's men did not charge the British ranks, but they were not idle. Hauling six cannon to the riverbank, the Americans zeroed in with incessant fire on the British cowering in the same uniforms they had worn now for weeks. Doused all day by a rain that came with violent thunder and lightning, they lay awake all night, teeth chattering from the cold.

One morning, the Mississippi managed to worsen their misery by overflowing its banks and soaking the troops even more thoroughly. It took a full day for the river to recede.

Through it all, the Americans continued the harassment that the

British considered unsporting. Not every assault was physical. American militiamen would steal close to a British guard position and throw down leaflets promising a hundred dollars and a plot of land to any man who deserted. Given their hardships and their bleak prospects, the sentinels began to steal away from their posts in numbers that disturbed their commanders.

When his flimsy roadway was open, Lambert sent the wounded back to the fleet first. Next went the baggage and supplies and support officers, until only the infantry and heavy artillery remained. Removing the most visible guns would alert the Americans to the evacuation; they were spiked and left in place.

On the evening of January 18, ten days after its inglorious rout, the British infantry stole away, regiment by regiment, moving as silently as when they slipped out of Washington. The march along the high road by the river went smoothly, but when the soldiers came to their pathway of reeds, the boots of the first men smashed them into the swamp, leaving the rest to propel themselves through mud up to their knees.

Inching forward under a starless sky, with no light to guide his steps, Lieutenant Gleig watched in horror as one soldier sank into the mud until, crying out for help, he disappeared up to his neck. Moving toward him, Gleig also sank to his chest. He grabbed gratefully at a leather canteen strap thrown out to him and pulled himself up to lie on the mud's surface. Gleig was dragged to safety as the first victim sank from sight.

By dawn, the troops had reached the huts called Fisherman's Village. Lambert called a halt, and the men threw themselves on the ground and slept for several hours. Lambert and his senior officers moved their gear into the deserted huts. The rest of the men tried to build fires, but the reeds flared up like straw and instantly went out.

For the next two days, the men got by with crumbs of biscuit and a small dot of rum. Growing up in England, Gleig had enjoyed hunting. When he saw ducks in the bog, he took a firelock and brought down three of them. The birds dropped into the water about twenty yards away, but Gleig's dog, more exhausted than his master, would not go after them. When he shot more ducks that fell into the lake a second time, Gleig pulled off his uniform except for his socks, broke through the crust of ice, and plunged in.

He retrieved a couple of birds to take back to camp, but ooze at the lake's bottom had sucked away one of his socks. Gleig knew that no civilian could ever understand why, at that moment, losing one wool sock was a calamity.

When Jackson discovered that General Lambert had led his men back to their boats, he sent along guards to make sure they were actually evacuating the area. Reassured, he wrote to the governor of Tennessee, "Louisiana may again say her soil is not trodden by the sacrilegious footsteps of a hostile Briton."

After the peace treaty was signed on Christmas Eve, it had gone immediately to London, where it was ratified four days later by the Prince Regent, who would become George IV. Couriers brought the document to a British war sloop, the *Favorite*, which sailed on January 2, 1815, and arrived in New York the evening of Saturday, February 11. The *Mercantile Advertiser*, a New York newspaper, printed five-by-six-inch sheets about the treaty and threw them from an office window. In a matter of minutes, they were posted all over the city, setting crowds to celebrate what the paper called "the great and joyful news of PEACE."

Although no one yet knew the terms, Americans would have agreed with John Quincy Adams, who wrote to his wife, "We have obtained nothing but peace and have made great sacrifices to obtain it. But our honor remains unsullied; our territory remains entire."

With the rest of the nation, Dolley Madison had been waiting to hear the fate of New Orleans. Six days after Jackson's victory she had written to Hannah Gallatin that she hoped for news that very day. "Our anxieties cannot be expressed," she wrote, since so much depended on the result.

Madison finally learned of Jackson's victory before Harrison Gray Otis and two fellow delegates from the Hartford Convention had the bad luck to arrive in the capital at a moment when the country was consumed by patriotic joy. After the New Englanders were granted a brief and embarrassing audience, they waited to return home until mockery from the opposition press had died down.

*　　*　　*

On February 14, Secretary of State Monroe presented the treaty to Madison, and celebrations sprang up around the capital. Senator Jonathan Roberts of Pennsylvania, a staunch Madison ally, left one party that evening to go to Octagon House and congratulate the president in person.

The household was quiet and dark. Roberts found Madison sitting alone in the parlor with no servants at his side. The contrast with the boisterous scene he had just left was so extreme that Roberts found himself apologizing. He had heard a rumor of peace, the senator said. Now he wondered whether it was mistaken.

"Take a seat," the president said, "and I will tell you all I know."

Madison confirmed that the reports were correct but said he was not ready to publish an official confirmation until the Senate ratified the treaty.

Impressed by Madison's self-control, Roberts marveled to himself, as he had before, at the man's composure. He had witnessed the same behavior even when every prospect had looked dark. Roberts worried that when the history of Madison's administration was written, that stoic aspect of his character would be lost.

The next morning, Madison submitted the treaty to the Senate, which ratified it unanimously. The *Niles' Weekly Register* headline reflected the country's reaction:

GLORIOUS NEWS
ORLEANS SAVED AND PEACE CONCLUDED.

WHO WOULD NOT BE AN AMERICAN?
LONG LIVE THE REPUBLIC!
ALL HAIL! LAST ASYLUM OF OPPRESSED HUMANITY!

Because of the magnitude of Jackson's victory, Madison could describe the treaty in far more ebullient language than John Quincy Adams had used. He began his statement on February 18 by asserting that the recent war had been necessary and its success "the natural result of the legislative council, of the patriotism of the people, of the public spirit of the militia, and of the valor of the Military and Naval Forces of Country."

The president warned Congress against unwise cuts in military spending. The American people were peaceable, but they had learned that their nature could not exempt them from the strife of a wider world. Preparing for war was the best way to ensure peace.

Madison concluded with the hope that the declaration of peace would not only mean friendship again between the United States and Great Britain but also would produce "happiness and harmony in every section of our beloved Country."

Henry Clay summed up the mood among his War Hawks: "Now, I can go to England without mortifications."

Andrew Jackson was determined not to throw away his epic success by letting down his guard prematurely. About the time Madison was issuing his victory resolution, Edward Livingston brought Jackson a report from the British fleet that the peace had been ratified. But confirmation from Washington had been held up in the post office, and Jackson did not receive official word until March 13.

For the two months since Jackson's victory, the Louisiana legislature had chafed under martial law, but he refused to lift its provisions or to send the militia back to their homes.

Tension with the townspeople was heightened by the anticlimactic loss of Fort Bowyer near Mobile. Brigadier General James Winchester had been released by the British after spending a year in Canada as a prisoner. Left in charge of the fort, he failed, not for the first time, to provide basic security. When the British took Bowyer during the afternoon of February 11, Jackson was badly chagrined. He wanted to retake the fort but was held back by rumors of the peace treaty.

"If an honorable peace," Jackson wrote to the governor of Mississippi, "I hail it with heartfelt satisfaction. If dishonorable, it will meet my hearty imprecations. But the Lord's will be done. The fall of Fort Bowyer is truly grating to my feelings."

Reliable news about the treaty ended Jackson's dream of retaliation. But by then he had other distractions.

*   *   *

The Louisiana members of the militia were especially resentful about having their service extended until Jackson could be satisfied that the peace was genuine. Creoles in the militia hit on the scheme of registering as French citizens and applying for discharge on that ground.

Jackson was infuriated by the ruse and ordered the French consul out of New Orleans, along with all French citizens. He forced them to travel 120 miles from the city, ostensibly because they might form a subversive third column.

On March 3, a member of the state assembly named Louaillier denounced the order in an anonymous newspaper letter. The writer was quickly identified, and Jackson sent soldiers to arrest him. When a federal judge ordered Louaillier's release on a writ of habeas corpus, Jackson ordered the judge arrested as well.

Jackson's directive revealed his sense of being surrounded by traitors and ingrates. An assembly resolution had thanked by name everyone who had saved the city—Carroll, Coffee, Adair—and omitted only their commanding general.

"You will be vigilant," Jackson cautioned the men he sent to imprison Judge Dominick Hall. "The agents of our enemy are more numerous than was expected."

Jackson's vindictive rage kept widening. When the district attorney applied to another judge for Hall's release, Jackson had both of those men arrested as well.

Louaillier was brought up before a court-martial on several charges, including the implausible accusation that he was a spy. The military court threw out all of them on the grounds that since the defendant was in neither the army nor the militia, a court-martial panel had no jurisdiction over him.

Jackson ignored that finding and kept Louaillier in prison while he exiled Judge Hall from the city. The next day, however, Jackson finally got official notification that the treaty had been ratified. Dismissing the state militias, he released his other prisoners and watched as the citizens of New Orleans welcomed back Judge Hall and the French consul.

＊   ＊   ＊

Then it was Hall's turn. On March 21, he ordered Jackson into court to show why he should not be cited for contempt for his refusal to honor the ruling on habeas corpus. Six days later, Jackson showed up in court with his aide, Major Reid. As Reid began to read Jackson's defense, he was cut off. The prosecution then made its case, but Jackson's attorney refused to respond. The next day, Jackson appeared again in court and issued a statement that began, "I will not answer interrogatories." Since he had been prevented from offering a defense, he said, he was ready to receive the court's punishment.

The courtroom was jammed with well-wishers, including a band of Lafitte's pirates. They were shouting curses against Hall until Jackson rose, turned to face them, and, with a gesture, commanded silence.

Judge Hall remarked, "The only question was whether the Law should bend to the General, or the General to the Law." He imposed a one-thousand-dollar fine but—given the defendant's service to the country—no imprisonment.

Jackson's admirers instantly raised the thousand dollars, but Jackson paid the fine himself and asked that the money be donated instead to the families of those who died defending the city. Cheering supporters pulled his carriage to the Exchange Coffee House, where Jackson spelled out a moral for the crowd to remember:

"Considering obedience to the laws, even when we think them unjustly applied, as the best duty of a citizen, I did not hesitate to comply with the sentence you have heard, and I entreat you to remember the example I have given you of respectful submission to the administration of justice."

With that cloud removed, Jackson was free to give himself over to the honors and awards being showered on him. Arriving in the city, Rachel Jackson won over local society women with her obviously kind heart. Short and plump, she created a sensation with her husband when they took to the dance floor and gave their wild version of "Possum Up De Gum Tree." Jackson towered over his wife like a pale wraith; to one observer, their bobbing up and down brought to mind "half-drunk Indians."

On April 6, the Jacksons left for Nashville, stopping along the way for dinners honoring Jackson as the hero of New Orleans. A small indication of the changes under way in the nation came when Thomas Jefferson left Monticello to offer up a toast to the victory.

Jackson no longer had to choke back his resentment over years of snubs and superiority from Jefferson and the landed gentry who had despised Jackson until the moment they needed his strength and courage.

Jackson's memory stretched back to the Revolution and stories of Jefferson hastily running away from Monticello as Redcoats came to capture him.

Now in a burst of withering sarcasm, Jackson paid off the rankling scores:

"I'm glad the old gentleman has plucked up courage enough to at least attend a banquet in honor of a battle."

James Monroe

Chapter Twenty-four

AFTERWARD
(1815–1861)

Much of Madison's wish for national harmony came true. From New Orleans, Jackson assured him that the Lafitte brothers had shown "courage and fidelity," and the president pardoned their past crimes. Across the rest of the country, the prevailing good spirits were buoyed by a prosperity that softened the memories of wartime hardship.

The exception was New England, which remained gripped by an economic depression that guaranteed the reelection in April of Massachusetts Governor Strong. Otherwise, southern cotton plantations thrived, and farmers sent grain and tobacco abroad from record harvests.

*   *   *

When casualties from the late war were added up, it appeared that about fifteen hundred ground troops, both regular army and militia, had been killed in action and another five thousand wounded. Apologists for the war pointed out that more men had often been killed in a single one of Napoleon's battles.

Estimates for the war's financial cost were equally imprecise—perhaps $80.5 million.

Pleading a lack of revenue, Congress resisted the military appropriations that Secretary Monroe requested and cut in half his recommendation for a peacetime army of twenty thousand men.

Sending his congratulations to Madison, Jefferson wrote that the defense of New Orleans should teach the nations of Europe that while Americans intended to take no part in their wars, neither would the country shrink from self-defense. He hoped that since England's pride had been spared because the treaty did not mention the "atrocity of impressment," the Foreign Ministry would willingly give up the practice. "Without this she must understand that the present is but a truce," Jefferson wrote. Peace could end the first time a British officer seized another American citizen.

Looking back on the war, Madison was less truculent. "If our first struggle was a war of our infancy," he wrote, "this last war was that of our youth."

In that hopeful vein, Madison suggested that if lessons were learned from both the Revolutionary War and the War of 1812, the result "may long postpone, if not forever prevent, a necessity for exerting the strength of our manhood."

Jefferson's had been a rare voice in mentioning impressment. With peace, America was turning inward to vast territories still unexplored. When Napoleon escaped from Elba and returned to power for one hundred days, no one proposed another Quasi-War. England agreed eventually to commercial terms that satisfied American businessmen, and Stephen Decatur sailed once again to the African coast and extracted a favorable treaty from the dey of Algiers.

＊　　　＊　　　＊

Madison found a suitable reward for each of the delegates he had sent to Ghent. John Quincy Adams was preparing to return to the United States in May 1815 when he was notified that he had been appointed minister plenipotentiary to Great Britain. To Gallatin, Madison offered the American ministry in France. James Bayard would go to Russia, and John Russell would take up his post in Sweden.

Henry Clay chose to return to Congress as Speaker of the House. And Bayard had no time to accept his nation's thanks. He died on March 8, 1815, during his return voyage to the United States.

While Gallatin was back in the United States before sailing to Paris, John Jacob Astor offered to sell him one-fifth of his fur-trading business, a share worth an estimated one hundred thousand dollars a year. Gallatin, now fifty-five, was tempted by the chance to provide for his family, but he went ahead and accepted instead the nine-thousand-dollar government position.

He continued to serve the country in treaty negotiations and diplomatic assignments until 1849, when he died at the age of eighty-eight. At the end of his life, Gallatin was warning about the danger to democracy in going to war against Mexico.

Madison was about to leave the presidency more popular than when he entered it, but debate had already begun about his performance as chief executive. No one had denied his brilliance at the Constitutional Convention when a federal United States emerged from the disunion and discord of the earlier confederation. Madison's temperament as a natural compromiser had served him then and again in the legislature when he led the newly born Republican faction.

The triumph of the Republicans had resulted, however, more from the Federalists' own instinct for self-destruction — their backbiting and repressive legislation, the brutal onslaught of Hamilton against John Adams. And Harrison Gray Otis and other Federalists would spend the rest of their lives trying to explain away the Hartford Convention.

Privately, Otis compensated for his party's impotence by insulting Madison. He called the president a "mean and contemptible little blackguard" and a "little pigmy" and assured his wife that, whatever Madison was claiming, the Federalist mission to Washington would somehow have succeeded.

Madison's judicious approach to government might have assured him a distinguished career on the bench. Instead, he was carried along to the presidency in Jefferson's wake, even though he was largely lacking in Jefferson's gift for the self-protective hypocrisy often termed political instinct.

And Otis was hardly the first to point out that Madison was short. Even men who admired his intellectual stature were inclined to mock his physical height. Washington and Jefferson before him had been tall, and John Adams had made up for his shorter size with an imposing corporeality. If Madison was a withered little applejohn, Adams was a full bushel.

Looming on the political horizon were Monroe and Jackson, casting shadows as imposing as those of the War Hawks who had pressed so relentlessly for war. Washington society had observed that even Madison's wife brought a more stately presence than his to the drawing room.

In the end, though, the course of Madison's presidency had not been determined by his physical size. Even if he could have looked them straight in the eye, he had not been inclined to face down Clay and the other Hawks. Madison was twenty years older than they were, but he too had risen in politics with that second generation of Americans who played no part in the Revolution. At a time when war was the highest measure of patriotism, men of his era welcomed the chance to stand up for their country. Although challenging Britain again had been an obsession for Clay and Calhoun, the new struggle soon became Mr. Madison's War in the public mind, and no evidence suggested that the label was distressing to him.

Launched by the promise of conquest and to avenge national honor, the War of 1812 was no triumph by traditional standards. After two and a half years, Madison had been grateful to preserve America's existing boundaries. He had witnessed the destruction of his capital during an invasion that sent his wife fleeing from their home, and his policies had pushed a prosperous sector of the country into economic recession and its people toward secession.

But Madison had also ridden out the bleakest months of the war without limiting the freedoms assured by the Bill of Rights. Unlike Jackson in New Orleans or America's subsequent wartime presidents, Madison did not impose martial law, restrict the press, round up suspected dissidents, or suspend the right of habeas corpus.

Instead, he adapted his philosophy to match the nation's wartime needs. In fact, critics accused him of using the war as a pretext for strengthening the central government in ways he had always claimed to resist. They pointed to bills he signed in April 1816 that chartered the national bank again, provided for a standing army and navy, imposed protective tariffs, and extended the war taxes.

Federalists said that the president was now admitting that they had been right all along.

But as his last act in office, on March 3, 1817, Madison vetoed a public works bill backed by Clay and Calhoun. The president granted that spending money to build roads and canals might increase the nation's prosperity, but he insisted that such expenditures must be authorized by a constitutional amendment.

To that, Calhoun had the unanswerable rebuttal. If Madison was now so devoted to a strict interpretation of the Constitution, "On what principle can the purchase of Louisiana be justified?"

To the end of Madison's administration, the blight of slavery remained unaddressed. On that explosive topic, he could expect no guidance from Jefferson, since both men claimed that their financial distress required them to hold on to their slaves.

When a young Virginian named Edward Coles freed his own slaves and moved north, he appealed to Jefferson to speak out for abolition. From Monticello, Jefferson wrote back, "This enterprise is for the young." Coles was not put off. He pointed out that Benjamin Franklin had been older than Jefferson when he went on arguing against the evils of slavery.

In Madison's case, he soothed his conscience with benign treatment. Visiting him at Montpelier, Attorney General Rush loyally praised the president as "a model of kindness to his slaves." And yet Madison made no attempt to resolve the issue of slavery, even though he understood its potential for disaster.

A year after the battle of Moraviantown, the British brought five charges of bad judgment and ineffectual leadership against Henry Proctor. The court found him guilty of four of them and recommended that he be publicly reprimanded and suspended without pay for six months. When the sentence was sent to the Prince Regent, he upheld only the reprimand.

George Prevost was also recalled to England in 1815 to answer the charges of mismanagement being pressed by James Yeo, but Prevost died of dropsy before his trial could begin.

Unlike his contemporaries in the army, George Cockburn suffered no loss of prestige from his role in the war. Returning to Britain, he was assigned the duty of conveying Napoleon into exile in St. Helena and staying there for seven months as his first custodian. Cockburn found Bonaparte sulky; the former emperor considered the admiral insulting.

Before his death in 1853, Cockburn served for many years on the British navy's Board of Admiralty, at one time unsuccessfully championing the discarded practice of impressment.

For George Gleig, army service had only diverted him temporarily from the career his family had chosen for him. He returned to Oxford for a master's degree at Magdalen College and in 1819 was married and ordained as an Anglican minister. Gleig was still only twenty-three.

His memoir of fighting under Wellington in northern Spain was published as a series of magazine articles called *The Subaltern*. Its success prompted Gleig to publish *Campaigns of the British Army at Washington and New Orleans*.

He wrote copiously on military and religious subjects and in middle age was appointed chaplain general of Britain's armed forces. Gleig was ninety-two when he died in 1888, seventy-four years from the time he had wept at the New Orleans grave of Charles Grey.

*   *   *

By surviving the many changes in Madison's cabinet, James Monroe had become well known if not especially popular. Because the northern states resented the hold Virginians had maintained on the presidency, Monroe did not present himself as yet another candidate from his home state. When he was able to reassure New York Republicans on that point, he won 183 electoral votes to the 34 cast for Rufus King, the candidate put forward by the hapless Federalists.

As his secretary of state, Monroe brought back John Quincy Adams from London, and he named John Calhoun as secretary of war. Adams had been abroad for almost nine years and his father was a leading Federalist which made his appointment surprising but well received. Adams had added substantial weight, his hair was gone, and his manner more forbidding than ever. Henry Clay hoped to succeed Monroe, and expected no challenge from his former sparring partner.

In July 1817, the *Columbian Centinel* in Boston, a steadfast Federalist newspaper, headed one of its social notes "Era of Good Feelings." The phrase became a widespread description of Monroe's presidency, although the Seminoles and Spaniards of Florida would not have agreed. Andrew Jackson claimed to be acting with President Monroe's approval when he invaded Florida and flew the American flag again over Pensacola. In the process, Jackson arrested two British citizens for supplying arms to the Indians and, when they were found guilty by a military court, ordered one shot, the other hanged.

Secretary of War Calhoun insisted that he had given Jackson permission to cross the Spanish border only if he were pursuing Seminole marauders. Clay and many other congressmen demanded that Jackson be punished for exceeding his authority.

Within Monroe's cabinet, Jackson was defended only by Adams, whose enthusiasm for expansion matched Jackson's own. Citing international law, Adams argued that Jackson had neither flouted the Constitution nor waged an illegal war against Spain.

Then, using Jackson's exploit as leverage, Adams went on to negotiate an advantageous treaty with Spain that extended the borders of the Louisiana Purchase to the northern boundary of present-day California, making the United States a transcontinental nation. Spain also relinquished claims to the Pacific Northwest and allowed the United States to buy Florida for $5 million. After consulting with Jackson, Adams agreed to one concession: The United States would give up any claim to Texas.

To his journal, Adams boasted that this Transatlantic Treaty was not only "the most important incident in my life" but "the most successful negotiations consummated by the Government of this Union."

As Monroe was grappling with a severe economic depression in 1819, he faced a crisis over the admission of the Missouri Territory to the union. Northern congressmen were threatening to block statehood unless slavery was eliminated from the new state's constitution.

In past years, John Quincy Adams had seemed indifferent to slavery, but he had come to see it as "the great and foul stain" upon the Union and was dismayed that Calhoun, a Yale graduate and the only cabinet officer Adams considered his intellectual equal, should be ardently against abolition.

A compromise preserved the balance of free and slave states by linking the creation of the state of Maine to Missouri's admission. But when Missourians proposed to bar all free blacks from migrating into their new state, Henry Clay negotiated a second compromise that prevented the Missouri constitution from limiting the rights of citizens from other states.

Privately, Adams wondered whether a better answer would have been to provoke a breach with the South, even if the result was a smaller United States "unpolluted with slavery." He noted in his journal, "If the union were to be dissolved, slavery is precisely the question upon which it ought to break."

Despite that crisis, Monroe's reelection was never in doubt. With the Federalist Party in tatters, Monroe received 321 votes to 1. The diehard governor of New Hampshire had embarrassed John Quincy Adams by casting that one protest vote for him.

Another historic debate marked Monroe's second term when Great Britain's secretary of foreign affairs suggested that his country and the United States join together to stop Spain from subduing its rebellious colonies in Latin America.

The question became whether Britain's navy should protect the hemisphere from European exploitation. When Monroe turned for advice to Jefferson and Madison, they both endorsed the idea.

Once again, Adams dissented. Recalling George Washington's warning against entangling alliances, he had already urged the House of Representatives never to go "abroad in search of monsters to destroy." Now, rather than waiting for a new crisis, Adams recommended that Monroe's administration proclaim to the world a clear statement of principles.

On December 2, 1823, Monroe sent to Congress the message that Adams had drafted. It announced that the American continent could no longer "be considered as subjects for future colonization by any European Power." The United States would consider such attempts "dangerous to our peace and safety."

The name for his warning only came twenty years after Monroe's death, but he had laid down the foundation of the Monroe Doctrine.

As Monroe's presidency drew to a close, he was plagued by rumors that he wanted a third term and might call out the army to achieve it. Monroe could quell that speculation, but he could not mend the rift when three of his cabinet members—Calhoun, Adams, and Secretary of the Treasury William Crawford—plus the Speaker of the House all became candidates in the campaign of 1824.

Clay had been sniping at Calhoun for a long while; and Crawford, a slave owner like Calhoun, had fallen out with Monroe over an attempt to define the slave trade as illegal piracy. Despite his cold and friendless manner, Adams's position made him a strong candidate, since Jefferson, Madison, and Monroe had all moved up to the presidency from the State Department.

Adams professed indifference to that prospect until John Russell, his former colleague from Ghent, tried to boost Clay's candidacy by accusing Adams of truckling abjectly to the British during the peace talks. The fury of his rebuttal made it clear that Adams was indeed a candidate.

And then there was Andrew Jackson. Appointed by Monroe as governor of Florida, he seemed to be in the running, although he had vowed, like Adams, that if he ever became president "it shall be without any exertion on my part."

*   *   *

In a campaign fueled largely by personalities, an unlikely alliance formed between Adams and Jackson. Adams claimed to venerate the general's service to the nation, while Jackson praised Adams for having both integrity and a first-rate mind. All the same, Jackson declined overtures to run as Adams's vice president.

When Calhoun withdrew abruptly from the race, he offered to serve as vice president with either Jackson or Adams.

During that period of jockeying, William Crawford developed erysipelas, an acute skin disease. His doctor apparently treated him with an overdose of lobelia that left Crawford speechless and nearly blind. Since his supporters did not reveal their candidate's infirmities, Crawford's showing in the election was strong enough to deny Clay a place as one of the three finalists to go before the House of Representatives.

Under Electoral College rules, the winner had to take thirteen of the twenty-four electoral votes. If no candidate got that majority, Calhoun, who had already been elected vice president, would assume the presidency on March 4, 1825.

Adams had lost the popular vote to Jackson by thirty-nine thousand votes. Now he threw himself into the kind of campaigning he had scorned, making the rounds of the few Federalists left in Congress and reassuring the Republicans about his loyalty.

To be elected, Adams would also have to put aside the differences with Clay that dated back to Ghent. In early January, Clay called on Adams and proposed a deal; Adams did not reveal its terms to his journal.

When the roll was called the following month, Adams won New England, New York, Maryland, and Illinois, and Clay delivered Kentucky, Ohio, Louisiana, and Missouri.

Elected the sixth president of the United States on the first ballot, Adams outraged Jackson and his followers by then naming Clay as his secretary of state.

Adams's term began nostalgically when Lafayette paid a farewell visit to America. After traveling to see Monroe, the marquis sidestepped the quicksand of American politics by calling on the senior

Adams in Massachusetts and on Jefferson and Madison in Virginia. Lafayette also traveled to New Orleans and then on to the Hermitage to congratulate Jackson in person on his world-renowned victory.

Despite peacetime cuts in the navy's budget, Stephen Decatur and Thomas Macdonough were among the naval veterans who had fared well. Decatur and his wife, Susan, could afford to commission the Capitol's architect, Benjamin Latrobe, to design a house for them on Washington's H Street, near the President's Mansion.

Macdonough had been promoted to captain, and for his capture of the British squadron, valued at $329,000, he was awarded $22,807, the war's biggest prize for a one-day battle. New York and Vermont deeded Macdonough real estate, and Connecticut put aside its antiwar sentiments to present him with matching pistols for saving the state from "imminent public danger."

Replacing Isaac Hull as commander of the Portsmouth Navy Yard, Macdonough lived quietly, tending to his investments, until he took command of one warship in 1818 and then, in 1824, of the *Constitution*.

The next year, Macdonough fell ill after a stop in Gibraltar and died aboard the merchant ship taking him back to the United States. He was approaching his forty-second birthday.

Oliver Perry died even younger. Promoted to captain, he was sent in 1819 on a mission to Venezuela, where he contracted yellow fever and died at the age of thirty-four. Buried first in Trinidad, his body was brought back to Newport, Rhode Island, and a memorial was erected at Put-in Bay.

For Captain James Barron, the years had been bleak since the navy had censured him for surrendering the *Chesapeake*. He had gone first to Copenhagen to try to support the wife and daughters he left behind in Virginia. When his five-year suspension ended, his family received a pension of fifty dollars a month; otherwise, Barron had to depend on charity from friends.

Returning to the United States in 1818, he sought reinstatement in the navy, but his application was endorsed by only one fellow officer—Jesse Duncan Elliott, who had also testified on his behalf at the original court-martial. In the meantime, Elliott's reputation had been fatally damaged when Oliver Perry accused him of misconduct during the battle of Lake Erie.

Elliott had challenged Perry to a duel, even though his countrymen now condemned dueling even more sharply than they had when Burr killed Hamilton. Perry responded that he would agree only if a court-martial absolved Elliott of Perry's charges.

Acting for the Board of Navy Commissioners, Decatur informed Perry that the government considered the case against Elliott too thin; there would be no investigation. The decision ended Elliott's hope for vindication but not his enthusiasm for dueling.

When Barron's reinstatement was blocked, he blamed Decatur. Egged on by Elliott, Barron sent wrathful letters to Decatur that escalated until a duel became inevitable.

The two commanders met at Bladensburg on March 22, 1819, along the stagecoach route between Washington and Baltimore. Over the past two decades, long before the field was drenched in blood by the British invasion, it had been a favorite locale for dueling. Fifty duels had been fought there, and men called Bladensburg's clearing "the Valley of Chance."

Inevitably, Barron had chosen Jesse Elliott as his second, but Decatur had trouble finding someone. Other navy officers said he had proved his courage many times over and should walk away from the challenge. At last, Decatur located an officer named William Bainbridge who agreed to accompany him to Bladensburg.

The previous night, Decatur and his wife had attended a cotillion given by John Quincy Adams. Appearing for the duel, Decatur seemed tired from the late hour but in good spirits. Neither he nor Barron had told their wives what they planned.

As the man who had received the challenge, Decatur could set the terms, but he seemed indifferent, and they agreed on rules that favored his opponent. Since Barron claimed to be nearsighted, the men would fire from eight paces—about twenty-four feet—rather than from the customary ten or twelve paces. And they could take aim with their pistols before the signal to fire instead of waiting until Bainbridge had counted off the signal.

When they reached the field, Decatur saw his challenger for the first time since he had served on Barron's court-martial board twelve years earlier. The code of honor required that duelists exchange no words except through their seconds, but Barron said clearly, "I hope, Commodore Decatur, that when we meet in another world, we shall be better friends than we have been in this."

Decatur, who intended to fire wide, answered, "I have never been your enemy, sir."

On Bainbridge's count of three, each man pulled the trigger, and it first seemed that both had been killed. Frightened that he might be implicated, Jesse Elliott rode off in Barron's carriage, leaving him to die. He returned only after one of Decatur's friends pursued him and shamed him into going back.

But Barron lived. As Decatur's carriage took him away, Barron called, "God bless you, Decatur," and got back a weak farewell.

When Decatur's friend rapped at the front door of his handsome house, Susan Decatur rose from breakfast with her nieces to find her husband dying on their doorstep.

As president, John Quincy Adams quickly cast off any misgivings about executive power as a threat to liberty. He recommended the kind of road and canal construction that Madison had vetoed, along with the creation of a Department of the Interior and a new Naval Academy. But when he sponsored funds for a national observatory and other projects for scientific research and exploration, westerners complained that his years in Europe had left Adams an elitist. Their suspicion was confirmed when he urged congressmen not to be "palsied by the will of their constituents."

Relations with Jackson's supporters were further strained when the Creeks rebelled against a Georgia treaty that deprived them of their rich farmland. They called the agreement fraudulent and killed the tribal chief who had betrayed them by accepting it.

The Senate had already ratified the treaty the day before Adams was sworn in, and he had signed it. But once the charges of fraud reached him, Adams embarked on a painstaking study of the controversy. After examining the disputed treaty, Adams concluded that the Creeks' grievance was legitimate, even though Jackson's supporters in Congress would block an outright revocation. A new agreement deeded the disputed land to the state of Georgia. The Creeks could either accept that decision or migrate still further west.

Isolated by choice in the White House, Adams was receiving warnings about his vice president. As Calhoun became a more determined advocate of the slave-owning states, he was said to be drifting into the Jacksonian camp, and Andrew Jackson had already concluded that Adams might not be the "man of real wisdom" he had once praised so highly.

More opposition had arisen from Senator Martin Van Buren of New York, who had managed William Crawford's presidential campaign but now was backing Jackson. Van Buren wrote to a friend, "You may rest assured that the reelection of Mr. Adams is out of the question."

So it proved. The election of 1828 was notable mainly for the smears and innuendo resurrected from past years. Adams was charged with falsifying his overseas expense accounts. Jackson's enemies claimed that his first, dubious marriage made him an adulterer and Rachel a bigamist of loose morals.

When the votes were counted, Calhoun was reelected vice president, and Jackson carried not only the South and West but also Pennsylvania, New York, Ohio, Indiana, Illinois, and Clay's home state of Kentucky.

In the Electoral College, the result was 178 for Jackson, 83 for John Quincy Adams, who joined his father in becoming the only men in America's brief history to be denied a second term. They were also the only two whose careers had been untainted by slavery.

For the senior Adams, the War of 1812 had revived his pride in his own youthful struggle against the British. Since his involuntary retirement in 1801, Adams had been questioning whether the American Revolution had truly improved the world. Quite possibly, he suspected, the years since 1776 had been an "age of Folly, Vice, Frenzy, Brutality, Daemons."

His two consolations had been the career of his eldest son and the increasing number of admiring visitors who called on him in Quincy. In his mellowed mood, Adams had yielded to the urging of mutual friends and written tentatively to Jefferson in 1812. The result was a warm correspondence that ran to 150 letters over the next fourteen years.

When the War of 1812 ended, Adams had weighed its results. He decided that Madison had proved that the Constitution could hold firm through both peace and war, that England could never again conquer America, and that, ship for ship, the U.S. Navy was now equal to any in the world.

It was not entirely to taunt Jefferson that Adams suggested that the Madison administration, despite its faults and blunders, "has acquired more glory, and established more Union, than all three predecessors, Washington, Adams and Jefferson, put together."

During the year of the peace treaty, both Adams and Jefferson began to fade. Jefferson's arthritis became severe and his enlarged prostate more painful. Adams lost most of his hearing, and cataracts clouded his sight until he had to be read to by his friends and grandchildren. After Abigail died in 1818, Adams seldom left the house.

Both men held on until 1826, when, in a coincidence too pat for fiction, each of them died on the Fourth of July. Adams was ninety, Jefferson eighty-three. Although they had renewed their friendship, their 1800 rivalry remained vivid to Adams. On his last afternoon, he had no way of knowing that Jefferson had died at one o'clock. Just before he lost his own struggle to breathe, Adams roused himself to whisper, "Thomas Jefferson survives."

A month after her husband's election as president, Rachel Jackson was escorted into Nashville to buy clothes suitable to her new position. When she finished shopping, she went to the office of a relative, a newspaper editor, to await her carriage.

There, she read for the first time what Jackson had been keeping from her—that her reputation had become an issue in the recent campaign.

When her companions came for her, they found Rachel huddled in a corner and crying inconsolably. Her health had been failing for years, but when she died just before Christmas, Jackson blamed her shock at discovering the newspaper articles. Holding John Quincy Adams responsible, he went off to Washington resolved not to make the customary duty call on the outgoing president.

By the time Jackson was sworn in on March 4, 1829, his followers had thrown off any mourning for Rachel Jackson, and they staged the most notorious inaugural party in American history. As the day began, their revelry was sedate. Frank Key surveyed the masses in front of the Capitol and pronounced the spectacle "sublime."

White-haired but erect, Jackson took the oath from Chief Justice John Marshall, who at seventy-four was a dozen years his senior. When the ceremony ended, Jackson set off on horseback for the White House, followed by a throng, white and black, of men, women, and children.

Refreshments had been arranged at the mansion, but no one expected the crush of uninvited guests, and the police had not been alerted. The vast crowd was so cheerfully uncontrollable that Jackson's friends had to lock arms around him and physically push away the hands extended for him to shake. At last, the new president escaped through a side door to a nearby hotel.

His well-wishers hardly missed him. In their rush for refreshments, they broke plates and glasses and jammed together so tightly they could not get to the doors. Desperate and suffocating, some jumped out of windows.

The hordes gradually thinned out, but by late afternoon, mobs of boys were still fighting and leaping with muddy boots on the damask chairs. One appalled political conservative was especially outraged to see "a stout black wench eating in this free country a jelly with a gold spoon in the President's House."

The party might have gone on until dawn if servants had not lured the stragglers outside by carrying tubs of punch to the lawn.

It was a gaudy kickoff for the Jacksonian era. The Jeffersonian Republicans were renaming themselves Democrats, while the last Federalists and other anti-Jackson factions were being called Whigs. Mocking the new president's intellectual limitations, those Whigs portrayed him as a donkey, but to Jacksonians that trusty and hardworking animal represented no slur, and they adopted it as their party symbol.

In naming his cabinet, Jackson rewarded his allies. As secretary of state, Van Buren from New York was able to reassure older politicians that the new administration would not reflect the inauguration's crudeness and disarray.

For his other appointments, Jackson tolerated a spoils system that caused even a sympathetic businessman to rail against departments that were "full of the laziest clerks," and men who were "paid large salaries for neglecting the public business."

Although Jackson was entering the White House as a widower, it was a social contretemps that demanded his early attention. When he had appointed Senator John Eaton of Tennessee as secretary of war, Jackson explained that he deserved to have at least one personal friend in his cabinet.

On New Year's Day, 1829, Eaton had married Peg O'Neil, the free-spirited daughter of a tavern owner. Peg's husband had died at sea; Washington rumors suggested he was a suicide, humiliated by her infidelities.

Even Eaton's friends thought the woman's reputation disqualified her as a bride. But for Jackson, the aspersions on her character recalled the recent attacks on Rachel. The president wrote that his late wife had considered Peg Eaton above reproach and that he himself believed her to be "as chaste as those who attempt to slander her."

Unconvinced, the ladies of Washington society took delight in snubbing her. Thrashing about in frustration, Jackson decided that Calhoun was stirring up the affair to plague him. Calling in his cabinet, Jackson told them to end the social quarantine that had resulted from what Van Buren termed "the Eaton malaria."

Carried away by his own gallantry, Jackson described Peg Eaton as being "as chaste as a virgin." The remark was widely ridiculed, and Henry Clay paraphrased Shakespeare on Cleopatra: "Age cannot wither nor time stale her infinite virginity." One Washington socialite spoke for her circle when she deplored Jackson's conduct and attributed his "violence and imbecilities" in the affair to his being "in his dotage."

Official business was crippled as the feud raged on between the capital's matrons and the president of the United States. Even Jackson's niece chose to move out from the White House rather than receive Mrs. Eaton, who, in any event, had begun to decline what few invitations still came her way.

In the end, Jackson felt that to resolve the matter he must purge his cabinet. Van Buren obliged him by resigning to become ambassador to Great Britain; Eaton went to Spain. During the confirmation debate seven months later, Calhoun cast the deciding vote against Van Buren's nomination, and Van Buren came home to await his turn in the White House.

In retirement, Dolley Madison had hoped to visit the Gallatins in Paris, but her husband showed no desire to travel. At first, Dolley sorely missed the glitter of Washington society, but by the time of the Peggy Eaton scandal, the mood in the capital had turned so venomous that she was glad to be out of it.

Payne Todd had come home as handsome and polished as his mother could wish but encumbered with sixty-five hundred dollars in gambling debts. Payne tried settling down at home. With only his parents and Madison's aged mother for company, however, he began to disappear for long periods. Often Dolley's only information about his whereabouts came from the creditors' letters that descended on Montpelier.

Dependent on the uncertain tobacco crop, the former president himself was pressed for cash, but he managed to pay off Payne's debts, often without telling Dolley. When she learned that the young man was in debtors' prison in Philadelphia, Dolley said the news wounded not merely her pride but her very soul. In all, Madison paid off about forty thousand dollars of his stepson's debts.

Dolley's brother could be no help. Drinking heavily and deeply in debt himself, he had given up a sinecure in the Tripoli consular office. And Richard Cutts, the husband of Dolley's sister Anna, declared bankruptcy during the financial panic in 1819. Madison bought their Washington house so that the Cuttses could go on living there.

Madison had always resisted selling his slaves, but eventually he was driven to let a relative in Louisiana buy sixteen of them.

Madison was spending his days in editing his papers, beginning with the notes he had taken during the Constitutional Convention thirty years earlier. Although the task wound up taking more than seven years, Madison persisted so that Dolley might be able to sell the papers one day if she needed cash.

In 1830, Madison was struck by the first of the rheumatic attacks that confined him to bed. Dolley passed her days at his bedside, not leaving Montpelier for months at a time until Madison died on June 28, 1836.

When Andrew Jackson was free to turn his mind to presidential policy, his objectives were clear: "The Federal Constitution must be obeyed, state rights preserved, our national debt *must be paid, direct taxes and loans avoided,* and the Federal Union preserved."

During his first term, a rebellion in Calhoun's South Carolina challenged that union. Many of the state's planters had moved to richer fields in Alabama and Mississippi, and Charleston had lost their trade. As revenues fell, Calhoun led a crusade against federal tariffs that he claimed penalized the cotton growers of his state.

South Carolinians took up the argument that Jefferson and Madison had made during the alien and sedition controversy and that some New Englanders had embraced during the Hartford Convention. Calhoun announced a policy of nullification: States could decide whether a federal measure was constitutional. If not, a state could refuse to enforce it.

After South Carolina passed its nullification ordinance, Jackson seemed ready to go to war. Instead, Henry Clay reached another compromise, and tariffs were scaled back over the next ten years to a level that Calhoun found acceptable.

In 1832, Jackson was reelected with Van Buren as his vice president. The president had vetoed a rechartering of the Bank of the United States on the grounds that its profits went to foreign stockholders and to America's richest investors. He ordered the government's deposits transferred instead to small local banks that were called "pet banks." But when a financial panic hit the country in 1837, his advisers had to scramble to find an effective substitute for the national bank he had dismantled.

Jackson, who knew the plight of the Indian tribes like few other Americans, had enforced with vigor the Indian Removal Act of 1830. When native chiefs in Georgia had first risen up, President Adams had sent federal troops to protect those who chose to stay. Jackson's secretary of war, Eaton, withdrew those troops.

Under the Removal Act, nearly one hundred thousand Cherokee, Shawnee, Delaware, Wyandot, and other tribes were compelled to accept new reservations across the Mississippi. As they were herded west, they fell sick and died by the hundreds along what came to be called the Trail of Tears.

Among the spokesmen for the West, Henry Clay was one of the few to attack the removal as dishonorable, although he observed "that there never was a full-blood Indian who took to civilization" and predicted the tribes' inevitable extinction.

During his farewell address in March 1837, Jackson expanded his opposition to a national bank to include a frontiersman's warning against the corporations that had begun to flourish across the nation.

"The laboring classes have little or no share in the direction of the great moneyed corporations," Jackson said, ". . . and unless you become more watchful and check this spirit of monopoly and thirst for exclusive privileges, you will in the end find that the most important powers of Government have been given or bartered away, and the control over your dearest interest has passed into the hands of these corporations."

By contrast, Jackson was bland in the benediction he offered to the tribes whose ruin he had helped to assure:

"This unhappy race—the original dwellers in our land—are now placed in a situation where we may well hope that they will share in the blessings of civilization."

*   *   *

In the first years after Jackson's war against the Creeks, two of his young recruits had followed parallel paths. Each man entered politics, each lost his wife, each moved to Texas. But after that, the fates of Davy Crockett and Sam Houston diverged dramatically.

Crockett had returned to Jackson's army in time to watch the British sail away from Pensacola late in 1814. When Jackson moved on to defend New Orleans, Crockett stayed on in Florida to protect against Seminole attacks. He returned home a militia sergeant at about the time his wife gave birth to a daughter.

During the next summer, Polly Crockett died, leaving her husband a widower with three small children. He soon married a local widow with two children of her own and, in 1817, he took his expanded family to the formerly Indian territory in western Tennessee.

Crockett drifted casually into politics, where his good nature and backwoods stories made him popular in the state legislature and then a curiosity in the House of Representatives. Known as "the Coonskin Congressman," Crockett found that not everyone relished his tall tales or his litany of boasts—how he could whip his weight in wildcats or hug a bear too close for comfort.

He entered Congress as a staunch ally of Andrew Jackson, but they clashed over frontier lands that had been allotted to veterans but were falling into the hands of speculators. When Jackson endorsed the measure to remove tribes to land west of the Mississippi, their break became complete.

"These are the remnants of a once powerful people," Crockett protested, "and they must be fairly treated." His stand cost him the election of 1831.

Whigs and Jackson's other political opponents embraced this frontiersman with his gift for sly ridicule, and they produced a book that purported to be Crockett's autobiography. When that volume and its sequel were both runaway successes, Crockett traveled to Philadelphia, New York, and Boston.

His attraction to the East was strong and mutual. After he had been taken to see Fanny Kemble, New York's reigning actress, he reported, "There's too many people in New York and too close together. But I'll tell you one thing. I went to the theatre and saw the prettiest play-acting lady in the world. She was like a handsome piece of changeable silk."

Up and down the country, he found "everybody seems anxious to get a peep at me." And many of them were urging him to run for president. He returned to Congress in 1835, but when he ran for reelection, he was narrowly defeated by a candidate with a wooden leg. During the campaign, Crockett had called him "Old Timbertoes."

With that loss, Davy Crockett announced that he was through with politics: "I'm going to Texas."

Crockett was now a hardy forty-nine, although he complained that because of an earlier attack of pleurisy he had "lost all my Red Rosy Cheeks that I have carryed So many years."

After Sam Houston recovered from his wounds at Horseshoe Bend, he applied to return to the peacetime army. At Jackson's request, he was assigned to staff duty at the Hermitage, where he became a trusted aide and a fellow member of the Freemasons. But Houston's heart remained with the Cherokees. When he went to plead their cause with Calhoun, he outraged Monroe's secretary of war by showing up in the full tribal regalia he had worn in his days as the Raven.

Indignant over the charges against him being spread by Jackson's enemies, Houston resigned from the army in 1818, one day before his twenty-first birthday. He studied law in Nashville and, trading on his wartime reputation, drifted into politics as Crockett had done. Elected state attorney general, Houston also advanced in the Tennessee militia to the rank of major general. As a cog in the Hermitage political machine, he went to Congress in 1823 in the same election that sent Jackson to the Senate.

The next year, Houston backed Jackson in the presidential contest he lost to John Quincy Adams. As Davy Crockett was pulling away, Sam Houston stayed loyal to Jackson and was rewarded with the governorship of Tennessee in 1827. His influence expanded the next year when Jackson became president.

Houston had always drunk heavily, but his social manners—more urbane than Crockett's—led Eliza Allen, the genteel daughter of a rich planter, to accept his marriage proposal. Just before she died, Rachel Jackson gave them a set of her own silver flatware as a wedding present.

Less than three months after the ceremony, the young bride ran back to her parents. Houston wrote to his father-in-law, "You can judge how unhappy I was, to think I was united to a woman that did not love me."

On bended knee, he begged Eliza to return to him; she refused.

Gossip about the brief marriage brought Houston no sympathy. He was burned in effigy, and mobs in Nashville became so hostile that it took the militia to disperse them. Houston came off a drinking jag, destroyed his personal papers, and resigned as governor.

He drifted back toward the Arkansas Territory, where he met Jim Bowie, a frontiersman who had been buying up land in San Antonio. When Houston began to spin grandiose fantasies about Texas, an alarmed Jackson wrote personally to warn him against any dreams of conquest.

Arriving at John Jolly's Cherokee camp after an eleven-year absence, Houston was greeted with music and dancing during a time that the Removal Act was driving other tribes further west. He tried again to mediate between Washington and the Cherokees and meanwhile married Tiana Rogers, a beautiful half-Scots, half-Cherokee widow, in a traditional tribal ceremony. With his marriage, Houston's transformation back to being the Raven seemed complete. He opened a trading post and wrote newspaper articles defending Indian rights.

In 1831, Alexis de Tocqueville sought out Houston for a book he was compiling on American democracy. He described the former governor as a towering figure of "physical and moral energy" and listened, over drinks, while Houston explained that brandy was "the main cause of the destruction of the natives of America."

During a lobbying trip to Washington, Houston beat up a hostile congressman so severely that the House of Representatives voted to arrest him. At President Jackson's suggestion, Houston hired part-time poet Frank Key as his lawyer. Although Key's defense tended to ramble, the House sentenced Houston to nothing more than a reprimand.

On the verge of forty, Houston was restless. Jackson had not lost faith in him, and he authorized Houston to head for Texas in 1832 to induce the Comanches to end their raids across the American border.

Three years later, established in the town of Nacogdoches, Houston's military rank made him the commander of an undisciplined militia. He was in charge when Antonio López de Santa Anna marched north with a sizeable Mexican army, expecting to seize Texas. Once in command, Santa Anna intended to end slavery and establish Catholicism again as the official religion.

On February 23, 1836, Santa Anna led three thousand veteran troops toward San Antonio de Bexar. A company of Texans led by Jim Bowie had recently occupied the town, usually called simply "Bexar," which Mexico had controlled for more than one hundred years. The community was isolated on a sweeping plain and distant by almost one hundred miles to the east and west from the nearest village.

Houston considered Bexar impossible to defend. He sent word to Bowie to retreat after he had stripped the armaments from a fortress called the Alamo that had been converted from a Spanish mission. But Bowie was defiant. "We will rather die in these ditches," he vowed, "than give it up to the enemy."

At that point, Davy Crockett showed up. In Nacogdoches, he had sworn his allegiance to the provisional government of Texas "or any future republican Government that may be hereafter declared." Most of Bexar's Mexicans had already fled, but Crockett's arrival with a band of comrades set off a round of gaiety and horseplay within Bowie's garrison.

Houston's next word from the Alamo was an urgent dispatch that Santa Anna had the garrison surrounded. Houston had already set off with a relief column when a new message told him he was too late. He wrote to a subordinate, "I am induced to believe from all the facts communicated to me that the Alamo has fallen, and all our men are *murdered!*"

What had happened at dawn on that Sunday morning of March 6, 1836, was quickly transformed into abiding myth. Fifty years later, a historian tracked down a Mexican woman who had been acting as a nurse to the Alamo's wounded defenders. She said she had been giving a drink of water to Jim Bowie, ill with typhoid fever, when one of Santa Anna's soldiers burst in and killed him.

The woman said that early in the fray Davy Crockett had been hit as he tried to edge out of the building. Other accounts had him captured and then stabbed to death. In any case, Crockett was among some 183 Texans slain at the Alamo that day, his body burned in a common pyre.

Estimates of the Mexican dead depended on who made them. The lowest figure was two hundred killed, the highest several times that many. Whatever Santa Anna's losses, he described the siege as only "a small affair."

But he had given Sam Houston's troops another potent rallying cry. When they defeated Santa Anna's army the following month at San Jacinto, they were shouting, "Remember the Alamo!"

Their echo reached to Aaron Burr in New York. Just before Madison declared war, Burr had been rebuffed by Napoleon in France and had managed to slip back into America. By that time, the scandal had faded sufficiently that clients would engage him for his undisputed talent as a lawyer.

Trying to remain inconspicuous in public, Burr suffered two private blows: His only grandchild died, and then the boy's mother, Burr's beloved daughter Theodosia, was lost at sea.

Still attractive to women, Burr managed to persuade a widow, Eliza Bowen Jumel, to marry him. Said to be one of America's richest women, she divorced him a year later for adultery. Burr was seventy-eight.

Shortly before he died in 1836, Aaron Burr exulted at the news of Sam Houston's victory at San Jacinto: "You see, I was right! I was only thirty years too soon. What was treason in me thirty years ago is patriotism today!"

Martin Van Buren's presidency had gone badly. The depression caused by the Panic of 1837 lingered on throughout his term, and he faced a crisis with England that might have set off another war.

Rebels from Ontario and Quebec had risen up against the British and crossed the border into the United States to launch guerrilla raids from Vermont and Buffalo. Van Buren issued a neutrality proclamation that was unpopular with those Americans who saw the revolutionaries as merely following, however belatedly, their own example. When an American was killed in a border clash, the *Rochester Democrat* called for revenge "not by simpering diplomacy but by blood."

Van Buren held firm in that instance, and he carried the day again by peacefully settling a border quarrel between Maine and New Brunswick, even though many in his party would have preferred a more muscular, Jacksonian solution.

But the Democrats renominated Van Buren, if with no great ardor. The Whigs presented William Henry Harrison, now sixty-eight, as the hero of battles nearly three decades old. Hoping for southern votes, they added John Tyler of Virginia as their vice president and marketed their ticket as "Tippecanoe and Tyler, Too," a slogan they etched into the American consciousness.

The Whigs took both houses of Congress, and Harrison won the Electoral College vote by a margin of nearly four to one.

But the new president barely had time to name Daniel Webster as his secretary of state before he died of pneumonia. After one month as vice president, Tyler moved to the White House and proved himself an unreconstructed states-rights Democrat who had only changed parties because he disliked Jackson. Webster resigned, along with the rest of Harrison's cabinet.

Tyler's faction faced an unexpected adversary in Congressman John Quincy Adams. Two years after he lost reelection, the voters of Plymouth, Massachusetts, sent the former president to the House of Representatives. From 1836, Adams had been leading the fight against the legislative maneuvering that preserved slavery. After eight years of parliamentary infighting, Adams got a rule repealed that had tabled any antislavery petitions. Four years later, he collapsed on the House floor at age eighty and died two days afterward.

Given the split in Tyler's ranks between northerners and his regional allies, the Whigs lost the next election to James Polk, a Democrat.

*   *   *

As a widow, Dolley Madison was depending on the sale of her husband's papers, which he had died believing would fetch one hundred thousand dollars—enough to cover his bequests to his alma mater in Princeton and to the new University of Virginia and still provide Dolley with a lifetime income.

But, ignoring every warning, she entrusted the negotiations to Payne Todd, who alienated every publisher except Harper and Brothers, and that firm would only offer a contract that assigned Dolley half the profits but also required her to assume half the risk. She could not afford the gamble. In the end, Congress bought three volumes of Madison's manuscripts for thirty thousand dollars.

The sale roused Dolley from the despair into which she had fallen. With her health and spirits restored, she moved back to Washington for its rounds of teas and parties. She still rouged her cheeks—a source of some disapproval during her White House days—and wore false jet-black curls under her turbans and headgear.

Seated next to her at dinner, one gallant added five years to her age when he reported that "the old lady is a very hearty, good-looking woman of about 75. I paid her the same attentions I should have done a girl of 15—which seemed to suit her fancy very well."

By 1840, still strapped for money, Dolley retreated again to Montpelier. John Jacob Astor lent her three thousand dollars, with her house in Washington as security. Finally, though, she had to agree to sell Montpelier with the condition that she could continue to live in the main house.

Traders came by regularly to bid on the slaves that Madison could never bring himself to set free. Dolley deeded forty slaves to her son, who was also carting off the mansion's books and manuscripts to pay his own debts. Dolley's creditors were demanding eleven thousand dollars by the time Congress bought a second lot of Madison's papers. She received five thousand dollars outright but an additional twenty thousand dollars was tied up in a trust that paid her only its income.

Through it all, Dolley kept smiling. She accepted the many invitations that greeted her final return to the capital, and she was James

Polk's guest at the White House in July 1848 for the laying of the cornerstone of the Washington Monument.

A year later, on July 12, Dolley was eased into a peaceful death by doses of opium. President Polk led the funeral procession from St. John's Episcopal Church, where she had been confirmed late in life.

When Dolley's son died two and a half years later, he set his remaining slaves free and bequeathed each of them a symbolic two hundred dollars from his encumbered inheritance.

Crushing the Mexicans and capturing their leader had established the new Republic of Texas, and Sam Houston became its first president. During his last full day as president, Andrew Jackson had recognized Texas. But when an independent republic proved impossible to sustain, Houston lobbied to have the United States annex Texas as a state.

After almost ten years, and over resistance from northern abolitionists, Texas was admitted to the Union in 1845. In the meantime, Tiana Houston had died of fever, and her widower, now forty-seven, married twenty-one-year-old Margaret Lea and began their family of eight children.

Elected to the U.S. Senate, Houston served fourteen years, even though his views were often at odds with those of many constituents who called him an "Indian lover" and pressed successfully for a belligerent policy toward Mexico that culminated in war.

Zachary Taylor, a veteran of the Indian Wars along the Wabash in 1812, led American troops to victory at the battle of Buena Vista and became America's latest military hero. In the treaty that followed, Mexico ceded two-fifths of its land to the United States, including California and New Mexico, in return for $15 million.

When the ailing James Polk declined to run for reelection in 1849, General Taylor became the successful Whig candidate. Nicknamed "Old Rough and Ready," Taylor survived in office until July 9, 1850, when he was killed by a combination of gastroenteritis and inept doctoring.

Vice President Millard Fillmore took over and appointed Daniel Webster once again as secretary of state. Together they saw California admitted as a free state, New Mexico granted territorial status, and the abolition of the slave trade in the District of Columbia. But when Webster and Henry Clay both died in 1852, the age of compromise was over.

Two more Democrats—Franklin Pierce and James Buchanan— served as one-term presidents, each trying to hold off the inevitable break over slavery. John C. Frémont, Buchanan's losing opponent in the election of 1856, had adopted the "Republican" label that the Jeffersonians had shed long before. Four years later, the election of a second Republican candidate, Abraham Lincoln, led South Carolina to secede from the Union on December 20, 1860, followed by ten more southern and western states.

In Texas, pressure had mounted on Sam Houston, now the state's governor, to join the Confederate States of America, and by a vote of 109 to 2, a Texas convention entered the Confederacy.

During the debate, Houston had retired to the Capitol basement, where he took up a piece of wood and began to whittle. When the delegates summoned him to return upstairs and endorse secession, Houston did not respond. At the third calling of his name, the convention declared the governorship vacant.

Houston knew what lay ahead: He saw his countrymen rushing to war without realizing that the first gun they fired would guarantee an end to slavery. For eighty-four years, tensions had bedeviled a Union that proclaimed liberty and went on trading in human life. When Sam Houston died on July 26, 1863, that contradiction had finally been confronted.

Another of Houston's predictions was borne out when the loss of life soon surpassed the bloodshed from Horseshoe Bend and San Jacinto— in fact, from every battle of the Revolution and the War of 1812. As Sam Houston had put it: "The civil war now being inaugurated will be as horrible as his Satanic Majesty could desire."

Acknowledgments

A welcome revival of interest in the American Revolution has taken place during the eighteen years since the publication of *Patriots: The Men Who Started the American Revolution*. America's first three presidents have been the subjects of several new biographies, as have Alexander Hamilton, Gouverneur Morris, John Jay, Thomas Paine, and many other leading figures.

This book takes up the nation's story from the conclusion of the Revolutionary War and carries it through to the end of America's second war with Great Britain. To solve the riddle of why such a seemingly avoidable war was fought at all requires a review of the three decades between the two peace treaties, especially because names and events from that era are likely to be only dimly familiar—the Alien and Sedition Acts, the X, Y, Z Affair, Citizen Genêt, the Louisiana Purchase, the Burr-Hamilton duel.

Historians differ on the best way to approach the past. The United States may have been carried forward on swift economic and political currents, but perhaps we may understand our history best by watching individual men and women as they struggle to keep afloat. That's why I prefer the approach of Samuel Eliot Morison, who urged young scholars to remember that history can be read for pleasure. James Parton had made that point in 1888, when he argued that historical writing need not be encyclopedic. "The art," he wrote, "is to be short where the interest is small, and long where the interest is great."

George Washington, John Adams, and Thomas Jefferson from *Patriots* appear again in these pages but changed now with age and new responsibilities. Sam Adams and John Hancock from the Revolution give way to James and Dolley Madison, William Henry Harrison, Zebulon Pike, and Oliver Perry. During a time when native tribes are being dispossessed, the formidable Tecumseh assumes a central role, along with his implacable antagonist, Andrew Jackson.

Writing the biography of one man may sometimes lead to becoming his advocate and suggesting that he was the dominant figure of his age. Presenting a broader canvas helps us to see these men and women as they looked to their contemporaries. Whatever the judgments in their lifetimes, most of the figures in this book emerge as remarkably intelligent or brave, or both.

With a few exceptions, they outlived the War of 1812. Since I consider it is high praise when nonfiction is said to read like a novel, I've provided a brisk survey as the last chapter to explain what happened to the book's characters later in life. Those few pages are not intended to provide a history of the next five decades.

Union 1812 owes a great debt, happily acknowledged, to the voluminous research by other women and men over the last two hundred years. In addition to the exhaustive work of Henry Adams, the superb modern studies include Robert V. Remini's *Jackson* and his *Henry Clay*; John Sugden's *Tecumseh*; and the biographies of Madison by Irving Brant and Ralph Ketcham.

When the late Fawn Brodie published her portrait of Jefferson in 1974, she was assailed for suggesting that he had fathered children with a slave. I've wished more than once that Professor Brodie had lived for the advent of DNA testing.

As a writer, I am lucky to live near the Huntington Library in San Marino, California, with its vast collection of Americana. I'm grateful to its staff, especially Jill Cogen and George Abdo; and Marsha Mullin, director of museum services at the Hermitage, was very helpful during a trip to Nashville. I have also drawn on the resources of the rare books collection at the University of Southern California's Doheny Library, the British Library in London and its newspaper archive in Colindale, and the Library of Congress in Washington.

During a memorable sail aboard the privateer *Lynx*, Captain Douglas Leasure, Michael Kellick, and Jeffrey Woods gave me a better understanding of the rigors of war at sea in 1812.

I want to thank Lynn Nesbit, my masterful literary agent for forty years, along with the extremely able team at Simon & Schuster: publisher David Rosenthal; the gifted editor Roger Labrie and associate editor Serena Jones; a skillful and painstaking copy editor, Sean Devlin; designer Jaime Putorti; art director Jackie Seow; cartographer Paul Pugliese; and in production, editor Al Madocs and manager John Wahler. Once again, Victoria Meyer as executive director of publicity has lent her talents to a book of mine, as has her associate, Julia Prosser.

Above all, *Union 1812* is dedicated to its editor. Alice Mayhew understood before I did that the men and women of *Patriots* deserved to be followed to their future triumph or disgrace. Alice's writers have all testified to the sensitivity and keen judgment she brings to every project. Through thirty years, and now five books together, I have relied heavily on those qualities—and on her friendship. Her gentle guidance was essential this time in drawing a coherent narrative from a turbulent era. Without Alice, there would be no book.

Notes

CHAPTER ONE. HOMECOMING (1783–1787)

4 "I was no longer a public man": Weintraub, 171.

4 "torpid state": George Washington, *Writings*, Fitzpatrick, ed., XXVII, 297.

4 "If you have any news": GW, *Writings*, Fitzpatrick, ed., XXVII, 347.

4 "I am not only retired": GW, *Writings*, Fitzpatrick, ed., XXVII, 317–18.

4 "might soon expect to be entombed": Bernier, 158.

4 bargain with his bibulous gardener: W. Wilson, 240.

4 he was forced to buy butter for their meals: W. Wilson, 251.

4 a year and a half passed before the day: W. Wilson, 238.

5 Another explanation might have been the false teeth: Rasmussen, 223–24.

5 "the taste of connoisseurs": Weintraub, 126.

6 "the little folks": Bryan, 255.

6 "a hope that she is translated": D. S. Freeman, 6, 229.

6 "had been long and well known": GW, *Writings*, Fitzpatrick, ed., XXVII, 301–2.

7 Washington was confronted by squatters: Beard, *Economic*, 145.

7 "A Mr. Noah Webster came here": GW, *Diaries*, IV, 142.

7 present in person his plan for a new system of government: Lossing, I, 25 note.

7 "shows that a mind like his": D. S. Freeman, 6, 27.

8 "unsettled and deranged": W. Wilson, 244.

8 "The touch of a feather": W. Wilson, 245.

8 "The Confederation appears to me": D. S. Freeman, 6, 48.

8 "We are either a united people": Washington, *Papers, Confederation*, 3, 420.

9 "My *opinion* is": D. S. Freeman, 6, 67.

9 "the people are yet ripe for such a measure": Washington, *Papers, Confederation*, 3, 601.

11 "It is one of the evils of democratical": Leibiger, 60.

12 They were convicted of high treason: M. Campbell, *Hull*, 227.

12 "I like a little rebellion": Madison, Peterson, ed., 102.

12 "The tree of liberty": Brodie, 311–12, cites Jefferson to William Stephens Smith, Nov. 13, 1787; Jefferson, *Papers*, Boyd, ed., XII, 356.

12 "a schoolteacher dressed up for a funeral": Allen Clark, 136.

12 "a country schoolmaster in mourning": Hunt-Jones, 11, cites the manuscript copy of the diary of Lord Francis Jeffrey.

12 "a withered little Apple-John": Brodie, 397.

12 speaking with a pronounced burr: Hunt-Jones, 4.

13 a fondness for racy jokes: James Morton Smith, I, 8.

13 "Who does not see": Koch, *Jefferson and Madison*, 24.

13 Washington said he believed: Leibiger, 49.

14 "What we have to do": Rutland, *Founding Father*, 12.

14 "lesser evil": Rutland, *Founding Father*, 12, cites letter from Jefferson to Edmund Pendleton, Feb. 4, 1787.

14 David Hume's essay: W. L. Miller, 54, 56.

15 "I am mortified beyond expression": Flexner, *New Nation*, 100.

15 Society of the Cincinnati: Custis, 409.

16 Madison assured him that: Leibiger, 67.

17 "No one can replace him, sir": Burstein, *Jefferson*, 172.

17 But, as Franklin wrote: Moran, vii, 152.

17 "radical": Ketcham, *Anti-Federalist*, 32–34, cites B. Hunt and J. B. Scott, eds., *The Debates of the Federal Convention of 1787* (New York, 1920), 592–95; also, Merrill Peterson, 107: Madison to Washington, April 16, 1787.

17 "harass each other": Madison, Peterson, ed., 10.

17 "right of coercion": Ketcham, *Madison*, 34.

CHAPTER TWO. PHILADELPHIA (1787–1788)

19 he smelled a rat: W. L. Miller, 62.

20 "Men of learning find nothing": Madison, *Debates*, xv.

20 one of the least prosperous: Schultz, 55.

22 that he thought kept him: Flexner, *Hamilton*, 41.

22 "Cement to the Union": W. L. Miller, 118.

22 As early as 1780, Hamilton: Letter to New York Congressman James Duane, Lossing, I, 25 note.

23 "abominable": James Morton Smith, I, 443.

23 William Jackson: Lossing, 1, 26.

23 Madison took on the chore: Madison, *Writings*, Hunt, ed., 2, 410–11.

24 "the work of many heads": Madison, *Writings*, Hunt, ed., 9, 533.

24 At the convention, however: Collier, 97.

34 keeping the minutes had almost killed him: Madison, *Debates*, xxii.

24 Hamilton rose to speak: Madison, *Debates*, 138.

24 "pork still, with a little change": Madison, *Debates*, 139 note.

25 Madison worried that Hamilton: Madison, *Debates*, 172.

25 "Take mankind in general": Madison, *Debates*, 175.

25 Hamilton's ideas visibly appalled: W. L. Miller, 171.

26 Washington regretted having been lured: W. L. Miller, 176.

26 "If to please the people": W. L. Miller, 177.

26 delegates spent most of their time: McDonald, 3.

26 Madison agreed to an Electoral College: McDougall, 303.

26 "did not lie between the large and small states": Kornblith, in Fraser, 42.

27 The first shipload of twenty Negroes: Elkins, 38–40.

27 Were the slaves citizens?: Mazyck, 92.

27 "The morality or wisdom": Mazyck, 93.

27 "infernal traffic": Mazyck, 93.

27 "if slavery be wrong": Mazyck, 505.

27 "Every master of slaves": Mazyck, 505.

28 He had first excluded: J. T. Wilson, 40–41; Wiencek, 204.

28 "a striking proof of your great poetical talents": Wiencek, 213.

28 "below the dignity of criticism": Binder, 57.

28 "The Mulatto fellow William": Hirschfeld, 106.

29 "We entered one of the huts": Hirschfeld, 54.

29 he made a point of recovering: Wiencek, 256.

29 "Either from habit": Hirschfeld, 54.

29 Lafayette knew that slavery: Mazyck, 91.

29 "a generous and noble proof": Mazyck, 94; P. L. Ford, 40, 26.

30 "to depend as little as possible": Madison, *Writings*, Hunt, ed., 2, 154.

30 "all the mischief": Jefferson, *Papers*, Boyd, ed., 12, 276; Schultz, 72.

31 sooner chop off his right hand: Schultz, 74.

31 To write and modify the Articles: Catherine Bowen, 8.

31 Madison's summation to Jefferson: Jefferson, *Papers*, Boyd, ed., 12, 103.

31 "absent a single day": Madison, *Writings*, Hunt, ed., 2, 410–11.
31 he had written out remarks: Madison, *Debates*, 653; quoted slightly differently in Moran, vii, 153.
32 "Thus, I consent, Sir": Madison, *Debates*, 654.
32 "like all men, abuse it": Billias, 179.
32 "anarchy and convulsion": Billias, 656.
33 At suppers around town: Catherine Bowen, 22; Collier, 114.
33 His diary entries: Washington, *Diaries*, 5, 155–85.
33 "I know not whose paper": Collier, 115.
33 But his face was no: Flexner, *Indispensable*, 207.
34 "But now at length": Madison, *Notes*, 659.
34 every southern congressmen voted for it: Kornblith in Fraser, 42.
35 Hamilton shared Madison's doubts: Hamilton, *Papers*, 4, 275–76.
35 "this will insure a wise choice": Hamilton, *Papers*, 4, 276.
35 "a superficial, self-conceited": Hamilton, *Papers*, 4, 281 note.
35 expressed again his highest regard: Hamilton, *Papers*, 4, 284.
35 Lafayette hoped the hostilities: Hamilton, *Papers*, 4, 282.
35 He thought everything useful: S. G. Brown, 54.
35 "their President seems like a bad edition": S. G. Brown, 54.
36 objected because no limit had been established: McCoy, 46.
36 urged states not to ratify: McCoy, 46.
36 Madison lectured his friend: Barbara Peterson, 148–49; Madison to Jefferson, Oct. 24, 1787.
36 "Publius": W. L. Miller, 188.
36 deadline pressure often required: W. L. Miller, 190.
37 "More, sir, than the *Green Dragon* could hold": Fowler, 170.
38 ratification in Massachusetts: Alexander, 207.
38 "They'll free your niggers": Brant, *Madison* (6 vols.), 3, 216.
38 "What can avail": Barbara Peterson, 157.
38 his voice was barely a whisper: Brant, *Madison* (6 vols.), 3, 218.
39 "Is it not self-evident": Brant, *Madison* (6 vols.), 3, 158–59.
39 cartoon of Nicholas: Brant, *Madison* (6 vols.), 3, 201.
39 Madison had resisted: Barbara Peterson, 162–63.
39 Jefferson wrote to George Washington: Brodie, 319.
39 "Do you enter into a compact first": Madison, Peterson, ed., 161.
40 George Clinton was leading: W. L. Miller, 213.
40 "in toto and forever": Rutland, 39.
40 The people of New York celebrated; John Miller, *Hamilton*, 213.
41 they often found him stuffy: Ammon, *Monroe*, 46.
41 Monroe had written to complain: Ammon, Monroe, 66.

CHAPTER THREE. WASHINGTON (1789–1797)

43   Washington would be giving up: Custis, 373.

44   Washington asked Morris: Custis, 349–50.

44   country was losing three hundred thousand pounds: Flexner, *Indispensable*, 214.

44   "The Defender of the Mothers": Custis, 393 note.

45   "It is done": D. S. Freeman, 6, 192.

45   Ames had been taking: Ames, 1, 567.

46   "only moments of ecstasy": S. G. Brown, 47.

46   "Here, it seems a man might pass": S. G. Brown, 48.

46   "The Revolution," Washington wrote: Bellamy, 362.

47   "half the earth desolated": Flexner, *Indispensable*, 274.

47   "The tender breasts of women": Brodie, 36.

47   "Every man should know his place": Brodie, 339.

47   "His Rotundity": McCullough, *Adams*, 408.

47   "they will despise him": Brodie, 338.

47   "If he could then have had one fibre": James Morton Smith, 1, 626.

48   The composition owed much: Bernier, 191; his translation of the document in France's Archives Nationales.

48   "as a model for them": James Morton Smith, 1, 629.

48   "Indeed, the scene is too interesting": James Morton Smith, 1, 626.

48   He ordered bars: Mapp, 271.

48   "rich, proud, hectoring, swearing": James Morton Smith, 1, 399.

48   "her blood and money to save us": James Morton Smith, 1, 29.

49   she had refused to leave Paris: Brodie, 314.

49   he encountered Alexander Hamilton: Jefferson, *Anas*, 668–69.

50   some of them began to buy up the bonds: Keats, 23.

50   Hamilton argued: Chernow, 298.

50   "Federal City": Flexner, *Indispensable*, 264.

51   "most disastrous consequences": Abigail Adams, Mitchell, ed., 49.

51   "Always an honest man": Brodie, 337.

51   Washington spoke of himself: Brodie, 339.

52   "disgrace the imbecility of school boys": Jefferson, *Papers*, Boyd, ed., 16, 261–62.

52   Bostonian named John Fenno: D. S. Freeman, 6, 397.

52   Readers could expect: Custis, 396.

52   "breadth of belly": D. S. Freeman, 6, 409.

52   Hamilton retaliated with attacks: Monroe, *Defense*, 3.

53   he always put his name to: Monroe, *Defense*, 54.

53   "His paper has saved the Constitution": Bellamy, 371.

53   "to destroy undue impressions": P. L. Ford, 264.

53   "the robbery and ruin": P. L. Ford, 264.

53   "the transmission of newspapers": Flexner, Washington, 2, 262.

54   "It's all over": Custis, 417.

55   Bache's *General Advertiser* used: D. S. Freeman, 6, 340 note.

56   would support France only in her defensive wars: Sturgis, 35.

56   Genêt began privately to dismiss: Chidsey, *Mr. Hamilton and Mr. Jefferson*, 46.

57   "endeavor to maintain a strict neutrality": Bellamy, 365.

57   "C. Volney needs no recommendation": P. L. Ford, 306.

57   *Little Sarah:* Jefferson, *Anas*, 133–39; Bellamy, 366.

58   "as inflammatory & declamatory": Ammon, *Genêt*, 101.

58   "got himself into one of those paroxysms": Bellamy, 371.

58   *"by god* he had rather": Bellamy, 371.

58   Rather than go home: Chidsey, *Mr. Hamilton*, 53.

59   "become at last tiresome": Flexner, *Washington*, 2, 265.

59   "the feelings of such men are always alive": Flexner, *Washington*, 2, 265.

60   "the bastard brat of a Scotch peddler": Harper, 75.

60   Jefferson took the opportunity: Washington, *Papers*, Chase, ed., 17, 185; Flexner, *Indispensable*, 267; Jefferson, *Anas*, 162–65.

61   Madison had challenged Hamilton's plan: James Morton Smith, 2, 666.

62   "I will frankly and solemnly declare": Flexner, *Indispensable*, 268.

62   "If a minority, and a small one": Flexner, *Indispensable*, 186–87.

62   A graduate of the University of Geneva: Lossing, 2, 1060 note.

63   "A happy issue": D. S. Freeman, 7, 202.

63   "we have fought, bled and conquered": D. S. Freeman, 7, 217.

63   "the misled have abandoned": Irving, 5, 297.

64   "Whiskey Boys" were marched: D. S. Freeman, 7, 227.

64   a day of public prayer: D. S. Freeman, 7, 229.

64   he had been engaged briefly: Ketcham, *Madison*, 109–10.

65   Jefferson had tried to console Madison: James Morton Smith, 1, 229.

65   a house sold to: Zall, *Dolley*, 1.

65   always sent her outdoors in: Clark, *Dolley*, 19.

65   kept in a bag: Cutts, 6.

65   Dolley learned to dance: Zall, *Dolley*, 4.

66   he would never leave her again: Cutts, 12.

66   but he was married to: Schachner, 72–79.

67   "Dear friend": Cutts, 15.

67   Dolley dressed carefully: Cutts, 15.

67   Dolley was now twenty-six: Lomask, 162.

67   his wife invariably rose: Clark, *Dolley*, 7.

67   "I think not": Cutts, 15–16.

67　He had decided: Clark, *Dolley*, 24.

68　British took some 250 American ships: Ferling, 338.

68　Madison's Republican faction: James Morton Smith, 2, 881.

69　"a ruinous bargain": James Morton Smith, 2, 884.

69　Washington made it clear: Flexner, *Indispensable*, 336–37.

70　Protesting the treaty outside: Bellamy, 374.

70　"his lips blistered to the bone": Monaghan, 389.

70　chapter of the Cincinnati: Monaghan, 392.

70　"Those," Hamilton said: Monaghan, 393.

70　"The cry over the treaty": Bellamy, 374.

71　"Mr. Madison looks worried to death": Combs, 185.

71　Albert Gallatin, now a Republican: Adams, *Gallatin*, 155.

72　Ames played to the drama: Ames, *Works*, 1, xxix–xxx.

72　"Tears enough were shed": Ames, *Works*, 1, xxx.

72　moved for a strategic adjournment: Mason, 36.

73　"frank, candid or friendly": Flexner, *Washington*, 4, 280.

73　"could scarcely be applied to a Nero": Flexner, *Washington*, 4, 281.

73　"the old fox was too cunning": Jefferson, *Anas*, 201.

74　"And they believe truly": Malone, 3, 483.

74　"the necessity of those overgrown": Irving, 5, 411–12.

74　"In offering to you, my countrymen": Irving, 5, 417–31.

Chapter Four. Adams (1797–1801)

75　"was as serene and unclouded": Bellamy, 375.

75　"For my own part, I should not pine": Bellamy, 376.

77　"I'll tell you what, the French republic": Chinard, 243.

77　Fencing with Jefferson: Jefferson, *Anas*, 185–87.

78　"The aspect of our politics": Brighton, 171.

78　"harlot" became "whore": Brighton, 171.

79　X, Y, and Z: The officials were Jean Conrad Hottinguer, Pierre Belamy, and Lucien Hauteval.

79　"I will never send another minister": Walker, 139.

79　"the victims of legal prostitution": Chidsey, *Hamilton*, 134.

79　his wife fell under the influence: Withey, 257–58.

80　"old, querulous, bald, blind": James Morton Smith, 2, 1003.

80　"pure sentiments and good principles": Ferling, 365.

81　Bache's vehement denunciations: Ferling, 367.

81　Albert Gallatin, who was: James Morton Smith, 2, 1099.

81　Lyon was convicted: Ferling, 367.

81　"cruel or violent": Ferling, 366.

82 "to disturb the public mind": D. S. Freeman, 7, 539.
82 "null, void, and of no force": James Morton Smith, 2, 1072.
83 "The greater part of the abuse": Abigail Adams, *Letters*, 216.
84 "Was there ever a more basely designing": Abigail Adams, *Letters*, 181.
84 Abigail Adams criticized the members: Withey, 257–58.
84 "there is no more chance of seeing a French army": Chidsey, *Hamilton*, 134.
85 Washington set the condition: Chidsey, *Hamilton*, 134.
86 "Let it go as it came": Abbott, 358.
86 "inflammatory quinsy": D. S. Freeman, 7, 640.
86 Although the patient: Sparks, 532–35.
87 Washington shared the prevailing fear: Bryan, 370.
88 "The new-time people don't know": Hirschfeld, 108.
88 Washington's scruples over his wife's slaves: Bryan, 378.
88 "He was, indeed, in every sense": Brodie, 414.
88 "First in war, first in peace": Custis cites speech of December 16, 1799.

CHAPTER FIVE. JEFFERSON (1801–1804)

89 John Adams confided: J. Q. Adams, *Life*, 2, 276.
90 Instead, Hamilton employed: Brodie, 441.
90 the Constitution's three-fifths clause: Garry Wills examines the three-fifths clause in *"Negro President."*
91 "Colonel Burr must have thought": Jefferson, *Anas*, 224.
91 "turned the conversation to something else": Brodie, 439.
92 had friends carry him: Ferling, 187.
92 "absolutely false": Ferling, 193.
92 His final break came: Fowler, 175.
92 "The storm we have passed through": Brodie, 449.
93 "every difference of opinion": Henry Adams, *Jefferson*, 1, 136.
93 Gallatin was left with: Henry Adams, *Jefferson*, 1, 163–64.
94 Christopher Perry: Dutton, 21.
94 Federalists "have retired into the Judiciary": Henry Adams, *Jefferson*, 1, 175.
94 "a mere rake, buck, blood and beast": Brodie, 451.
95 listed in his accounts as "charity": Gordon-Reed, 61.
95 "keeps and for many years has kept": Brodie, 464.
96 "bears a strong likeness": Gordon-Reed, 64.
96 "no virgin or matron ever had cause": Brodie, 471.
96 "The serpent you cherished and warmed": Brodie, 471.
96 "Another year has come around": Brodie, 488.

97 Congress agreed to send gifts: Thomas Watson, 6.

97 "Appropriations to foreign intercourse": James Morton Smith, 1, 10; Gordon-Reed, 232.

97 "Millions for defence, but not one cent for tribute": Dutton, 22.

98 he considered all of Washington's documents "sacred": Brighton, 171.

98 "I have not yet begun to fight": Krafft, 43.

98 Slipping aboard with three-inch: McKee, 196–98.

99 Thomas Macdonough: Forester, 208.

99 William Eaton proposed: Brighton, 242.

99 wrote a five-thousand-word: Brighton, 267.

99 Tobias Lear, at the age of: Brighton, 329.

100 the settlement was destined to become: *Louisiana Purchase*, 7.

100 due to diseases: *Louisiana Purchase*, 14.

100 seize New Orleans by force: *Louisiana Purchase*, 41.

101 "a neighbor might as well ask me to sell": DeConde, *This Affair of Louisiana*, 36.

101 "destined beyond a doubt": DeConde, *This Affair*, 38.

101 "from that moment we must marry ourselves": *Louisiana Purchase*, 43.

102 "The Mississippi is to them everything": *Louisiana Purchase*, 46.

102 "Perhaps nothing since the revolutionary war": *Louisiana Purchase*, 47.

102 The sale would also break French law: *Louisiana Purchase*, 50.

102 Napoleon in his bath: Hosmer, 80–96.

103 "are thoroughly sick of it": Bernier, 273.

104 "nothing will be effected here": *Louisiana Purchase*, 49.

104 "You know the temper": Hosmer, 162.

105 "We have lived long": *Louisiana Purchase*, 50.

105 Monroe was finally received: House of Representatives, 169.

105 "for our descendants": *Louisiana Purchase*, 40.

106 "We must leave it to yourself": Jones, 40.

106 He instructed Clark: Donnelly, 79; Fresonke and Spence, eds., 5.

106 "others like thick-skinned beasts": Brant, 151.

106 Madison was expressing apprehension: Hosmer, 64.

107 Federalist newspapers jeered: Hosmer, 151; Hasting, in Bannon, ed., 48.

107 the cabal had next approached: Henry Adams, *Jefferson*, 1, 755–839.

108 John Laurens: Chernow, 117.

108 Early on the morning of: Schachner, 158, 240.

109 "O Burr, O Burr": Schachner, 255.

109 "A man of intelligence": Burr, 210.

Chapter Six. Andrew Jackson (1805–1807)

111 had murdered their grandfather: Colyar, 17.

112 bounties for Indian scalps: Sumner, 7.

112 "snick-a-snack": O'Brien, 9.

112 "Stop and submit": Jenkins, 38.

113 he always kept a pair: Parton, *Life of Andrew Jackson*, 1, 154.

113 Robards threatened to "haunt" her: Parton, *Life of Andrew Jackson*, 1, 151.

113 "tall, lank, uncouth-looking": Sumner, 1, 16.

114 "a golden moment": DeConde, *This Affair*, 180.

114 "a call under present existing": James, *Andrew Jackson: The Border Captain*, 104.

114 "He could never speak on account": Sumner, 1, 16.

114 "to effect a separation of the Western part": Melton, 53.

115 proposing instead a daring coup d'etat: Malone, *Jefferson*, 6, 235.

115 A man named Charles Dickinson: Remini, *Andrew Jackson*, 1, 137–38.

116 "Great God!" he exclaimed: Parton, *Life of Andrew Jackson*, 1, 299.

116 "Oh, I believe that he has pinked me": Parton, *Life of Andrew Jackson*, 1, 300.

116 He downed the whole quart: Coit, *Andrew Jackson*, 25.

117 "the barbarous and pernicious practice": Parton, *Life of Andrew Jackson*, 1, 302.

117 regarded Jackson as a lawless outcast: Parton, *Life of Andrew Jackson*, 1, 305.

117 "die in the last ditch": Melton, 111.

117 "You have heard of the screws": Melton, 116.

117 "I fear treachery": Henry Adams, *Jefferson*, 1, 801.

Chapter Seven. Zebulon Pike (1805–1807)

120 "Distance eight miles": Pike, Coues, ed., 475.

120 his soldiers had to cram: Whiting, 231.

120 overcome with ennui: Whiting, 247.

120 "all the elegant hams": Whiting, 256–57.

121 Pike told Wilkinson he would pretend: Jacobs, 224.

121 This second expedition: Whiting, 261.

121 "found it very difficult": Pike, Hart, ed., 126.

121 "Arose hungry, dry": Pike, Hart, ed., 126.

122 "I believe no human being": Pike, Hart, ed., 128.

122 Frémont would explore: Hollon, 128.

122 "that the ravens had left us": Pike, Hart, ed., 129.

123 "instant death": Whiting, 270.

123 "Send this evening six or eight": Pike, Coues, ed., 627.

124 "There was really a handsome display": Pike, Coues, ed., 627.

124 "Language cannot express": Pike, Coues, ed., 714.

124 Pike had returned with two grizzly cubs: Malone, *Jefferson*, 6, 208.

124 "The general will probably be surprised": Pike, Coues, ed., 593.

124 "his services were held in high esteem": Hollon, 217.

124 "This is indeed a deep, dark": Chidsey, *Louisiana*, 174.

125 Burr's guilt was "beyond question": Chidsey, *The Great Conspiracy*, 94.

126 On the street, his denunciations: Coit, *Andrew Jackson*, 29.

126 "darted a flash of indignation": Chidsey, *The Great Conspiracy*, 115.

126 "go home, see their wives": Chidsey, *The Great Conspiracy*, 117.

127 "I cannot descend to your level": Jacobs, 240, quotes John Randolph of Roanoke, 1, 315.

CHAPTER EIGHT. EMBARGO (1807–1808)

129 had set sail that month: Tucker and Reuter, *Injured Honor*, 1.

130 a sailor's citizenship ran: Zimmerman, 21–23.

130 an Order in Council: Headley, *The Second War with England*, 1, 21.

131 "a few fir-built things": Paine, 92.

131 "You had better": Tucker and Reuter, *Injured Honor*, 6, cites testimony of Gordon, "Court of Enquiry & Court Martial," 102, 121.

131 "You may do as you please": Tucker and Reuter, *Injured Honor*, 8.

132 "For God's sake, fire one gun": Cooper, 17.

132 discharged a solitary shot: Henry Adams, *Madison*, 830.

132 The other three: The three black sailors were William Ware, Daniel Martin, and John Strachan, who had jumped ship from the British *Melampus* and signed on with the *Chesapeake*. The first two carried their "protections"—notarized certificates of their citizenship. The hanged man was John Wilson, a white British subject. Joseph Wilson, 73–74.

132 stormed the British ship *Melampus*: Tucker and Reuter, *Injured Honor*, 101.

133 "can only be done by red-hot": Tucker and Reuter, *Injured Honor*, 108.

133 Barron's officers urged: Tucker and Reuter, *Injured Honor*, 100.

133 "death before dishonor": Tucker and Reuter, *Injured Honor*, 103.

133 "The British may laugh": Dutton, 36.

133 "never since the battle of Lexington": Brodie, 560, cites Jefferson to DuPont de Neumours, July 14, 1807.

133 it was a cheap and expedient: Bradford Perkins, *Prologue*, 51.

133 said he worked even harder: Brodie, 561.
133 revolution every twenty years: Sears, 85.
134 "great bunglers": Mayo, 263.
134 told Madison to draft: James Morton Smith, 3, 1476–78.
134 "I confess," he confided: Jefferson, *Memoirs*, Randolph, ed., 4, 180.
134 "peaceable coercion": Jefferson, Peterson, ed., 131.
134 Napoleon added to: James Truslow Adams, 326.
134 Exports from New England dropped: James Truslow Adams, 327.
135 Thirty thousand of America's: Krafft, 62.
135 soup kitchens: Engle, 92.
135 expanded the power of customs: Jefferson, *Reference*, Peterson, ed., 132.
135 "Dambargo": Engle, 93.
135 guardian of a Boston orphan: Sears, 71.
135 Massachusetts alone controlled: Sears, 145.
135 Federalists had entered into: James Truslow Adams, 328.
135 "This embargo law is certainly": Jefferson, *Writings*, Ford, ed., 9, 202, August 11, 1808.
136 "has kept us in hot water": Brodie, 564, cites Jefferson to Thomas Leiper, Jan. 21, 1809.
136 "I think one war is enough": Jefferson, *Writings*, Ford, ed., 9, 201.
137 "My father has been all his lifetime": Quincy, 5.
138 "the most valuable public character": Quincy, 19.
138 "firm and dispassionate course": Quincy, 102.
138 "I could wish to please my parents": Remini, *Adams*, 39.
138 "you have too honest a heart": Quincy, 104.

CHAPTER NINE. MADISON (1809–1812)

141 a suit made entirely: Allen C. Clark, 99.
142 "have been very dear to each other": Brodie, 556.
142 "I have ever viewed Mr. Madison": Ammon, *Monroe*, 273.
143 "Here's to thy absent broadbrim": Clarke, 143.
143 "the exposure of their swelling breasts": James Morton Smith, 3, 1566.
144 "mobs of boys to see what will not often": Zall, *Dolley*, 34.
144 "half a cake of soap": Catherine Bowen, 13.
144 "I wish so, too": Clarke, 102.
144 "The crowd there was excessive": James Morton Smith, 3, 1563.
145 "I have sent for you, sir": Bobbe, 131.
145 "life of indolence": Bobbe, 141.
145 "Your people, sir!": Henry Adams, *Jefferson*, 2, 61.
146 a state whose population: Mason, 79.

147 "I am for resistance by the *sword*": Remini, *Clay*, 60.

147 "all of the enemies to public liberty": McCoy, 14, cites Madison, Political Observations, April 20, 1795, in Hutchinson, *Papers of James Madison* (Chicago, 1962), 15, 518.

148 "*une bonne grosse femme de la classes bourgeoise*": Ketcham, *Madison*, 496.

148 "botch of a bill": Ketcham, *Madison*, 499.

149 "to see, ere long, the *new* United States": Remini, *Clay*, 66.

149 "I am not for stopping at Quebec": Clarke, 327 note.

150 his bulky dog: Brant, *Madison* (6 vols.), 5, 381.

151 "They have entered this house": Bruce, 1, 370.

151 "We are next told": Jenkins, 44.

151 "may alarm himself with the disorganizing": Calhoun, *Papers*, Meriwether, ed. 1, 81.

152 "crafty contrivance and insatiate cupidity": Madison, Peterson, ed., 294

152 Depression had struck England: Charles Campbell, 26.

153 "That a body containing 100 lawyers": James Morton Smith, 3, 1677–78.

153 "Where are your armies?": Brant, *Fourth*, 495.

153 "You know of our embargo": Dolley Madison, *Selected Letters*, 163.

154 A year earlier: Headley, *The Second War*, 2, 212.

154 "Relying on the patriotism of the nation": Joseph Wilson, 74–75.

154 "We are to have war then?": Bradford Perkins, *Prologue to War*, 42, cites Jefferson to Charles Pinckney, Feb. 2, 1812.

154 "iniquitous": Brant, *Madison* (6 vols.), 6, 27.

155 The setting for the celebration: Ketcham, *Madison*, 447.

155 "Still, you have time to read": Allen C. Clark, 141.

155 "amounted to but 2,000 persons": Egan, 176–77.

155 "always talked to me of war as a duel": Mayo, 474.

155 "A great many people here are afraid": Mayo cites Foster diary, April 18, 1812.

156 He sent out an aide: Mayo, Foster diary, June 15, 1812.

156 Madison looking "ghastly pale": Mayo, Foster diary, June 15, 1812.

CHAPTER TEN. TECUMSEH (1812)

157 he insisted on an interpreter: Ridout, 135.

158 Shawan was the southernmost: Raymond, 2.

158 Before his birth: Sugden, *Life*, 15, 37.

158 "Shooting Star": Raymond, 26.

158 reprisal for an Indian raid: Raymond, 23–24.

159 Lecturing his elders against such brutality: Berton, 60.

159 Tenskwata assured the tribe: Raymond, 50–51.

159 "It is the drink of the Evil Spirit": Clarke, 317.

159 "grew from the scum": Maria Campbell, 315.

160 "vainly trying to lead his brothers": Sugden, 163.

160 serving as aide-de-camp: Cleaves, 13.

161 Harrison sponsored a law: H. Montgomery, 66.

162 the Indians thought of heaven: Lawson, 191.

162 Lawson had already written: Lawson, xix.

162 tribes resented the insult: Kelsay, 20.

162 An enemy's dried scalp: Kelsay, 21.

162 He observed that they: Harrison, 89–95.

163 Brant stayed for two years: Wood, 21.

163 then traveled to England: Wood, 43.

164 "Without being united": Calloway, 214.

164 "My son, keep your eyes fixed": Raymond, 69.

164 Tecumseh paddled down the Wabash: Drake, 124–30.

164 "perhaps one of the finest-looking": Raymond, 71.

166 Harrison decided that: Edmunds, *Shawnee*, 189.

166 "Well, as the Great Chief is to determine": Raymond, 73; Sugden, *Life*, 202.

167 "I have been particularly instructed": Brant, *Madison* (6 vols.), 5, 385.

167 "in the most peremptory terms": Brant, *Madison* (6 vols.), 5, 385.

168 he persuaded his warriors: Edmunds, *Shawnee*, 111.

169 took the dark stallion: Edmunds, *Shawnee*, 112.

169 Americans scalped and mutilated: Edmunds, *Shawnee*, 114.

169 the casualty figures did not justify: Edmunds, *Shawnee*, 115.

170 His wife was to blame: Edmunds, *Shawnee*, 114.

170 "General Harrison made war": Raymond, 86.

170 "those I left at home": Raymond, 85.

170 possessed more integrity: Harrison, 39.

171 at Britain's Fort Malden: Sugden, *Life*, 272.

171 except for potatoes: Sugden, *Life*, 274.

171 "My British father will not deny me": Raymond, 86.

171 "I will suffer my bones": Raymond, 88.

Chapter Eleven. William Hull (1812)

174 He protested that for thirty: Clarke, 329 note.

174 "a mere matter of marching": Berton, 15; Hickey, 73.

174 "We can take Canada": Clarke, 327 note.

174 His white constituents numbered: Clarke, 307.

175 several essential commitments: Maria Campbell, ix.

175 "Return, Jonathan": Lossing, I, 255 note.

176 "Conquer or Die": Hickey, 81.

176 riding its officer out: Clarke, 331 note.

176 Abraham Hull provided: Berton, 94.

176 "Circumstances have recently": Henry Adams, *Madison*, 500.

177 "Sir," he wrote: Clarke, 333.

177 immersion in petty details: Henry Adams, *Madison*, 571.

177 Their farms were laid out: Henry Adams, *Madison*, 500; Brock, 243.

178 If they could guarantee: Clarke, 342.

178 "you are authorized to commence": Clarke, 335–56.

178 "The British have established": Henry Adams, *Madison*, 503.

179 "Inhabitants of Canada": Thompson, 103–5.

180 "It is all important": Henry Adams, *Madison*, 504.

180 the residence of a British colonel: Edgar, 229.

180 he sent out troops: Thompson, 106.

180 But the French farmers: Berton, 136.

Chapter Twelve. Isaac Brock: Detroit (1812)

182 people of Massachusetts resisted going: Henry Adams, *Madison*, 505.

182 "Who is it to have the command": Clarke, 391 note.

182 so when the enemy appeared: Sugden, *Life*, 287.

183 seven hundred packs of furs: Clarke, 343 note.

183 "Our general is losing all the confidence": Sugden, *Life*, 286.

183 ordering each man to arrive: Ridout, 129.

183 Hull's papers told Brock: Edgar, 218.

184 "It can be demolished when found necessary": Edgar, 219.

184 "All your wants shall be supplied": Edgar, 217.

184 "I, however, talk loud": Edgar, 215.

184 "hard as nails": Berton, 83.

185 "By the Lord Harry, sir!": Brock, xx.

185 Brock's open bateau: Brock, xxii.

185 Hull sent out: Raymond, 92.

186 Nicked by a bullet: Sugden, *Life*, 297.

187 a petition was circulating: Sugden, *Life*, 298.

187 was welcoming Isaac Brock: Raymond, 99.

187 "I have fought against the enemies": Brock, xxiv.

188 "This is a man": Raymond, 102.

188 He unrolled a long peel: Raymond, 103.

188 "were ready to shed their last drop of blood": Raymond, 104.

188　"A more sagacious or more gallant": Henry Adams, *Madison*, 524.

188　"but I answer that the state": Henry Adams, *Madison*, 524.

188　"I have decided on crossing": Brock, xxii.

189　"Tecumseh, *go* fight Yankee": Brock, xxii note.

189　round little hat: Richard Rush to Benjamin Rush, June 20, 1812. Benjamin Rush Papers, Library of Congress.

189　"speedy, a just and an honorable": *National Intelligencer*, June 20, 1812.

189　Congress had finally: Turner, 4.

189　was widely known to be: Brant, *Madison* (6 vols.), 6, 25.

190　"I trust they will move soon": Clarke, 392.

191　Detroit's fort was: Ridout, 142.

191　"The force at my disposal authorizes me": Raymond, 105.

191　"I have no reply to make": Ridout, 140.

191　the same Lieutenant Hancks: Ridout, 141.

192　moved to the forefront: Brock, xxiii.

192　Abraham Hull then took out: Berton, 179.

192　He sent forward an officer: Brant, *Madison* (6 vols.), 6, 79.

193　Hull had been sitting: Brant, *Madison* (6 vols.), 6, 77.

193　"I have done what my conscience": Berton, 183.

193　it was run up the pole: Berton, 182.

193　"I hasten to apprize your excellency": Raymond, 109.

194　Brock intended to praise: Raymond, 109.

194　removed the silk sash: Brock, 247.

194　At the traditional surrender: Ridout, 144, 145 note.

194　The men he left: Berton, 186.

195　Hull's papers were destroyed: Maria Campbell, x.

195　"the general appears to be about sixty": Brock, 273.

196　Madison directed Dearborn: Brant, *Madison* (6 vols.), 6, 56.

196　One evening, Dolley: Moore, 276.

196　"our red children": Moore, 277.

196　on nearby Greenleaf's Point: Brant, *Madison* (6 vols.), 6, 69; Moore, 276.

196　Madison used the occasion: Brant, *Madison* (6 vols.), 6, 69.

197　Few in Madison's audience: Moore, 277.

197　"I find myself worn down": Moore, 277.

198　cabinet members answered yes: Brant, *Madison* (6 vols.), 6, 75.

198　"Do you not tremble with resentment": Moore, 278.

198　his comptroller, Richard Rush: Brant, *Madison* (6 vols.), 6, 75.

198　"gasconading booby": Moore, 278.

CHAPTER THIRTEEN. ISAAC HULL (1812)

199 "as the die is now cast": Hickey, 53.

200 "are you for your country or against it": Hickey, 55.

200 "there are but two parties": Hickey, 55.

200 "hazard everything most dear": Hickey, 57.

200 "to destroy the freedom of speech": Hickey, 61.

200 set off another riot: Hickey, 66.

202 "The crew are as yet unacquainted": Roosevelt, 47 note.

202 got an enlistment bounty: William S. Dudley, 138–39.

202 he had sailed his frigate: William S. Dudley, 153; Roosevelt, 43–44.

204 "caused me to make this communication": William S. Dudley, 165.

205 On the afternoon of August 19: Hull's account, William S. Dudley, 244.

205 The surviving British: Hollis, 163–64.

206 That lenient judgment contrasted: Isaac Hull, 9.

206 "Hurray! Her sides are made of iron!": Hollis, 165.

206 caused one British newspaper: Hollis, 173–74.

206 "Captain Hull, who has immortalized": Nevins, 51.

207 "May danger from abroad": Hollis, 172.

207 "uncommonly handsome": Isaac Hull, 29.

207 "I do not mind the day of the battle": Isaac Hull, 29.

CHAPTER FOURTEEN. ISAAC BROCK: QUEENSTON (1812)

209 "I have received so many letters": Edgar, 267.

210 "though landed only two hours": Edgar, 271.

210 "I shall suspend": Edgar, 278.

210 "I agree in opinion with you": Brock, 303–4.

211 "I fear that Hull's surrender": Brock, 437.

211 "bold, and, I regret to say": Brock, 313.

212 "They die very fast": Edgar, 281.

212 "Although the regiment has been ten years": Edgar, 281.

212 "At all events, we must calculate": Edgar, 285.

213 "willing, well-disposed characters": Edgar, 298.

213 the frisky ten-year-old horse: Malcomson, *A Very Brilliant Affair*, 144, notes that Prevost's predecessor, Sir James Craig, asked Brock to take the horse when Craig returned to England the previous year but doubts whether Alfred was shipped to Upper Canada.

213 Henry Dearborn claimed: Brant, *Madison* (6 vols.), 6, 92.

213 Only two of Van Rensselaer's: Berton, 232–33.

214 a solid sheet of fire: Berton, 233.

214 He borrowed a coat: Malcomson, *Affair*, 138.

214 lost a struggle with the helmsman: Berton, 234.

214 "a scene of confusion": Malcomson, *Affair*, 141.

215 finished that stirrup cup: Brock, Appendix 23, 211; Malcomson, *Affair*, 141–42, questions whether he stopped at Captain Powell's house.

215 passed the York Company: Breton, 238.

215 entered the British gun enclosure: Edgar, 303.

216 "Are you much hurt, sir?": Malcomson, *Affair*, 153.

216 "For heaven's sake, tell us": Edgar, 308.

217 Brock had deplored: Malcomson, *Affair*, 97.

217 In the end, one: Malcomson, *Affair*, 193, 196.

218 The Quebec *Gazette*: Brock, 325.

218 newspaper in Montreal: Brock, 327.

CHAPTER FIFTEEN. JOHN ARMSTRONG, JR. (1813)

220 "the greatest army this New World": Henry Adams, *Jefferson*, 2, 591.

221 annex the Floridas: Egan, 180.

221 "its minister does not know French": Skeen, *Armstrong*, 105; Quimby, 173.

221 "We are a nation of Quakers": Skeen, *Armstrong*, 120.

222 "to harmonize with him": Skeen, *Armstrong*, 123.

222 "Two of them have cost us": James Morton Smith, 3, 1707.

223 "Citizens!": Syrett, 58–60.

223 "by an ambition to rival": Syrett, 62.

223 "constitutional scruples": Sumner, 35.

224 "to take for granted that every volunteer": Buell, 265.

224 "You will on receipt of this letter": Brant, *Fourth*, 533.

224 two thousand volunteers eight hundred miles from home: Brant, *Fourth*, 533.

224 "violently insubordinate": Coit, *Andrew Jackson*, 35.

224 "Gentlemen, I cannot believe that the distinguished": Buell, 267.

225 "We can lie on our horses": Colyar, I, 53.

225 when Wilkinson sent recruiters: Jenkins, 52.

CHAPTER SIXTEEN. YORK (1813)

227 as they chatted: J. Q. Adams, *Memoirs*, 2, 268.

228 Now the count asked: Bemis, *John Quincy Adams*, 186.

228 Gallatin had also pushed: Kuppenheimer, 85–86; Hickey, 122.

229 "Will Federalists subscribe to the loan?": Lossing, 2, 1009 note.

230 John Payne Todd: Ketcham, *Madison*, 552.

231 Armstrong insisted that Dearborn: Henry Adams, *Madison*, 726.

231 he put on a pair himself: Whiting, 289 note.

231 "If success attends my steps": Mahon, 142.

232 major, Benjamin Forsyth: Whiting, 301.

232 "By God," Pike shouted: Quimby, 227.

232 He had trained his men: Mahon, 142.

233 set off a huge explosion: Quimby, 227.

233 Pike had bent forward: Whiting, 305.

234 Dearborn denied that he had ordered: Mahon, 143.

234 Chauncey tried to make: Wood, 109.

234 British had returned and built: Lossing, 2, 591.

234 "My dear Clara": Hollon, 217.

235 "Sir," Captain Chauncey had written: Cruikshank, 247.

CHAPTER SEVENTEEN. OLIVER PERRY (1813)

237 the army's strength: Skeen, *Armstrong*, 134–35.

238 "the imbecility, and inexperience": Henry Adams, *Madison*, 676.

239 "He went and sat down on it": Mason, 88.

239 along the Raisin River: Henry Adams, *Madison*, 685–86.

240 "only conjecture": Cleaves, 143.

240 three hours to prepare for inspection: Mahon, 224.

241 "strewed with mangled bodies": Cleaves, 149.

241 stuck them on a picket fence: Cleaves, 150.

243 "Are there no men here?": O'Brien, 31.

243 threatened to kill the next: Henry Adams, *Madison*, 693.

243 "I have also to observe that in this instance": Henry Adams, *Madison*, 697.

244 "We have determined to maintain this place": Henry Adams, *Madison*, 695.

244 throwing down canteens of water: Lyman, 117.

244 "It is worthy of notice": Henry Adams, *Madison*, 698.

244 Britain's strategists agreed: Dutton, viii.

245 "No person on earth": Hickey, 140.

245 taking with him the British brig: Roosevelt, 141.

245 Perry and Lawrence had served: Dillon, 28.

246 "Don't Give Up the Ship": Forester, 159.

246 "Think of my situation": Bancroft, *Erie*, 140.

246 "a motley set of Negroes": Lyman, 123.

246 one sailor out of every ten: Joseph Wilson, 78.

246 "I have yet to learn": Bancroft, *Erie*, 140.

246 "Would it not have been as well": Dutton, 111–12.

247 the cut "might influence my judgment": Dillon, 181.

247 "Sir, I am under the disagreeable": Dutton, 113.

247 "It is right you should reap": Dutton, 125.

247 "You ought to consider that the first duty": Dutton, 130.

248 "our Father with One Arm": Hickey, 132.

248 "I expect to find the Yankee brigs": Lyman, 127.

248 scows that were called "camels": Roosevelt, 142, cites J. F. Cooper, vol. ii, 389.

249 Harrison had brought along: Bancroft, *Erie*, 145.

249 When they arrived on the *Lawrence*: Cleaves, 185.

250 soldiers and novice Canadians: Henry Adams, *Madison*, 701.

250 the British had to feed: Hickey, 132.

250 "I don't care": Dutton, 145.

251 The cost of the rum: Dutton, 147

251 By one calculation: Bancroft, *Erie*, 153.

251 "You ought to use great caution": Paine, 55.

251 owed his superior command: Forester, 159.

252 J. J. Yarnell: Barnes, 154.

252 Tecumseh had paddled out: Sugden, *Last*, 37.

253 Red Sticks had attacked: Sugden, *Life*, 350–53.

253 while he played cards: Shackford, 201.

255 a Narragansett Indian: Barnes, 155.

255 The American losses: Roosevelt, 149, notes that ninety-six Americans were wounded, and three died soon afterward.

255 Dulaney Forrest: Barnes, 154.

Chapter Eighteen. William Henry Harrison (1813)

257 not to be sent into Canada: Cleaves, 190.

258 "Of Captain Elliott, already so well-known": Dillon, 162.

258 "Old King Mountain": Hickey, 137.

258 evacuate the nearby town: Dillon, 166.

259 "coming out of his hole": Sugden, *Life*, 356.

259 Proctor had hoped: Sugden, *Last*, 51.

259 "of the very first quality": Sugden, *Last*, 50.

260 "Father! Listen to your children": Sugden, *Last*, 55.

260 "You always told us": *Proctor Court Martial*, 381–82.

261 Proctor who was vowing: Sugden, *Last*, 57.

262 Johnson had represented: Meyer, 81.

262 ordered one man shot: Cleaves, 191.

262 "The revenge of a soldier": Lossing, 2, 546.

263 "a series of continued blunders": Henry Adams, *Madison*, 709.

263 Johnson vetoed Harrison's plan: Cleaves, 194.

264 "let no man grumble": Cleaves, 195.

264 "We do not know what he is gone for": Sugden, *Last*, 77.

265 Kentuckians returned with scalps: Cleaves, 198.

265 the "Forlorn Hope": Cleaves, 199.

266 Colonel Elliott came to Warburton: Sugden, *Last*, 84; Sugden, *Life*, 365.

266 "Very well": Sugden, *Last*, 89.

267 "downright murder": Cleaves, 200.

267 "Father! Have a big heart": Cleaves, 200.

267 he seemed exuberant: Sugden, *Last*, 122.

268 when Harrison returned: Meyer, 131.

268 "Brother, take my place": Meyer, 132.

269 "The American backwoodsmen ride better": Dillon, 172.

269 managed to shoot an Indian: Cleaves, 203.

269 Harrison wanted Proctor protected: Cleaves, 203.

269 Kentuckians marveled at the elegance: Cleaves, 203.

269 Indian babies drowned: Lossing, 2, 555 note 2.

270 "Rumpsey dumpsey": Sugden, *Last*, 252 note.

CHAPTER NINETEEN. CREEK WARS (1813–1814)

271 "a sort of family quarrel": Kuppenheimer, 87.

273 On stage: Colyar, 9.

273 "Our forbearance has been despised": Mahon, 377.

273 Hull finally faced: William Hull, *Reports*, 35–119.

373 "Hickory Ground": Bassett, 90.

274 When the British began: Corkran, 253.

274 "When friends ask for property": Debo, 75.

275 But Andrew Jackson: Lossing, 2, 758.

275 but back in Nashville: Meigs, *Benton*, 71.

275 swore to friends that he would horsewhip: James, *Jackson*, 161.

276 "I'll keep my arm": Remini, *Course*, 185.

276 a gift for swearing that was widely celebrated: Parton, 1, 463.

277 welcomed the white feathers: Lossing, 2, 763.

277 Crockett's grandfather had come: Derr, 39.

277 "I was plaguy well pleased with her": Derr, 57.

277 "If every man would wait": Crockett, Shackford, ed., 72.

278 "a goat could have preference": Crockett, Shackford, ed., 75.

278 "I kept it all to myself": Crockett, Shackford, ed., 81.

278 "We shot men like dogs": Crockett, Shackford, ed., 88.

278 "So sullen is the Indian": Crockett, Shackford, ed., 89.

279 Jackson came upon a child: Remini, *Course*, 194.

279 He named the boy Lincoya: Parton, 1, 439.

279 "looked like they had been stewed": Crockett, Shackford, ed., 90.

279 "Sharp Knife": Derr, 62.

279 a needless assault against a Hillabee faction: Parton, 1, 453.

280 Crockett joined the men: Crockett, Shackford, ed., 94–95.

281 "always delighted to be in the very thickest": Crockett, Shackford, ed., 96.

281 Jackson led them immediately: Lossing, 2, 774.

282 single six-pound cannon: Lossing, 2, 775.

282 "personal firmness, popularity and exertions": Lossing, 2, 776.

282 A respected chieftain: Derr, 62.

283 Woods's execution: Parton, 1, 508–9.

284 "I began to feel": Crockett, Shackford, ed., 99–100.

284 called him "John Jolly": Braider, 22.

284 "the wild liberty of the Red Men": Braider, 22.

284 disrupted a militia meeting: James, *Raven*, 20.

284 "wandering along the bank of streams": James, *Raven*, 23.

285 "Indian University": James, *Raven*, 25.

285 Coffee's friendly Creeks swam across the Tallapoosa: Bassett, 117.

285 Lemuel P. Montgomery: James, *Raven*, 33; Alabama's capital is named for him.

285 An arrow struck: James, *Raven*, 33.

286 a cloud passed overhead: Houston, Day, ed., 12.

286 The tally counted 560 Creek bodies: Parton, 1, 520

286 Left alone, not expecting: Houston, Day, ed., 15.

288 commission as major general: Skeen, *Armstrong*, 176.

289 Creeks agreed to give up: Debo, 83; Buchanan, 300.

289 arranged a special exemption: Buchanan, 295.

Chapter Twenty. Dolley Madison (1814)

292 "most malicious insinuations": Cleaves, 222.

292 The U.S. Navy captured 254 British ships: Heidler, 429.

293 imports and exports dropped: Benn, 55.

293 But John Calhoun was able: Merrill Peterson, 43.

294 "had ever proved more vindictive": Gleig, *Campaigns*, 5.

294 A high point came: Gleig, *Campaigns*, 68.

295 Cockburn said, he intended: Lossing, 2, 945 note. Lossing does not give

a specific date; the episode apparently took place after the burning of Washington. Parker was killed during a subsequent skirmish near Chestertown, Maryland, on the night of August 30, 1814.

295 Disgusted British officers regarded: Lossing, 2, 944.

295 Dolley wrote to a friend: Brant, *Fourth*, 339.

296 "No! No! Baltimore is the place": Skeen, *Armstrong*, 189.

296 Monroe and Secretary of the Navy Jones: Brant, *Fourth*, 566.

296 John Adams wrote: Ketcham, *Madison*, 566.

297 Monroe had been pushing: Skeen, *Armstrong*, 189.

297 "in case of actual or menaced invasion": Skeen, *Armstrong*, 190.

297 a staff consisting of: Lossing, 2, 919–20.

298 British were bragging: Lossing, 2, 920.

298 On paper at least: Lossing, 2, 922.

298 George Gleig stepped: Gleig, *Campaigns*, 107–11.

299 "Well, be it so": Lord, 97–98.

300 "engrossed by a variety": Dolley Madison, *Selected Letters*, 190.

300 One British soldier compared: Ketcham, *Madison*, 576.

300 "of short duration": Stagg, 416.

300 Dolley sensed Madison's concern: Zall, *Dolley*, 57.

300 protect his official documents: Cutts, 100.

301 "who are in high spirits": Dolley Madison, *Selected Letters*, 192.

301 the British marched: Gleig, *Campaigns*, 114–18.

302 Winder estimated his strength: Pitch, 72.

303 Winder had started: Marine, 85–89, quotes Winder, American State Papers, Military Affairs, v. 1.

303 So far, the British: Gleig, *Campaigns*, 121–22.

304 The Americans lost: Henry Adams, *Madison*, 1012; Ketcham, *Madison*, 578, puts British casualties at perhaps 100 dead and 300 or 400 wounded.

304 Dolley Madison had risen: Dolley Madison, *Selected Letters*, 193.

305 Jean Pierre Sioussat: Lord, 153; his name is sometimes spelled without the *t*.

305 "I have always been an advocate": Zall, *Dolley*, 63.

305 "Mr. Madison comes not": Dolley Madison, *Selected Letters*, 193.

305 "Clear out!": Zall, *Dolley*, 59; Dolley Madison, *Memoirs*, 167.

306 "The precious portrait": Dolley Madison, *Selected Letters*, 194.

306 Ross sent out an aide: Lossing, 2, 932, note 2.

307 Captain Thomas Tingey: Lord, 162.

308 "I hope, sir": Pitch, 114, cites William Gardner letter, *Federal Republican*, September 16, 1814.

308 "I would rather protect, than burn": Dolley Madison, *Memoirs*, 164.

308 places had been laid out: Lord, 146.

308 "It is he who has got you into this scrape": Ketcham, *Madison*, 579.

309 pronounced very good: Hickey, 199.

309 Cockburn took for himself: Zall, *Dolley*, 60.

310 offices of the *National Intelligencer:* Lossing, 2, 933, note 2.

310 "Be sure that all the 'c's are destroyed": Lord, 176.

310 The British deputy adjutant: Pitch, 143.

310 Ross's troops retraced: Lossing, 2, 937.

311 Barney, having been: Marine, 102.

311 They sent a delegation: Lossing, 2, 940 note.

311 "It is impossible that men could behave better": Lord, 220.

312 indulged in vengeful thoughts: Dolley Madison, *Memoirs*, 166.

313 "our bitterness relented": Zall, *Dolley*, 62.

313 brought villagers from nearby: Ketcham, *Madison*, 580.

313 Even before the British raid: A. C. Clark, 85.

313 Picking his way: Ketcham, *Madison*, 581.

314 One British soldier caught: Pitch, 116.

314 "James Madison lost it": Hickey, 202.

314 "make as good a sheep walk": Skeen, *Armstrong*, 199.

314 "every officer would tear off his epaulets": Ketcham, *Madison*, 582.

315 offered Madison a choice: Skeen, *Armstrong*, 200.

315 "With men of such imbecility": Skeen, *Armstrong*, 201.

315 "whose nature and habits forbid him": Skeen, *Armstrong*, 202.

316 Key had come to make: Pitch, 191.

316 "not from any opinion of his own merit": Pitch, 192.

317 "No, I shall sup in Baltimore tonight": Pitch, 197.

317 "Remember, boys, General Ross rides": Marine, 191.

317 He sent out light: Lossing, 2, 950.

318 "My dear wife": Lossing, 2, 952.

318 rum cask as his coffin: Hickey, 203.

318 "It is impossible to conceive": Hickey, 203.

318 "he would have destroyed Washington": Pitch, 203.

318 about accepting a "contribution": Pitch, 203.

318 found them ignorant: Pitch, 192.

319 "It is my desire": Lord, 274.

320 charged the army $405.90: Lord, 275.

320 Yet only four men: Lossing, 2, 956 note.

320 Going through his head: Lord, 296.

321 "O say!": Key's original first stanza, Lossing, 2, 957.

Chapter Twenty-one. Ghent (1814)

323 "Two third of the period allotted to the life": J. Q. Adams, *Diary*, Adams, ed., 7, 657.

324 "that same dogmatical, overbearing manner": Parsons, 117.

324 "the fickle goddess": Clement Eaton, 16.

324 In renting the home: Van Deusen, 101.

324 "They sit after dinner": J. Q. Adams, *Diary*, Nevins, ed., July 8, 1814.

325 accepting that peremptory invitation: J. Q. Adams, *Diary*, Adams, ed., 3, 3.

325 Gallatin's son compared him: Dangerfield, 64.

325 But he sized up Swiss-born Gallatin: Van Deusen, 100.

326 "If this encroachment of Great Britain": Bemis, *John Quincy Adams*, 196.

327 "must shift for themselves": Morse, 80.

327 "that what I had written was too long": J. Q. Adams, *Diary*, Adams, ed., 3, 21.

327 "To surrender both the rights of sovereignty": Dangerfield, 69.

328 Adams went to talk with Goulburn: J. Q. Adams, *Diary*, Adams, ed., 3, 25–29.

328 "destined by Divine Providence": Parsons, 115.

329 "That is, if you send us away": Morse, 86.

330 "the misfortune at Washington": J. Q. Adams, *Writings*, Ford, ed., 5, 1814–16, 149.

330 His army was the largest: Henry Adams, *Madison*, 978.

331 Prevost's new arrivals recalled: Hitsman, 254.

331 troops that amounted to fewer: Roosevelt, 207.

331 thirty-nine-gun *Confiance*: Skaggs, *Macdonough*, 120.

332 Macdonough gathered his officers: Lossing, 2, 866.

333 Macdonough was knocked unconscious: Paine, 182.

333 He had laid out kedge: Forester, 214.

333 Of nearly 900 men: Roosevelt, 208, 210.

333 He argued to his superiors: Hitsman, 264.

334 When Liverpool offered Wellington: Forester, 220.

334 "a defeat still more disastrous": Henry Adams, *Madison*, 1207.

334 "20 million acres of the cream": Remini, *American Empire*, 232.

334 "An Eye for an Eye": Jackson to Gonzales Manrique, August 24, 1814, Jackson Papers, Library of Congress.

335 American eagle would now be soaring: Jackson to War Department, August 24, 1814, Jackson Papers, Library of Congress.

335 "there will be bloody noses": Remini, *American Empire*, 237.

335 "peace and friendship on honorable terms": Rutland, *Founding Father*, 230.

336 seized Bangor and Machias: Forester, 220.

336 "Mr. Clay lost his temper": Morse, 89.

336 "much too important to be conceded for the mere liberty": Morse, 89.

337 "The situation in which I am placed": Bemis, *John Quincy Adams*, 196.

337 volunteering for the regular army: Lossing, 2, 1012; Ammon, *Monroe*, 338.

337 riddled with cheaters: Henry Adams, *Madison*, 1062.

338 "If he does not retract": Morison, *Otis*, 240.

339 agreed to meet in Hartford: Lossing, 2, 112–13.

339 "inconceivable idea": J. Q. Adams, *Memoirs*, III, 20.

339 The art of beating: Rogers, 86.

339 Liverpool wrote to Castlereagh: Bemis, *Diplomatic History*, 166–71.

339 cost Britain more than 10 million pounds: Henry Adams, *Madison*, 1209.

340 "not very unfavorable": Van Deusen, 105.

340 federal army major had stationed: Lossing, 2, 1013.

340 Marat, Danton, and Robespierre: Morison, *Otis*, 361.

340 "wise and manly": Henry Adams, *Madison*, 1110.

340 "intelligent and honest men": Morison, *Otis*, 361.

340 "We are going to keep you young hotheads": Henry Adams, *Madison*, 1111.

340 "From the moment that the British possess": Morison, *Otis*, 364.

340 gave the British command in Halifax: Morison, *Otis*, 364.

341 "Blue-Light Federalist": Hickey, 257–58.

341 The final recommendations: Lossing, 2, 1014 note.

342 "the time for a change is at hand": Henry Adams, *Madison*, 1114.

342 in 1798 with the Virginia Resolutions: Henry Adams, *Madison*, 1114.

342 threatened him with physical harm: Henry Adams, *Madison*, 1113.

342 the discrepancy, while unfortunate: J. Q. Adams, *Memoirs*, 3, 126.

342 Adams told Gambier that: Nagel, 220.

CHAPTER TWENTY-TWO. NEW ORLEANS (1814–1815)

343 British ships failed to capture: Lossing, 2, 1021.

344 "The steady firmness of my troops": Bassett, 141.

344 Britain's troops had plundered: Remini, *American Empire*, 243.

344 Secretary Monroe's letter instructing: Bassett, 142.

344 newspapers back home: Lossing, 2, 1023.

345 Slaves who brought: Remini, *Battle*, 27.

345 who had seized almost fourteen hundred: Heidler, 429.

345 The American ship names reflected: Headley, *Second War*, 2, 263.

345 "I have never ceased to be a good citizen": Lossing, 2, 1019.

345 He would receive a naval commission: Bassett, 151.

346 At the last census: Remini, *Battle*, 26.

346 "Jackson's come!" Lossing, 2, 1024.

346 "You are now a Major Generals lady": Remini, *Battle*, 15.

347 "hellish banditti": Remini, *American Empire*, 252.

347 married the sister of a prominent Creole: Latour, xvii.

347 The imprisoned pirates had promised: George Poindexter to James Monroe, Feb. 15, 1815, Monroe Papers, New York Public Library.

347 When they finally met: Remini, *American Empire*, 253.

348 "Our country has been invaded": Bassett, 155–56.

348 "Through a mistaken policy": Bassett, 156.

348 "Be pleased to keep to yourself": Bassett, 157.

349 They intended to travel: Remini, *Battle*, 55.

349 the local government appeared to be: Bassett, 213.

350 Jackson declared martial law: Bassett, 174.

350 Suspending the right: Lossing, 2, 1028.

350 "the differences of language": Stagg, 497.

350 Jackson sent many: Bassett, 171.

351 froze the tops of their water tanks: Hickey, 209.

351 "the reverse of agreeable": Brooks, 164.

351 eating Christmas dinner in New Orleans: Remini, *Battle*, 69.

352 Inflating America's strength: Henry Adams, *Madison*, 1151.

352 lounged on the front porch: Remini, *Battle*, 66.

352 "Catch him or kill him!": Remini, *Battle*, 67.

353 "By the Eternal": Remini, *Battle*, 70.

353 "Gentlemen, the British are below": Lossing, 2, 1029.

353 "Major-General Jackson has received": Bassett, 217–18.

354 "Louisianians!": Lossing, 2, 1030.

354 George Gleig observed: Remini, *Battle*, 63.

354 Daniel Patterson: Bassett, 165 note, observes that although Jackson and others called Patterson "Commodore," that rank was not established in the United States until 1862; Patterson's official title was "Master-Commander."

354 ridiculed their general's obsession: Brooks, 137.

355 Gleig and his friend Captain Grey: Gleig, *Campaigns*, 290.

355 "Now, boys, give it to them": Brooks, 144.

356 A burst of fire proved: Gleig, *Campaigns*, 291–92.

356 Looking around for his friend: Gleig, *Campaigns*, 295.

356 "Save the guns, my boys": Lossing, 2, 1031.

357 recently drafted militiamen: Lossing, 2, 1033.

358 Locating Grey's pale and bloody corpse: Gleig, *Campaigns*, 300–303.

358 His killed, wounded: Henry Adams, *Madison*, 1156.

359 Eating in a barn: Gleig, *Campaigns*, 309.

359 Tennessee riflemen were creeping: Remini, *Battle*, 103.

359 To Gleig and his fellow: Gleig, *Campaigns*, 314.

359 Jackson had drawn most: Lossing, 2, 1035; Henry Adams, *Madison*, 1155; Latour, 84.

360 either to halt the enemy: Bassett, 184.

360 an earldom and possibly the governorship: Remini, *Battle*, 87.

360 his brother-in-law Wellington was suggesting: Henry Adams, *Madison*, 1158.

361 "We will storm the American lines": Remini, *Battle*, 89.

361 the animal stopped a few paces: Gleig, *Campaigns*, 315.

361 with horses commandeered: Latour, 91.

361 open sustained fire against the *Carolina*: Latour, 86.

362 He had concluded that living: Gleig, *Campaigns*, 317.

362 Gleig worried that they were: Gleig, *Campaigns*, 321.

362 hogsheads of sugar they found: Gleig, *Campaigns*, 324.

363 He could draw on ten: Henry Adams, *Madison*, 1166.

363 headquarters in the Macarty farmhouse: Latour, 95.

363 Jackson had passed the night: Derby, 189.

363 When the shelling died: Remini, *Battle*, 115.

364 "the growling of a chained dog": Gleig, *Campaigns*, 328.

364 Forty-fourth Regiment seemed to have: Bassett, 194.

366 into the tops of their heads: Gleig, *Campaigns*, 335.

366 John Adair, who had led: Bassett, 203.

366 "What more do you want?": Remini, *Battle*, 154.

367 British soldiers seeming to rise: Remini, *Battle*, 156.

368 refused to take orders from: Bassett, 201.

369 The man's insufferable bragging: Gleig, *Campaigns*, 343.

CHAPTER TWENTY-THREE. PEACE (1815)

371 a courier reached Washington: Brant, *Fourth*, 586.

372 He had refused: Rutland, *Madison*, 581.

372 he favored the Unitarians: Brant, *Fourth*, 586.

372 renewed its call for Madison's impeachment: Brant, *Fourth*, 587.

373 the sentinels began to steal away: Gleig, *Campaigns*, 348.

373 Inching forward under: Gleig, *Campaigns*, 352.

373 When he saw ducks: Gleig, *Campaigns*, 356.

374 "Louisiana may again say": Remini, *Battle*, 182.

374 "the great and joyful news of PEACE": Lossing, 2, 1064.

374 "We have obtained nothing but peace": Parsons, 120.

374 "Our anxieties cannot be expressed": Dolley Madison, *Selected Letters*, 197.

374 Otis and two fellow delegates: Banner, 348.

375 "Take a seat": James Morton Smith, 3, 1754.

375 GLORIOUS NEWS: Remini, *Battle*, 198.

375 "the natural result of the legislative council": Madison, Peterson, ed., 354–56.

376 "Now, I can go to England": Van Deusen, 107.

376 "If an honorable peace": Bassett, 212, cites Jackson to Governor Gabriel Holmes, February 21, 1815.

377 "You will be vigilant": Bassett, 225.

378 "The only question was whether": Bassett, 228.

378 "Considering obedience to the laws": Bassett, 230.

379 "I'm glad the old gentleman has plucked up": Burke Davis, 149.

CHAPTER TWENTY-FOUR. AFTERWARD (1815–1861)

381 "courage and fidelity": Latour, 341.

382 When casualties from the late war: Henry Adams, *Madison*, 1243–44.

382 "atrocity of impressment": James Morton Smith, 3, 1764; Jefferson letter, March 23, 1815.

382 "If our first struggle was a war": Brant, *Madison* (6 vols.), 6, 380; Madison to Charles Ingersoll, January 4, 1818.

383 "mean and contemptible": Brant, *Madison* (6 vols.), 6, 370.

384 "little pigmy": Otis to his wife, February 20, 1815, Massachusetts Historical Society.

385 "On what principle can the purchase of Louisiana": Henry Adams, *Madison*, 1285.

385 "This enterprise is for the young": Freehling, 130.

386 "a model of kindness": Ketcham, *Madison*, 608.

386 The court found him: Antal, 375.

386 Prevost was also recalled: Antal, 389.

386 Cockburn found Bonaparte: Morriss, 121–41.

386 unsuccessfully championing the discarded: Morriss, 280.

386 For George Gleig: Gleig, *Subaltern*, unnumbered introduction.

387 When he was able to reassure: Ammon, *Monroe*, 357.

387 "Era of Good Feelings": Dangerfield, 95.

388 "the most important incident in my life": Remini, *Adams*, 56.

388 "the great and foul stain": Parsons, 160.

388 "unpolluted with slavery": Parsons, 162.

388 With the Federalist Party: Ammon, *Monroe*, 459.

389 "abroad in search of monsters": Parsons, 149.

389 "be considered as subjects for future colonization": Remini, *Adams*, 60.

390 an acute skin disease: Ammon, *Monroe*, 530.

391 "imminent public danger": Skaggs, *Macdonough*, 147.

392 "the Valley of Chance": DeKay, *Decatur*, 200.

393 "I hope, Commodore Decatur, that when we meet": DeKay, *Decatur*, 203.

393 the kind of road and canal construction: Parsons, 180.

393 "palsied by the will of their constituents": Parsons, 181.

394 "man of real wisdom": Parsons, 186.

394 "You may rest assured": Parsons, 190.

395 "age of Folly, Vice": Ferling, 213.

395 Adams had weighed its results: Brant, *Madison* (6 vols.), 4, 378.

395 "has acquired more glory": Brant, *Madison* (6 vols.), 4, 603.

395 "Thomas Jefferson survives": McCullough, 646.

396 "a stout black wench": Bassett, 424.

397 adopted it as their party symbol: Morison, *History*, 2, 161–62.

397 "full of the laziest clerks": Bassett, 456.

397 "as chaste as those who attempt to slander her": Bassett, 463.

397 "the Eaton malaria": Bassett, 464.

397 "Age cannot wither nor time stale": Morison, *History*, 2, 167.

398 "violence and imbecilities": Bassett, 471.

398 Payne Todd had come home: Dolley Madison, *Selected Letters*, 220.

399 first of the rheumatic attacks: Dolley Madison, *Selected Letters*, 223.

399 "The Federal Constitution must be obeyed": Morison, *History*, 2, 164.

400 "that there never was a full-blood Indian": Remini, *Adams*, 156.

400 "The laboring classes have little or no share": Jackson, *Farewell Address*.

400 "This unhappy race—the original dwellers": Morison, *History*, 2, 194.

401 Crockett stayed on in Florida: Crockett, Shackford, ed., 34.

401 "These are the remnants": Rourke, 135.

401 "There's too many people in New York": Rourke, 146.

402 "I'm going to Texas": Rourke, 149.

402 "lost all my Red Rosy Cheeks": Crockett, Shackford, ed., 282.

403 "You can judge how unhappy I was": Williams, 67.

403 where he met Jim Bowie: Williams, 75.

403 "physical and moral energy": Williams, 92.

404 "We will rather die": Rourke, 206.

404 "or any future republican Government": Crockett, Shackford, ed., 218.

404 "I am induced to believe": Crockett, Shackford, ed., 225.

405 "a small affair": Derr, 249.

405 "You see, I was right!": Parton, *Burr,* 319.
406 "not by simpering diplomacy but by blood": Morison, *History,* 2, 211.
407 She still rouged her cheeks: Hunt-Jones, 13.
407 "the old lady is a very hearty": Dolley Madison, *Selected Letters,* 320.
408 set his remaining slaves free: Dolley Madison, *Selected Letters,* 325.
409 "The civil war now being inaugurated": Williams, 346.

Bibliography

Abbott, John S. C. *George Washington*. New York, 1898.

Adams, Abigail. *New Letters, 1788–1801*. Steward Mitchell, ed. Boston, 1947.

Adams, Henry. *History of the United States During the Administration of James Madison*. Earl N. Harbert, ed. New York, 1986.

——. *History of the United States During the Administration of Thomas Jefferson*. Earl N. Harbert, ed. 2 vols. New York, 1986.

——. *The Life of Albert Gallatin*. Philadelphia, 1879.

——. *The Lives of James Madison and James Monroe*. Boston, 1850.

Adams, James Truslow. *The Living Jefferson*. New York, 1936.

Adams-Jefferson Letters. Lester J. Cappon, ed. Williamsburg, Va., 1987.

Adams, John Quincy.

——. *Diary: 1794–1845*. Allan Nevins, ed. New York, 1951.

——. *Diary from 1795 to 1848*. Charles Francis Adams, ed. 12 vols. Philadelphia, 1874–77.

The Life of John Adams. Completed by Charles Francis Adams. 2 vols. Philadelphia, 1871.

——. *The Russian Memoirs*. Charles Francis Adams, ed. Philadelphia, 1874.

——. *Writings*. Worthington Chauncy Ford, ed. Vol. IV, 1811–13. New York, 1914.

Adams, William Howard. *Gouverneur Morris: An Independent Life*. New Haven, Conn., 2003.

Alexander, John K. *Samuel Adams: America's Revolutionary Politician*. New York, 2002.

Amar, Akhil Reed. *The Bill of Rights*. New Haven, Conn., 1998.

Ames, Fisher. *Works*. Seth Ames, ed. 2 vols. Enlarged by W. B. Allen. Indianapolis, Ind., 1983.

Ammon, Harry. *The Genet Mission.* New York, 1973.

——. *James Monroe.* New York, 1971.

Antal, Sandy. *A Wampum Denied: Procter's War of 1812.* Ontario, Canada, 1997.

Atherton, Gertrude. *A Few of Hamilton's Letters.* New York, 1903.

Auchinleck, G. *A History of the War Between Great Britain and the United States During the Years 1812, 1813, and 1814.* Toronto, 1855.

Austin, James T. *The Life of Elbridge Gerry.* 2 vols. Boston, 1828–29.

Baldwin, Joseph G. *Party Leaders.* Hallandale, Fla., 1855, 1972.

Bancroft, George. *History of the Battle of Lake Erie.* New York, 1891.

——. *Martin Van Buren to the End of His Public Career.* New York, 1889.

Banner, James M. *To the Hartford Convention: The Federalists and the Origins of Party Politics in Massachusetts, 1789–1815.* New York, 1970.

Banning, Lance. *The Sacred Fire of Liberty: James Madison and the Founding of the Federal Republic.* Ithaca, N.Y., 1995.

Bannon, John Francis, ed. *The Greatest Real Estate Deal in History.* St. Louis, Mo., 1953.

Barbuto, Richard V. *Niagara 1814: America Invades Canada.* Lawrence, Kans., 2000.

Barnes, James. *Naval Actions of the War of 1812.* New York, 1896.

Bartlett, Irving H. *John C. Calhoun.* New York, 1993.

Bassett, John Spencer. *The Life of Andrew Jackson.* New York, 1925, 1967.

Beirne, Francis F. *The War of 1812.* New York, 1949.

Bellamy, Francis R. *The Private Life of George Washington.* New York, 1951.

Bemis, Samuel Flagg. *Diplomatic History of the United States,* New York, 1942.

——. *John Quincy Adams and the Foundations of American Foreign Policy.* New York, 1949.

Benn, Carl. *The War of 1812.* New York, 2002.

Berkin, Carol. *Revolutionary Mothers: Women in the Struggle for America's Independence.* New York, 2005.

Bernhard, Winfred E. A. *Fisher Ames: Federalist and Statesman.* Williamsburg, Va., 1965.

Bernier, Oliver. *Lafayette.* New York, 1983.

Berton, Pierre. *The Invasion of Canada.* Canada, 2001.

Billias, George Athan. *Elbridge Gerry: Founding Father and Republican Statesman.* New York, 1976.

Binder, Frederick M. *The Color Problem in Early National America as Viewed by John Adams, Jefferson and Jackson.* The Hague, Netherlands, 1968.

Bobbe, Dorothie. *Mr. and Mrs. John Quincy Adams.* New York, 1930.

Borden, Morton. *The Federalism of James A. Bayard.* New York, 1968.

Borneman, Walter R. *1812: The War That Forged a Nation.* New York, 2004.

Bowen, Catherine Drinker. *Miracle at Philadelphia.* Boston, 1966.

Bowen, Clarence Winthrop, ed. *The History of the Centennial Celebration of the Inauguration of George Washington as First President of the United States.* New York, 1892.

Bradford, M. E. *Founding Fathers: Brief Lives of the Framers of the United States Constitution.* Lawrence, Kans., 1981.

Braider, Donald. *Solitary Star: A Biography of Sam Houston.* New York, 1974.

Brant, Irving. *The Bill of Rights.* Indianapolis, Ind., 1965.

———. *The Fourth President.* Indianapolis, Ind., 1970.

———. *James Madison.* 6 vols. Indianapolis, Ind., 1950–53.

———. *James Madison and American Nationalism.* Princeton, N.J., 1968.

Brighton, Ray. *The Checkered Career of Tobias Lear.* Portsmouth, N.H., 1985.

Brock, Isaac. *Letters.* Ferdinand Brock Tupper, ed. London, 1845.

Brodie, Fawn M. *Thomas Jefferson: An Intimate History.* New York, 1974.

Brookheiser, Richard. *America's First Dynasty.* New York, 2002.

Brooks, Charles B. *The Siege of New Orleans.* Seattle, 1961.

Brown, Ralph Adams. *The Presidency of John Adams.* Lawrence, Kans., 1975.

Brown, Roger H. *The Republic in Peril: 1812.* New York, 1964.

Brown, Stuart Gerry. *Thomas Jefferson.* New York, 1963.

Brown, Walt. *John Adams and the American Press.* Jefferson, N.C., 1995.

Bruce, William Cabell. *John Randolph of Roanoke.* 2 vols. New York, 1922.

Bryan, Helen. *Martha Washington: First Lady of Liberty.* New York, 2002.

Buchanan, John. *Jackson's Way.* New York, 2001.

Buel, Richard, Jr. *America on the Brink: How the Political Struggle Over the War of 1812 Almost Destroyed the Young Republic.* New York, 2005.

Buell, Augustus C. *History of Andrew Jackson.* 2 vols. New York, 1904.

Burns, Edward McNall. *James Madison, Philosopher of the Constitution.* New Brunswick, N.J., 1938.

Burns, James MacGregor, and Susan Dunn. *George Washington.* New York, 2004.

Burr, Aaron. *Correspondence of Aaron Burr and His Daughter Theodosia.* New York, 1929.

Burstein, Andrew. *The Inner Jefferson.* Charlottesville, Va., 1995.

———. *The Passions of Andrew Jackson.* New York, 2003.

Caffrey, Kate. *The Twilight's Last Gleaming.* New York, 1977.

Calhoun, John C. *Papers.* Robert L. Meriwether, ed. Vol. 1. Columbia, S.C., 1959.

———. *Works.* New York, 1853.

Calloway, Colin G. *Crown and Calumet: British-Indian Relations, 1783–1815.* Norman, Okla., 1953.

Campbell, Charles S. *From Revolution to Rapprochement: The United States and Great Britain, 1783–1900.* New York, 1974.

Campbell, Maria. *Revolutionary Service and Civil Life of General William Hull.* New York, 1848.

Chambers, William Nisbet. *Old Bullion Benton: Senator from the New West.* Boston, 1956.

——. *Political Parties in a New Nation: American Experience, 1776–1809.* New York, 1963.

Chernow, Ron. *Alexander Hamilton.* New York, 2004.

Chidsey, Donald Barr. *Andrew Jackson, Hero.* Nashville, Tenn., 1970.

——. *The Great Conspiracy.* New York, 1967.

——. *Louisiana Purchase.* New York, 1972.

——. *Mr. Hamilton and Mr. Jefferson.* Nashville, Tenn., 1975.

——. *The Wars in Barbary.* New York, 1971.

Chinard, Gilbert, ed. *George Washington as the French Knew Him.* Princeton, N.J., 1940.

——. *Honest John Adams.* Boston, 1933.

Clark, Allen C. *Life and Letters of Dolley Madison.* Washington, D.C., 1914.

Clark, Bennett Champ. *John Quincy Adams.* Boston, 1933.

Clark, William. *Dear Brother: Letters to Jonathan Clark.* James J. Holmberg, ed. New Haven, Conn., 2002.

Clarke, James Freeman. *History of the Campaign of 1812.* New York, 1848.

Clay, Henry. *Papers.* James F. Hopkins, ed. Vol. 1. Lexington, Ky., 1959.

Cleaves, Freeman. *Old Tippecanoe: William Henry Harrison and His Time.* New York, 1939.

Coit, Margaret L. *Andrew Jackson.* Cambridge, Mass., 1965.

——. *John C. Calhoun: American Portrait.* Boston, 1950.

Cole, Donald B. *Martin Van Buren and the American Political System.* Princeton, N.J., 1984.

Coles, Harry L. *The War of 1812.* Chicago, 1965.

Collier, Christopher, and James Lincoln Collier. *Decision in Philadelphia.* New York, 1986.

Colton, Calvin. *Henry Clay.* 6 vols. New York, 1857.

Colyar, A. S. *Life and Times of Andrew Jackson.* Vol. 1. Nashville, Tenn., 1904.

Combs, Jerald A. *The Jay Treaty.* Berkeley, Calif., 1970.

Conner, Susan P. *The Age of Napoleon.* Westport, Conn., 2004.

Cooper, J. Fenimore. *History of the Navy of the United States of America.* New York, 1854.

Corkran, David H. *The Creek Frontier: 1540–1783.* Norman, Okla., 1967.

Crane, William Carey. *Select Literary Remains of Sam Houston of Texas.* Dallas, Tex., 1884.

Crockett, David. *An Autobiography.* New York, 1903.

——. *Davy Crockett's Own Story, As Written by Himself.* New York, 1955.

——. *A Narrative of the Life.* Shackford and Fomsbee, eds. Lincoln, Nebr., 1987.

Cruikshank, E. *The Documentary History of the Campaign Upon the Niagara Frontier in the Year 1813.* Part II. Welland, Canada, 1905.

Cusick, James G. *The Other War of 1812.* Gainesville, Fla., 2003.

Custis, George Washington Parke. *Recollections and Private Memoirs of Washington.* New York, 1860.

Cutts, Lucia Beverly. *Memoirs and Letters of Dolley Madison.* Boston, 1886.

Dahl, Robert A. *How Democratic Is the American Constitution?* New Haven, Conn., 2003.

Dangerfield, George. *The Era of Good Feelings.* Gloucester, Mass., 1793.

Davis, Burke. *Old Hickory.* New York, 1977.

Davis, David Brion. *The Problem of Slavery in the Age of Revolution, 1770–1823.* New York, 1999.

Davis, William C. *The Pirates Laffite.* New York, 2005.

Debo, Angie. *Road to Disappearance.* Norman, Okla., 1941.

——. *This Affair of Louisiana.* Baton Rouge, La., 1976.

DeConde, Alexander. *The Quasi-War.* New York, 1966.

DeKay, James Tertius. *The Battle of Stonington.* Annapolis, Md., 1990.

——. *A Rage for Glory: The Life of Commodore Stephen Decatur, USN.* New York, 2004.

Derby, James C. *Memoirs of General Andrew Jackson.* New York, 1845.

Derr, Mark. *The Frontiersman.* New York, 1993.

Dillon, Richard. *We Have Met the Enemy.* New York, 1978.

Dixon, Peter. *Canning: Politician and Statesman.* London, 1976.

Dobbins, W. W. *Battle of Lake Erie.* Erie, Pa., 1913, 1929.

Documentary History of the Ratification of the Constitution. Merrill Jensen et al., eds. Madison, Wisc., 1976–.

Dodd, William E. *Statesmen of the Old South, or From Radicalism to Conservative Revolt.* New York, 1911.

Donnelly, Joseph Peter. "Explorers, Beaver Pelts and Wagon Trains," in *The Greatest Real Estate Deal in History*, John Francis Bannon, ed. St. Louis, Mo., 1953.

Doster, James F. *Creek Indians.* 2 vols. New York, 1974.

Doutrich, Paul E. *Jacksonian Democracy.* Westport, Conn., 2004.

Drake, Benjamin. *Life of Tecumseh.* Cincinnati, Ohio, 1841.

Dudley, Wade G. *Splintering the Wooden Wall: The British Blockade of the United States, 1812–1815.* Annapolis, Md., 2003.

Dudley, William S., ed. *The Naval War of 1812, A Documentary History.* Washington, D.C., 1985.

Duncan, Dayton. *Scenes of Visionary Enchantment: Reflections on Lewis and Clark.* Lincoln, Nebr., 2004.

Dunn, Susan. *Jefferson's Second Revolution.* Boston, 2004.

Dutton, Charles J. *Oliver Hazard Perry.* New York, 1935.

Dwight, Theodore. *History of the Hartford Convention.* Boston, 1833.

Dye, Ira. *The Fatal Cruise of the* Argus: *Two Captains in the War of 1812.* Annapolis, Md., 1994.

Eaton, Clement. *Henry Clay and the Art of American Politics.* Boston, 1957.

Eaton, John Henry. *The Life of Andrew Jackson.* Philadelphia, 1824; New York, 1971.

Edgar, Matilda. *General Brock.* Toronto, 1910.

Edmunds, R. David. *The Shawnee Prophet.* Lincoln, Nebr., 1983.

——. *Tecumseh and the Quest for Indian Leadership.* Boston, 1984.

Egan, Clifford L. *Neither Peace Nor War: Franco-American Relations, 1803–1812.* Baton Rouge, La., 1983.

Egerton, Douglas R. *Charles Fenton Mercer and the Trial of National Conservatism.* Jackson, Miss., 1989.

Elkins, Stanley. *Slavery.* New York, 1963.

Ellis, Joseph J. *American Sphinx: The Character of Thomas Jefferson.* New York, 1997.

——. *His Excellency George Washington.* New York, 2004.

Eltin, John R. *Amateurs, To Arms!* Chapel Hill, N.C., 1991.

Engle, Eloise, and Arnold S. Lott. *America's Maritime Heritage.* Annapolis, Md., 1975.

Englund, Steven. *Napoleon: A Political Life.* New York, 2004.

Erney, Richard Alton. *The Public Life of Henry Dearborn.* Ph.D. dissertation, Columbia University, New York, 1957; published New York, 1979.

Erwin, Andrew. *Jackson's Negro Speculations.* Pamphlet, Library of Congress, 1828.

Everest, Allan S. *The War of 1812 in the Champlain Valley.* Syracuse, N.Y., 1981.

Farquhar, Michael. *Great American Scandals.* New York, 2003.

Fehrenbacher, Don E. *The Era of Expansion: 1800–1848.* New York, 1969.

Ferling, John. *Adams vs. Jefferson: The Tumultuous Election of 1800.* New York, 2004.

Fitz-Enz, David G. *The Final Invasion: Plattsburgh, the War of 1812's Most Decisive Battle.* New York, 2001.

——. *John Adams: A Life.* Knoxville, Tenn., 1992

Fleming, Thomas. *Affectionately Yours, George Washington.* New York, 1967.

——. *The Louisiana Purchase.* Hoboken, N.J., 2003.

Flexner, James Thomas. *George Washington: Anguish and Farewell (1793–1799).* Boston, 1972.

——. *George Washington and the New Nation (1783–1793).* Boston, 1970.

——. *Washington: The Indispensable Man.* Boston, 1974.

——. *The Young Hamilton.* Boston, 1978.

Ford, Henry Jones. *Alexander Hamilton.* New York, 1920.

Ford, Paul Leicester. *The True George Washington.* Philadelphia, 1896.

Forester, C. S. *The Naval War of 1812.* London, 1957.

Fowler, William M., Jr. *Samuel Adams: Radical Puritan.* New York, 1997.

Fraser, Steve, and Gary Gerstle, eds. *Ruling America.* Cambridge, Mass., 2005.

Freehling, William W. *The Road to Disunion.* Vol. 1. New York, 1990.

Freeman, Douglas Southall. *George Washington.* 7 vols. Vol. 7 completed by John Alexander Carroll and Mary Wells Ashcroft. New York, 1954–75.

Freeman, Joanne B. *Affairs of Honor.* New Haven, Conn., 2002.

Fresonke, Kris, and Mark Spence, eds. *Lewis & Clark.* Berkeley, Calif., 2004.

Gardiner, Robert, ed. *The Naval War of 1812.* Annapolis, Md., 1998.

Geer, Curtis M. *The Louisiana Purchase and the Westward Movement.* Vol. VIII of *The History of North America.* Philadelphia, 1904.

Gerry, Elbridge. *Letterbook: Paris 1797–1798.* Russell W. Knight, ed. Salem, Mass., 1966.

——. *Some Letters: 1784–1804.* Worthington Chauncey Ford, ed. Brooklyn, N.Y., 1896.

Gilman, Daniel C. *James Monroe.* Boston, 1899.

Gleig, George R. *The Campaigns of the British Army at Washington and New Orleans.* London, 1847.

——. *The Subaltern.* London, 1825.

Gordon-Reed, Annette. *Thomas Jefferson and Sally Hemings: An American Controversy.* Charlottesville, Va., 1997.

Greenblatt, Miriam. *War of 1812.* New York, 2003.

Haley, James L. *Sam Houston.* Norman, Okla., 2002.

Hamilton, Alexander. *Papers.* 27 vols. Harold C. Syrett, ed. New York, 1961–87.

Hamilton, Allan McLane. *The Intimate Life of Alexander Hamilton.* New York, 1910.

Hannay, James. *History of the War of 1812.* Toronto, 1905.

Harper, John Lamberton. *American Machiavelli: Alexander Hamilton and the Origins of U.S. Foreign Policy.* Cambridge, England, 2004.

Harrison, William Henry. *Aborigines of the Ohio Valley.* Chicago, 1883.

Hasting, Martin Franklin. "How the Deal Was Made." In *The Greatest Real Estate Deal in History,* John Francis Bannon, ed. St. Louis, Mo., 1953.

Hatzenbuehler, Ronald L., and Robert L. Ivie. *Congress Declares War*. Kent, Ohio, 1983.

Hay, Thomas Robson, and M. R. Werner. *The Admirable Trumpeter: A Biography of General James Wilkinson*. Garden City, N.Y., 1941.

Headley, J. T. *The Lives of Winfield Scott and Andrew Jackson*. New York, 1852.

——. *The Second War with England*. 2 vols. New York, 1853.

Heidler, David S., and Jeanne T. Heidler, eds. *Encyclopedia of the War of 1812*. Santa Barbara, Calif., 1997.

Henriques, Peter R. *He Lived as He Died*. Mount Vernon, Va., 2001.

Hickey, Donald R. *The War of 1812: A Forgotten Conflict*. Urbana, Ill., 1989.

Higginbotham, Don. *George Washington: Uniting a Nation*. Latham, Md., 2002.

Hirschfeld, Fritz. *George Washington and Slavery*. Columbia, Mo., 1997.

History of the American War of 1812, From the Commencement Until the Final Termination Thereof on the Memorable Eighth of January 1815. Freeport, N.Y., 1970.

Hitsman, J. Mackay. *The Incredible War of 1812*. Toronto, Canada, 1999.

Hollis, Ira N. *The Frigate* Constitution: *The Central Figure of the Navy Under Sail*. Boston, 1900.

Hollon, W. Eugene. *The Lost Pathfinder: Zebulon Montgomery Pike*. Norman, Okla., 1949.

Horsman, Reginald. *The Causes of the War of 1812*. Philadelphia, 1962.

——. *The War of 1812*. New York, 1969.

Hosmer, James K. *The History of the Louisiana Purchase*. New York, 1902.

House of Representatives. *Purchase of the Territory of Louisiana*. State Papers and Correspondence. Washington, D.C., 1903.

Houston, Sam. *The Autobiography*. Donald Day and Harry Herbert Ullom, eds. Norman, Okla., 1954.

——. *The Writings*. Amelia W. Williams and Eugene C. Barker, eds. Vol. 1. Austin, Tex., 1938.

Hull, Isaac. *Papers*. Gardner Weld Allen, ed. Boston, 1929.

Hull, William. *Report of the Trial of Brig. Gen. William Hull, Commanding the North-Western Army of the United States by a Court Martial, Held at Albany, Monday 3 January, 1814 and Succeeding Days*. Lt. Col. Forbes, stenographer.

Hunt-Jones, Conover. *Dolley and the "Great, Little Madison."* Washington, D.C., 1977.

Irving, Washington. *Life of George Washington*. 5 vols. New York, 1859.

Jackson, Andrew. *Farewell Address*. The World's Famous Orations. Vol. 1. William Jennings Bryan, ed. New York, 1906.

——. *Memoirs*. Auburn, N.Y., 1845.

——. *Memoirs.* John H. Eaton, ed. Philadelphia, 1839.

Jacobs, James Ripley. *Tarnished Warrior: Major-General James Wilkinson.* New York, 1938.

James, Marquis. *Andrew Jackson: The Border Captain.* Indianapolis, Ind., 1933.

——. *The Raven: A Biography of Sam Houston.* London, 1929.

Jay, John. *The Correspondence and Public Papers, 1763–1781.* 4 vols. Henry P. Johnson, ed. New York, 1890.

——. *Diary During the Peace Negotiations of 1782.* New Haven, Conn., 1934.

——. *The Making of a Revolutionary: Unpublished Papers 1745–1780.* Richard B. Morris, ed. New York, 1975.

Jefferson, Thomas. *The Complete Anas.* Franklin B. Sawvel, ed. New York, 1903.

——. *The Jefferson Cyclopedia.* John P. Foley, ed. New York, 1900.

——. *Jefferson Himself.* Bernard Mayo, ed. Boston, 1942.

——. *The Literary Bible.* Gilbert Chinard, ed. Baltimore, 1928.

——. *Memoirs, Correspondence and Private Papers.* 4 vols. Thomas Jefferson Randolph, ed. London, 1829.

——. *Papers.* Julian P. Boyd, ed. Princeton, N.J., 1950–97.

——. *A Reference Biography.* Merrill D. Peterson, ed. New York, 1986.

——. *Writings.* 10 vols. Paul Lester Ford, ed. New York, 1892–99.

Jenkins, John S. *The Life of John Caldwell Calhoun.* New York, undated.

Jenkinson, Isaac. *Aaron Burr: His Personal and Political Relations with Thomas Jefferson and Alexander Hamilton.* Richmond, Ind., 1902.

Jones, Landon Y. *William Clark and the Shaping of the West.* New York, 2004.

Kahn, Paul W. *The Reign of Law.* New Haven, Conn., 1997.

Kaminski, John P. *George Clinton: Yeoman Politician of the New Republic.* Madison, Wisc., 1993.

Karsner, David. *Andrew Jackson: The Gentle Savage.* New York, 1929.

Kaster, Peter J. *The Nation's Crucible: The Louisiana Purchase and the Creation of America.* New Haven, Conn., 2004.

Keats, John. *Eminent Domain: The Louisiana Purchase and the Making of America.* New York, 1973.

Kelsay, Isabel Thompson. *Joseph Brant 1743–1807: Man of Two Worlds.* Syracuse, N.Y., 1984.

Kennedy, Roger G. *Burr, Hamilton and Jefferson: A Study in Character.* New York, 1999.

——. *Mr. Jefferson's Lost Cause.* New York, 2003.

Ketcham, Ralph. *The Anti-Federalist Papers and the Constitutional Convention Debates.* New York, 1986.

——. *James Madison, A Biography.* New York, 1971.

Klinck, Carl F., ed. *Tecumseh: Fact and Fiction in the Early Records.* Englewood Cliffs, N.J., 1961.

Koch, Adrienne, ed. *Jefferson.* Englewood Cliffs, N.J., 1971.

——. *Jefferson and Madison: The Great Collaboration.* New York, 1950.

——. *Madison's "Advice to My Country."* Princeton, N.J., 1966.

Kornblith, Gary J., and John M. Murri. "The Dilemmas of Ruling Elites in Revolutionary America," in Fraser and Gerstle, *Ruling America.*

Krafft, Herman F., and Walter B. Norris. *Sea Power in American History.* New York, 1920.

Kuppenheimer, L. B. *Albert Gallatin's Vision of Democratic Stability.* Westport, Conn., 1996.

Lane, Ann J., ed. *The Debate over Slavery: Stanley Elkins and His Critics.* Urbana, Ill., 1971.

Lanier, John J. *Washington: The Great American Mason.* New York, 1922.

Latour, Arsene Lacarriere. *Historical Memoir of the War in West Florida and Louisiana in 1814–15.* Gene A. Smith, ed. Gainesville, Fla., 1999.

Lavender, David. *Climax at Buena Vista: The American Campaigns in Northeastern Mexico 1846–47.* Philadelphia, 1966.

Lawson, John. *History of North Carolina.* Richmond, Va., 1937.

Le Couteur, John. *The War Diaries of, Merry Hearts Make Light Days.* Donald E. Graves, ed. Ottawa, 1994.

Leibiger, Stuart. *Founding Friendship. George Washington, James Madison, and the Creation of the American Republic.* Charlottesville, Va., 1999.

Levin, Phyllis Lee. *Abigail Adams.* New York, 1987.

Levy, Leonard W. *Origins of the Bill of Rights.* New Haven, Conn., 2001.

Lewis, Jan Ellen, and Peter S. Onuf, eds. *Sally Hemings & Thomas Jefferson.* Charlottesville, Va., 1999.

Lomask, Milton. *Aaron Burr.* 2 vols. New York, 1979, 1982.

Lord, Walter. *The Dawn's Early Light.* New York, 1972.

Lossing, Benson J. *The Pictorial Field-Book of the War of 1812.* 2 vols. New York, 2001.

Louisiana Purchase: An Exhibition Prepared by Louisiana State Museum. New Orleans, La., 1953.

Lyman, Olin L. *Commodore Oliver Hazard Perry and the War on the Lakes.* New York, 1905.

Madison, Dolley. *Memoirs and Letters.* Lucia Beverly Cutts, ed. Boston, 1886.

——. *Selected Letters.* David B. Mattern and Holly C. Shulman, eds. Charlottesville, Va., 2003.

Madison, James. *A Biography in His Own Words.* Merrill D. Peterson, ed. New York, 1974.

——. *Letters and Other Writings.* 4 vols. Philadelphia, 1867.

——. *The Mind of the Founder.* Marvin Meyers, ed. Hanover, Vt., 1981.

——. *Notes of Debates in the Federal Convention of 1787.* Adrienne Koch, ed. Athens, Ohio, 1966.

——. *The Papers.* 4 vols. J. C. A. Stagg, ed. Charlottesville, Va., 1999.

——. *The Papers.* Presidential Series. Robert Allen Rutland et al., eds. Charlottesville, Va., 1984–.

——. *The Papers.* Secretary of State Series. David B. Mattern et al., eds. Charlottesville, Va., 1999.

——. *The Writings.* Vol. VIII. Gaillard Hunt, ed. New York, 1908.

——. *Writings.* Jack N. Rakov, ed. New York, 1999.

Madison, James, Alexander Hamilton, and John Jay. *The Federalist Papers.* Isaac Kramnick, ed. London, 1987.

Magoon, E. L. *Living Orators in America.* New York, 1849.

Mahon, John K. *The War of 1812.* Gainesville, Fla., 1972.

Malcomson, Robert. *H. M. S. Detroit: The Battle for Lake Erie.* Annapolis, Md., 1990.

——. *Lords of the Lake: The Naval War on Lake Ontario 1812–1814.* Annapolis, Md., 1998.

——. *A Very Brilliant Affair: The Battle of Queenston Heights, 1812.* Annapolis, Md., 2003.

Malone, Dumas. *Jefferson and His Time.* 6 vols. Boston, 1948–62.

Manceron, Claude. *The Wind from America.* Nancy Amphoux, trans. New York, 1978.

Mapp, Alf J., Jr. *Thomas Jefferson: A Strange Case of Mistaken Identity.* New York, 1987.

Marine, William M. *The British Invasion of Maryland, 1812–1815.* Baltimore, 1913.

Mason, Jeremiah. *Memoir and Correspondence.* Cambridge, Mass., 1873.

May, Ernest R. *The Making of the Monroe Doctrine.* Cambridge, Mass., 1975.

Mayo, Bernard. *Henry Clay: Spokesman of the New West.* Boston, 1937.

Mazyck, Walter H. *George Washington and the Negro.* Washington, D.C., 1932.

McClure, C. H. *Early Opposition to Thomas Hart Benton.* Columbia, Mo., 1916.

McCoy, Drew R. *The Last of the Fathers: James Madison and the Republican Legacy.* Cambridge, England, 1989.

McCullough, David. *John Adams.* New York, 2001.

McDonald, Forrest. *The Presidency of George Washington.* Lawrence, Kans., 1974.

McDougall, Walter A. *Freedom Just Around the Corner: A New American History 1585–1828*. New York, 2005.

McKee, Christopher. *Edward Preble: A Naval Biography*. Annapolis, Md., 1972.

McLeod, Alexander. *A Scriptural View of the Character, Causes and Ends of the Present War*. New York, 1815.

Meigs, William M. *The Life of John Caldwell Calhoun*. 2 vols. New York, 1917.

——. *The Life of Thomas Hart Benton*. Philadelphia, 1904.

Melton, Buckner F. *Aaron Burr*. New York, 2002.

Meyer, Leland Winfield. *The Life and Times of Colonel Richard M. Johnson of Kentucky*. New York, 1932.

Miller, John C. *Alexander Hamilton: Portrait in Paradox*. New York, 1959.

Miller, Melanie Randolph. *Envoy to the Terror: Gouverneur Morris & the French Revolution*. Dulles, Va., 2005.

Miller, William Lee. *The Business of May Next*. Charlottesville, Va., 1992.

Mitchell, Broadus. *Alexander Hamilton: The National Adventure, 1788–1804*. New York, 1962.

Mitchell, Broadus, and Louise Pearson Mitchell. *A Biography of the Constitution of the United States*. New York, 1964.

Molotsky, Irvin. *The Flag, the Poet and the Song: The Story of the Star-Spangled Banner*. New York, 2001.

Monaghan, Frank. *John Jay*. New York, 1935.

Monroe, James. *Defense of Jefferson and Freneau Against Hamilton*. Philip M. Marsh, ed. Oxford, Ohio, 1948.

Montgomery, H. *The Life of Major-General William H. Harrison, Ninth President of the United States*. New York, 1857.

Montgomery, M. R. *Jefferson and the Gun-Men*. New York, 2000.

Moore, Virginia. *The Madisons*. New York, 1979.

Moran, Thomas Francis. *The History of North America*. Vol. VII. Philadelphia, 1904.

Morgan, Edmund S. *Benjamin Franklin*. New Haven, Conn., 2002.

——. *The Birth of the Republic*. Chicago, 1992.

——. *The Genius of George Washington*. New York, 1980.

Morison, Samuel Eliot. *Dissent in Three American Wars*. Cambridge, Mass., 1970.

——. *Harrison Gray Otis: The Urbane Federalist*. Boston, 1969.

——. *The Oxford History of the American People*. 2 vols. New York, 1994.

Morriss, Roger. *Cockburn and the British Navy in Transition*. Columbia, S.C., 1997.

Morse, John T. *John Quincy Adams*. Boston, 1886.

Muller, Charles G. *The Darkest Day: The Washington–Baltimore Campaign During the War of 1812.* Philadelphia, 2003.

Nagel, Paul C. *John Quincy Adams: A Public Life, A Private Life.* New York, 1997.

Nevins, Allan. *American Press Opinion: Washington to Coolidge.* Boston, 1928.

O'Brien, Sean Michael. *In Bitterness and In Tears: Andrew Jackson's Destruction of the Creeks and Seminoles.* Westport, Conn., 2003.

O'Connell, Frank A., ed. *National Star-Spangled Banner Centennial.* Baltimore, 1914.

Paine, Ralph D. *The Fight for a Free Sea.* New Haven, Conn., 1920.

Parmet, Herbert S., and Marie B. Hecht. *Aaron Burr: Portrait of an Ambitious Man.* New York, 1967.

Parrington, Vernon L. *The Colonial Mind 1620–1800.* New York, 1974.

Parsons, Lynn Hudson. *John Quincy Adams.* Madison, Wisc., 1998.

Parton, James. *Life and Times of Aaron Burr.* New York, 1858.

——. *Life of Andrew Jackson.* 3 vols. New York, 1860–61.

——. *Presidency of Andrew Jackson.* Robert V. Remini, ed. New York, 1967.

Patterson, Benton Rain. *The Generals: Andrew Jackson, Sir Edward Pakenham, and the Road to the Battle of New Orleans.* New York, 2005.

Paullin, Charles Oscar. *Commodore John Rodgers: A Biography.* Cleveland, Ohio, 1910.

Perkins, Bradford. *Castlereagh and Adams: England and the United States 1812–1823.* Berkeley, Calif., 1964.

——. *Prologue to War: England and the United States 1805–1812.* Berkeley, Calif., 1961.

Perkins, James Breck. *France in the American Revolution.* Boston, 1911.

Peskin, Allan. *Winfield Scott and the Profession of Arms.* Kent, Ohio, 2003.

Peterson, Barbara Bennett. *George Washington, America's Moral Exemplar.* New York, 2005.

Peterson, Merrill D. *The Great Triumvirate: Webster, Clay, and Calhoun.* New York, 1987.

Peterson, Norma Lois. *The Presidencies of William Henry Harrison & John Tyler.* Lawrence, Kans., 1989.

Petrie, Charles. *George Canning.* London, 1932.

Pike, Zebulon M. *Arkansaw Journal.* Stephen Hardin Hart and Archer Butler Hulbert, eds. Denver, Colo., 1932.

——. *The Expeditions.* Elliott Coues, ed. New York, 1895.

——. *The Journals.* 2 vols. Donald Jackson, ed. Norman, Okla., 1966.

Pitch, Anthony S. *The Burning of Washington.* Annapolis, Md., 2000.

Poage, George Rawlings. *Henry Clay and the Whig Party*. Chapel Hill, N.C., 1936.

Powell, J. H. *Richard Rush, Republican Diplomat*. Philadelphia, 1942.

Pratt, Julius W. *Expansionists of 1812*. New York, 1925.

Proctor Court Martial. War Office Papers, Public Records Office, WO 71/243, Kew, England.

Quimby, Robert S. *The U.S. Army in the War of 1812: An Operational and Command Study*. East Lansing, Mich., undated.

Quincy, Josiah. *Memoir of the Life of John Quincy Adams*. Boston, 1858.

Randall, Henry S. *Life of Thomas Jefferson*. 3 vols. New York, 1858.

Rasmussen, William M. S., and Robert S. Tilton. *George Washington: The Man Behind the Myths*. Charlottesville, Va., 1999.

Ratner, Lorman A. *Andrew Jackson and His Tennessee Lieutenants*. Westport, Conn., 1997.

Raymond, Ethel. *Tecumseh*. Toronto, 1920.

Recollections of the Early Republic. Joyce Appleby, ed. Boston, 1997.

Reid, John, and John Henry Eaton. *The Life of Andrew Jackson*. University of Alabama, 1974.

Remini, Robert V. *Andrew Jackson*. 3 vols. Baltimore, 1988.

———. *Andrew Jackson and the Course of the American Empire 1767–1821*. New York, 1977.

———. *Andrew Jackson & His Indian Wars*. New York, 2001.

———. *The Battle of New Orleans*. New York, 1999.

———. *Henry Clay: Statesman for the Union*. New York, 1991.

———. *John Quincy Adams*. New York, 2002.

Richardson, John. *War of 1812*. Brockville, Ontario, 1842.

Ridout, Thomas G. *Ten Years of Upper Canada in Peace and War, 1805–1815*. Matilda Edgar, ed. Toronto, 1890.

Ritcheson, Charles R. *Aftermath of Revolution: British Policy Toward the United States*. Dallas, Tex., 1969.

Rives, William C. *History of the Life and Times of James Madison*. 3 vols. Boston, 1868.

Rogers, Joseph M. *The True Henry Clay*. Philadelphia, 1904.

Rogow, Arnold A. *A Fatal Friendship: Alexander Hamilton and Aaron Burr*. New York, 1998.

Roosevelt, Theodore. *The Naval War of 1812*. New York, 1999.

Ross, Maurice. *Louis XVI*. New York, 1976.

Rossiter, Clinton. *The American Quest 1790–1860*. New York, 1971.

Rourke, Constance. *David Crockett*. Lincoln, Nebr., 1998.

Rutland, Robert Allen. *James Madison: The Founding Father*. Columbia, Mo., 1987.

———. *James Madison and the Search for Nationhood.* Washington, D.C., 1981.

———. *The Presidency of James Madison.* Lawrence, Kans., 1990.

Schachner, Nathan. *Aaron Burr.* New York, 1937.

Schlesinger, Arthur M., Jr. *The Age of Jackson.* Boston, 1946.

Schultz, Harold S. *James Madison.* New York, 1970.

Sears, Louis Martin. *Jefferson and the Embargo.* Durham, N.C., 1927.

Sellers, Charles. *Andrew Jackson: A Profile.* New York, 1971.

Shackford, James Atkins. *David Crockett: The Man and the Legend.* Chapel Hill, N.C., 1956; Lincoln, Nebr., 1986.

Sheads, Scott Sumpter. *Guardian of the Star-Spangled Banner.* Baltimore, 1999.

Sheppard, George. *Plunder, Profit, and Paroles: A Social History of the War of 1812 in Upper Canada.* Montreal, 1994.

Simon, James F. *What Kind of Nation.* New York, 2001.

Skaggs, David Curtis, and Gerard T. Altoff. *A Signal Victory: The Lake Erie Campaign 1812–1813.* Annapolis, Md., 1997.

———. *Thomas Macdonough: Master of Command in the Early U. S. Navy.* Annapolis, Md., 2003.

Skeen, C. Edward. *Citizen Soldiers in the War of 1812.* Lexington, Ky., 1999.

———. *John Armstrong, Jr. 1758–1843.* Syracuse, N.Y., 1981.

Slaughter, Philip. *Christianity: The Key to the Character and Career of Washington.* New York, 1896.

Smith, Elbert B. *Magnificent Missourian: The Life of Thomas Hart Benton.* Westport, Conn., 1957.

Smith, James Morton, ed. *The Republic of Letters: The Correspondence Between Thomas Jefferson and James Madison, 1776–1826.* 3 vols. New York, 1995.

Smith, Page. *John Adams.* Garden City, N.Y., 1962.

Sparks, Jared. *The Life of George Washington.* Boston, 1860.

Spaulding, E. Wilder. *His Excellency George Clinton.* New York, 1938.

Spivak, Burton. *Jefferson's English Crisis.* Charlottesville, Va., 1979.

Stagg, J. C. A. *Mr. Madison's War.* Princeton, N.J., 1983.

Stapleton, Augustus Granville. *George Canning and His Times.* London, 1859.

Stevenson, James. *The War of 1812 in Connection with the Army Bill Act.* Montreal, 1892.

Stuart, Reginald C. *The Half-way Pacifist: Thomas Jefferson's View of War.* Toronto, 1978.

Sturgis, Amy H. *Washington Through Monroe, 1789–1825.* Westport, Conn., 2002.

Sugden, John. *Tecumseh, A Life*. New York, 1997.

——. *Tecumseh's Last Stand*. Norman, Okla., 1985.

Sumner, William Graham. *Andrew Jackson*. Vol. 1. Boston, 1899.

Swanson, Neil H. *The Perilous Fight*. New York, 1945.

Syrett, Harold C. *Andrew Jackson: His Contribution to the American Tradition*. Indianapolis, Ind., 1953.

Syrett, Harold C., and Jean G. Cooke, eds. *Interview in Weehawken: The Burr-Hamilton Duel as Told in the Original Documents*. Middletown, Conn., 1960.

Temperley, H. W. V. *Life of Canning*. London, 1905.

Thomas, John L., ed. *John C. Calhoun: A Profile*. New York, 1968.

Thompson, David. *History of the Late War Between Great Britain and the United States of America*. Niagara, B.C., Canada, 1832.

Tucker, Glenn. *Dawn Like Thunder: The Barbary Wars and the Birth of the U.S. Navy*. Indianapolis, Ind., 1963.

Tucker, Spencer C., and Frank T. Reuter. *Injured Honor: The* Chesapeake-Leopard *Affair*. Annapolis, Md., 1996.

——. *Stephen Decatur: A Life Most Bold and Daring*. Annapolis, Md., 2005.

Turner, Wesley B. *British Generals in the War of 1812 High Command in the Canadas*. Montreal, 1999.

Updyke, Frank A. *The Diplomacy of the War of 1812*. Baltimore, 1915.

U.S. House of Representatives. *Purchase of the Territory of Louisiana*. State Papers and Correspondence. Washington, D.C., 1903.

Van Deusen, Glyndon V. *The Life of Henry Clay*. Boston, 1937.

Vidal, Gore. *Inventing a Nation: Washington, Adams, Jefferson*. New Haven, Conn., 2003.

Wait, Eugene M. *Adams vs. Jackson*. Huntington, N.Y., 2001.

——. *America and the War of 1812*. Commack, N.Y., 1999.

Walker, Francis A. *The Making of the Nation, 1783–1817*. London, 1896.

Walsh, Correa Moylan. *The Political Science of John Adams*. New York, 1915.

Ward, John William. *Andrew Jackson: Symbol for an Age*. New York, 1962.

Washington, George. *Diaries*. Donald Jackson and Dorothy Twohig, eds. Vols. 4, 5. Charlottesville, Va., 1978, 1979.

——. *Papers*. Confederation Series, 6. Dorothy Twohig, ed. Charlottesville, Va., 1997.

——. *Papers*. Vol. 11. Philander D. Chase, ed. Charlottesville, Va., 2002.

——. *Writings*. 39 vols. John C. Fitzpatrick, ed. Washington, D.C., 1931–44.

Watson, Paul Barron. *The Tragic Career of Commodore James Barron*. New York, 1942.

Watson, Thomas E. *The Life and Times of Thomas Jefferson*. New York, 1903.

Webster, Daniel. *The Papers*. Vol. 1. Charles M. Wiltse, ed. Hanover, N.H., 1974.

Webster, Homer J. "William Henry Harrison's Administration of the Indiana Territory." Publications, Indiana Historical Society. Vol. IV, no. 3. Indianapolis, Ind., 1907.

Weintraub, Stanley. *General Washington's Christmas Farewell*. New York, 2003.

Welsh, William Jeffrey, and David Curtis Skaggs, eds. *War on the Great Lakes*. Kent, Ohio, 1991.

Wheelan, Joseph. *Jefferson's Vendetta*. New York, 2005.

———. *Jefferson's War: America's First War on Terror, 1801–1805*. New York, 2003.

Whiting, Henry. *Life of Zebulon Montgomery Pike*. Jared Sparks, ed. Boston, 1845.

Wiencek, Henry. *An Imperfect God: George Washington, His Slaves and the Creation of America*. New York, 2003.

Williams, John Hoyt. *Sam Houston*. New York, 1993.

Wills, Gary. *James Madison*. New York, 2002.

———. *"Negro President": Jefferson and the Slave Power*. New York, 2003.

Wilson, Joseph T. *The Black Phalanx*. New York, 1994.

Wilson, Woodrow. *George Washington*. New York, 1896.

Wiltse, Charles M. *John C. Calhoun–Nationalist, 1782–1828*. Indianapolis, Ind., 1944.

———. *The New Nation: 1800–1845*. New York, 1961.

Withey, Lynne. *Dear Friend: A Life of Abigail Adams*. New York, 1981.

Wolcott, Oliver. *Memoirs of the Administrations of Washington and John Adams*. George Gibbs, ed. New York, 1846.

Wood, William. *The War with the United States*. Toronto, 1920.

Zall, Paul M. *Dolley Madison*. Huntington, N.Y., 2001.

———. *George Washington Laughing*. Hamden, Conn., 1989.

———. *Washington on Washington*. Lexington, Ky., 2003.

Zimmerman, James Fulton. *Impressment of American Seamen*. New York, 1925.

Index

Adams, Abigail, 12, 48, 51, 71, 75, 79–80, 83–84, 96, 138, 145, 395

Adams, John: and Adams (J. Q.) in Russia, 145; appearance of, 384; and British attack on Washington, 296; and Burr, 91; death of, 394; and elections, 76, 89, 90, 91, 92; and factionalism, 52; as foreign emissary, 136–37; Franklin's relationship with, 17, 51; and Ghent treaty, 337; and Hamilton, 60, 64, 76, 84, 91, 312, 383; and Hartford Convention, 340; inauguration of, 75, 144; and Jay treaty with Britain, 71, 72; Jefferson's relationship with, 23, 35, 76–77, 78, 83, 94, 394; and Lafayette, 391; as leading Federalist, 387; on Madison administration, 394; Madison's relationship with, 20, 76–77, 296; personality and character of, 42, 90; and Philadelphia Convention, 19, 20, 23; prediction about U.S. of, 101; retirement of, 96; and social class, 60; and Treaty of 1783, 337; as vice president, 41, 42, 51, 64; views about War of 1812 of, 394; and Washington's death, 88; Washington's relationship with, 84; as Washington's successor, 51

Adams, John Quincy: Abigail's relationship with, 138; Adams's views about, 138; and British attack on Washington, 330; childhood and youth of, 136–37; and Clay, 390; and Clinton, 142; in congress, 138, 406; death of, 406; and Decatur, 392; as Democrat, 138; and elections, 389, 390, 394, 402; and embargo, 138; and expansion of U.S., 387–88; as Federalist, 138; and Ghent

treaty, 272, 323–25, 327–30, 336–37, 339, 342, 374, 375, 389, 390; and Jackson, 387–88, 390, 393–95; and Jefferson, 144; and Louisiana Purchase, 138; and Madison's inauguration, 144; marriage of, 137–38; ministerial appointments of, 137–38, 383; and Monroe Doctrine, 389; personality and character of, 138, 324, 325; as president, 390–91, 393–94; professional career of, 137–38, 144–45; in Russia, 94, 137, 145, 227–28, 230; as secretary of state, 387–88; and slavery, 388, 394, 406; and Tyler, 406; Washington's views of, 137, 138

Adams, Samuel, 19–20, 37–38, 76, 92, 135, 136

Adams, William, 325–27

African Americans, 246, 317, 348. *See also* slavery

Alabama, Indians in, 253, 273–90

Alamo, 404–5

Albany, New York, 182, 273, 331

Alexander (czar of Russia), 227–28, 230, 271–72, 328

Alexandria, Virginia, British attack on, 298, 299, 302, 311–12, 314

Alien and Sedition Acts, 80–84, 89, 92, 94–96, 399

American Revolution, 6, 44, 48, 56, 163–64, 336, 382, 394

Ames, Fisher, 45, 71–72

Amherstburg, and War of 1812, 258, 259–60, 263, 292

Annapolis, Maryland, 10, 16, 350

Armstrong, John Jr.: army complaints about, 314; and British attack on Washington, 295–97, 301–3, 305, 311,

465

Photo Credits

Page 3. The Washington family at Mount Vernon. Courtesy of the Mount Vernon Ladies' Association

Page 19. Madison addressing the Virginia Convention. Collection of The New-York Historical Society, Accession # 1947.414

Page 21. Alexander Hamilton. Library of Congress, Prints & Photographs Division, LC-USZ62–96268

Page 43. Washington reviewing the Whiskey Rebellion army. © Bettmann / CORBIS

Page 75. Abigail Adams. Gilbert Stuart, *Abigail Smith Adams (Mrs. John Adams)*, Gift of Mrs. Robert Homans, Image © 2006 Board of Trustees, National Gallery of Art, Washington

Page 75. John Adams. Gilbert Stuart, *John Adams*, Gift of Mrs. Robert Homans, Image © 2006 Board of Trustees, National Gallery of Art, Washington

Page 89. Thomas Jefferson. *Thomas Jefferson* by Rembrandt Peale (#55), White House Historical Association (White House Collection)

Page 111. Andrew Jackson. The Hermitage, Home of Andrew Jackson, Nashville, Tennessee

Page 111. Rachel Donelson Jackson. The Hermitage, Home of Andrew Jackson, Nashville, Tennessee

Page 119. Zebulon Pike. Getty Images

Page 129. The *Chesapeake* and *Leopard* battle near Hampton Roads. William Gilkerson

Page 137. John Quincy Adams. © Bettmann / CORBIS